Halal Tourism and Artificial Intelligence

Halal Tourism and Artificial Intelligence: New Approaches for a New Generation

EDITED BY

ANUKRATI SHARMA
University of Kota, India

SHRUTI ARORA
Modi Institute of Management & Technology, India

AND

HÜSEYIN PAMUKÇU
University of Afyon Kocatepe, Turkey

emerald
PUBLISHING

United Kingdom – North America – Japan – India – Malaysia – China

Emerald Publishing Limited
Emerald Publishing, Floor 5, Northspring, 21-23 Wellington Street, Leeds LS1 4DL.

First edition 2026

British Library Cataloguing in Publication Data
A catalogue record for this book is available from the British Library

ISBN: 978-1-80686-166-8 (Print)
ISBN: 978-1-80686-165-1 (Online)
ISBN: 978-1-80686-167-5 (Epub)

Printed and bound by CPI Group (UK) Ltd, Croydon, CR0 4YY

INVESTOR IN PEOPLE

For being there in quiet moments and in confusion, in hope and in chaos.
For the patience, the laughter, the late-night conversations,
and the silent understanding.
This is for the way we lift each other up, even on the hardest days.

Contents

About the Editors

Anukrati Sharma is the Professor in the Department of Commerce and Management at the University of Kota (A State Govt. University) in Kota, Rajasthan, India. She is the Director of the Skill Development Centre and Chairperson of the Women Cell at the same University. She is also Dean (Honorary) of Tourism and Hospitality at Vishwakarma Skills University, Jaipur (A Govt. State University). She is a teachers-elected BoM (Board of Management) Member of University of Kota. She worked three years (January 06, 2021–January 06, 2024) as the Head of the Department of Commerce and Management, University of Kota. She has many edited books with reputed publishers like Emerald, IGI Global, CABI, Apple Academic Press, Routledge, and Springer. She has attended various International Conferences and visited many countries.

Shruti Arora is an Associate Professor at Modi Institute of Management and Technology, Kota, Rajasthan, India, with over 17 years of experience in the education sector. She specializes in Marketing, Tourism, Events, International Business, and Customer Relationship Management. Since July 2024, she has been serving as an Academic Counsellor at IGNOU. She previously worked as Guest Faculty at the University of Kota (January 2021–January 2024) and as a Trainer/Expert Lecturer under PMKVY 4.0 from February to September 2024.

She has participated in numerous international conferences and has several research publications to her credit, including contributions to Routledge, Emerald, Springer, and IGI Global. Her authored book *Event Management and Marketing* (ISBN: 978-93-86608-61-1) was approved as a CBSE and Government of M.P. learning resource. She has edited books with Apple Academic Press, Emerald, and CABI and is working on several upcoming international edited volumes.

She co-led a major research project funded by the Mahatma Gandhi National Council of Rural Education, completed in June 2024. She also served as a BRICS Community of Practice (2022–2024) Researcher to foster cross-national academic collaboration. She is a Member of editorial boards including *SEMANT Journal* and *BRICS Plus Journal* and is Associate Editor of *IJAER* since February 2025.

She holds an Indian patent and has been recognized as a keynote and invited speaker at prestigious international conferences. Her work on "Food Walk Tourism" has been featured in the *Encyclopedia of Tourism Management and Marketing* (Edward Elgar Publishing, 2022). She received the Best Women Researcher Award by INSPIRA in 2024 and served as a manuscript reviewer for *Exploresearch* Journal. Additionally, she acts as both internal and external examiner for academic assessments.

Hüseyin Pamukçu received his bachelor's degree from Mustafa Kemal University in 2011, his master's degree from Afyon Kocatepe University in 2014, and his doctorate from Sakarya University in 2017. He started his academic career at Kastamonu University in 2013. He started to work as a Research Assistant in 2013 and as a Doctor Lecturer in 2018 in the Department of Tourism Management of the Faculty of Tourism at the University of Kastamonu. As of February 2021, he has continued his studies at the Faculty of Tourism, University of Afyon Kocatepe as Assistant Professor. In May 2021, he was successful in the Inter-University Board exam and received the title of Associate Professor. He, who continues to work as an Associate Professor in the Department of Gastronomy and Culinary Arts at the same university, is married and has two children.

List of Contributors

Mustapha Ahachmi	Mons University, USA
Abdullah Akmaz	Mersin University, Turkey
Ahmad Albattat	Asia Pacific University of Technology and Innovation, Malaysia
Mansoor Ali	Kohat University of Science and Technology, Pakistan
Syed Immamul Ansarullah	University of Kashmir, India
Orhan Batman	Sakarya University of Applied Sciences, Turkey
Saurabh Bharti	Manipal Academy of Higher Education, India
Sulekha Chourasiya	Dr. Harisingh Gour Vishwavidyalaya (Central University), India
Fatma Reyhan Ekiz	Mersin University, Turkey
Fatima Zahra Fakir	Padova University, Italy
Akif Gökçe	Sakarya Uygulamalı Bilimler Üniversity, Turkey
Abdulbaki Güçlü	Kirklareli University, Türkiye
Mohammad Sobri Bin Hamid	Universiti Sultan Zainal Abidin (UniSZA), Malaysia
Sheikh Ikhlaq	Cyber-Enterprise Security-Deloitte, India
Sumaya Iqbal	University of Kashmir, India
Muhammad Idrees ul Islam	University of Kashmir, India
Mohamed Jaafari	University Sultan Moulay Slimane, Morocco
Nohman Khan	Asia Pacific University of Technology and Innovation, Malaysia
Gizem Kiper	Sakarya University of Applied Sciences, Turkey
Vahit Oguz Kiper	Sakarya University of Applied Sciences, Turkey
Neeraj Kumar	Dr. Harisingh Gour Vishwavidyalaya (Central University), India
Mohamed Louza	University Cadi Ayyad, Morocco
Gobinathan Manickam	Asia Pacific University of Technology and Innovation, Malaysia
Priyakrushna Mohanty	Christ University, India
Anabela Monteiro	Eudoxia Research University, USA
Irfan Nawaz	Federal Ministry of Human Rights, Pakistan
Nazirullah -	Universiti Sultan Zainal Abidin, Malaysia
Betül Öztürk	Izmir University of Economics, Turkey

Manvinder Singh Pahwa	Dr. Harisingh Gour Vishwavidyalaya (Central University), India
Ayush Singh Parihar	Dr. Harisingh Gour Vishwavidyalaya (Central University), India
Ravindra Kumar Perumal	Asia Pacific University of Technology and Innovation, Malaysia
Sabeeha Rahman	Allama Iqbal Open University, Pakistan
S.K.L.J. Ramanayaka	Sri Lanka Institute of Tourism & Hotel Management, Sri Lanka
Birendra Kishore Roy	Manipal University, India
Che Wan Nur Safraa	Monash University, Malaysia
Ayush Sahu	Dr. Harisingh Gour Vishwavidyalaya (Central University), India
Manabhanjan Sahu	SVKM's Narsee Monjee Institute of Management Studies, India
Sharanya M	Christ University, India
Anukrati Sharma	University of Kota, India
CS. Surti Sharma	University of Kota, India
Vivek Sharma	Government Mahendra Karma Girls College, India
Ashutosh Singh	Dr. Harisingh Gour Vishwavidyalaya (Central University), India
Ahmad Puad Mat Som	Universiti Sultan Zainal Abidin, Malaysia
Kaplan Uğurlu	Kirklareli University, Türkiye
Ihtisham Ullah	Asia Pacific University of technology and Innovation, Malaysia
Tyba Yousuf	SSM College of Engineering, India

Preface

The combination of tourism and technology in recent years has created astonishing prospects for creativity, customization, and inclusion. Among the many changing aspects of the global travel industry, Halal tourism has become a vibrant and quickly expanding sector that embraces the transformational potential of emerging technology, particularly artificial intelligence (AI), while also catering to the particular demands of Muslim tourists. This edited book, *Halal Tourism and Artificial Intelligence: New Approaches for a New Generation*, presents a timely and thorough analysis of how technological developments, digital tools, and AI-driven solutions are changing the face of Halal tourism across diverse cultural, geographic, and socioeconomic contexts. This book examines the relationship between digital revolution and Halal tourism by bringing together a wide variety of academic viewpoints. In order to lay the groundwork for more in-depth investigations into ecosystem management, including regional studies like those concentrating on Malaysia and Portugal and generational analyses of digital pilgrimage experiences, this edited book begins with chapters that highlight fundamental approaches to integrating AI within Halal tourism. Innovative case studies and technical advancements in environmental management and hospitality are used to address the issue of sustainability and show how the Halal tourist sector is in line with international sustainability objectives. Examining how AI and other technologies like IoT and digitalization are changing backend operations, service delivery, and destination marketing in addition to improving passenger experiences takes up a large amount of this edited book. Important topics covered in other chapters include curriculum development, intercultural cooperation, and the moral issues required to create an inclusive and sustainable future for Halal travel. Academics, researchers, legislators, and business executives with an interest in the relationship between technology, religion, and tourism are the target audience for this book. This volume offers a comprehensive understanding of how AI and digital innovation are not only instruments for expansion but also catalysts for changing expectations, experiences, and values in the field of Halal tourism by fusing the viewpoints of several disciplines. We believe this collection of scholarly work from Turkey, India, Portugal, Belgium, Italy, Malaysia, Pakistan, Sri Lanka, and Morocco will spark meaningful dialog, inspire future research, and guide the development of more inclusive, intelligent, and sustainable tourism ecosystems for the generations to come.

We wish to thank all the contributors for their hard work.

Dr. Anukrati Sharma
Dr. Shruti Arora
Dr. Hüseyin Pamukçu

Chapter 1

Technological Innovation and Artificial Intelligence Approach in Halal Tourism

Abdullah Akmaz[a] *and Fatma Reyhan Ekiz*[b]

[a]*PhD Faculty Member, Faculty of Tourism, Mersin University, Turkey*
[b]*Department of Tourism Guidance, Institute of Social Sciences, Mersin University, Turkey*

1. Introduction

The concept of halal, which carries considerable weight in Islamic tradition, has garnered attention from multiple fields recently, resulting in an expansion of its implications. The definition provided by the Turkish Language Institution, "not contrary to religious rules, not forbidden" (Tayar & Doğan, 2019, p. 63), resonates with the etymological origins of "hall" and "hıll," which denote "the removal of an obstacle or being set free" (Orum, 2018, p. 173). This concept, once predominantly linked to the culinary realm, has now broadened its scope to include a diverse array of sectors, spanning cosmetics, medical products, banking, finance, and tourism services. The evaluation of halal standards takes place in a complex mix of ethical and religious settings in different areas, indicating that halal includes not just religious factors but also cultural, social, and economic aspects. Nonetheless, the domain of halal tourism has surfaced as a prominent industry, witnessing considerable expansion and increasing demand, especially in Asian and Middle Eastern countries (Rahman et al., 2022, p. 63). In response to this progress and growth, many countries have started to implement novel tourism initiatives, facilities, and infrastructural improvements to meet the demands of consumers seeking halal tourism (Samori et al., 2016, p. 131). It is obvious that, similar to numerous fields in modern society, the introduction of groundbreaking applications within the tourism sector, driven by technological advancements, is reshaping the anticipations and experiences of consumers interested in halal tourism. This evolution is likewise shaping the competitive dynamics among enterprises functioning within this market. The emergence of digital technology has fundamentally altered the way consumers perceive and engage with its

Halal Tourism and Artificial Intelligence: New Approaches for a New Generation, 1–10

doi:10.1108/978-1-80686-165-120261001

incorporation into their daily lives. The transformation of personal lifestyles and consumption behaviors has significantly impacted tourist demands, facilitating the rise of novel forms of tourism, including halal tourism. The global Muslim demographic has expanded, and their increasing economic prosperity has resulted in a heightened interest in travel, leisure, and entertainment opportunities that align with their religious values (Baysal, 2017, p. 90; Yıldız & Yıldız, 2018, p. 774). This situation has established halal tourism as a domain with considerable revenue prospects within the spectrum of alternative tourism categories. The halal industry offers significant economic prospects for both Muslim and non-Muslim nations and is regarded as a considerable niche sector within the global market (Bakar & Rosbi, 2019, p. 48). In a world that is becoming ever more interconnected, the progression of technological opportunities and applications provides consumers with a range of conveniences while also nurturing beneficial consumer behaviors such as satisfaction, loyalty, and a sense of attachment to businesses. Nevertheless, the tools utilized in the progression of halal tourism, such as artificial intelligence (AI), cloud computing, advanced robotic systems, and the Internet of Things, also raise potential security and safety issues for consumers (Mukherjee et al., 2022, p. 41). The accommodation sector is influenced by this development and is progressively engaging with various stakeholders in the tourism industry to provide services that adhere to halal standards (Büyükşalvarcı & Dinç, 2019, p. 1035). The expansion of the internet presents considerable marketing benefits for lodging businesses. By leveraging e-commerce and e-business processes, organizations can achieve cost reductions and expand their customer reach in a timely and efficient manner (Karamustafa et al., 2002, p. 52). The aim of this investigation is to disclose the impact of AI, autonomous technology, and a variety of technology applications on the halal tourism sector. Additionally, it will disclose the most recent technological advancements and offer recommendations to both private and public institutions in this regard.

2. The Concept and Scope of Halal Tourism

Modern consumers exhibit a heightened level of discernment and awareness in their buying behaviors, shaped by a multitude of influencing factors. Alongside personal attributes like age, gender, worldview, and education, the influence of religious and belief systems is paramount in molding consumption behaviors. The belief systems held by individuals significantly influence a diverse array of consumption behaviors, encompassing both the products they select and those they consciously eschew (Kardeş & Kıngır, 2017, p. 33). Consequently, brands utilize religious elements as powerful tools in their marketing strategies and communication endeavors. Within this framework, halal tourism has surfaced as a tourism paradigm designed to cater to the needs of Muslim travelers seeking services that resonate with their religious principles (Kunt, 2022, p. 997). This form of alternative tourism emerged as significant in the latter quarter of the 20th century and has attracted considerable attention in both academic research and industry applications in the first quarter of the 21st century (Akmaz, 2020, p. 401). The foundation of halal tourism comprises accommodation facilities, food and beverage establishments, travel agencies, transportation and transfer services, banking institutions, and the entertainment sector that adhere to Islamic norms. Nonetheless, the assessment of halal tourism may also include the appraisal of the values and sensitivities of travelers who practice Judaism and Christianity, alongside the delivery of services that align with these principles. Turkey is no longer a prominent destination providing services tailored for Muslim guests within the realm of halal tourism. It occupies a significant position due to the existence of "Kosher" enterprises that offer food and beverages in alignment with Jewish customs, catering to the demands of Jewish travelers (Akmaz & Akmeşe, 2023). Additionally, in partnership with Muslim nations such as Malaysia and Indonesia, countries from various geographical regions, including India, Egypt, Dubai, Switzerland, Australia, Spain, and Thailand, are formulating distinctive marketing strategies to appeal to conservative travelers (Tunç & Sayın, 2019, p. 398). This activity highlights the growing global significance of halal tourism and the development of a competitive environment among various places.

2.1. Halal Product

Halal products, produced in compliance with Islamic regulations and permissible for eating, are a prominent preference among Muslim consumers. The key features of these products include not using any ingredients that are considered haram (forbidden) and being made according to specific religious rules (Kurtoğlu & Çiçek, 2013, p. 182). Consumers' religious convictions significantly influence their purchasing decisions, establishing the foundation for the development of the halal product concept (Özçelik Yorulmaz & Akçi, 2020, p. 1219).

Soygüden (2020) characterizes a halal product as one that is not only permissible for eating and use from a religious standpoint but is also pure, clean, and devoid of health hazards. The notion of halal cuisine has its roots in the earliest human history and has been influenced by religious regulations. The account of Adam and Eve consuming the prohibited fruit and their subsequent expulsion from paradise exemplifies the significance of the halal and haram divide. This divide has existed across various cultures and religions throughout history and is still assessed from religious and ethical viewpoints (Türker, 2020, p. 88). As a result, certification and auditing organizations have arisen to standardize halal food (Özçelik Yorulmaz & Akçi, 2020, p. 1219).

According to Sürme et al. (2018) and Tayar and Doğan (2019, p. 63), halal tourism comprises, among other things, tourism services that are designed in accordance with the religious sensitivities of devout individuals. This is a result of their efforts to connect their lives with their religious beliefs and values. There is a greater possibility for halal tourism as a result of the encouragement within Islam for Muslim individuals who reside in various geographical regions to prefer halal products and services (İstanbullu Dinçer & Erkol Bayram, 2017, p. 27). Creating a large tourism market for countries and enterprises can be accomplished through the implementation of halal tourism, which is conducted in accordance with the standards that are established by Islam. This can be accomplished not only by generating revenue from domestic tourists but also by taking into consideration the potential demand from other countries that have Muslim populations. According to Pamukçu and Sarıışık (2017, p. 94), increasing investments in this particular field can result in substantial contributions to the economy.

2.2. *Halal Certificate*

According to Islamic regulations, reputable and authorized institutions provide the halal certificate, an essential document. It serves as evidence that the products in question have been made in a manner that is both hygienic and dangerous. This certification offers official confirmation that manufacturing businesses comply with specified halal criteria in their production procedures with regard to the manufacturing of their products. Malaysia is widely acknowledged as the first nation in the world to establish a halal certification system (Akbulut et al., 2020, p. 111). This is particularly true in the food industry, where Malaysia has been a pioneer. The halal certification system gives Muslim consumers the assurance that they can make informed decisions about the food goods they purchase. According to Baltacı and Kodalak (2022, p. 95), halal food is becoming an increasingly appealing choice not just for Muslims but also for a growing number of consumers who are not of Muslim faith. This appeal is primarily due to the high manufacturing standards and high level of hygiene that it possesses. Taking all these factors into consideration, Star-K Kosher Certification, which is the only "Kosher" agency that is recognized on a global scale and provides local services in Turkey, is a prominent institution that also provides certification services in this field for consumers who are not Muslims. The concept of halal certification has particularly evolved in countries where the Muslim population is a minority. This evolution is driven by the need for individuals to keep their religious identity and maintain consumption habits that are in accordance with their beliefs (Çukadar, 2017, p. 191). Halal certifications ensure that products and services are in accordance with the Sharia laws that govern both Muslims and non-Muslims. According to Altunöz Sürücü et al. (2021, p. 68), consumers are more likely to choose businesses that hold this accreditation since they are able to fulfill particular expectations more effectively.

2.3. *Halal Hotel*

The importance of the accommodation industry, which is a major component of the travel and tourism sector, is continuously increasing as a result of several causes, including globalization, technological improvements, and rising income levels. The increasing tendency of individuals to travel further increases the strategic function that accommodation establishments play within the tourist sector, as stated by Oktay and Özgür (2008, p. 164). On the other hand, establishments that provide lodging are confronted with a demand structure that is subject to fluctuations on a daily, weekly, monthly, and seasonal basis (Çuhadar & Kayacan, 2005, p. 24).

Hotel establishments are companies that offer fundamental services to their visitors, including lodging, food and beverage, and other amenities. Halal hotels,

Customers of halal-concept hotels seek information on hotel websites concerning halal certification, food and beverage offerings, prohibitions on alcohol and gambling, mosque facilities, privacy provisions, gender-specific areas, religious activities, and proximity to faith tourism sites (Pamukçu & Arpacı, 2016, p. 150). Addressing the requirements of travelers with religious sensitivity is essential for the efficient delivery of halal tourism services. Consequently, alongside the rising demand, it is essential to examine tourist profiles, expectations, and requirements and to devise technology-enhanced solutions.

Applications that are powered by AI, chatbots, and personal assistants can provide halal-conscious travelers with assistance in making well-informed decisions and managing their travel procedures in a more effective manner. While chatbots are able to answer consumer inquiries at any time of the day or night with lightning-fast response times, personal assistants that have been designed expressly for the halal tourism market make it possible for travelers to conveniently obtain information about destinations and take advantage of services that are provided in real time (Pamukçu & Tekin, 2022, p. 150). According to Akgün (2023), chatbots not only provide information about the hotel and its amenities, but they also provide direction regarding businesses and services located in the vicinity of the hotel and in the location more generally.

Wearable technologies powered by AI have emerged as a notable innovation in the realm of halal tourism recently. Smartwatches specifically function to deliver reminders for users' religious obligations. These criteria encompass prayer times, iftar and suhoor schedules, and other crucial moments pertinent to religious observance. Şeyhanlıoğlu and Zengin (2022, p. 129) assert that the implementation of AI-based applications in tourism businesses can enhance tourist experiences, potentially improving the company's perceived image. Ören and Ören (2024, p. 64) assert that the extensive adoption of modern technologies in the hospitality sector, including AI, robotics, and augmented reality, will facilitate the delivery of technologically sophisticated services and allow for the personalization of guest experiences.

5. Conclusion and Recommendations

In today's quickly digitalizing world, the notion of halal tourism, which prioritizes religious sensitivities in the tourism sector, has become an area of interest not just for those who identify as Muslim but also for a broad customer base that is sensitive to values that are founded on faith. The outcomes of this study suggest that technological improvements have the potential to make the essential principles of halal tourism more effective and accessible to a wider audience. Specifically, applications that are based on AI are thought to provide substantial contributions to the creation of individualized experiences in service delivery, the enhancement of customer happiness, and the optimization of operational procedures. When addressing the issue of halal tourism, it is necessary to take a comprehensive strategy that takes into account not just the religious underpinnings of the industry but also its cultural, social, and economic aspects. Considering this, it is recommended that digitalization-based strategies be developed in both the management of destinations and the administration of customer interactions by utilizing the opportunities provided by AI.

It is of the utmost necessity for businesses that provide halal tourist services to accelerate the processes of digital transformation by implementing technologies that leverage AI into their organizational structures. This is particularly relevant in the context of the industry's guidelines. People may discover that cutting-edge solutions like chatbots, smart assistants, and wearable technology are essential components when they look for vacations that align with their religious sensibilities. However, it is of the highest importance that businesses not only make investments in technological improvements but also provide reliable information regarding the compatibility of these services with halal standards. This is one of the biggest necessities. Additionally, the training of personnel in this profession in both digital literacy and religious sensitivity can be regarded as a factor that directly affects the quality of service that is offered. This is due to the direct correlation between these two aspects and the provision of services. Also, working together with important private and public groups to create sustainable policies and set halal tourism standards locally and globally, along with developing new technology-based systems, could make halal tourism more popular and competitive worldwide. This is because these policies will lead to the establishment of halal tourism standards at both the local and international levels.

References

Akbulut, M., Daştan, Ş., Can, E., & Sipahioglu, O. (2020). Awareness of young consumers regarding halal certification and its effects on food preference: The case of Kayseri Province. *Journal of Halal and Ethical Research, 1*(2), 110–121.

Akgün, A. (2023). Artificial intelligence-supported applications for hotel activities. *Selçuk Tourism and Informatics Research Journal, 3*, 1–21.

Akmaz, A. (2020). The concept of halal tourism and an evaluation on halal tourism practices in Turkey. *Journal of International Social Research, 13*(74), 398–405.

Akmaz, A., & Akmeşe, H. (2023). *Halal tourism and hotel management: Concepts, applications and literature*. Detay Publications.

Akpur, A. (2023). Exploring the capabilities of Chatgpt as a travel consultant: A study on generative artificial intelligence in tourism marketing. *International Journal of Current Tourism Research, 7*(2), 93–105.

Altunöz Sürücü, Ö., Kıroğlu, H. S., Kargiglioğlu, Ş., & Karaçağ, S. (2021). An evaluation on halal tourism practices within the framework of Islamic sensitivities: Halal hotels. *Turkish Journal of Tourism Research, 1*(2), 64–77.

Arslan, K. (2020). Artificial intelligence and its applications in education. *Western Anatolian Journal of Educational Sciences, 11*(1), 71–88.

Bakar, N. A., & Rosbi, S. (2019). Robust framework of Halal certification process with the integration of artificial intelligence method. *Journal of Islamic, Social, Economics and Development, 4*(20), 47–55.

Baltacı, M., & Kodalak, O. (2022). Halal tourism in Turkey and the world. *Eurasian Tourism Research Journal, 3*(2), 92–102.

Başer, M. Y., & Olcay, A. (2022). Artificial intelligence technology in smart tourism. *Gaziantep University Journal of Social Sciences, 21*(3), 1795–1817.

Baysal, D. (2017). Halal tourism in Turkey. *Black Sea International Journal of Science, 36*, 89–103.

Büyükşalvarcı, A., & Dinç, İ. (2019). Halal tourism: Its place in Turkey and a brief comparative evaluation of Turkey-Malaysia. *Journal of International Social Research, 12*(66), 1032–1041.

Cabi Bilge, A. (2023). Potential and implemented applications of ChatGPT, an artificial intelligence-supported language model, in the tourism sector. *Journal of Recreation and Tourism Research, 10*(3), 139–155.

Çalık, İ., & Pekerşen, Y. (2020). A qualitative research on the halal hotel awareness of halal concept hotel managers. *Atatürk University Journal of Institute of Social Sciences, 24*(1), 397–414.

Çuhadar, M., & Kayacan, C. (2005). Forecasting occupancy rate in accommodation establishments using artificial neural networks: An experiment on accommodation establishments in Turkey. *Anatolia: Journal of Tourism Research, 16*(1), 24–30.

Çukadar, M. (2017). Consumer behaviors on halal food. *Gaziosmanpaşa University Journal of Agricultural Faculty (JAFAG), 34*(3), 190–200.

Ercan, F. (2020). The use of artificial intelligence technologies and application examples in tourism marketing. *Ankara Hacı Bayram Veli University Journal of Tourism Faculty, 23*(2), 394–410.

İbiş, S. (2019). Robotization in the tourism industry. *Turkish Journal of Tourism Research, 3*(3), 403–420.

İbiş, S. (2025). The use of artificial intelligence technologies in gastronomy tourism: The case of ChatGPT. *Journal of Current Tourism Research, 9*(1), 109–131.

İstanbullu Dinçer, F., & Erkol Bayram, G. (2017). Halal tourism from an Islamic perspective. *International Journal of Turkish World Tourism Research, 2*(1), 26–42.

Karamustafa, K., Biçkes, D. M., & Ulama, Ş. (2002). A study on evaluating the internet websites of accommodation establishments in Turkey. *Erciyes University Journal of Economics and Administrative Sciences Faculty, 19*, 51–92.

Kardeş, N., & Kıngır, S. (2017). A rising tourism type in Turkey: Halal tourism. *Journal of Management Economics Literature Islamic and Political Sciences, 2*(1), 32–46.

Kayıkçı, M. Y., & Bozkurt, A. K. (2018). Z and Alpha generations in the digital age, robots and artificial intelligence applications in tourism. *Social Sciences Texts, 2018*(1), 54–64.

Kunt, S. (2022). Evaluation of holiday experiences of foreign customers who purchased services from "Muslim-Friendly" hotels in Turkey: Halalbooking. Com foreign customer reviews (2017–2021). *Turkey Studies-Social Sciences, 17*(5), 989–1005.

Kurtoğlu, R., & Çiçek, B. (2013). A research on determining consumers' perceptions, attitudes and expectations about halal products. *Eskişehir Osmangazi University Journal of Economics and Administrative Sciences, 8*(3), 181–205.

Mukherjee, A., Rajendran, S. D., & Wahab, S. N. (2022). Technology strategy in boosting halal tourism activities. In A. Hassan & N. A. Abdul Rahman (Eds.), *Technology application in aviation, tourism and hospitality: Recent developments and emerging issues* (pp. 41–56). Springer Nature Singapore.

Oktay, E., & Özgür, E. (2008). Efficiency analysis of accommodation establishments. *Journal of Social Sciences, 10*(1), 164–175.

Ören, T., & Ören, V. E. (2024). *Accommodation businesses trends*. Duvar Publications.

Orum, F. (2018). The legal analysis of the verses regarding the authority of the messenger of Allah to determine halal-haram in the Holy Quran within the framework of the concepts of "Tayyib" and "Khabith". *Kalemname, 3*(6), 166–233.

Özçelik Yorulmaz, D., & Akçi, Y. (2020). The effect of attitudes towards halal food consumption on purchase intention (the case of Adıyaman). *Kahramanmaraş Sütçü İmam University Journal of Social Sciences, 17*(2), 1218–1238.

Öztürk, K., & Şahin, M. E. (2018). A general overview of artificial neural networks and artificial intelligence. *Takvim-i Vekayi, 6*(2), 25–36.

Pamukçu, H., & Arpacı, Ö. (2016). Analysis of websites of halal concept hotel businesses. *Çatalhöyük International Tourism and Social Research Journal*, *1*, 147–160.

Pamukçu, H., & Sarıışık, M. (2017). A general evaluation on the concept and development of halal tourism. *Journal of International Economic and Administrative Sciences*, *3*(1), 82–98.

Pamukçu, H., & Tekin, Ö. A. (2022). *Muslim-friendly tourism and the turkey experience: Conceptual discussions, criticisms and suggestions*. Nobel Publications.

Rahman, M. K., Akter, S., Hossain, M. M., & Hassan, A. (2022). Hajj and halal tourism event: Application of technology. In A. Hassan (Ed.), *Application of technology in tourism fairs, festivals, and events in Asia* (pp. 63–75). Springer Singapore.

Samori, Z., Salleh, N. Z. M., & Khalid, M. M. (2016). Current trends on Halal tourism: Cases on selected Asian countries. *Tourism Management Perspectives*, *19*, 131–136.

Şeyhanlıoğlu, H. Ö., & Zengin, B. (2022). The reflection of digitalization and social media on Muslim-friendly tourism. *Journal of Hotel and Tourism Issues*, *4*(2), 123–134.

Şimşek, M. (2019). Halal hotel concept as a basic element of halal tourism. *Journal of Halal Life*, *1*(1), 35–43.

Şimşek, M. (2023). Artificial intelligence in tourism. In İ. Kalemci Tüzün & M. Öksüz (Eds.), *Multifaceted researches in the field of tourism II* (pp. 147–160). Özgür Publications.

Soygüden, A. (2020). The effects of prayer and nutrition practices in Islam on obesity. *Akademiar Journal of Academic Islamic Studies*, *9*, 99–125.

Sürme, M., Olcay, A., & Karaçil, G. (2018). Bibliometric profile of halal tourism field. *Iğdır University Journal of Social Sciences*, *15*, 389–408.

Tayar, M., & Doğan, M. (2019). Halal Slaughtering. *Academic Platform Journal of Halal Lifestyle*, *1*(2), 62–76.

Tunç, M. G., & Sayın, A. A. (2019). Evaluation of supplier selection within the scope of halal tourism. *Journal of Academic Social Science Studies*, *7*(99), 396–409.

Türker, S. (2020). Halal and safe food. *Journal of Halal and Ethical Research*, *2*(1), 85–97.

Yıldız, S., & Yıldız, Z. (2018). The reflection of Islam on tourism: Halal tourism. *Mehmet Akif Ersoy University Journal of Social Sciences Institute*, *10*(26), 770–781.

Yılmaz, Y., Akgün, A., & Kınay, H. (2020). A qualitative research on the usability of hotel management systems in halal tourism practices in hotels. *Safran Culture and Tourism Research Journal*, *3*(2), 182–207.

Yorulmaz, D. Ö., & Akçi, Y. (2020). The effect of attitudes towards halal food consumption on purchase intention (the case of Adıyaman). *Kahramanmaraş Sütçü İmam University Journal of Social Sciences*, *17*(2), 1218–1238.

Chapter 2

The Influence of Innovative Technologies and AI on Halal Tourism: Trends, Instruments, and Transformation

Birendra Kishore Roy

Department of Hotel Management, FoMCA, Manipal University Jaipur, India

Abstract

In the past few years, hospitality and tourism sector has experienced many significant changes by adapting to digital transformation. Many international hotels are using artificial intelligence in the form of robot chefs, which are specialized in performing a wide range of tasks by giving certain commands. Providing authentic service by maintaining service quality within a specific time remains a challenge for service providers in this industry. In a niche tourism sector where food is the priority for a specific group who are passionate about experiencing only Halal foods, for the mass production houses, it remains a challenge to provide standard products only by maintaining manual support. This chapter explains how artificial intelligence (AI) and automation are helping Halal tourism to improve service excellence. It elaborates on how advanced technology is supporting the operational needs of Muslim travelers, as they mainly seek Halal cuisine at a specific destination. What upgraded technical advancements, like voice recognition systems or the auto bots and service robots, or AI-driven mechanisms, have the possibilities in delivering service excellence in Halal tourism are also discussed in this chapter. This chapter explains that Halal tourism enterprises have a possible outcome if they adapt new technology to fulfill the needs of major communities. The research will help tourism policymakers and stakeholders obtain new strategies for greater success.

Keywords: Halal tourism; niche tourism; artificial intelligence; automation; Muslim; community; digital transformation

Halal Tourism and Artificial Intelligence: New Approaches for a New Generation, 11–21

doi:10.1108/978-1-80686-165-120261002

1. Introduction: A World in Motion, a Faith in Practice

Essentially, traveling is all about getting about, seeing new places, and making new friends. Constantly changing preferences, global events, and, most significantly in our day, the unrelenting advancement of technology transformed the ever changing global environment of tourism and hospitality, reflecting this dynamism. An enormous digital upheaval has just swept across the sector, changing the whole nature of trip planning, booking, execution, and dissemination. This is more than simply a change in the way websites and applications work; it is a fundamental shift toward expedited communication, simplified operations, and individualized user experiences. In today's rapidly changing world, organizations cannot afford to miss out on the opportunities presented by the digital transformation. A substantial and rapidly expanding current Halal tourism exists within this enormous sea of travel. Travel planned within the explicit goal of conforming to the Islamic principles and values is more than just Muslim tourism; it is travel for Muslims. The special demands for Muslims have turned into a multi billion dollar industry, with products made in accordance with Islamic law, species designated for prayer, an atmosphere that values modesty, and interest free financial transactions being the driving forces behind it all. While it is true that Halal tourists use this time search engines and booking sites as the general public, they face specific challenges when trying to ensure the genuineness of the products they purchase, most notably, the food that is central to Halal diets (Hidayat Hidayat, 2023).

This chapter explores a crucial meeting points, which are how new technologies, especially the intelligence of algorithms (AI) and the precision of automation, are being brought to bear on the challenges and aspirations of Halal tourism. As Muslim travelers increasingly expect journeys that are smooth, dependable, and sensitive to their faith, the old ways of doing things relying solely on manual checks and human diligence begin to show their strain. How can a large hotel guarantee that every meal from its kitchen meets strict Halal standards? How can service remain excellent and consistent when dealing with culturally specific needs? How can the complex operational demands of providing truly Halal compliant experiences be met efficiently? All of these enquiries lead to technological concerns. To mitigate these issues, automated processes and artificial intelligence could be a possible solution. Imagine an artificial intelligence system that effortlessly navigates the complex network of Halal ingredient suppliers and a kitchen where robotic arms meticulously adhere to Halal preparation protocols. Think of virtual assistants who can understand cultural settings, robots that can quietly daily her food, or even an AI system that can instantaneously determine whether a product is Halal. These are not any type of science fiction or fragmented reality or even any imagination; rather, they are cutting edge technology with the potential to revolutionize Halal tourism (Suhartanto et al., 2021; Vargas-Sánchez & Moral-Moral, 2019).

This investigation will focus on the significant technical impact. To begin with, by comprehending the characteristics that set Halal tourism apart, including its fundamental principles, its impressive expansion, and the particular demand of Muslim tourists that characterize this business. To provide the groundwork for the

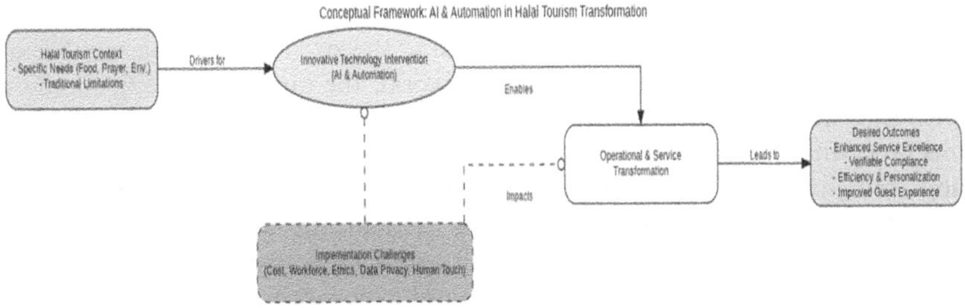

Fig. 2.1. Conceptual Framework. *Source*: By author.

adaptation of these technologies for Halal purposes, the authors have decided to take as a first step and examine the larger digital change that is redefining the whole hospitality industry. The main focus of this chapter is on the ways in which technology interacts with the daily reality of Halal travel through the develop- ment of digitalization for the global Halal food tourism industry (Hidayat Hidayat, 2023). The author has demonstrated how AI in food systems and automated serving procedures, intelligent customization, and other advanced mechanisms may cooperate to improve service quality, guarantee that compliance isn't just a calm but a verifiable reality, and improve the overall experience. It could be more understandable if elaborated through examples, such as AI creating meals with only approved foods, automatic systems that provide prayer alerts and navigational guidance, and chatbots who are skilled at answering questions about religion. However, the author has considered the intricacies to avoid any biases. What are the prices? What adaptations does the workforce make? What about the privacy of data? And most importantly, how can we make sure that technology complements rather than replaces the moral and spiritual core of Halal travel? "Ultimately, this book chapter shed light upon the influences of future of food tourism which includes investors, policy makers, hotel managers, and tour operators, by demonstrating how technology can be used not only for financial gain but also for increased success, sustainability, and authentic service in the thriving, rising Halal sector. The idea is if any Halal tourism establishments requires to satisfy the demands of modern Muslim tourists and establish a sustainable advantage is less of a choice and more of a requirement to carefully embrace AI and automation as explained by the previous practitioners (Battour et al., 2022; Wulandari et al., 2025).

Fig. 2.1 presents the author's conceptual framework, which maps out the relationships among technology adoption (AI, robotics, IoT), operational processes (food preparation, prayer assistance, data management), and ultimate service outcomes (quality, consistency, trust) in Halal tourism.

2. Understanding Halal Tourism: Growth, Principles, and Traveler Priorities

The phrase "Halal tourism," which includes ideas like Muslim friendly or "Sharia compliant" travel, has solidly transformed from a unique or niche tourism market to a significant sector of the international travel sector. Because of a number of interrelated reasons, including the size and growing number of youth Muslim population throughout the world, the quality of living standard and social status signifies the Muslim majority, and therefore the desire of Muslims everywhere to make sure that their vacations don't conflict with their religious principles, the growth of this type of tourism is often out stripping that of traditional tourism. Understanding the fundamental tenets of this sector as well as the unique needs of the visitors it caters to is essential to appreciating its importance. Making sure the whole travel experience is in accordance with the Islamic law (Sharia) is the fundamental goal of Halal delicacies. This implies that everything must be appropriate (Halal), avoiding everything expressly prohibited (Haram), including where one lives, what one eats, activities, and services obtained (Boğan & Sarıışık, 2019; Syahr et al., 2023).

This supply of Halal food and drinks is without a doubt the most important and often non negotiable condition. This is for more than just abstaining from alcohol and meat. In the preparation of Muslim food, a specific method of the slaughter process is mostly used, also known as "Zabiha," and follows strict proto- cols to ensure that none of the non Halal substances are mixed in at any point throughout the process (preparation, storage, cooking, and serving). Certification by reportable Halal authorities is ideal for reassuring travelers. The assurance of obtaining authentic Halal cuisine is a major determinant for many Muslim tourists when selecting their location, airline, and lodging. This offers a huge operational problem for tourist companies. It takes extraordinary dedication, strong processes, and sometimes substantial financial support to maintain these high standards daily, maintain supply chains to get certified products consistently, and educate employees to comprehend and adhere to stringent Halal rules. Inaccurate information regarding an ingredient or a kitchen mishap that results in contamination are examples of failures that can quickly destroy confidence and seriously harm a provider's reputation in the Muslim community (Chantarungsri & Alam, 2024).

Aside from eating, having access to suitable places of worship is quite important. Muslims face the Kaaba in Mecca, called the Qibla, during their five daily ritual prayers, or salat, at predetermined times. As pilgrims require clean, easily accessible, and appropriately situated locations to fulfill this religious duty. Some examples of such places are mosques in the area, prayer rooms (Musallas) in hotels, shopping malls, and airports, or even just a quiet area in their hotel room. Important supplementary materials consist of easily accessible data on the times of daily prayers (which vary according to place and date) and precise, legible indications indicating the direction of Qibla. Guests of hotels that take their Muslim community seriously may find prayer mats and their religious books in their rooms (Mohsin et al., 2016).

In addition, those who practice Halal tourism also look for places that reflect the Islamic principles of humility, family, and community. This may manifest as a deserve for lodging that provides amenities targeted toward certain genders, such as designated swimming hours or gender specific poles and fitness centers. Other popular choices include family shows and movies that do not feature adult themes, gambling, or alcohol, as these are all considered sinful according to Islamic law. Islamic cultural standards are well appreciated in general. While people's degrees of observation vary, having these amenities available greatly increases a property's or destination's perceived value. Additionally, many Muslim tourists choose hotels that do not serve alcohol or at least have rooms that do not have many words with alcoholic beverages, as well as restaurants and public spaces that are specifically marked as alcohol free (Azwar & Usman, 2025).

The tourist business has inherent challenges in meeting this variety of requirements, consequently, and reliability using conventional techniques. In the past, humans were the mainstay in providing these specialized services. Sorting through a paper certificate to verify Halal food could be necessary, staff awareness of procedures could be inconsistent, and giving precise, up to date information about the prayer timings or nearby Halal options relies on having knowledgeable staff on hand at the appropriate time something that isn't always guaranteed. In adios, where Muslims constitute a minority tourist infrastructure was not designed to accommodate their demands, scaling this service has proven to be a tremendous challenge (Ahyani et al., 2021). Consistently providing Halal service across multiple hotels in a chain or even within a single massive resort was an ongoing problem for the management team at the earliest stage. Initially, there was a lack of reliable information on the Halal choices for travelers, who had a hard time finding this information either for booking or after they arrived. Because of these information gaps and operational bottlenecks, the limitations of traditional methods were brought to light, and a window of opportunity for technological solutions was opened. The fundamental requirements of Halal tourism revolve around the following regulations proving compliance, having up to date, correct data, same to be well suited to be met by technology, especially by means of systems that provide accuracy, verification, and immediate information delivery (Rahman et al., 2020).

3. The Digital Reshaping of Hospitality: Context for Change

A true renaissance has occurred in the luxury and tourism sectors as a result of technological advancements, which have utterly dismantled long standing methods of operational logic, guest interaction models, and resource management. This shit could not have possible without modern analytical system, who is algorithms filter through vast amount of data (suggest booking histories, spending patterns, and guest ratings) to provide instantaneous, highly personalized suggestions, forecast occupancy rates, and adjust hotel prices accordingly. Human receptionists may now manage more complex, high value interactions by handling basic in room inquiries using chatbots and voice assistants. The use of advanced monitoring technologies to analyze public space traffic patterns and optimize security is going on in the background (Tseng et al., 2022). In addition to the new physical robots that work at the front desk, serve food, carry items of luggage, or even follow precise "robot chef" recipes that ensure every last detail of Halal compliance, robotic process automation technology is also used for back office tasks like report generation, data analysis, and interpretation. The IoT is the glue that holds this smart layer together; it uses smart sensors embedded into a building's surfaces. An attentive, energy efficient, and uptime-optimized guest centric environment is made possible by the interconnection of RADIUS devices and systems, such as the IoT. Guests may control the temperature and lighting with their voice or smartphone app, and energy monitoring systems can detect when anything needs fixing before it breaks. The interplay of automation, recentralization, IoT, and virtual platforms goes beyond the sum of its parts to create data driven architecture. This design increases efficiency, promotes customization, and opens the door to new revenue streams (Agil et al., 2021). Hotels of all kinds, from high end resorts to low cost motels, are you saying these technologically advanced strategies to please the increasing needs of their client, offering prompt, individualized service, safe labor costs, and running more ecologically responsible operations in the Halal travel industry. This all compassing digital framework ensures rigorous adherence, real service, and greater visitor delight, and it contains the most costly solutions to the unique problems of charity (Raya, 2022).

4. Where Technology Meets Tradition: Enhancing the Halal Travel Experience

Combining state of the art technology with these specific requirements of Halal tourism produces a very effective synergy. Collectively, they provide practical solutions to ongoing operational issues and pave the way for enhanced service quality. Technology offers precise, efficient, and transparent solutions to the basic problems faced by Muslim tourists and businesses that follow Muslim principles, as opposed to human approaches that hear inconsistent, unscalable, and legally verifiable evidence. Multiple touchpoints are becoming possible throughout the Halal tourist journey as a result of this fusion, including the procurement and serving of food, the exchange of information, and the customization of experiences (Aan Jaelani et al., 2021). Be mindful of the vital realm of Halal food. This offers a level of variable tracking that goes beyond conventional paper trails. However, relying on reliable, always present automated solutions rather than relying only on human oversight to ensure complete complaints has the dual benefit of boosting kitchen productivity and instilling a sense of trust. Customers who are concerned about their adherence to Halal standards are being better served by automatic non food service procedures. Apart from preparing the food, automation can handle room service, ensuring that Halal meals are delivered promptly and maybe even offering an alternative to the contact list that some customers want. This can be done while lowering the probability of errors when the hotel is busy (Huda et al., 2021). These intelligent robots can navigate hotels and other hospitality establishments to control the multiple accommodation facilities and provide a discreet amount of help. Much more standard facilities like housekeeping services, whether automated or human operated, are sure to impress guests of all religions and those with no faith. Therefore, the Halal tourism experience has the potential to be enhanced by incorporating these technologies for data management, task automation, the Internet of Things (IoT), and responsive spaces with analytics for deep understanding. This should make the experience more consistent, tailored to each individual, and in harmony with the core beliefs of Muslim tourism (Asa et al., 2024; Feizollah et al., 2021).

5. Navigating the Path Forward: Challenges and Opportunities

Although there are several obstacles in the way of general adaptation, the idea of a technology advanced Halal tourism industry is appealing. If stakeholders want to fully capitalize on the possibilities of this technological transformation, it is as critical to acknowledge and carefully handle the obstacles as it is to recognize the benefits. Considerable expense is one of the main obstacles in this relevant field. Implementing advanced AI systems, purchasing robotic machinery, updating building infrastructure for IoT devices, and integrating various digital platforms all require a substantial financial outlay. These upfront expenses may be a significant deterrent for independent, smaller hotels or companies that operate in underdeveloped areas, thereby dividing the Halal tourist sector into two groups tech haves and have nots (Katuk et al., 2021). The long term budget must include continuing expenses for upkeep, software upgrades, and specialist technical assistance. Humans, in particular their abilities and flexibility, are another important factor. Advanced AI and robotics systems need a person with specialized technical knowledge to operate and maintain; these abilities may not be easily accessible everywhere. Assisting the current hospitality workers with adaptation is equally crucial. In addition to learning how to operate new technologies, stop members also need to be trained to collaborate with automatic procedures and may switch their attention to jobs that call for special human abilities, such as empathy, complicated problem solving, cultural sensitivity, and real warmth. It is normal to be resistant to change, and what is that technology is taking jobs away is legitimate (Masood et al., 2023). Transparency, retaining expenditures, and a singular emphasis on how technology may enhance human roles rather than just replace them are all necessary for managing this shift. When it comes to the personal information that drives customization, data security and privacy are crucial issues that cannot be compromised. Systems are fueled by data, which includes visitor preferences, trip patterns, and maybe even details on religious adherence. It is crucial to make sure that these data are gathered morally, kept safely using reliable techniques, utilized openly with visitors' permission, and conforms with a complicated network of global data protection regulations (such as the GDPR in Europe) (Marlinda et al., 2023). A security lapse might permanently erode visitor confidence, especially in the neighborhood where people often place a grade value on privacy. Additionally, there are significant ethical issues unique to Halal settings. AI algorithms that are used to filter material or make suggestions need to be properly crafted and regularly checked to make sure they do not unintentionally encourage actions or content that is harmful or prohibited (Haram) in an Islamic context. To prevent prejudices, the AI must have inherent cultural awareness. For example, a tourist activity recommendation AI has to comprehend Islamic views on entertainment, proper social behavior, or attire. To do this right, technology developers and specialists in Halal standards and Islamic law must work together continuously. Lastly, technology runs the danger of producing an impersonal, cold, and efficient experience. Fundamentally, hospitality and tourism are all about connecting with others. While repetitive activities may be expertly handled by automation, it's important to strike the correct balance between the convenience of technology and real, warm human connection. Rather than taking the place of the fundamental components of welcoming, caring, and culturally sensitive service of which are particularly crucial in niche industries like Halal tourism-technology should be used to improve the visitor experience. Over automation may deprive tourists of the very personal touch and authenticity they want (Azam et al., 2024). Despite these struggles, using technology thoughtfully opens up a world of options. To begin with, there is no denying the possibility of substantial increases in cost reduction and operational efficiency. Second, improving profitability and significant long term financial gains may result from streamlining processes, making the best use of personnel and resources, cutting down on expensive mistakes, and automatic respective operations. Third, technology makes it possible for a much greater level of variable quality control and uniformity. This is especially important for preserving the integrity of Halal across several services or locations on the same property. Fourthly, having the potential to provide extremely convenient and highly customized services gives you a significant competitive edge. More client satisfaction and repeat business result from better offering to the unique requests of Muslim travellers, from direct access towards Halal information plus personalized recommendations to simple control over the hotel surroundings. Therefore, the AI and automation may be used by Helen to resume industry to create a more efficient, significant, and complaint, and guest focus future by deliberately impressing in the potential and handling the hurdles with foresight (Kurniawan et al., 2025; Rasul, 2019).

6. Conclusion: Weaving a Future of Faith aligned Travel

The introduction of advanced automation and artificial intelligence is not only a passing fad; rather, it signifies a fundamental change that has the potential to completely transform the Halal travel industry. As discussed, the specific necessities of individual Muslim tourist, the necessity of assured Halal food, easily available prayer facilities, small surroundings, and reliable information – create special operational requirements. The inherent constraints of manual procedures and human effectiveness in addressing these criteria make traditional methods ineffective in terms of scalability, consistency, and verifiable evidence. Nonetheless, the digital revolution that is sweeping the hotel industry provides full support tools. Improved service quality, streamlined operations, and individualized care in the Halal tourist industry are all within reach with the use of AI, robots, the IoT, and intelligent data analytics author have seen the possibilities. AI is adding new levels of precision to food preparation and Halal supply chains, with automatic solutions such as the robot chefs guaranteeing Street adherence to guidelines. Though smart robotics and intelligent chatbots are ready to rapidly answer faith specific queries, automation simplifies service delivery. AI creating travel experience is catered not just to tastes but also to morals, thereby enabling Muslim visitors to feel very visible and valued. Intelligent surroundings predict requirements, including Qibla orientation and prayer timings. Data analytics provide the understanding required for ongoing adaptation and improvement. Because of this convergence, practitioner/author: have made great strides in overcoming previous obstacles, and now we can look forward to the future when travel is not only fun but also consistently in line with Islamic beliefs. Still, accepting this future calls for knowledge and cautious navigation. The challenges are real, the high barrier to entry, the necessity of training current employees to adapt to new ways of working, the critical ethical obligation to keep technology in line with Islamic principles, and absolute necessity of protecting guests' personal information. It will be a constant balancing effort to find the ideal that makes UP technical efficiency and priceless human warmth. Overcoming these obstacles calls for strategic investment, dedication to training and ethical growth, strong security policies, and honest communication among Islamic scholars, hotel managers, and digital developers. Still, the benefits of doing it correctly are really large. Providers of Halal tourism that cleverly use these technologies will have a leg up in the competitive goal market thanks to increased efficiency, more reliable service, better customer loyalty, and stellar reputation. Establishing and ecosystem that encourages this innovation through improved infrastructure, focused funding, unambiguous ethical standard, and digital skills programs is essential for legislators and destination managers to gain a greater portion of this crucial market and guarantee its long term growth. Looking forward, hello tourism's impact on artificial intelligence and automation will probably only become more pronounced. Through this present study, researchers confirm that robotics will definitely continue to evolve to improve the service quality with the help of automation to achieve greater cultural awareness and dexterity. It is also undeniable that with the essence of modification and upgraded technology innovation, AI is not only going to change the Halal tourism sector but also it is going to change the perception of Muslim tourists around the globe. The timely distribution of services and a strategic and ethical approach will attract a greater number of guests in coming future, which will provide a dynamic and responsive impact in the global tourism sector. Research driven and led by stakeholder corporations, the road ahead promises further innovation and long lasting profitability in this important tourism and hospitality sector (Hanafiah et al., 2022).

References

Aan Jaelani, D., Firdaus, S., Sukardi, D., Bakhri, S., & Muamar, A. (2021). *EVALUATION Journal: ROSA DOS VENTOS-Turismo e Hospitalidade Title: Smart city and Halal tourism during the Covid-19 pandemic in Indonesia (Cidade Inteligente e Turismo Halal durante a Pandemia Covid-19 na Indonésia)*. https://mail.google.com/mail/u/0/?ik=cd98aaa350&view=pt&search=all&permthid=thread-f%3A1720331432761272529&simpl=msg-f%3A1720331

Agil, A., Rakhmad, N., & Hidayat, W. N. (2021). *Halalan.Id: Design and build Halal tourism application to develop Halal smart city in East Java.*

Ahyani, H., Mahfud, M., Waluyo, R., Ulya, W., & Muharir, M. (2021). The potential of Halal food as a driver of the economic development in regional community. *Jurnal Pariwisata Terapan*, *4*(2), 163.

Asa, G. A., Fauk, N. K., McLean, C., & Ward, P. R. (2024). Medical tourism among Indonesians: A scoping review. *BMC Health Services Research*, *24*(1), 49. https://doi.org/10.1186/s12913-023-10528-1

Azam, M. S. E., Muflih, B. K., & Al Haq, M. A. (2024). Intersection between modern technologies and Halal tourism. *The Journal of Muamalat and Islamic Finance Research*, *21*(1), 16–31. https://doi.org/10.33102/jmifr.546

Azwar, A., & Usman, A. H. (2025). Artificial intelligence in the halal industry: Trends and global research opportunities. *International Journal of Halal Industry*, *2025*(1), 46–67. https://doi.org/10.20885/IJHI.v

Battour, M., Salaheldeen, M., & Mady, K. (2022). Halal tourism: Exploring innovative marketing opportunities for entrepreneurs. *Journal of Islamic Marketing*, *13*(4), 887–897. https://doi.org/10.1108/JIMA-06-2020-0191

Boğan, E., & Sarıışık, M. (2019). Halal tourism: Conceptual and practical challenges. *Journal of Islamic Marketing*, *10*(1), 87–96. https://doi.org/10.1108/JIMA-06-2017-0066

Chantarungsri, C., & Alam, A. (2024). *Sustainable strategies for Halal tourism infrastructure in the digital age: Integrating architecture, urban planning, and technology*.

Feizollah, A., Mostafa, M. M., Sulaiman, A., Zakaria, Z., & Firdaus, A. (2021). Exploring halal tourism tweets on social media. *Journal of Big Data*, *8*(1), 72. https://doi.org/10.1186/s40537-021-00463-5

Hanafiah, M. H., Hasan, M. R., & Mat Som, A. P. (2022). Managing modern Muslim travellers: Emerging trends and issues for Islamic tourism destinations. *Tourism and Hospitality*, *3*(4), 908–918. https://doi.org/10.3390/tourhosp3040058

Hidayat Hidayat. (2023). Development strategies for Halal tourism in Indonesia through the smart tourism approach. *International Conference on Digital Advance Tourism, Management and Technology*, *1*(2), 178–187. https://doi.org/10.56910/ictmt.v1i2.35

Huda, N., Rini, N., Muslikh, M., & Hidayat, S. (2021). Developing a strategic model for Halal tourism in Aceh. *International Journal of Religious Tourism and Pilgrimage*, *9*(1), 70–82. https://doi.org/10.21427/0y6f-gh36

Katuk, N., Ku-Mahamud, K. R., Kayat, K., Abdul Hamid, M. N., Zakaria, N. H., & Purbasari, A. (2021). Halal certification for tourism marketing: The attributes and attitudes of food operators in Indonesia. *Journal of Islamic Marketing*, *12*(5), 1043–1062. https://doi.org/10.1108/JIMA-03-2020-0068

Kurniawan, T., Islam, M. F., Gazi, M. A. I., & Hossain, M. B. (2025). Halal tourism research in Indonesian context: A bibliometric analysis. *Discover Sustainability*, *6*(1), 254. https://doi.org/10.1007/s43621-025-00959-7

Marlinda, A. P., Al-Fadhat, F., Cipto, B., & Jubba, H. (2023). Halal tourism as a strategic option for South Korean tourism. *Journal of Islamic Marketing*, *14*(5), 1276–1290. https://doi.org/10.1108/JIMA-03-2021-0074

Masood, A., Hati, S. R. H., & Rahim, A. A. (2023). Halal cosmetics industry for sustainable development: A systematic literature review. *International Journal of Business and Society*, *24*(1), 141–163. https://doi.org/10.33736/ijbs.5609.2023

Mohsin, A., Ramli, N., & Alkhulayfi, B. A. (2016). Halal tourism: Emerging opportunities. *Tourism Management Perspectives*, *19*, 137–143. https://doi.org/10.1016/j.tmp.2015.12.010

Rahman, M., Moghavvemi, S., Thirumoorthi, T., & Rahman, M. K. (2020). The impact of tourists' perceptions on halal tourism destination: A structural model analysis. *Tourism Review*, *75*(3), 575–594. https://doi.org/10.1108/TR-05-2019-0182

Rasul, T. (2019). The trends, opportunities and challenges of halal tourism: A systematic literature review. *Tourism Recreation Research*, *44*(4), 434–450. https://doi.org/10.1080/02508281.2019.1599532

Raya, M. K. F. (2022). Wali Pitu in Bali: Inventing new halal tourism destinations in contemporary Indonesia. *Contemporary Islam, 16*(2–3), 475–505. https://doi.org/10.1007/s11562-022-00503-8

Suhartanto, D., Dean, D., Wibisono, N., Astor, Y., Muflih, M., Kartikasari, A., Sutrisno, R., & Hardiyanto, N. (2021). Tourist experience in Halal tourism: What leads to loyalty? *Current Issues in Tourism, 24*(14), 1976–1990. https://doi.org/10.1080/13683500.2020.1813092

Syahr, Z. H. A., Syaifullah, D. H., Buyamin, B., & Sally, N. U. (2023). *Sustainable development goals concept overview in the digital service halal certification in Indonesia* (pp. 73–83). https://doi.org/10.1007/978-981-99-5146-8_6

Tseng, M. L., Ha, H. M., Tran, T. P. T., Bui, T. D., Lim, M. K., Lin, C. W., & Helmi Ali, M. (2022). Data-driven on sustainable food supply chain: A comparison on Halal and non-Halal food system. *Journal of Industrial and Production Engineering, 39*(6), 430–457. https://doi.org/10.1080/21681015.2022.2040622

Vargas-Sánchez, A., & Moral-Moral, M. (2019). Halal tourism: State of the art. *Tourism Review, 74*(3), 385–399. https://doi.org/10.1108/TR-01-2018-0015

Wulandari, A., Narimawati, U., & Syafei, M. Y. (2025). The influence of Halal friendly attributes on visit intention mediated by destination image and artificial intelligence adoption in tourist destinations: Pengaruh Atribut Ramah Halal terhadap Minat Berkunjung yang Dimediasi oleh Citra Destinasi dan Adopsi Kecerdasan Buatan di Destinasi Wisata. *EKOMABIS: Jurnal Ekonomi Manajemen Bisnis, 6*(01), 1–16. https://doi.org/10.37366/ekomabis.v6i01.2294

Chapter 3

Halal Tourism in Portugal: A Digital Renaissance of the Routes of Gharb al-Andalus

Anabela Monteiro

Universidade Europeia, Lisbon, Portugal

Abstract

This chapter explores the potential of Halal tourism in Portugal, focusing on cultural heritage, identity, and digital innovation. Building on the legacy of Gharb al-Andalus, the chapter proposes the revitalization of tangible and intangible Islamic heritage to create inclusive and meaningful tourist experiences. Key locations that evidence the Islamic presence in Portugal are identified and contextualized with a view to integrating them into itineraries that are authentic and rooted in cultural memory.

The chapter also examines how Halal tourism can be combined with digital tools, such as artificial intelligence (AI), augmented reality, and digital storytelling, to create immersive and personalized experiences for Muslim and spiritually motivated travelers. Portugal's preparedness for this tourism sector is assessed by identifying its current strengths, shortcomings, and prospects.

It proposes a strategic approach to integrating Halal tourism into sustainable development policies, with the aim of positioning Portugal as an innovative, inclusive, and culturally significant destination. Included in the chapter is a three-day itinerary entitled "Echoes of Al-Andalus: Living Islamic Traditions in Portugal," merging cultural visits, immersive digital experiences, and Halal-certified services.

Halal Tourism and Artificial Intelligence: New Approaches for a New Generation, 23–38

Published under exclusive licence by Emerald Publishing Limited
doi:10.1108/978-1-80686-165-120261004

Ultimately, the chapter advocates a digital renaissance of the Gharb al-Andalus routes where memory, heritage, and technology converge to offer new paradigms for spiritual and identity-based tourism.

Keywords: Halal tourism; Portugal; Gharb al-Andalus; Islamic heritage; cultural legacy

1. Introduction

Halal tourism is a growing segment of the global tourism industry that attends to the cultural and religious needs of Muslim travelers by providing services that align with Islamic principles. Beyond food and accommodation, it encompasses an appreciation of cultural and spiritual identity. In Portugal, this development aligns with a renewed interest in the Islamic heritage of Gharb al-Andalus, the westernmost region under Muslim rule in the Iberian Peninsula.

This chapter analyses Halal tourism in Portugal through the lens of Islamic heritage, exploring how historical memory and digital innovation can converge to support inclusive, culturally significant tourism. By recovering overlooked sites, revaluing heritage, and integrating technology, Portugal has great potential to establish itself as a Halal-friendly destination.

The chapter concludes with a proposed three-day itinerary called "Echoes of Al-Andalus: Living Islamic Traditions in Portugal," designed to offer Muslim travelers a meaningful and contemporary experience that combines heritage, spirituality, and immersive technologies.

2. Gharb al-Andalus: Islamic Heritage as a Tourist Resource

2.1. Historical Importance of Gharb al-Andalus

The term Gharb al-Andalus is used to describe the westernmost part of Islamic territory in the Iberian Peninsula during the medieval period. It was part of a larger geographical area called al-Andalus. The word "Gharb" comes from the Arabic word for "west" and is used to talk about the area that is now Portugal and part of western Andalusia. This area, including major cities such as Silves, Beja, and Lisbon (al-Lixbūnā), became part of the political, cultural, and economic activities of the western Islamic world and developed its distinct identity within al-Andalus (Nunes, 2015; Picard, 2000).

The first Muslims arrived in the Iberian Peninsula in 710. They came across the Strait of Gibraltar and settled in a region called al-Andalus, which covered most of the Peninsula. The western region of the Gharb al-Andalus had Silves as one of its main capitals for several hundred years. The conquest and administration of these territories show not only military success but also the establishment of a cultural, religious, and scientific system that had a profound effect on the region (Fletcher, 2006; Picard, 2000).

To understand the real importance of Gharb al-Andalus, we need to understand the bigger picture of Islamic thought and mobility. The experience of the Prophet Muhammad, who travelled himself, had a big effect on Islam. Islam sees knowledge and travel as ways to improve spiritually and intellectually. Prophetic hadith states, "Travelling in search of knowledge is an obligation for every Muslim," reinforcing the link between mobility, knowledge, and cultural development (Glick, 1995).

The combination of this itinerant spirit with the dynamism of commercial and diplomatic networks in the medieval Islamic world facilitated the circulation of people, ideas, and goods between East and West. Al-Andalus, and the Gharb in particular, became favored spaces for Muslims, Christians, and Jews to coexist, fostering religious tolerance, free trade, and scientific and philosophical research (Kennedy, 2014; Menocal, 2009). This peaceful coexistence gave rise to a hybrid culture, evident in architecture, agriculture, music, and oral traditions that persisted beyond the reconquest.

In the context of Gharb al-Andalus, cities such as Lisbon (al-Lixbūnā), Silves, and Beja played a key role in connecting people and ideas. As Nunes (2015) shows, Lisbon became a place where people from all over the world met and got together to talk about books and ideas, showing how full of life the area was. This local literary production was connected to the major centers of al-Andalus while showing the Gharb's specificities, confirming its status as a peripheral yet creative space within the Western Islamic world.

The work of Christophe Picard (2000) is important for the study of Gharb al-Andalus because it combines Arabic sources and modern historical writing in a very good way. As Boissellier (2003) explains, Picard shows the complexity of politics, economics, and culture in the region, highlighting its important position within the Western Islamic world. The legacy of Gharb al-Andalus is still visible in the southern Iberian Peninsula, in things like the layout of cities, water systems, the names of places, and cultural practices. It is very important to understand this history if we want to appreciate the Peninsula as a place where different cultures met and to think about ideas of movement, living together, and sharing knowledge.

2.2. Main Places and Regions with Islamic Heritage in Portugal

The Islamic period in Portugal began when the Muslims took over the Iberian Peninsula in the 8th century. The Reconquista was a long process that lasted almost 700 years. It was marked by sporadic territorial gains and losses between Muslim and Christian factions. This led to the creation of Christian kingdoms and counties, helped by support from Christian Europe and division within the Muslim empire (Torres, 2021).

To better understand the history of Muslim domination in Portuguese territory, this work uses a framework of four major phases, based on Mattoso's proposal in *História de Portugal*, Vol. I (1992).

2.2.1. 1st Period – Conquest and Initial Consolidation (711–828)

The Muslim conquest of the Iberian Peninsula began in the early 8th century, after they had taken control of North Africa. Tariq ibn Ziyad, leading newly converted Berbers, took advantage of the internal divisions in the Visigoth kingdom. The Battle of Guadalete (711) led to the death of King Rodrigo and the swift occupation of territory, including the capital Toledo, which surrendered without a fight.

2.2.2. 2nd Period – Autonomy of the Peninsular West (828–929)

From the late 8th century, the western part of the Iberian Peninsula was relatively free from the rule of the emirate of Córdoba, as shown by revolts. These included the Berber uprising in Mérida (828–835) and the revolts led by Abd ar-Rahman ibn Marwan al-Jilliqi, who founded Badajoz with the emir's permission. During this time, the city was captured by Christians in 878. After al-Jilliqi died, power was shared among local leaders in Badajoz, Beja, Mértola, and Ossónoba. But Abd ar-Rahman III took control and stopped this autonomy. This autonomy was later repressed by Abd ar-Rahman III, who consolidated Umayyad rule in the western peninsula (916–930) after declaring himself caliph.

2.2.3. 3rd Period – Umayyad Centralization and Fragmentation in Taifas (929–1086)

The Umayyads consolidated their power, but their rule was not consistent, and there were many small kingdoms (929–1086).

The Umayyad caliphate was becoming stronger, and Córdoba was being controlled from the center. This meant that the western region was losing its independence. Al-Mansur ibn Abi Amir got more soldiers, including Berbers and Christian mercenaries. They won battles and took back Coimbra and sacked Santiago de Compostela. But there was a lot of dissatisfaction, and the caliphate was declining, so it broke into smaller parts in 1031. Taifa kingdoms appeared, including Huelva, Santa Maria (Ossónoba), Mértola, Silves, Lisbon, and Badajoz. The Christian kingdoms of León and Castile advanced because of their rivalry with Seville. Between 1055 and 1085, there were major conquests, including Coimbra and Toledo. Muslim rulers then asked the Almoravids for help, who were a powerful group in the area.

2.2.4. 4th Period – Decline and End of Islamic Rule (1086–1249)

The Almoravids arrived in 1086, marking the end of Islamic rule in Portugal. This period was marked by a move toward centralization in North Africa. Even though they had won some battles, like the one at Zalaca, the Almoravid empire still declined because of religious intolerance and poor management of money. The Almohad dynasty brought a brief resurgence with the second taifas (1144–1151), led by Ibn Qasi in Mértola, Silves, and Ossónoba. His assassination made it quicker for the Christians to take back control. After the Almohad defeat at Navas de Tolosa in 1212, Muslim territory in western Iberia quickly got smaller. Afonso III took control of Silves and Faro in 1249, which marked the end of Islamic rule in Portugal.

It is very important to identify these four periods of history. This helps us to understand where Islamic influence was strong in Portugal. This history helps us reflect on ideas of mobility, coexistence, and knowledge exchange.

2.3. Localities with Islamic Heritage in Portugal – Summary

Although it is often thought of as being in the south, there is also evidence of Islamic presence in the north of Portugal. This has left historical, archeological, and cultural traces in various regions. As this text shows, there is evidence that people lived in the Algarve to Beira Interior, including Lisbon, Évora, and Coimbra, for more than 500 years. It had a big impact on how cities were organized, the names of places, buildings and architecture, and culture.

Identifying and celebrating these places help us understand shared intercultural history and supports new types of cultural and spiritual tourism. Table 3.1 gives information about important Portuguese sites with Islamic heritage. It includes the historical names of the sites, what they were used for during the Muslim period, and the heritage elements that can still be seen or are recorded (Fig. 3.1).

Table 3.1. Localities with Islamic Heritage in Portugal – Summary.

Current Locality	Historical Name	Function During Islamic Period	Current Remains and Legacy
Silves	Madīnat Shilb	Capital of a taifa; political and military center of the Gharb	Castle, walls, cistern, ceramic remains (Liberato et al., 2021)
Mértola	Madīnat Saŷūṭala	Taifa center and strategic outpost on the Guadiana River	Islamic Museum, mosque-church, ceramic finds (Camara et al., 2023)
Beja	Al-Bajja az-Zayt	Administrative and military center; shared by local clans	Archeological remains, toponymy (Oliveira Marques, 1985; Picard, 2000)
Lisboa	Al-Ushbūna	Important port city; commercial and defensive hub	São Jorge Castle, urban layout, ceramic remains (Fernandes, 2019; Tavares, 2009)
Faro	Al-Farūn/ Al-Hārūn	Coastal city under the Taifa of Huelva; maritime relevance	Urban traces and archeological remains in the Municipal Museum (Fernandes, 2019; Tavares, 2009)
Coimbra	Qulunbirya	Brief Muslim rule; reconquered by Christians in 878	Islamic archeological remains underground (Mattoso, 1992; Oliveira Marques, 1985)

(*Continued*)

Table 3.1. (*Continued*)

Current Locality	Historical Name	Function During Islamic Period	Current Remains and Legacy
Idanha-a-Velha	Al-Antaniya	Refuge and base for revolts against Córdoba (al-Jilliqi)	Visigothic and Muslim ruins; ongoing archeological research (Mattoso, 1992; Oliveira Marques, 1985)
Lagos	Al-Zāwiya	Possible subdivision of the Algarve territory ruled by the Banū Hārūn	Toponymy and possible archeological structures (Fernandes, 2019; Tavares, 2009)
Lamego	[Unknown]	Conquered by Christians during the León and Castile campaigns	Castle and documented Visigothic and Islamic occupation (Mattoso, 1992; Oliveira Marques, 1985)
Viseu	Bijāw	Frontier town with residual Islamic presence	Toponymy and limited archeological remains (Mattoso, 1992; Oliveira Marques, 1985)
Évora	Al-Yabura	Important Alentejo Centre; sacked in 913 and reconquered in the 1230s	Castle, walls, continuous occupation (Gomes, 2015; Picard, 2000)
Aljustrel	Al-Lustr	Conquered by the Portuguese in 1234; modest earlier Islamic presence	Limited archeological remains; toponymy (Mattoso, 1992; Oliveira Marques, 1985)
Alcácer do Sal	Al-Qasr al-Bajja / Al-Qasr Abū Dānis	Major urban and defensive hub on the Sado River; link between interior and coast	Castle, Islamic urban layout, ceramic finds (Liberato, 2021; Paths of Faith, 2024)
Palmela	Balmallah	Strategic defense point between the Tagus and Sado estuaries	Castle with Islamic structures; documented ceramics (Liberato et al., 2021; Paths of Faith, 2024)
Tavira	Qaryat Ṭabīra	Commercial port linked to the kingdom of Niebla	Castle, Islamic cistern, ceramic finds (Fernandes, 2019; Liberato, 2021)
Ribat da Arrifana	Ribāt	Fortified religious complex (ribat); site of contemplation and defense	Ribat ruins, ongoing archeology, spiritual and touristic value (Boscaglia, 2023; Ribat da Arrifana, 2025)

Source: Author (2025).

has been important in history. At São Jorge Castle, medieval graffiti shows what people were doing for religious reasons and in their daily lives (Alves et al., 2024).

Islamic ceramics are very important for understanding society and the economy in Gharb al-Andalus. The CIGA Group has divided ceramics into two groups: every day and luxury.

Museums in Mértola, the historic center of Silves, and the "Islamic Lisbon" project show how archeology can encourage authentic, dialog-based halal tourism. These heritage sites help people find their identity and value tourism.

New projects like the Paths of Faith project have found evidence of Islamic heritage in Alcácer do Sal, Palmela, Tavira, Mértola, and the Alcáçova de Santarém, showing where Islam was present in Portugal. The Gharb al-Andalus Route is an example of how tourism and spirituality can be combined at these sites. It offers visitors the chance to experience the history and intercultural values of al-Andalus (Paths of Faith, 2024).

4. Heritage as a Bridge to Ancestral and Spiritual Tourism

The rediscovery of the Islamic legacy in Portugal has emerged as an opportunity for the development of forms of tourism that transcend the mere visit to monuments, focusing on experiences that reconnect identity, spirituality, and culture. This tendency is of pertinence to Muslim diaspora travelers and tourists who are interested in authentic spiritual experiences (de Pinho & Santos, 2021; Santos, 2015).

(a) Ancestral tourism and identity reconnection
Ancestral tourism enables individuals from the Muslim diaspora to explore their historical and cultural roots. In Portugal, the Islamic legacy is palpable in locales such as Mértola, Silves, and Lisbon, offering a tangible connection to the nation's historical past. The experience of touring these cities, exploring their historic districts, and visiting museums dedicated to the Andalusian legacy allows for a deep immersion in the history and culture of their ancestors (Boscaglia, 2023; Vidal, 2019).

(b) Experiencing reconnection through spiritual tourism
The phenomenon of spiritual tourism in Portugal has witnessed a notable surge, propelled by initiatives that underscore the nation's religious and cultural heritage. These initiatives have been instrumental in creating spaces that encourage reflection and contemplation, thereby fostering a deeper connection with the country's spiritual and cultural essence. The Mértola Islamic Festival, for instance, is a biennial event that celebrates Andalusian culture through musical performances, culinary traditions, and handicrafts, thereby fostering intercultural dialogue (Mértola Islamic Festival, 2025). The Ribat da Arrifana in Aljezur serves as a remarkable exemplar of a space dedicated to spirituality and retreat. It stands as a rare Islamic religious complex preserved within Portuguese territory, offering a significant cultural and historical landmark.

(c) Halal tourism: initiatives and resources
In response to the emergence of this niche market, Portugal has been undertaking measures to adapt its infrastructure and services to cater to the needs of this segment of the tourism sector. The Portugal Halal platform is an online resource that identifies certified accommodation, restaurants, and places of worship, thereby positioning the country as a welcoming destination for Muslim visitors (Portugal Halal, 2020).

In this context, the Casa da Cultura Islâmica e Mediterrânica (House of Islamic and Mediterranean Culture) in Silves is a notable cultural institution. It is a cultural space housed in a historic building that was renovated using traditional techniques, and its architecture incorporates elements of Islamic and Mediterranean arts (VisitPortugal, 2024). Concurrently operating with the Silves Center for Luso-Arab Studies (CELAS), the House fosters exhibitions, conferences, Arabic language instruction, and cultural dialogue initiatives. Its incorporation into thematic itineraries, such as those delineated by the Paths of Faith project, serves to underscore its function as a nexus between heritage, spirituality, and identity.

5. Is Portugal Ready for Halal Tourism?

Halal tourism is growing quickly and is set to be worth $350 billion by 2030 (Publituris, 2025). Portugal has a lot going for it: safety, friendliness, a variety of food, and a rich culture. But to make the right decisions for the company, the current offer, barriers, and opportunities must be assessed.

(a) Current Halal offer: key components
Portugal has taken some steps but still doesn't have a national plan for halal tourism. The PortugalHalal project says there are not enough certified services and not enough people know about them (Monteiro et al., 2021). The main problems are that there is not enough special training and that communication with Muslim travelers is not good enough. Domingues and Almeida (2024) say that tour operators don't know much about this. International models, such as CrescentRating's Halal Tourism Executive Program, offer solutions though implementation in Portugal is limited.

(b) Barriers: cultural ignorance, low visibility, and stigma
Common barriers include lack of knowledge about Halal requirements, low international visibility as a Halal destination, and persistent stigma around Islam in the West (Domingues & Almeida, 2024; Monteiro et al., 2021). These issues hinder trust and repeat visitation among Muslim tourists.

(c) Strong points: safety, hospitality, food, and culture
Portugal stands out as a safe, welcoming destination where its gastronomic offerings can be adapted to halal requirements. Islamic heritage in places like Mértola, Silves, Lisbon, and Alcácer do Sal makes it appealing to both religious and spiritually motivated travelers (Portugal Halal, 2020; Vidal, 2019).

(d) Opportunities: territorial valorization and integrated tourism
Halal tourism can enhance low-density areas by linking heritage with sustainable, cultural, and religious tourism (Domingues & Almeida, 2024). Initiatives like Paths of Faith and cross-border partnerships with Andalusia strengthen the Gharb al-Andalus brand.

6. Halal Tourism and AI: New Ways for a New Generation

6.1. Storytelling and Digital Scripts in Promoting Gharb al-Andalus

People in Portugal are becoming more interested in the Islamic heritage of the country. Digital tools such as interactive storytelling, augmented reality, and personalized itineraries are helping to spread this interest. Projects like Paths of Faith use this approach through themed routes with historical content, maps, videos, and stories that you can access by scanning QR codes. In cities like Mértola, Silves, and Lisbon, there are mobile apps that use your location to offer historical tours designed for modern Halal tourism (Boscaglia, 2023; VisitPortugal, 2024).

These tools help people learn about the past and make visitors from the Muslim world and other parts of the world feel welcome. Digital storytelling is now an important way to give a voice to people who have been ignored or stopped from speaking. By symbolically bringing back the legacy of Gharb al-Andalus, it supports the reinterpretation and revitalization of historical spaces (Battour et al., 2021; Santos, 2015).

6.2. Personalizing Halal Tourism Through AI

The use of AI in Halal tourism is changing how personalized experiences are designed. AI tools suggest Halal-certified options for routes, places to stay, and restaurants, considering dietary restrictions, prayer times, and cultural preferences. These suggestions adapt in real time to the user's profile, digital history, and interests (Battour et al., 2021; Vargas-Sánchez & Moral-Moral, 2018).

Chatbots that can understand different cultures and languages, as well as AI systems that can predict what customers want, can make services more efficient and improve customer experience in the hospitality industry. These tools help overcome language and cultural differences, making Muslim tourists happier and more loyal (Battour et al, 2022; CDIAL Halal, 2024; Elbendary et al., 2021; Salaam Gateway, 2024).

Interest in AI is especially strong among Generation Z and Muslim millennials, who want to travel in a way that feels real but also uses technology.

6.3. Collaborative Digital Platforms and Content Generation

The growth of user-generated content (UGC) is a big opportunity for Halal tourism. Muslim tourists share their experiences on social media, like blogs, Instagram, TikTok, and YouTube. They promote places of Islamic heritage by sharing real stories and interesting photos (de Pinho & Santos, 2021; Vargas-Sánchez & Moral-Moral, 2018).

These platforms act as living archives, encouraging the Muslim community to take part in creating their own heritage. Recommendations from qualified cultural moderators help shape the image of a destination, build trust among potential visitors, and attract new demographics (Portugal Halal, 2020; Salaam Gateway, 2024).

6.4. Future Opportunities and Integration into Public Policies

The digitalization of Halal tourism offers Portugal a unique opportunity to position itself as an innovative, inclusive, and culturally enriching destination. A Gharb al-Andalus Digital Route, built on storytelling, AI, and UGC, could encourage identity-based and spiritual tourism, especially in less populated regions such as the Alentejo and interior Algarve (Boscaglia, 2023; Monteiro et al., 2021).

To do this, projects must align with public strategies for tourism, digital transformation, and cultural heritage. Working with Turismo de Portugal, local authorities, and research centers will be very important. Research from around the world shows that when technology and culture come together, it makes tourists want to come back repeatedly. This also creates long-lasting benefits for the economy and for the area's reputation (Battour et al., 2021; Nuraini & Sucipto, 2021; Oliveira Borges, 2017).

The suggested tour, called Echoes of Al-Andalus, is a good example of these plans. It is a tour that includes everyone and which gives visitors a real experience of the culture.

7. Halal Roadmap Proposal – Gharb al-Andalus Portugal: "Echoes of Al-Andalus: Living Islamic Traditions in Portugal"

Echoes of Al-Andalus: Living Islamic Traditions in Portugal is a three-day itinerary (Table 3.2) that combines Islamic heritage with immersive digital experiences, designed for Halal tourism. It includes visits to Lisbon, Silves, and Mértola. It uses technologies such as virtual and augmented reality, mobile apps with geolocated storytelling, and cultural workshops.

The itinerary includes Halal meals, spiritual places, and places to stay, creating an experience that is culturally rich and inclusive. Each day has QR codes with links to maps, audio guides, and multimedia content. The program shows how Islamic heritage, when combined with digital tools and designs that are respectful of culture, can create new and exciting opportunities for sustainable, spiritual, and identity-based tourism.

8. Conclusion

The valorization of Islamic heritage in Portugal is a strategic opportunity to reposition the country as an inclusive, sustainable, and culturally differentiated tourist destination. As asserted by Picard (2000) and Menocal (2009), the Gharb al-Andalus was a milieu of coexistence and profound cultural exchange,

Table 3.2. Digital Itinerary – Echoes of Al-Andalus: Living Islamic Traditions in Portugal.

Day	Location	Activities & Experiences	Meals	Accommodation
1	**Lisbon (al-Ushbūna)**	Visit to São Jorge Castle with virtual reality (Islamic city & mosque reconstruction) Multilingual digital guide (Arabic, English, Portuguese) with geolocation & prayer times Halal shopping and prayer space suggestions via app	*Lunch*: *Mezze* (Halal, Middle Eastern) *Dinner*: *Zubir Churrasqueira* (Martim Moniz)	*The Leaf Boutique* Hotel, Rua do Conde de Redondo, Lisbon
2	**Silves (Madīna Shilb)**	Transfer to Silves Guided tour of Silves Castle with AR app Digital storytelling walks through old medina	–	–
	Portimão (Burj Munt)	Transfer to Portimão Free time with app-guided cultural and spiritual suggestions	*Lunch*: *Annapurna Indian Restaurant* (Halal) *Dinner*: At hotel	*Bela Vista Hotel & Spa – Relais & Châteaux*, Praia da Rocha
3	**Mértola (madīna Sayūṭala)**	Transfer to Mértola Visit to Islamic Museum and mosque-church Ceramics workshop (glazing & geometric design) with CIGA artisans Geolocated storytelling tour	*Picnic lunch* with Halal ingredients	–
	Alcácer do Sal (al-Qasr al-Baja)	Stop to visit old town Brief contextualization of Islamic heritage Final transfer to Lisbon	–	*The Leaf Boutique Hotel*, Lisbon
	Lisbon (Closing Session)	Closing session with sharing of experiences Presentation of digital film of the trip	*Dinner*: Halal buffet dinner in private room	–

Source: Author (2025).

whose legacy remains manifest in the urban layout, toponymy, irrigation systems, archeological objects, and local traditions. This phenomenon, though at times rendered imperceptible, can be re-activated in the present through conscious and technological tourism practices.

Halal tourism, a rapidly expanding sector (Battour et al., 2021; Vargas-Sánchez & Moral-Moral, 2018), has emerged as a potentially significant economic catalyst in regions with a historical Islamic presence. The integration of AI, digital storytelling, and georeferenced applications facilitates the creation of personalized and culturally sensitive experiences, as evidenced by the studies conducted by Battour et al. (2021) and initiatives such as the Paths of Faith project (2024).

However, as Monteiro et al. (2021) and Domingues and Almeida (2024) have highlighted, significant challenges persist, including a shortage of certified infrastructures, inadequate international visibility, and limited cultural preparation of tourism agents. To overcome the barriers, there is a necessity for investment in specialized training, liaison with local communities, and the integration of Halal tourism into public policies on sustainable tourism and heritage.

The establishment of a Gharb al-Andalus Digital Route, integrating historical narrative, identity inclusion and digital tools, has the potential to serve as a catalyst for territorial cohesion and a plural reinterpretation of the past. Portugal could recover a significant part of its history, strengthen ties with the Muslim diaspora and assert itself as an innovative and welcoming destination in the context of the global Islamic economy.

Portugal has the opportunity not only to rediscover its Islamic legacy but also to emerge as a global reference for inclusive, digital, and heritage-based Halal tourism.

References

Alves et al. (2024). Grafitos medievais no Castelo de São Jorge (Séculos XIV–XV): Novos estudos. *Portvgalia*, 45.

Battour et al. (2021). *Artificial intelligence applications in Halal tourism to assist Muslim tourist journey*. International conference on emerging technologies and intelligent systems (pp. 861–872). Springer. https://doi.org/10.1007/978-3-030-85990-9_68

Bento, A. M., & Costa, M. C. (2023). O tambor islâmico da rua da Cadeia (Silves). *Revista do Museu de Arqueologia e Etnologia*, *41*, 75–94.

Boissellier, S. (2003). Christophe Picard, Le Portugal musulman (VIIIe–XIIIe siècle). *Histoire & Sociétés Rurales*, *19*, 268–271. https://doi.org/10.3917/hsr.019.0253

Boscaglia, F. (2023). *Património Islâmico: formação no Turismo de Portugal*. https://fabrizioboscaglia.com

Bugalhão, J. (2025). Da mesquita à catedral, percurso por um lugar central em Lisboa. *Medievalista*, 37. https://journals.openedition.org/medievalista/9317

Camara, C., Gonçalves, M. J., Mirão, J. A., Gómez Martínez, S., & Beltrame, M. (2023). Morpho-functional, decorative and petrographic study of Islamic glazed/unglazed ceramics from the cities of Évora, Mértola and Silves. *Estudos do Quaternário/ Quaternary Studies*, *23*, 29–46. https://doi.org/10.30893/eq.v0i23.215

Castro Gomes, M. L. (2023). *Língua portuguesa: história e formação*. Editora Intersaberes.

CDIAL Halal. (2024). *A ascensão do turismo Halal: o que você precisa saber*. https://cdial-Halal.com.br

de Pinho, J. A., & Santos, M. C. (2021). Ancestral tourism and identity building: Narratives of return among the descendants of Portuguese Sephardic Jews. *Heritage*, *3*(4), 1423–1441. https://doi.org/10.3390/heritage3040081
Domingues, J., & Almeida, S. (2024). Exploring the potential of halal tourism in a non-Muslim destination: The case of Portugal. *International Journal of Religious Tourism and Pilgrimage*, *11*(6).
Faulstich, E., & Carvalho, E. A. (2006). Aspectos de herança da língua árabe na língua portuguesa. *Debate Terminológico*, *2*.
Fernandes, H. (2018). Os madjus através do espelho: Algumas glosas em torno da incursão de 844. *Mil Anos da Incursão Normanda ao Castelo de Vermoim*, 87.
Fernandes, H. (Ed.). (2019). *Atlas das cidades islâmicas em Portugal*. INCM.
Festival Islâmico de Mértola. (2025). https://www.festivalislamicodemertola.com
Fletcher, R. A. (2006). *Moorish Spain*. University of California Press.
Glick, T. F. (1995). *From Muslim fortress to Christian castle: Social and cultural change in Medieval Spain*. Manchester University Press.
Gomes, M. (2015). *Silves muçulmana: da capital de taifa ao centro de memória*. Arqueologia Medieval em Portugal: 30 anos depois (pp. 115–132).
Gomes, R., & Gomes, M. (1995). Silves: Vestígios de uma cidade islâmica. *Revista Arqueologia Medieval*, *3*, 53–79.
Gomes, R. V. (2002). O século XX e a Arqueologia Muçulmana em Portugal. *Arqueologia e História*, *54*, 203–214.
Gomes, R. V. (2025). Testemunhos de instrumentos musicais islâmicos (sécs. VIII–XIII). *CEM – Cultura, Espaço & Memória*, *18*.
Kennedy, H. (2014). *Muslim Spain and Portugal: A political history of al-Andalus*. Routledge.
Liberato, M., Inácio, I., Lopes, G., Santos, C. D., Bugalhão, J., Catarino, H., & Gonçalves, M. J. (2021). Cerâmica de tradição islâmica em contexto português: Séculos XII–XIV. *Medievalista,* 30. https://doi.org/10.4000/medievalista.4554
Mattoso, J. (1992). *História de Portugal* (Vol. *I*). Círculo de Leitores.
Menocal, M. R. (2009). *The ornament of the world*. Hachette UK.
Monteiro et al. (2021). *PortugHalal project: A strategic path for Portugal*. https://www.researchgate.net/publication/357559265
Neto, J. P. (2006). *Mértola Islâmica: Território e Identidade*. Campo Arqueológico de Mértola.
Nunes, N. M. L. (2015). Al-Lixbūnā, uma cidade cosmopolita do al-Andalus. In *Territórios da Lisboa Medieval* (pp. 99–110).
Nuraini, S., & Sucipto. (2021). Comparison halal food regulation and practices to support halal tourism in Asia: A review. *IOP Conference Series: Earth and Environmental Science, 733*(1), 012044. https://doi.org/10.1088/1755-1315/733/1/012044
Oliveira Borges, M. (2017). A importância estratégica do conhecimento do território em Sintra no período islâmico. *Anuario de Historia Regional y de las Fronteras*, *22*(2), 17–48.
Oliveira Marques, A. H. de. (1985). *História de Portugal* (Vol. *I*). Palas Editores.
Paths of Faith. (2024). https://www.pathsoffaith.com/pt-pt/legado-islamico
Perrando, I. (2003). El árabe andaluz y la clasificación de los dialectos neo-árabes. *Alif Nün*, *19*, 9.
Picard, C. (2000). *Le Portugal musulman (VIIIe–XIIIe siècle)*. Maisonneuve & Larose.
Portugal Halal. (2020). https://www.portugalHalal.com
Publituris. (2025). *Turismo Halal valerá 350 mil milhões até 2030*. https://www.publituris.pt
Salaam Gateway. (2024). *How AI is powering the future of the Islamic economy*. https://salaamgateway.com

Santos, C. (2015). "Procurando as minhas raízes": Narrativas de identidade no turismo ancestral. *Antropológicas*, *28*(1), 145–166.
Tavares, A. A. (2009). *A cidade islâmica no Ocidente peninsular*. IGESPAR.
Torres, M. (2021). *A reconquista cristã da Península Ibérica*. RTP Ensina. https://ensina.rtp.pt
Vargas-Sánchez, A., & Moral-Moral, M. (2018). Halal tourism: State of the art. *Tourism Review*, *74*(3), 385–399.
Vidal, M. (2019). *Islamic traces in Portugal's past*. The New Arab. https://www.newarab.com
VisitPortugal. (2024). *Casa da Cultura Islâmica e Mediterrânica*. https://www.visitportugal.com

Chapter 4

Generations Z and Y's Virtual Voyage: Exploring Hajj and Umrah Through the Digital Lens

Mustapha Ahachmi[a], *Fatima Zahra Fakir*[b] *and Akif Gökçe*[c]

[a]*Mons University, City of Mons, Belgium*
[b]*Padova University, City of Padova, Italy*
[c]*Sakarya Uygulamalı Bilimler Üniversity, City of Sapanca, Turkey*

Abstract

This study examines generational differences in adopting immersive digital technologies, virtual reality (VR), augmented reality (AR), and artificial intelligence (AI), within virtual religious tourism, specifically Hajj and Umrah. It compares Generations Y and Z in terms of behavioral intention (BI) and actual usage of virtual pilgrimage platforms, applying the Unified Theory of Acceptance and Use of Technology 2 (UTAUT2). Core constructs include performance expectancy (PE), effort expectancy (EE), social influence (SI), facilitating conditions (FC), hedonic motivation (HM), price value (PV), and habit (H), with generation as a moderating variable.

Based on survey data from 396 Muslims in North Africa and Europe, analyzed via Partial Least Squares Structural Equation Modeling (PLS-SEM), results show that Gen Z responds more to HM, PV, and habit, while Gen Y is more influenced by EE, SI, and FC. BI strongly predicts use for both groups. The study extends UTAUT2 to immersive faith-based technologies and offers insights for designing inclusive, engaging digital pilgrimage platforms. It is one of the first to explore intergenerational adoption of immersive tech in Islamic spiritual tourism.

Keywords: Virtual religious tourism; Generations Z and Y; UTAUT2; immersive technologies; Virtual Hajj and Umrah

Halal Tourism and Artificial Intelligence: New Approaches for a New Generation, 39–51

doi:10.1108/978-1-80686-165-120261005

1. Introduction

Virtual tourism is transforming the travel industry through VR and immersive technologies that redefine traditional models. As digitalization progresses, VR improves accessibility for those with physical limitations and serves as a marketing tool (Tussyadiah et al., 2018). Hyper-realistic simulations extend attraction reach, personalize experiences, and promote sustainable tourism (Buhalis & Amaranggana, 2014), while aiding heritage preservation through reconstructions. When combined with AI and AR, VR enhances smart tourism by delivering real-time, context-aware content (Boes et al., 2016).

Tourism stakeholders use VR to boost engagement and decision-making. Hotels, theme parks, and cruise lines offer 360-degree previews to reduce uncertainty and drive bookings (Bilro et al., 2018). It supports experiential marketing by letting users preview services (Brakus et al., 2009) and promotes eco-tourism through low-carbon alternatives (Buhalis & Law, 2008). Yet, adoption is limited by costs, access, and authenticity concerns (Hunter et al., 2015). While enriching tourism, VR still falls short of replicating full sensory experiences (Tussyadiah et al., 2018). Future research should examine hybrid models that blend VR with physical travel.

1.1. Digital Transformation in Religious Tourism

Religious tourism is being transformed by immersive technologies like AR, VR, and AI. These tools digitally reconstruct sacred sites and offer interactive, educational, and spiritually immersive experiences (Gombault & Allal-Chérif, 2021). AR recreates monuments in real time, VR enables virtual pilgrimages, and AI supports personalization and heritage preservation.

In Islam, pilgrimage includes Hajj, an obligatory rite for those able, and Umrah, a recommended ritual performed year-round (Safiullah et al., 2024; Shah, 2024). Hajj entails structured rites like Ihram, Tawaf, Sa'i, Arafat, and Jamarat, while Umrah focuses on Ihram, Tawaf, Sa'i, and Tahalul. Both signify devotion, purification, and renewal (Abdul Shukor & Kattiyapornpong, 2024). Virtual tools like VR and AI enhance access to Mecca and Medina, addressing barriers such as cost, health, and geopolitics. Though not a replacement, they offer inclusive, emotionally resonant spiritual engagement (De Luca et al., 2023).

1.2. Generational Shifts in Technology Adoption

Digital tourism adoption highlights key differences between Generation Y (1981–1994) and Generation Z (1995 onward), shaped by distinct digital experiences and expectations. Millennials value authenticity, ethical engagement, and experiential consumption, often guided by peer content and reviews (Eastman & Liu, 2012). In contrast, Gen Z favors immediacy, personalization, and immersive interaction, influenced by short-form content and cross-platform integration (Lissitsa & Kol, 2016).

While both generations are digitally fluent, their engagement with VR, AR, and AI in virtual religious tourism varies. Gen Z embraces interactive and cost-effective innovations more readily, whereas Millennials may need more support to adopt immersive platforms. This is especially pertinent for Hajj and Umrah, where virtual simulations offer alternative spiritual experiences. However, the emotional authenticity of physical pilgrimage remains hard to replicate. This study explores these generational dynamics using the UTAUT2 model (Venkatesh et al., 2012), focusing on BI and age as a moderating factor, offering insight into how digital natives and adopters engage with virtual religious rites.

2. Theoretical Framework

2.1. The Unified Theory of Acceptance and Use of Technology

The UTAUT2, proposed by Venkatesh et al. (2012), expands the original model by incorporating HM, PV, and Habit (H) alongside PE, EE, SI, and FC to explain BI and usage behavior (UB), moderated by factors such as age and gender. In the context of Hajj and Umrah, UTAUT2 provides a relevant framework for understanding the adoption of immersive technologies like VR, AR, and AI, which simulate rituals such as Tawaf and Saai, lowering access barriers while enhancing spiritual engagement.

Each construct plays a distinct role: PE reflects perceived spiritual enrichment; EE relates to ease of use, especially for Millennials; SI involves social and religious endorsement; and FC includes infrastructure needs. HM strongly appeals to Gen Z's preference for emotional and immersive content, while PV reflects cost sensitivity among young users. Habit, supported by digital religious practices, eases transition into immersive formats. UTAUT2's application across various sectors (Alalwan et al., 2017; Tamilmani et al., 2019) confirms its versatility. In virtual religious tourism, it captures cognitive, emotional, and structural factors shaping adoption across generational lines, supporting the design of inclusive digital pilgrimage experiences.

2.2. Research Model

The hypothesized model was constructed using the exogenous variables (PE, EE, SI, FC, HM, PV, H, BI, and UB) (see Table 4.1). Additionally, Gen Y refers to Generation Y (Millennials, born 1981, 1994/96), while Gen Z represents Generation Z (born 1995/97 and after). The M hypotheses indicate the moderating effects of age (Gen Y vs. Gen Z) on the relationships between independent variables and BI or UB. Fig. 4.1 presents the theoretical model.

3. Methodology

3.1. Sample

In this study, we aim to investigate the factors influencing the adoption of virtual Umrah and Hajj services among Generations Y and Z Muslims across Morocco,

Table 4.1. Researcher Hypothesis.

Direct Effects
On BI
- *H1. PE has a significant effect on BI*
- *H2. EE has a significant effect on BI*
- *H3. SI has a significant effect on BI*
- *H4a. FCs have a significant effect on BI*
- *H5. HM has a significant effect on BI*
- *H6. PV has a significant effect on BI*
- *H7a. HB has a significant effect on BI*
On use behavior (UB)
- *H4b. FCs have a significant effect on UB*
- *H7b. HB has a significant effect on UB*
- *H8. BI has a significant effect on UB*
Moderating effects of age (Gen Y vs. Gen Z)
- *M1. The relationship between PE and BI is moderated by age, with Gen Z emphasizing interactivity and Gen Y prioritizing functional benefits*
- *M2. The relationship between EE and BI is moderated by age, with Gen Z perceiving virtual pilgrimage as easier to use than Gen Y*
- *M3. The relationship between SI and BI is moderated by age, with Gen Y being more influenced by peer and family recommendations*
- *M4a. The relationship between FCs and BI is moderated by age, with Gen Y requiring more technological support and guidance*
- *M4b. The relationship between FCs and UB is moderated by age, with Gen Y being more dependent on technical infrastructure*
- *M5. The relationship between HM and BI is moderated by age, with Gen Z placing greater emphasis on enjoyment and immersive experiences*
- *M6. The relationship between PV and BI is moderated by age, with Gen Y being more price-sensitive in evaluating the cost–benefit trade-off*
- *M7a. The relationship between HB and BI is moderated by age, with Gen Z developing stronger habitual engagement with digital religious platforms*
- *M7b. The relationship between HB and UB is moderated by age, with Gen Z displaying higher habitual engagement in virtual pilgrimage platforms*

Algeria, Tunisia, Italy, France, and Belgium. Data were collected through a structured questionnaire distributed via a non-probabilistic sampling method, resulting in 465 responses in total. However, after screening for completeness and consistency, 396 valid responses were retained for analysis. Valid questionnaires were utilized for data analysis.

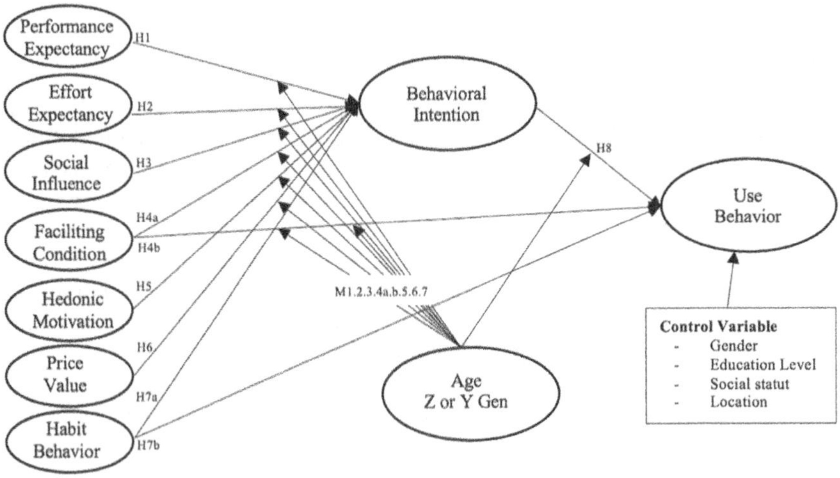

Fig. 4.1. Research Framework.

3.2. Variables Measures

This study utilized a survey adapted from the UTAUT2 by Venkatesh et al. (2012) to examine the adoption of virtual Umrah and Hajj services. The questionnaire was customized to this religious context, incorporating constructs such as PE, EE, SI, FC, HM, PV, habit, BI, and UB, all measured on a five-point Likert scale.

Prior studies emphasize the role of attitudinal and socio-demographic factors, such as education, gender, and location, in shaping technology adoption in religious contexts (Madan & Yadav, 2018). Differences between European and North African Muslims show higher skepticism among the latter. Moreover, religiosity negatively correlates with digital engagement (Lissitsa & Kol, 2016), prompting its inclusion as a control variable due to its potential moderating effect on technology acceptance.

3.3. Data Analysis

The study employed principal component analysis with Varimax rotation to explore the measurement model's structure, identifying three components with strong loadings, minimal cross-loadings, and acceptable reliability (Hair et al., 2019). Confirmatory factor analysis in SPSS confirmed construct validity, with fit indices (CFI, TLI, RMSEA) meeting recommended thresholds (Hu & Bentler, 1999). For hypothesis testing, PLS-SEM using SmartPLS 4 was applied, given its suitability for theory building and handling moderate sample sizes and non-normal data (Hair et al., 2021). This approach enabled robust assessment of reliability, validity, and path significance, ensuring methodological rigor in a digital technology context (Sarstedt et al., 2022).

4. Results

4.1. Descriptive Statistics of Measurement

Table 4.2 presents the descriptive statistics of the 396 respondents, 269 from Generation Y and 127 from Generation Z, revealing notable generational differences in gender, marital status, education, and location. Generation Y includes 62% males and 73% females, while Generation Z consists of 38% males and 27% females, indicating a slightly higher female presence among older respondents. Marital status differs markedly: 80% of Gen Y are married versus only 20% of Gen Z. Educational levels also contrast, with 85% of Gen Y holding high school diplomas, while 56% of Gen Z possess university degrees, showing a greater pursuit of higher education among younger participants.

Geographically, 62% of the total sample resides in North Africa and 38% in Europe, yet generational disparities are evident: Generation Y is more evenly distributed (43% in North Africa, 58% in Europe), while Generation Z is more concentrated in North Africa (57%) compared to Europe (42%). These findings underscore key socio-demographic shifts, highlighting that Generation Z is less likely to be married, more likely to have pursued higher education, and predominantly based in North Africa, all of which may influence their perceptions of digital religious experiences and the adoption of virtual pilgrimage technologies.

4.2. Structural Equation Modeling

To test the research model and hypotheses, data analysis was conducted using SmartPLS 3.0, a tool for PLS-SEM. This method is well-suited for small to moderate samples and complex, exploratory models due to its minimal distributional

Table 4.2. Descriptive Statistics.

Variable		Gender		Social Status		Education			Location	
		M	F	M	NM	NHSG	HSG	UD	NA	EU
Gen Y	Freq	113	156	189	52	47	121	73	106	86
(*N* = 269)	%	62%	73%	80%	32%	54%	85%	44%	43%	58%
Gen Z	Freq	69	58	46	109	40	21	94	141	63
(*N* = 127)	%	38%	27%	20%	68%	46%	15%	56%	57%	42%
Total	Freq	182	214	235	161	87	142	167	247	149
(*N* = 396)	%	46%	54%	59%	41%	22%	36%	42%	62%	38%

M: Male; F: Female | GY: Generation Y (1995<); GY: Generation Z (<1995) | M: Married; NM: Non-married | NHSG: Non-high School Graduate; HSG: High School Graduate; CD: College's Degree | NA: North Africa; EU: Europe.

Source: Authors' calculations.

assumptions (Hair et al., 2021). A bootstrapping procedure with 5,000 resamples was employed to assess the significance of path coefficients, with corresponding *t*-values used to evaluate hypothesis support.

Following Anderson and Gerbing's (1988) two-step SEM approach, the measurement model was first examined for reliability, convergent validity, and discriminant validity. Key indicators included factor loadings, Cronbach's alpha, composite reliability (CR), and average variance extracted (AVE) (Fornell & Larcker, 1981; Hair et al., 2019). Results confirmed that all constructs met accepted psychometric criteria, as detailed in Table 4.3.

4.2.1. Measurement Model Evaluation

An exploratory factor analysis was conducted in SPSS to examine the latent structure of the measurement items and their alignment with theoretical constructs. All Kaiser–Meyer–Olkin values exceeded the 0.60 threshold, confirming sampling adequacy. The explained variance ranged from 54.8% to 91.3%, indicating strong construct representation. Cronbach's alpha values for all constructs were above 0.70 (Hair et al., 2021), supporting internal consistency and structural validity.

Subsequently, the measurement model was assessed using SmartPLS 3, following Hair et al. (2010) and Fornell and Larcker (1981). Convergent validity was confirmed by factor loadings above 0.70, and by Cronbach's alpha, rho_A, CR, and AVE values all exceeding recommended thresholds. Discriminant validity was verified via the Fornell–Larcker criterion, with each construct's AVE square root exceeding its inter-construct correlations, confirming the model's empirical distinctiveness.

Table 4.3. Correlation Matrix for All Sample.

Construct	PE	EE	SI	FC	HM	PV	HB	BI	UB
PE	**0.864**	0.514	0.452	0.351	0.734	0.791	0.455	0.326	0.242
EE	0.569***	**0.886**	0.514	0.508	0.626	0.663	0.378	0.591	0.423
SI	0.463***	0.437***	**0.868**	0.682	0.442	0.325	0.634	0.721	0.547
FC	0.522***	0.541**	0.516***	**0.888**	0.571	0.676	0.781	0.675	0.713
HM	0.517**	0.494***	0.552***	0.491***	**0.897**	0.527	0.567	0.241	0.503
PV	0.538***	0.516***	0.568**	0.517**	0.591***	**0.872**	0.698	0.782	0.678
HB	0.432**	0.579***	0.424***	0.484***	0.523***	0.412**	**0.880**	0.771	0.473
BI	0.558***	0.591***	0.471***	0.539***	0.475**	0.552***	0.562***	**0.871**	0.589
UB	0.332**	0.373**	0.413**	0.433**	0.458**	0.448**	0.426**	0.394**	**0.871**

Bolded values on the diagonal are the square root of the AVE, below the diagonal is the Fornell & Larcker value | ***$p < 0.01$, **$p < 0.05$, *$p < 0.1$ | PE, performance expectancy; EE, effort expectancy; SI, social influence; FC, facilitating conditions; HM, hedonic motivation; PV, price value; HB, habit behavior; BI, behavioral intention; UB, use behavior.

Source: Authors' calculations.

To evaluate the measurement model's reliability and validity, convergent and discriminant validity were assessed using CR, AVE, rho_A, and item loadings (see Table 4.4). All constructs demonstrated high internal consistency, with Cronbach's alpha ranging from 0.887 to 0.931, and CR values between 0.932 and 0.962, exceeding the 0.70 threshold. AVE values were above 0.50, and item loadings exceeded 0.68, confirming convergent validity.

Discriminant validity was verified using the Fornell–Larcker criterion (Table 4.3), with the square root of each construct's AVE greater than its correlations with other constructs. For instance, PE's AVE square root (0.864) surpassed its highest inter-construct correlation (0.791 with PV), confirming construct distinctiveness across the model.

Multicollinearity was assessed via variance inflation factor (VIF) indicating no multicollinearity concerns. BI (2.144) and UB (2.096) reported the highest VIFs, but remained within acceptable limits.

The correlation matrix (Table 4.3) revealed strong, significant associations between PV and BI (0.782, $p < 0.01$), and between Habit and BI (0.771, $p < 0.01$). FC also correlated strongly with habit (0.781) and UB (0.713), underscoring their role in adoption. These results confirm the measurement model's robustness and justify progression to structural model analysis.

4.2.2. Structural Model

This study used comparative structural equation modeling to examine technology adoption in virtual pilgrimage across Generation Z (Model 2) and Generation Y (Model 3) using an extended UTAUT2 framework (see Table 4.5). The models

Table 4.4. Validity and Reliability.

Construct	Item Loading	rho_A	AVE	CR	VIF	α
PE	0.747	0.756	0.747	0.932	1.425	0.903
EE	0.689	0.792	0.786	0.941	1.357	0.912
SI	0.694	0.761	0.753	0.951	1.273	0.892
FC	0.702	0.794	0.789	0.946	1.351	0.917
HM	0.716	0.817	0.805	0.958	1.417	0.909
PV	0.717	0.772	0.761	0.962	1.364	0.887
HB	0.732	0.782	0.774	0.948	1.294	0.919
BI	0.689	0.771	0.759	0.939	2.144	0.902
UB	0.721	0.764	0.771	0.952	2.096	0.931

PE, performance expectancy; EE, effort expectancy; SI, social influence; FC, facilitating conditions; HM, hedonic motivation; PV, price value; HB, habit behavior; BI, behavioral intention; UB, use behavior.

Source: Authors' calculations.

Table 4.5. Estimation Results for Hypotheses.

	Model 1		Model 2		Model 3	
Path	**β**	**t-Value**	**β**	**t-Value**	**β**	**t-Value**
H1	0.201***	3.375	0.263	3.873	0.261**	5.215
H2	0.275**	4.285	0.179***	2.575	0.025**	0.092
H3	0.071	0.053	0.018	0.035	0.013	0.102
H4a	0.104**	3.215	0.103	0.055	0.054	0.112
H4b	0.067	1.212	0.036	1.775	0.082	0.895
H5	0.174*	2.675	0.138*	2.224	0.182*	2.169
H6	0.128*	1.775	0.248***	4.713	0.201**	1.792
H7a	0.057	0.067	0.069	0.062	0.074	0.115
H7b	0.021	0.039	0.007	0.031	0.011	0.172
H8	0.174**	2.662	0.212**	3.371	0.149**	2.641
Moderation Effect			**AGE = Gen Z**		**AGE = Gen Y**	
M1			0.192**	2.341	0.205**	3.273
M2			0.174*	1.992	0.201*	3.159
M3			0.063	0.072	0.019	0.058
M4a			0.119**	2.917	0.102	1.492
M4b			0.029	0.095	0.011	0.047
M5			0.152*	1.973	0.112*	1.562*
M6			0.096*	1.375	0.141*	2.092
M7a			0.025	0.017	0.003	0.002
M7b			0.009	0.023	0.012	0.022
M8			0.145**	2.061	0.182**	2.405
Control						
C1			0.246**	4.316	0.205*	3.403
C2			0.285***	3.421	0.218***	4.717
C3			0.293***	5.138	0.271***	3.926
C4			0.158*	1.482	0.209*	2.096
R^2						
BI	0.761		0.684		0.712	
UB	0.729		0.513		0.594	
SRMR			0.056		0.063	

***$p < 0.01$, **$p < 0.05$, *$p < 0.1$.

Source: Authors' calculations.

showed strong explanatory power, with R^2 values for BI ranging from 0.684 to 0.761 and for UB from 0.513 to 0.729, indicating high and moderate variance explained, respectively. Model fit was satisfactory, with SRMR values below the 0.08 threshold (Hair et al., 2017), and all fit indices within acceptable ranges, confirming the robustness of the structural model for future empirical investigation.

4.2.3. Direct Effects Across Models

The structural model showed that BI was significantly influenced by PE, EE, HM, PV, and Habit, while SI was not. This suggests that virtual pilgrimage adoption is primarily driven by perceived usefulness, ease of use, enjoyment, affordability, and habitual behavior. Generational analysis revealed that Gen Z's BI was shaped by PE ($\beta = 0.32$), HM ($\beta = 0.35$), PV ($\beta = 0.20$), and Habit ($\beta = 0.30$), with EE and SI proving non-significant, indicating a preference for engaging, value-driven, and routine-based usage.

Conversely, Gen Y's BI was influenced by PE ($\beta = 0.25$), EE ($\beta = 0.30$), SI ($\beta = 0.22$), and HM ($\beta = 0.18$), highlighting a stronger focus on usability and social validation, while PV and Habit were not significant. BI strongly predicted UB across groups, overall ($\beta = 0.53$), Gen Z ($\beta = 0.55$), and Gen Y ($\beta = 0.50$). For Gen Z, Habit impacted UB ($\beta = 0.22$), but FC did not, whereas Gen Y's UB was significantly influenced by FC ($\beta = 0.25$), not Habit. These findings underscore generational differences: Gen Z favors intrinsic and habitual drivers, while Gen Y relies more on usability and external support.

4.2.4. Moderation Effects by Generation

The multi-group analysis revealed significant generational moderation effects. PE influenced BI in both Gen Z ($\beta = 0.32, p < 0.001$) and Gen Y ($\beta = 0.25, p < 0.01$), with a stronger effect among younger users, suggesting greater emphasis on usefulness among digital natives. EE and SI were significant only for Gen Y (EE: $\beta = 0.30$; SI: $\beta = 0.22$), indicating older users are more influenced by ease of use and social norms.

FC affected UB in Gen Y ($\beta = 0.25$), but not Gen Z, who showed a stronger response to HM (HM: $\beta = 0.35$) than Gen Y ($\beta = 0.18$), reflecting Gen Z's experiential focus. PV influenced BI only in Gen Z ($\beta = 0.20$), pointing to higher cost sensitivity, while Habit significantly impacted both BI ($\beta = 0.30$) and UB ($\beta = 0.22$) in Gen Z but was non-significant for Gen Y. BI strongly predicted UB in both generations (Gen Z: $\beta = 0.55$; Gen Y: $\beta = 0.50$; $p < 0.001$), confirming its central role across cohorts.

5. Discussion

This study reinforces the relevance of the UTAUT2 model in explaining virtual pilgrimage adoption, revealing distinct generational patterns between Generation Y and Z. Consistent with prior research (Bilynets et al., 2024), PE and HM emerged as key drivers across both cohorts, though more strongly for Gen Z, who value both the functionality and emotional richness of technology. In the context of Hajj and Umrah, PE encompasses not only efficiency but also the capacity of digital platforms to simulate sacred rites like Tawaf and Arafat, supporting spiritual preparation without replacing the physical journey. Gen Z, in particular, embraces immersive formats as part of their broader digital religiosity.

Generational contrasts appeared in EE and FC, with Gen Y placing greater importance on usability, ritual guidance, and technical infrastructure (Katoch & Rana, 2023), while Gen Z navigates these technologies with greater ease. SI significantly shaped Gen Y's intention, reflecting reliance on community validation, whereas Gen Z demonstrated a more autonomous approach to spiritual engagement, favoring personalized digital exploration over external approval.

Habit Behavior (HB) proved more predictive for Gen Z, likely due to their routine use of digital religious tools, apps, livestreams, and online communities, making virtual Hajj and Umrah a natural extension of their spiritual lives. In contrast, Gen Y requires more reinforcement for such practices to become habitual. PV significantly influenced Gen Z's intentions, reflecting sensitivity to the high costs of physical pilgrimage and preference for affordable, digital alternatives. Gen Y, however, prioritized authenticity and depth over cost-efficiency.

BI remained the strongest predictor of UB, consistent with earlier studies (Bilynets et al., 2024; Katoch & Rana, 2023), though actual usage also depended on emotional connection, infrastructure, and spiritual alignment. Concerns over authenticity or religious legitimacy may still deter some, especially older users. These findings highlight the importance of tailoring virtual pilgrimage platforms to generational expectations: Gen Y values usability and religious validation, while Gen Z seeks immersive, personalized, and cost-effective experiences. Adapting design accordingly can foster spiritually meaningful and inclusive digital engagement, reaffirming UTAUT2's applicability to one of Islam's most sacred practices.

6. Conclusion

This study applied the UTAUT2 model to explore immersive technology adoption in virtual religious tourism, with a focus on generational differences between Generation Y and Generation Z. The findings reveal that Gen Z is primarily influenced by HM, PV, and habit, while Gen Y responds more to EE, SI, and FC. BI strongly predicts UB across both cohorts, confirming the model's robustness. These insights not only validate UTAUT2 in a novel religious context but also underscore the moderating role of age and digital fluency in shaping adoption patterns. The importance of experiential and economic drivers among younger users supports the extension of traditional technology acceptance models to account for evolving user expectations in immersive environments.

Beyond theoretical contributions, the study offers practical guidance for developers and marketers of virtual pilgrimage platforms. Gen Y favors usability, technical support, and credibility, while Gen Z is drawn to interactive, personalized, and gamified features. Tailoring experiences accordingly can enhance engagement across age groups. Nevertheless, the cross-sectional design and culturally specific sample limit generalizability. Future research should adopt longitudinal and cross-cultural approaches and consider additional moderators such as digital literacy, personality traits, or spiritual orientation to strengthen explanatory power and adaptability of UTAUT2 in faith-based, immersive technological contexts.

References

Abdul Shukor, S., & Kattiyapornpong, U. (2024). Muslim travellers: A bibliometric analysis. *Journal of Islamic Marketing*, *15*(4), 1054–1077. https://doi.org/10.1108/JIMA-11-2022-0302

Alalwan, A. A., Dwivedi, Y. K., & Rana, N. P. (2017). Factors influencing adoption of mobile banking by Jordanian bank customers: Extending UTAUT2 with trust. *International Journal of Information Management, 37*(3), 99–110. https://doi.org/10.1016/j.ijinfomgt.2017.01.002

Anderson, J. C., & Gerbing, D. W. (1988). Structural equation modeling in practice: A review and recommended two-step approach. *Psychological Bulletin, 103*(3), 411–423. https://doi.org/10.1037/0033-2909.103.3.411

Bilro, R. G., Loureiro, S. M. C., & Guerreiro, J. (2018). Exploring online customer engagement with hospitality services: A comparison between virtual and augmented reality. *Journal of Hospitality Marketing & Management*, *27*(6), 581–607. https://doi.org/10.1080/19368623.2018.1506375

Bilynets, I., Trkman, P., & Knežević Cvelbar, L. (2024). Virtual tourism experiences: Adoption factors, participation and readiness to pay. *Current Issues in Tourism, 27*(22), 3658–3675. https://doi.org/10.1080/13683500.2023.2268809

Boes, K., Buhalis, D., & Inversini, A. (2016). Smart tourism destinations: Ecosystems for tourism destination competitiveness. *International Journal of Tourism Cities*, *2*(2), 108–124. https://doi.org/10.1108/IJTC-12-2015-0032

Brakus, J. J., Schmitt, B. H., & Zarantonello, L. (2009). Brand experience: What is it? How is it measured? Does it affect loyalty? *Journal of Marketing*, *73*(3), 52–68. https://doi.org/10.1509/jmkg.73.3.052

Buhalis, D., & Amaranggana, A. (2014). Smart tourism destinations. In Z. Xiang & I. Tussyadiah (Eds.), *Information and communication technologies in tourism 2014* (pp. 553–564). Springer International Publishing. https://doi.org/10.1007/978-3-319-14343-9_28

Buhalis, D., & Law, R. (2008). Progress in information technology and tourism management: 20 years on and 10 years after the Internet, the state of eTourism research. *Tourism Management*, *29*(4), 609–623. https://doi.org/10.1016/j.tourman.2018.06.002

De Luca, V., Barba, M. C., D'Errico, G., Nuzzo, B. L., & De Paolis, L. T. (2023). A user experience analysis for a mobile mixed reality application for cultural heritage. *Virtual Reality*, *27*(4), 2821–2837. https://doi.org/10.1007/s10055-023-00840-w

Eastman, J. K., & Liu, J. (2012). The impact of generational cohorts on status consumption: An exploratory look at generational cohort and demographics on status consumption. *Journal of Consumer Marketing*, *29*(2), 93–102. https://doi.org/10.1108/07363761211206348

Enkatesh, V., Thong, J. Y. L., & Xu, X. (2012). Consumer acceptance and use of information technology: Extending the unified theory of acceptance and use of technology. *MIS Quarterly*, *36*(1), 157–178. https://doi.org/10.2307/41410412

Fornell, C., & Larcker, D. F. (1981). Evaluating structural equation models with unobservable variables and measurement error. *Journal of Marketing Research*, *18*(1), 39–50. https://doi.org/10.1177/002224378101800104

Gombault, A., & Allal-Chérif, O. (2021). The expansion of virtual spaces of superstar and star museums during the COVID-19 lockdown. In F. D. Molli & M. Vecco (Eds.), *The metamorphosis of cultural and creative organizations* (pp. 192–207). Routledge. https://doi.org/10.4324/9781003134671

Hair, J. F., Babin, B., & Krey, N. (2017) An assessment of structural equation modeling applications in the journal of advertising. *Journal of Advertising, 46*(1), 163–177. https://doi.org/10.1080/00913367.2017.1281777

Hair, J. F., Black, W. C., Babin, B. J., & Anderson, R. E. (2010). *Multivariate data analysis* (7th ed.). Prentice Hall.

Hair, J. F., Black, W. C., Babin, B. J., & Anderson, R. E. (2019). *Multivariate data analysis*. https://thuvienso.hoasen.edu.vn/handle/123456789/10308?locale-attribute=vi

Hair, J. F., Hult, G. T. M., Ringle, C. M., & Sarstedt, M. (2021). *A primer on partial least squares structural equation modeling (PLS-SEM)* (3rd ed.). Sage Publications. https://doi.org/10.1007/978-3-319-57413-4_15

Hu, L. T., & Bentler, P. M. (1999). Cutoff criteria for fit indexes in covariance structure analysis: Conventional criteria versus new alternatives. *Structural Equation Modeling: A Multidisciplinary Journal, 6*(1), 1–55. https://doi.org/10.1080/10705519909540118

Hunter, W. C., Chung, N., Gretzel, U., & Koo, C. (2015). Constructivist research in smart tourism: A case of VR-based heritage tourism. *Asia Pacific Journal of Information Systems, 25*(4), 647–664. https://doi.org/10.14329/apjis.2015.25.1.103

Katoch, R., & Rana, A. (2023). Online spiritual meets (OSMs) and user behavior–A divine application of technology during COVID-19. *Computers in Human Behavior, 139,* 107514. https://doi.org/10.1016/j.chb.2022.107514

Lissitsa, S., & Kol, O. (2016). Generation X vs. Generation Y – A decade of online shopping. *Journal of Retailing and Consumer Services, 31*, 304–312. http://dx.doi.org/10.1016/j.jretconser.2016.04.015

Madan, K., & Yadav, R. (2018). Understanding and predicting antecedents of mobile shopping adoption: A developing country perspective. *Asia Pacific Journal of Marketing and Logistics, 30*(1), 139–162. https://doi.org/10.1108/apjml-02-2017-0023

Safiullah, M., Anchal, & Parveen, N. (2024). *Brand building through CSR initiatives during Hajj and Umrah: A study of tourism industry*. Corporate social responsibility, corporate governance and business ethics in tourism management: A business strategy for sustainable organizational performance. https://doi.org/10.1108/978-1-83608-704-520241006

Sarstedt, M., Ringle, C. M., & Hair, J. F. (2022). Partial least squares structural equation modeling. In C. Homburg, M. Klarmann, & A. Vomberg (Eds.), *Handbook of market research*. Springer. https://doi.org/10.1007/978-3-319-57413-4_15

Shah, A. A. (2024). Enhancing Hajj and Umrah rituals and crowd management through AI technologies: A comprehensive survey of applications and future directions. *IEEE Access, 12*, 161820–161841. https://doi.org/10.1109/ACCESS.2024.3487923

Tamilmani, K., Rana, N. P., Prakasam, N., & Dwivedi, Y. K. (2019). The battle of Brain vs. Heart: A literature review and meta-analysis of "hedonic motivation" use in UTAUT2. *International Journal of Information Management, 46*, 222–235. https://doi.org/10.1016/j.ijinfomgt.2019.01.008

Tussyadiah, I. P., Wang, D., Jung, T. H., & tom Dieck, M. C. (2018). Virtual reality, presence, and attitude change: Empirical evidence from tourism. *Tourism Management, 66*, 140–154. http://dx.doi.org/10.1016/j.tourman.2017.12.003

Venkatesh, V., Thong, J. Y. L., & Xu, X. (2012). Consumer acceptance and use of information technology: Extending the unified theory of acceptance and use of technology. *MIS Quarterly, 36*(1), 157–178. https://doi.org/10.2307/41410412

Chapter 5

Influencer Marketing in Halal Tourism: A Study on Muslim Traveler's Trust and Engagement

Neeraj Kumar and Manvinder Singh Pahwa

Department of Commerce, Dr. Harisingh Gour Vishwavidyalaya (Central University), India

Abstract

This study explores the role of influencer marketing in the halal tourism industry in shaping Muslim travelers' trust (TR) and engagement (ENG). With the growing influence of social media, this research examines the impact of influencers' attributes – credibility, authenticity, content quality (CQ), and alignment with Islamic values – on Muslim travelers' perceptions and behaviors. A quantitative survey of 384 Muslim travelers who follow halal tourism influencers was conducted, with participants completing a structured questionnaire, and whose data were analyzed using structural equation modeling (SEM). The results suggest that alignment with Islamic values was the strongest predictor of trust which is then followed by authenticity and credibility, establishing that research participants may engage in religiously or culturally sensitive content that is genuine in nature. The visually stimulating and quality of content were found to be significant influencers driving ENG, with visually stimulating posts generating more interaction than other posts. Trust was found to mediate the relationship between influencers' characteristics and intention to visit (INT) to promoted destinations, while ENG also acted to amplify INT. This study highlights the unique interplay of religious and marketing variables in the context of halal tourism, providing valuable information that destination marketers, travel service providers, and influencers can apply to shape effective and culturally responsive tourism, destination, and marketing strategies. As a recommendation, the research suggests

Halal Tourism and Artificial Intelligence: New Approaches for a New Generation, 53–71

doi:10.1108/978-1-80686-165-120261006

long-term relationships with influencers and communicating halal certification transparently, the study stresses the importance of TR and ENG with Muslim travelers.

Keywords: Halal tourism; influencer marketing; Muslim traveler's; travel behavior; Islamic values

1. Introduction

In the last decade, the international tourism industry has grown and diversified significantly, with sub-markets added to service different demographic segments of consumers. One of specialized markets that are growing in terms of numbers and share is the halal tourism to meet demand of Muslim travelers around the world (El-Gohary, 2016). Halal tourism as tourism products and services respects the Islamic requirements and meets Muslim tourists' needs in terms of places of prayer, halal food, no alcohol areas, and family environment (Battour & Ismail, 2016).

Influencer marketing at the same time revolutionized the way of travel decision journey, social media influencers positioning as opinion leaders who redefine consumer thought and behavior. Tourism (Xu & Pratt, 2018) has adopted the use of influencer marketing as an important strategy in many fields. This traditional marketing ploy uses people with reputation and audience following behind accommodations, destinations, or travel experience to do promotion on social media (Lou & Yuan, 2019).

In particular for halal tourism, influencer marketing implies opportunities and challenges specifically. Muslim travelers have shown a tendency to demand certain amenities and services that are abiding both to belief, preferences of people in matters of religion religious practices and values, trusted information sources help them plan their trips (Han et al., 2019). To solve this information gap, social media influencers specializing in halal travel have been developed to share real reviews, recommendations, and experiences about halal accommodations and travel destinations (Oktadiana et al., 2016).

Although the role of halal tourism and influencer marketing has been getting more and more popular, there is a lack of research which has focused on their intersection. This study seeks to fill this gap by examining the moderating effect of different components of influencer marketing on Muslim traveler's TR and ENG. To be specific, this research investigates the relationship between influencer attributes (credibility, CQ, authenticity, and Islamic value alignment) and perceptions/trust/behaviors of the Muslim travelers.

The results of this study add insights on how to use influencer marketing successfully in halal tourism industry for destination marketers, travel service providers, and actual influencers to take action. This research identifies TR and ENG-influencing factors for Muslim traveler which is useful information in creating more effective communications resonating to this potential key consumer group.

Research Objectives

1. To examine how influencer attributes like credibility and authenticity and Islamic values alignment (IVA) affect Muslim travelers' trust in halal tourism influencers.
2. To analyze the impact of CQ, visual appeal (VA), and IVA on Muslim travelers' ENG with halal tourism influencer content.
3. To investigate the relationships between TR, ENG, and INT destinations endorsed by halal tourism influencers.
4. To provide evidence-based recommendations for tourism marketers and influencers to effectively engage Muslim travelers through religiously aligned content strategies.

2. Literature Review and Development of Hypothesis

2.1. Halal Tourism

Halal tourism is a niche within the tourism industry and caters to the religious as well as cultural requirements of Muslim travelers. It refers to a multitude of services and facilities applicable based on the tenets of Islam, such as halal foods, prayer areas, sex segregated recreation areas, and alcohol-free zones (Battour & Ismail, 2016). The halal tourism market is projected to grow in the recent years at a Rapid rate and its market value is expected to exceed USD 220 Billion (Global Muslim Travel Index, 2022) accounting to USD 400 Billion by 2026.

Research by Mohsin et al. (2016) says Muslim travelers are more likely to search for destinations and accommodation that reflects their own religious requirements accordingly. Halal tourism goes beyond prayer facilities and halal food, as mentioned by El-Gohary (2016) who adds that it represents all aspects of Islamic value in service delivery such as decency, ethics, and gender sensitiveness.

2.2. Influencer Marketing in Tourism

Influencer marketing is thought to have changed the way travel destinations and services are advertised toward future tourists. On social media, tourism influencers, as defined by Xu and Pratt (2018), are individuals with high credibility in specific travel niches who can shape destination image and travel decisions through the content they create or endorse. Many of these influencers will post their own personal travel experiences, reviews, and recommendations on Instagram, YouTube, and travel blogs.

Gretzel (2018) also defines the tourism context that the influencers perform three types of roles as information source, opinion leader, and experience co-creator. The transparency of authentic stories about locations and travel experiences tend to elicit a more powerful response from audiences than the fact-based advertising (Lou & Yuan, 2019). Researches of Femenia-Serra et al. (2019) reveal the strong effect of travel influencers on awareness, image formation, and intention for destination among their audience.

2.3. *Credibility and Authenticity in Influencer Marketing*

Credibility and authenticity of influencer are crucial in the effectiveness of marketing. Schouten et al. (2020) defined influencer credibility (IC) as expertise, trustworthiness, and attractiveness. In the tourism, this expertise is a kind of an intellectual capital corresponding to knowledge and experience of a given influencer traveler, whereas authenticity implies credibility regarding honesty and objectivity (Xu & Pratt, 2018).

Authenticity which is authentic and sincere has been a core issue in Influencer Marketing (Audrezet et al., 2020). Perceived authenticity is an important antecedent to followers' trust in influencer generated content and positive purchase intention (Lou & Yuan, 2019).

Authenticity may further extend to the influencer practicing Islam, his personal understanding of the concept (Battour et al., 2017) in halal tourism for instance.

From these considerations, we suggest the subsequent hypotheses:

H1. IC positively affects Muslim travelers' trust.

H2. Influencer authenticity (IA) positively affects Muslim travelers' trust.

2.4. *Content Quality and Visual Appeal*

Influencer CQ and presentation is key to how your audience engage with and perceive you. When content is good, it has informative value, entertaining value and professional appearance (Lou & Yuan, 2019).

In marketing of tourism, it is essential that the content is attractive visual because it has to attract traveler's and give a destination's image (Laudi & Mouchniss, 2018).

Kim and Fesenmaier (2017) research reveals that aesthetically travel imagery triggers emotional impact and more attractions in destination. In addition, the quality content can be even demanded from halal tourism especially as information of halal facilities and services must be accurate and detailed (El-Gohary, 2016).

Therefore, we hypothesize:

H3. CQ positively affects Muslim travelers' ENG.

H4. VA positively affects Muslim travelers' ENG.

2.5. *Alignment with Islamic Values*

Wilson and Liu (2010) note that, for Muslim consumers, adherence to Islamic values is an important criterion that influenced purchase behavior in these and other related product categories. For me, in halal tourism – this alignment is across different aspects of travel experiences and its representation (Battour et al., 2017).

Oktadiana et al. (2016) hypothesize that Muslim audiences trust influencers that exhibits content respect for and recognition of Islamic principles. The study of Muslim travelers suggests that marketing recognizes and respects their religious needs and values (Han et al., 2019).

Based on these insights, we propose

H5. Alignment with Islamic values positively affects Muslim traveler's trust.

H6. Alignment with Islamic values positively affects Muslim traveler's ENG.

2.6. Trust and Engagement

Trust mediates the relationship between attributes of the influencer and consumer responses in influencer marketing effectiveness (Lou & Yuan, 2019).

Trust in information sources considerably influences the travel decision-making processes (Femenia-Serra et al., 2019), tourism being the field of study.

ENG (likes, comments, shares, and others) supports with consumers knowledge (Valentini et al., 2018). The content that influencers post deals with the level of consumer ENG (Schouten et al., 2020). *Administrate*: Higher ENG, higher consumer influencer relationship, and stronger marketing effects.

Trust in travel influencers is found to predict more ENG with the involved platforms and stronger destination visit intentions, built upon Xu and Pratt (2018). On this relationship, we hypothesize:

H7. Trust in halal tourism influencers positively affects Muslim travelers' ENG.

H8. Trust in halal tourism influencers positively affects INT endorsed destinations.

H9. ENG with halal tourism influencer content positively affects INT endorsed destinations.

3. Methodology

3.1. Research Design

This study was conducted with a quantitative research methodology, using structured questionnaire survey to investigate the associations of influencer marketing aspects on trust among Muslim travelers and INT destination. The study used a cross-sectional design where data were collected from Muslim travelers using the social media platforms who follow halal tourism influencer.

3.2. Sampling and Data Collection

This research focused on Muslim travelers (18 years and above) who regularly follow at least one halal tourism influencer on Instagram, YouTube, or travel website like Facebook and/or travel blogs. Respondents that fit the above requirement were purposively selected to be part of the study.

The sample size was based on the recommendation of Hair et al. (2010) for SEM, which recommends a minimum of 10 respondents per parameter estimated. According to our measurement model with 28 observed variables a sample size of 280 was desired; above all, we could not allocate incomplete responses. We also sent survey to 450 people to sample for likely respondents due to the uncertainty around responses not being complete.

Between February and April 2025, data were collected by an online survey through:

1. Social media platforms (Instagram, Facebook, Twitter)
2. Muslim travel forums and communities
3. Halal tourism influencers' comment sections (with permission)
4. Muslim student associations in universities across five countries

3.3. Measurement Instrument

The questionnaire was established and modified according to halal tourism and influencer marketing themes. The 5-point Likert scale items were measured per construct and ranged from 1 = Strongly disagree to 5 = Strongly agree. Table 5.1 includes measurement items for each construct and their sources.

Table 5.1. Measurement Items and Sources.

Construct	Items	Source
IC	IC1: The halal tourism influencers I follow are knowledgeable about halal travel	Adapted from Ohanian (1990)
	IC2: The halal tourism influencers I follow are experienced in halal travel	
	IC3: The halal tourism influencers I follow are qualified to provide information about halal travel	
	IC4: The halal tourism influencers I follow are trustworthy in their recommendations	
IA	IA1: The halal tourism influencers I follow share genuine travel experiences	Adapted from Audrezet et al. (2020)
	IA2: The halal tourism influencers I follow are honest about both positive and negative aspects of destinations	
	IA3: The halal tourism influencers I follow demonstrate consistency between their stated values and content	
	IA4: The halal tourism influencers I follow clearly disclose sponsored content	
CQ	CQ1: The halal tourism influencers I follow provide detailed information about halal facilities	Adapted from Lou and Yuan (2019)
	CQ2: The halal tourism influencers I follow share useful travel tips for Muslim travelers	
	CQ3: The halal tourism influencers I follow create well-organized content	

Table 5.1. (*Continued*)

Construct	Items	Source
	CQ4: The halal tourism influencers I follow provide accurate information	
VA	VA1: The halal tourism influencers I follow post high-quality images and videos	Adapted from Kim and Fesenmaier (2017)
	VA2: The halal tourism influencers I follow use aesthetically pleasing visuals	
	VA3: The halal tourism influencers I follow create visually engaging content	
IVA	IVA1: The halal tourism influencers I follow respect Islamic principles in their content	Adapted from Battour et al. (2017)
	IVA2: The halal tourism influencers I follow emphasize halal aspects of travel experiences	
	IVA3: The halal tourism influencers I follow promote modest and family-friendly activities	
	IVA4: The halal tourism influencers I follow understand Muslim travelers' needs	
TR	TR1: I trust the information provided by the halal tourism influencers I follow	Adapted from Lou and Yuan (2019)
	TR2: I believe the halal tourism influencers I follow have my best interests in mind	
	TR3: I can rely on the halal tourism influencers I follow for accurate information about halal travel	
ENG	ENG1: I regularly like posts from the halal tourism influencers I follow	Adapted from Valentini et al. (2018)
	ENG2: I often comment on posts from the halal tourism influencers I follow	
	ENG3: I frequently share content from the halal tourism influencers I follow	
	ENG4: I actively participate in discussions on the halal tourism influencers' platforms	
INT	INT1: I am likely to visit destinations recommended by the halal tourism influencers I follow	Adapted from Xu and Pratt (2018)
	INT2: I prefer destinations endorsed by the halal tourism influencers I follow	
	INT3: I would choose a destination promoted by the halal tourism influencers I follow over one that is not	

3.4. Data Analysis

IBM SPSS 26.0 and AMOS 26.0 software was used for the stage wise data analysis. Descriptive statistics were performed initially to describe the respondent-level and social media use patterns among respondents. Second, confirmatory factor analysis (CFA) was used as measurement model testing reliability and convergent/discriminant validity. Third, SEM was used to analyze if the hypothesized relationships among constructs. *Mediation analyses*: Mediating role of trust and ENG in influence on INT endorsed destinations.

4. Results

4.1. Demographic Profile

The demographic profile of the 384 respondents is present in Table 5.2. The sample consisted of slightly more females 54.7% than males 45.3%. The largest age group is 25–34 years 42.7%, followed by 18–24 years 30.5%. In terms of education, most respondents had bachelor's degrees 43.8% or postgraduate qualifications 32.0%.

Table 5.2. Demographic Profile of Respondents (N = 384).

Demographic Variables	**Categories**	**Frequency**	**Percentage**
Gender	Male	174	45.3%
	Female	210	54.7%
Age	18–24 years	117	30.5%
	25–34 years	164	42.7%
	35–44 years	73	19.0%
	45–54 years	22	5.7%
	55 years and above	8	2.1%
Education level	High school or less	37	9.6%
	Bachelor's degree	168	43.8%
	Postgraduate degree	123	32.0%
	Professional qualification	56	14.6%
	Others	16	4.2%
Annual travel frequency	1–2 times	157	40.9%
	3–4 times	142	37.0%
	5–6 times	58	15.1%
	More than 6 times	27	7.0%

4.2. Social Media Usage and Influencer Following Patterns

Table 5.3 presents respondents' social media usage and influencer following patterns. Instagram emerged as the most popular platform for following halal tourism influencers 84.9%, followed by YouTube 68.5% and Facebook 41.4%. Most respondents 45.8% followed between 3 and 5 halal tourism influencers, while 28.6% followed more than 5 influencers. The primary reasons for following these influencers included seeking travel inspiration 78.6%, obtaining information about halal facilities 76.3%, and learning about Muslim-friendly destinations 69.5%.

Table 5.3. Social Media Usage and Influencer Following Patterns ($N = 384$).

Variables	Categories	Frequency	Percentage
Platforms used to follow halal tourism influencers	Instagram	326	84.9%
	YouTube	263	68.5%
	Facebook	159	41.4%
	Travel Blogs	132	34.4%
	Snapchat	127	33.1%
	Twitter	84	21.9%
Number of halal tourism influencers followed	1–2	98	25.5%
	3–5	176	45.8%
	6–10	83	21.6%
	More than 10	27	7.0%
Frequency of ENG with halal tourism influencers' content	Daily	107	27.9%
	Several times a week	145	37.8%
	Once a week	76	19.8%
	Several times a month	42	10.9%
	Once a month or less	14	3.6%
Primary reasons for following halal tourism influencers	Travel inspiration	302	78.6%
	Information about halal facilities	293	76.3%
	Knowledge about Muslim-friendly destinations	267	69.5%

(*Continued*)

Table 5.3. (*Continued*)

Variables	Categories	Frequency	Percentage
	Travel tips and advice	249	64.8%
	Reviews of accommodations and restaurants	231	60.2%
	Personal connection with influencer	118	30.7%
	Entertainment	96	25.0%

4.3. Reliability and Validity Analysis

CFA was conducted to assess the measurement model. The results revealed satisfactory fit indices: χ^2/df = 1.986, CFI = 0.947, TLI = 0.940, RMSEA = 0.051, SRMR = 0.043. Table 5.4 presents the reliability and convergent validity statistics for all constructs.

Table 5.4. Reliability and Convergent Validity Results.

Construct	Items	Factor Loading	Cronbach's α	CR	AVE
IC	IC1	0.842	0.889	0.891	0.673
	IC2	0.825			
	IC3	0.798			
	IC4	0.816			
IA	IA1	0.813	0.874	0.876	0.639
	IA2	0.789			
	IA3	0.805			
	IA4	0.786			
CQ	CQ1	0.821	0.896	0.897	0.685
	CQ2	0.845			
	CQ3	0.810			
	CQ4	0.834			
VA	VA1	0.866	0.904	0.905	0.761
	VA2	0.889			
	VA3	0.864			
IVA	IVA1	0.834	0.908	0.909	0.714
	IVA2	0.855			

Table 5.4. (*Continued*)

Construct	Items	Factor Loading	Cronbach's α	CR	AVE
	IVA3	0.842			
	IVA4	0.849			
TR	TR1	0.857	0.887	0.889	0.728
	TR2	0.835			
	TR3	0.865			
ENG	ENG1	0.782	0.883	0.885	0.658
	ENG2	0.824			
	ENG3	0.834			
	ENG4	0.803			
INT	INT1	0.846	0.871	0.872	0.694
	INT2	0.831			
	INT3	0.819			

Note: CR, composite reliability; AVE, average variance extracted.

All factor loadings exceeded the recommended threshold of 0.7, indicating good item reliability. Cronbach's alpha and composite reliability (CR) values for all constructs were above 0.8, demonstrating high internal consistency. The average variance extracted (AVE) values ranged from 0.639 to 0.761, exceeding the 0.5 threshold and confirming convergent validity.

Discriminant validity was assessed by comparing the square root of AVE for each construct with its correlations with other constructs. As shown in Table 5.5, the square root of AVE for each construct (diagonal values) was greater than its correlations with other constructs, confirming discriminant validity.

Table 5.5. Discriminant Validity Results.

Construct	IC	IA	CQ	VA	IVA	TR	ENG	INT
IC	**0.820**							
IA	0.573	**0.799**						
CQ	0.612	0.549	**0.828**					
VA	0.486	0.421	0.632	**0.873**				
IVA	0.594	0.627	0.541	0.467	**0.845**			
TR	0.684	0.721	0.609	0.489	0.748	**0.853**		
ENG	0.512	0.487	0.637	0.673	0.513	0.583	**0.811**	
INT	0.563	0.582	0.548	0.532	0.612	0.675	0.646	**0.833**

Note: Diagonal values (in bold) represent the square root of AVE.

Table 5.6. Results of Hypothesis Testing.

Hypothesis	Path	Standardized Coefficient (*β*)	*t*-value	*p*-value	Result
H1	IC → TR	0.326	5.782	<0.001	Supported
H2	IA → TR	0.374	6.423	<0.001	Supported
H3	CQ → ENG	0.298	4.843	<0.001	Supported
H4	VA → ENG	0.437	7.156	<0.001	Supported
H5	IVA → TR	0.451	7.839	<0.001	Supported
H6	IVA → ENG	0.175	3.127	0.002	Supported
H7	TR → ENG	0.263	4.218	<0.001	Supported
H8	TR → INT	0.418	6.856	<0.001	Supported
H9	ENG → INT	0.385	6.279	<0.001	Supported

4.4. Hypothesis Testing

SEM was employed to test the hypothesized relationships. The structural model demonstrated good fit: χ^2/df = 2.134, CFI = 0.938, TLI = 0.930, RMSEA = 0.054, SRMR = 0.046. Table 5.6 presents the results of hypothesis testing.

All hypotheses were supported by the data. IC (β = 0.326, p < 0.001), authenticity (β = 0.374, p < 0.001), and IVA (β = 0.451, p < 0.001) were significant predictors of trust, supporting *H1*, *H2*, and *H5*. CQ (β = 0.298, p < 0.001), VA (β = 0.437, p < 0.001), and IVA (β = 0.175, p = 0.002) positively influenced ENG, supporting *H3*, *H4*, and *H6*. Trust significantly affected both ENG (β = 0.263, p < 0.001) and INT (β = 0.418, p < 0.001), supporting *H7* and *H8*. Finally, ENG had a significant positive effect on INT (β = 0.385, p < 0.001), supporting *H9*.

4.5. Mediation Analysis

Mediation analysis was conducted to examine the indirect effects of influencer attributes on INT through trust and ENG. The results are presented in Table 5.7.

The results indicated that trust partially mediated the relationships between IC, authenticity, IVA, and INT endorsed destinations. ENG fully mediated the relationship between CQ and INT and partially mediated the relationships between VA, IVA, and INT.

5. Discussion and Theoretical Implications

The strong impact of IVA on trust aligns with previous research by Battour et al. (2017) and Han et al. (2019), who emphasized the importance of religious considerations in Muslim consumers' decision-making processes. This finding extends the existing influencer marketing literature, which has predominantly focused on

Table 5.7. Results of Mediation Analysis.

Path	Direct Effect	Indirect Effect	Total Effect	Mediation Type
IC → TR → INT	0.121 ($p = 0.036$)	0.136 ($p < 0.001$)	0.257 ($p < 0.001$)	Partial
IA → TR → INT	0.146 ($p = 0.021$)	0.156 ($p < 0.001$)	0.302 ($p < 0.001$)	Partial
IVA → TR → INT	0.173 ($p = 0.012$)	0.188 ($p < 0.001$)	0.361 ($p < 0.001$)	Partial
CQ → ENG → INT	0.098 ($p = 0.086$)	0.115 ($p < 0.001$)	0.213 ($p < 0.001$)	Full
VA → ENG → INT	0.127 ($p = 0.042$)	0.168 ($p < 0.001$)	0.295 ($p < 0.001$)	Partial
IVA → ENG → INT	0.173 ($p = 0.012$)	0.067 ($p = 0.003$)	0.240 ($p < 0.001$)	Partial

mainstream markets, by highlighting the unique role of religion-specific attributes in specialized tourism contexts.

IA emerged as the second strongest predictor of trust, supporting Audrezet et al.'s (2020) assertion that genuineness and sincerity are fundamental elements in effective influencer marketing. In the halal tourism context, authenticity appears to be particularly important as Muslim travelers seek reliable information about religiously appropriate travel options. This finding reinforces Lou and Yuan's (2019) work on authenticity in influencer marketing while adding the dimension of religious authenticity.

The significant impact of IC on trust confirms the findings of Schouten et al. (2020) and extends them to the halal tourism context. For Muslim travelers, perceived expertise in halal travel matters is an essential component of credibility, highlighting the specialized knowledge requirements for influencers in this niche market.

5.1. Content Characteristics and ENG

The study found that VA ($\beta = 0.437$) had the strongest effect on ENG, followed by CQ ($\beta = 0.298$) and IVA ($\beta = 0.175$). The primacy of VA aligns with Kim and Fesenmaier's (2017) research emphasizing the emotional impact of esthetically pleasing travel imagery. This finding suggests that even in religiously oriented tourism contexts, the sensory and esthetic aspects of content remain crucial ENG drivers.

CQ's significant effect on ENG supports Lou and Yuan's (2019) findings on the importance of informative and well-presented content. In halal tourism specifically, quality appears to be associated with comprehensive and accurate information about halal facilities and services, extending previous understanding of CQ to include religion-specific information needs.

The relatively lower but still significant impact of IVA on ENG (compared to its strong effect on trust) suggests that while religious considerations are essential for establishing credibility, they may play a secondary role in driving interactive behaviors once trust is established. This nuance contributes to a more refined understanding of how religious values function differently across various stages of consumer response in specialized tourism contexts.

5.2. Trust, Engagement, and Intention to Visit

The findings confirmed significant relationships between TR, ENG, and INT endorsed destinations. Trust emerged as a stronger predictor of visit intention ($\beta = 0.418$) than ENG ($\beta = 0.385$), highlighting the paramount importance of establishing credibility in influencer marketing for halal tourism. This aligns with Femenia-Serra et al.'s (2019) emphasis on trust as a critical factor in travel decision-making but extends it to religiously oriented tourism contexts.

The significant effect of TR on ENG ($\beta = 0.263$) supports Xu and Pratt's (2018) assertion that trust in travel influencers leads to higher levels of content interaction. This relationship demonstrates the sequential nature of consumer response, where trust establishment precedes active ENG behaviors.

The role of TR and ENG as mediators in the relation between influencer characteristics and the INT offers a deeper insight into the psychological processes that influence how influencer marketing impacts travel Decision. This finding contributes to the theoretical framework of influencer marketing by illuminating the complex pathways of influence in specialized tourism contexts.

5.3. Theoretical Contributions

This study makes several notable theoretical contributions. First, it integrates theories from influencer marketing, consumer trust, and religious tourism to develop a comprehensive model that explains Muslim travelers' responses to halal tourism influencers. This integration addresses the gap identified by El-Gohary (2016) regarding the need for specialized marketing theories for religiously oriented tourism.

Second, the research extends existing influencer marketing models by incorporating religion-specific factors, particularly the alignment with Islamic values. This extension challenges the universality of generic influencer marketing theories and highlights the need for context-specific adaptations in diverse market segments.

Third, the study provides empirical evidence for the differential effects of influencer attributes on TR versus ENG, contributing to a more nuanced understanding of consumer response mechanisms in specialized tourism contexts. This differentiation enhances the theoretical precision of influencer marketing models by recognizing the distinct pathways through which marketing factors affect various consumer outcomes.

Finally, the research establishes a validated measurement instrument for assessing influencer effectiveness in halal tourism, addressing the methodological gap identified by Battour and Ismail (2016) regarding the need for specialized measurement tools in religious tourism research.

6. Practical Implications

The findings of this study offer valuable practical implications for various stakeholders in the halal tourism ecosystem, including destination marketers, travel service providers, and social media influencers.

6.1. Implications for Destination Marketers

Destination marketing organizations (DMOs) seeking to attract Muslim travelers should carefully select influencers based on their alignment with Islamic values, authenticity, and credibility. The strong impact of these factors on trust suggests that influencer selection criteria should extend beyond follower count and ENG metrics to include religious knowledge and cultural sensitivity.

DMOs should provide selected influencers with comprehensive information about halal facilities, prayer spaces, and other Muslim-friendly services at their destinations. This would enhance CQ, which our findings show significantly impacts ENG. Additionally, DMOs should facilitate high-quality visual content creation by organizing familiarization trips that showcase photogenic aspects of halal-friendly facilities and experiences.

The significant relationship between TR, ENG, and visit intention suggests that DMOs should prioritize long-term influencer partnerships over one-off campaigns. Such sustained collaborations allow for trust development between influencers and their followers, which our research indicates is a crucial precursor to destination visit decisions.

6.2. Implications for Travel Service Providers

Hotels, restaurants, and other travel service providers catering to Muslim travelers should develop influencer partnership programs that emphasize transparent disclosure of their halal credentials. Our finding that authenticity significantly impacts trust suggests that open and honest presentation of halal compliance levels is more effective than exaggerated claims.

Service providers should invest in creating visually appealing environments for their halal offerings, as VA strongly influences ENG. This might include esthetically pleasing presentation of halal food, attractive prayer spaces, and visually distinctive halal certificates displayed prominently.

The strong impact of IVA on trust suggests that travel service providers should educate their partnered influencers about the Islamic principles underlying their services. This knowledge transfer would enable influencers to communicate religious compliance more effectively, enhancing perceived alignment with Islamic values.

6.3. Implications for Halal Tourism Influencers

Influencers specializing in halal tourism should focus on building credibility through demonstrated knowledge of Islamic principles relevant to travel. This might include explaining the religious basis for halal certifications, discussing prayer time accommodations, or highlighting modest dress considerations at various destinations.

Our findings on the importance of authenticity suggest that halal tourism influencers should maintain transparency about sponsored content and provide balanced reviews that acknowledge both positive and negative aspects of destinations from a Muslim traveler's perspective. This honest approach is likely to enhance trust more effectively than exclusively positive portrayals.

The strong effect of VA on ENG indicates that halal tourism influencers should invest in high-quality photography and videography equipment and skills. Additionally, they should develop distinctive visual styles that effectively showcase halal-friendly aspects of destinations while maintaining esthetic appeal.

CQ's significant impact on ENG suggests that halal tourism influencers should develop systematic approaches to reviewing and presenting halal facilities and services. This might include standardized rating systems for halal food authenticity, prayer facility accessibility, or family-friendliness of accommodations.

7. Limitations and Future Research Directions

While this study provides valuable insights into influencer marketing in halal tourism, several limitations should be acknowledged, which also point to directions for future research.

7.1. Methodological Limitations

The self-reported measures of ENG and visit intention may be subject to social desirability bias. Future studies could complement survey data with actual ENG metrics from social media platforms and real travel behavior tracking to enhance validity.

The use of purposive sampling may limit the generalizability of findings. Future research should aim for more representative sampling frames, possibly using probabilistic sampling methods across more diverse Muslim populations.

7.2. Conceptual Limitations

This study focused primarily on social media influencers and did not examine traditional Muslim authorities or religious leaders who may also influence travel decisions. Future research could compare the effectiveness of secular travel influencers versus religious authorities in shaping halal tourism choices.

The research examined general halal tourism influencers without distinguishing between different types (e.g., family travel specialists, adventure halal tourism influencers, luxury halal travel influencers). Future studies could investigate how influencer specialization affects their effectiveness across different Muslim traveler segments.

The study did not address cross-cultural variations in Muslim travelers' responses to influencer marketing. Future research could examine how cultural factors moderate the relationships between influencer attributes and consumer responses in different Muslim-majority and Muslim-minority countries.

7.3. Future Research Directions

Several promising directions for future research emerge from this study:

1. *Generational differences*: Examining how different generations of Muslim travelers (e.g., Gen Z, Millennials, Gen X) respond to various aspects of influencer marketing in halal tourism.
2. *Multi-platform strategies*: Analyzing the effectiveness of cross-platform influencer campaigns that span various social media platforms with different content formats (e.g., Instagram photos, YouTube videos, blog articles).
3. *Content analysis*: Conducting qualitative content analysis of successful halal tourism influencers to identify specific narrative strategies, visual techniques, and religious framing approaches that enhance effectiveness.
4. *Co-creation processes*: Exploring how co-creation between influencers, destinations, and followers' shapes halal tourism experiences and perceptions through interactive social media ENG.
5. *Ethical considerations*: Investigating ethical issues in halal tourism influencer marketing, such as authenticity in religious representation, transparency in commercial relationships, and potential conflicts between commercial and religious values.
6. *Resilience during crises*: Examining how halal tourism influencers affected destination recovery and Muslim traveler confidence during and after global crises such as the COVID-19 pandemic.

8. Conclusion

This study investigated the impact of influencer marketing on Muslim travelers' TR, ENG, and INT endorsed destinations in the context of halal tourism. The findings reveal that influencer attributes (credibility, authenticity, CQ, VA, and alignment with Islamic values) significantly affect Muslim travelers' responses through both direct and mediated pathways.

The research highlights the distinctive nature of influencer marketing in halal tourism, where religious considerations play a crucial role alongside traditional marketing factors. Alignment with Islamic values emerged as the strongest predictor of trust, underscoring the importance of religious authenticity in this specialized market segment. VA and CQ were primary drivers of ENG, suggesting that esthetic and informational aspects remain fundamental even in religiously oriented tourism contexts.

The significant relationships between TR, ENG, and visit intention demonstrate the sequential process through which influencer marketing affects travel decisions. Trust establishment appears to be a critical prerequisite for both active ENG and destination visit consideration, highlighting the importance of credibility-building strategies in halal tourism marketing.

These findings have important implications for destination marketers, travel service providers, and influencers operating in the halal tourism space. The research suggests that effective influencer marketing in this context requires a careful balance between religious sensitivity, authentic representation, high-quality content, and VA.

As halal tourism continues to grow globally, understanding the unique dynamics of influencer marketing in this sector becomes increasingly important. This study contributes to this understanding by providing empirical evidence for the factors that enhance marketing effectiveness in this specialized context. Future research building on these findings will further illuminate the complex interplay between religious considerations, digital marketing strategies, and travel decision-making in the evolving landscape of halal tourism.

References

Audrezet, A., de Kerviler, G., & Guidry Moulard, J. (2020). Authenticity under threat: When social media influencers need to go beyond self-presentation. *Journal of Business Research, 117*, 557–569.

Battour, M., & Ismail, M. N. (2016). Halal tourism: Concepts, practices, challenges and future. *Tourism Management Perspectives, 19*, 150–154. https://doi.org/10.1016/j.tmp.2015.12.008

Battour, M., Ismail, M. N., Battor, M., & Awais, M. (2017). Islamic tourism: An empirical examination of travel motivation and satisfaction in Malaysia. *Current Issues in Tourism, 20*(1), 50–67. https://doi.org/10.1080/13683500.2014.965665

El-Gohary, H. (2016). Halal tourism, is it really Halal? *Tourism Management Perspectives, 19*, 124–130. https://doi.org/10.1016/j.tmp.2015.12.013

Femenia-Serra, F., Gretzel, U., & Alzua-Sorzabal, A. (2019). Instagram travel influencers in #TheBaqueCountry. In B. Stangl & J. Pesonen (Eds.), *Information and communication technologies in tourism 2019* (pp. 213–224). Springer.

Global Muslim Travel Index. (2022). *Mastercard-CrescentRating Global Muslim Travel Index 2022*. CrescentRating.

Gretzel, U. (2018). Influencer marketing in travel and tourism. In S. Sigala & U. Gretzel (Eds.), *Advances in social media for travel, tourism and hospitality: New perspectives, practice and cases* (pp. 147–156). Routledge.

Hair, J. F., Black, W. C., Babin, B. J., & Anderson, R. E. (2010). *Multivariate data analysis* (7th ed.). Pearson.

Han, H., Al-Ansi, A., Olya, H. G., & Kim, W. (2019). Exploring halal-friendly destination attributes in South Korea: Perceptions and behaviors of Muslim travelers toward a non-Muslim destination. *Tourism Management, 71*, 151–164. https://doi.org/10.1016/j.tourman.2018.10.010

Kim, J., & Fesenmaier, D. R. (2017). Sharing tourism experiences: The posttrip experience. *Journal of Travel Research, 56*(1), 28–40. https://doi.org/10.1177/0047287515620491

Lou, C., & Yuan, S. (2019). Influencer marketing: How message value and credibility affect consumer trust of branded content on social media. *Journal of Interactive Advertising, 19*(1), 58–73. https://doi.org/10.1080/15252019.2018.1533501

Mohsin, A., Ramli, N., & Alkhulayfi, B. A. (2016). Halal tourism: Emerging opportunities. *Tourism Management Perspectives, 19*, 137–143. https://doi.org/10.1016/j.tmp.2015.12.010

Ohanian, R. (1990). Construction and validation of a scale to measure celebrity endorsers' perceived expertise, trustworthiness, and attractiveness. *Journal of Advertising*, *19*(3), 39–52. https://doi.org/10.1080/00913367.1990.10673191

Oktadiana, H., Pearce, P. L., & Chon, K. (2016). Muslim travellers' needs: What don't we know? *Tourism Management Perspectives*, *20*, 124–130. https://doi.org/10.1016/j.tmp.2016.08.004

Schouten, A. P., Janssen, L., & Verspaget, M. (2020). Celebrity vs. influencer endorsements in advertising: The role of identification, credibility, and product-endorser fit. *International Journal of Advertising*, *39*(2), 258–281. https://doi.org/10.1080/02650487.2019.1634898

Valentini, C., Romenti, S., Murtarelli, G., & Pizzetti, M. (2018). Digital visual engagement: Influencing purchase intentions on Instagram. *Journal of Communication Management*, *22*(4), 362–381. https://doi.org/10.1108/JCOM-01-2018-0005

Wilson, J. A., & Liu, J. (2010). Shaping the halal into a brand? *Journal of Islamic Marketing*, *1*(2), 107–123. https://doi.org/10.1108/17590831011055851

Xu, X., & Pratt, S. (2018). Social media influencers as endorsers to promote travel destinations: An application of self-congruence theory to the Chinese Generation Y. *Journal of Travel & Tourism Marketing*, *35*(7), 958–972. https://doi.org/10.1080/10548408.2018.1468851

Chapter 6

Sustainable Halal Tourism: QR-code Menu in the Restaurant Industry

Betül Öztürk

Gastronomy and Culinary Arts Department, Izmir University of Economics, Izmir, Turkey

Abstract

The period following the onset of the global pandemic known as "COVID-19," in conjunction with the accelerated implementation of advanced digital technologies, including augmented reality (AR), virtual reality (VR), and the Internet of Things (IoT), has precipitated substantial transformations in various sectors, notably operations, service, and hospitality. The widespread adoption of scannable barcodes as a digital transformation instrument has facilitated the transition to online menus, which are hosted on the internet and can be accessed by scanning quick response (QR) codes in restaurants. Given the pervasiveness and accelerated growth of this technology, it is imperative to understand consumer perceptions and their subsequent effects on restaurant operators. This chapter proposes a conceptual framework that explores the influence of menu presentation, both in the form of QR codes and traditional paper back menus, on restaurant perceptions and consumer engagement and the integration of QR code payment systems within restaurant infrastructure. A review of the extant literature reveals a need for further research in this area, particularly concerning the digitalization of the restaurant industry and customer perceptions. The objective of this chapter is to address this gap by conducting a trough examination of the relationship between the utilization of QR code as a menu presentation and a payment tool and its impact on tourism and sustainability.

Keywords: QR code systems; QR code restaurant menu; sustainable restaurant; sustainable tourism; sustainable halal tourism

Halal Tourism and Artificial Intelligence: New Approaches for a New Generation, 73–86

Published under exclusive licence by Emerald Publishing Limited
doi:10.1108/978-1-80686-165-120261007

Introduction

The tourism industry is multifaceted and interdisciplinary field characterized by intricate supply chain connections (Fauzi, 2023). This characteristic of the industry underscores its potential for promoting sustainable development despite its inherent challenges. The United Nations World Tourism Organization (UNWTO) established the initial definition of sustainable tourism in 1996 with the publication of the emergence of the Brundtland Report (UN, 1987) which is characterized sustainable tourism as *tourism which leads to management of all areas, in such a way, that the economic, social and environmental needs are being fulfilled with the cultural integration, ecological processes, biodiversity and supporting the development of societies* (Janusz & Bajdor, 2013). In 2005, a guide for the more sustainable development of the tourism sector was published as a cooperative work by the World Tourism Organization (WTO) and the United Nations Environmental Programme (UNEP). The objective of this guide was twofold: first, to integrate the environmental sustainability into the decision-making process within the tourism industry, and second, to disseminate the technical know-how and build business networks to catalyze sustainability in the tourism sector (UNEP & WTO, 2005). In 2017, UNWTO declared the International Year for more sustainable tourism (UNTWO, 2017). In the alignment with the UN Sustainable Development Goals delineated in the Future Agenda 2030: Sustainable Development Goals, UNTWO has identified five pivotal domains for deliberation: inclusive and sustainable economic growth, social inclusiveness, employment and poverty reduction, resource efficiency, environmental protection and climate change, cultural values, diversity and heritage, mutual understanding, peace, and security (UNTWO, 2017). The sustainable development of tourism is an evolving process that is encountering novel challenges in the context of shifting technological applications and tourism consumption patterns (Streimikiene et al., 2021). This transformation is a critical aspect of promoting sustainability in tourism, encompassing both environmental and social dimensions, as well as economic dimensions of sustainability (Gössling, 2021).

The tourism industry is a highly dynamic one, encompassing a wide array of sectors, including transportation, accommodations, hospitality, and food services. This multifaceted nature of the tourism industry is characterized by a high degree of diversity and heterogeneity including the hotels, restaurants, and travel agencies from the private to the public sector provide services and goods to the tourists (Mandal & Saravanan, 2019). Beginning in the late 20th century, the scientific and technological has had a profound impact on the industry and its various sectors, particularly with the introduction of new information and communication technologies. These developments have also had significant societal and cultural ramifications, influencing diverse aspects of human activity. The Internet revolution has had a profound impact on the travel and tourism industry, characterized by an escalation in the level of interaction among industry stakeholders (Romero Dexeus, 2019). The advent of Tourism 4.0, a novel paradigm integrating Industry 4.0 technologies such as the IoT, cloud computing, artificial intelligence (AI), AR, and VR, has been defined as significant development in this context (Gomes et al., 2024). The integration of these technologies in conjunction with the robotization and big data analytics has resulted in enhanced operational efficiency, sustainability, and the emergence of innovative business models within the sharing economy. This paradigm shift has implications for both the tourism sector and the adaptation of tourists and local communities to digital innovation.

Sustainable Restaurants in the Tourism Industry

The relevance of tourism to food consumption is attributable to the substantial quantity of food prepared by the various food service providers involved in catering to tourists in both leisure and business contexts. This encompasses food stalls, restaurants, cafeterias, canteen kitchens, fast-food chains, diners, trains, aircraft, ferries, and cruise ships (Gössling et al., 2011). In the context of the diversity of the food services, restaurants emerge as the predominant destination of choice for consumers, seeking either sustenance or culinary experiences. The heightened awareness among consumers regarding sustainability has also had a significant impact on developments in the restaurant industry. The renowned organizations such as Michelin Guide (Huang et al., 2023) and Gault & Millau guide have initiated commendations for chefs who incorporate sustainability principles in their culinary process. Consequently, these restaurants are often classified as green restaurants (Öztürk, 2024). Nevertheless, the considerable transition toward technological instruments has begun to be acknowledged in the realm of business management. The transition encompasses the collection of data and the evaluation of the restaurant infrastructure from various perspectives. The National Restaurant Association (NRA) has announced its adaption of digital technologies related to the cost management, with a focus on adjusting ingredient amounts to prevent food loss and waste (NRA, 2025). This transformation results in the integration of QR code systems within the restaurant infrastructure. This digitalization revealed the restaurants in which the sustainable developments are implemented in all dimensions – environmental, social, and economics – as illustrated in Fig. 6.1.

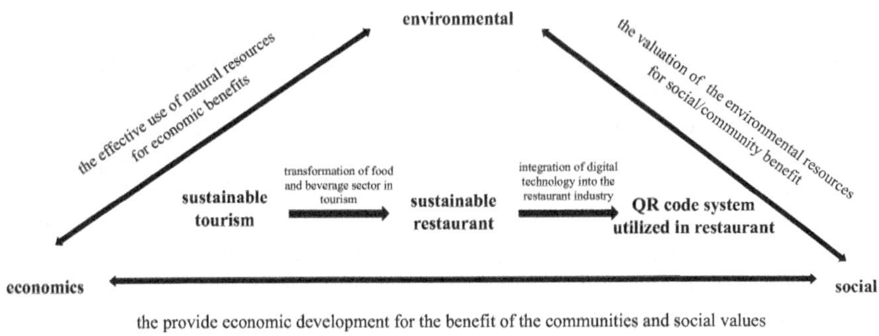

Fig. 6.1. The Potential of QR Code Systems to Facilitate a Technological Transition in the Tourism and Restaurant Industries, with a Focus on Sustainability.

QR Code

QR system was originally developed by the Japanese company Denson-Wave (Azmadi et al., 2022) for the purpose of tracking the car parts in automotive industry (Intal et al., 2020). The QR code is composed of intertwined squares in three corners of a square box. This square is linked to an internet webpage, a portable document file (pdf), a text file, or a picture (Büyükkol Köse & Çetin, 2024). The widespread use of smart phones with their wireless connection to the Internet capability enables the introduction of the QR code as a visual interface connecting and accessing from portable devices. The integration of wireless interned with automated identification and data capture technologies such as barcodes and QR codes has also facilitated more cost-effective and reliable data sharing over the internet (Nguyen, 2022). The implementation is designed for diverse objectives, including the facilitation of mobile payments in retail settings (Yamin & Abdalatif, 2024), the multimedia elements as part of exhibitions in museum-like spaces (Pérez-Sanagustín et al., 2016), getting maps while traveling globally (Udvaros & Forman, 2024), the ability to join wi-fi networks (Şeker et al., 2024), the implementation of the loyalty programs in marketing and advertising (Höpken et al., 2012; Onyinyechi et al., 2021), and the incorporation of knowledge tools on food labels (Rotsios et al., 2022).

In the restaurant industry, the utilization of QR code applications plays a pivotal role in enhancing consumer satisfaction (Kılıç et al., 2023) and optimizing restaurant's operational efficiency (Intal et al., 2020; Zakri et al., 2024). The implementation of QR codes in the restaurant industry is categorized into two distinct uses in the contact point of the consumers. The first pertains to the presentation of the restaurant's menu, and the second involves the integration of a payment terminal to facilitate electronic money transfers. Fig. 6.2 is a flowchart illustrating the application of QR codes in a restaurant environment, with a particular emphasis on the integration of these codes into the restaurants' menu and payment options.

QR Code Menus in the Restaurant Industry

Technological advancements have revealed that human activities have led to significant developments in business operations. These developments have evolved into growth and transformation, as well as strategic points such as the stability and predictability of efficiency achieved through technology and technological tools (Nguyen, 2022). The advent of the pandemic has underscored the potential for existing interactions, both personal and sectoral, to be integrated into comprehensive social automation and data extraction systems. This transformation is most evident in the advent of the QR code menu ordering application or system in the restaurant industry, which facilitates the exchange of user transaction data through preexisting digital infrastructures and platforms.

As it is illustrated in Fig. 6.3, a QR code, prominent location or display on the dining table, serves as the interface for the workflow of the restaurant's QR code menu ordering system. Subsequent scanning the QR code, a digital menu either

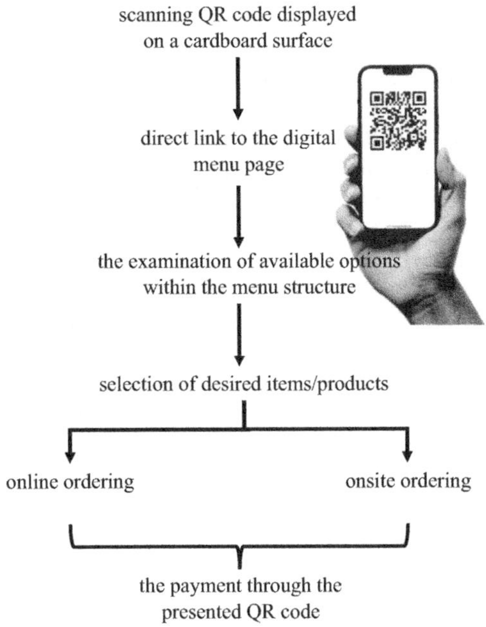

Fig. 6.2. Flowchart Illustrating the Application of QR Codes in a Restaurant, Including the Restaurant Menu and Payment Options.

Fig. 6.3. QR Code Menu on Restaurant Table.

a web-based menu or pdf menu on the consumers' smartphone is presented, allowing the consumer to browse the available options in the menu structure. The ordering process can be categorized into two distinct service models, contingent upon the operational framework and management system of the restaurant. The first model entails the utilization of a QR code menu ordering application, which is exclusively composed of food items that are prepared and served in the restaurant kitchen. In this scenario, the consumer initiates the order by requesting the food items from the waiter (Bawazir et al., 2023). The second option involves online ordering, wherein consumers select the desired food items without the need for physical interaction with a waiter (Paul et al., 2020). In the latter scenario, the order is transferred directly to the kitchen for preparation. In both scenarios, QR code technology enables access to the digital menu through mobile applications providing consumers with convenient access to information regarding nutritional values, allergen information, ingredient traceability (Gagić, 2016; Mu et al., 2019), and food type based on religious requirements such as halal and kosher (Ahamed et al., 2024; Aisyah et al., 2019; Tan et al., 2020; Vuksanović et al., 2021).

A restaurant menu functions as a medium for facilitating communication between consumers and restaurateurs. Moreover, it serves as a guide for chefs, delineating the types of ingredients and equipment required in the kitchen and the personnel with the necessary qualifications to utilize them (Ozdemir & Caliskan, 2014). The ongoing rise in consumer awareness regarding health and well-being in the post-pandemic era has also led to heightened expectations of transparency concerning the food items featured on restaurant menu (Brewer & Sebby, 2021; Fakih et al., 2016). The menu information dimensions have been identified as a critical factor in shaping consumers' attitudes and behavioral intentions toward restaurants, with menu design identified as pivotal element in this regard (Fakih et al., 2016). Furthermore, QR code menus have the capacity to incorporate multimedia elements such as images and videos (Nie et al., 2025) which increases their appeal to consumers. Additionally, AR-based interactive menus on digital platforms have been proposed to enhance consumer engagement (Nur Amin et al., 2022).

Conventional menus are typically paper based, necessitating the consumption of considerable quantities of paper (Kılıç et al., 2023; Ozturkcan & Kitapci, 2023). The paper-based menu types tend to become damaged or lost during a dining experience or operation. Consequently, restaurants are compelled to publish new menus attract consumers' and facilitate order-service operations (Iskender et al., 2023). QR code menus offer a contactless menu option in comparison to conventional menus such as single-page, laminated, or paper-based menus. The advent of the COVID-19 pandemic and the subsequent post-pandemic era have led to a shift in consumers' attitude toward to paper-based menus due to concerns regarding hygiene and health (Al-Zyoud, 2023; Khare & Alkonda, 2023; Laporte et al., 2023). QR code menus have also to decrease the language barriers in the popular tourism destinations along with the service accuracy and table turnover (Xinyu & Garg, 2023). The enhanced functionality of advanced QR code menus has the capability to assess the consumers' preferences, reviews, and ratings on the food that they order and the service they receive and also the satisfaction of the customers in the context of the technology adaption (Kim et al., 2018; Shahril et al., 2024; Singh et al., 2022).

QR Code Payment Applications in Restaurant Industry

During the ongoing pandemic, individuals have experienced heightened social isolation, which has subsequently driven their interest in mobile applications. Consequently, in the post-pandemic era, companies across various sectors have expedited their pursuit of more dependable solutions to ensure the well-being and security of their users (Şat & Ayazlar, 2022). QR code applications are defined as self-service technological tools that allow fast access to big data or cloud within seconds (Vuksanović et al., 2021). Their user-friendly nature and rapid adaptability across diverse age groups have contributed to proliferation of QR codes in various sectors including finance, where they have emerged as a means of facilitating transactions (Jiang et al., 2021). The tourism industry, like other sectors, has begun integrating QR codes providing information to tourists (Katlav, 2020), marketing (Ahmed & Damodharan, 2022), advertisement (Çeltek, 2017), and payment tools for various purposes, including payments at travel agencies, museums, hotels, and restaurants (Lou et al., 2017).

The QR code payment system is comprised of a sequential series of actions, initiated by creation of a square image intended for scanning. This process is instrumental in facilitating the digitalization of restaurant operations in a detailed manner. The customers utilize their mobile devices' camera functionality to scan QR codes, which facilitate access to either restaurant's menu or payment particulars. The database encompasses the menu items' cost and management details enabling the restaurant to not only analyze sales and customer order data but also evaluate the menu design based on the selling numbers of the menu items. Fig. 6.4 summarizes the interaction between the restaurant and its customers through the medium of the QR code system.

Sustainable Development by Implementing QR Code System in Restaurant Industry

The implementation of a QR code system in the restaurant industry has been shown to demonstrated sustainable development across three distinctive domains:

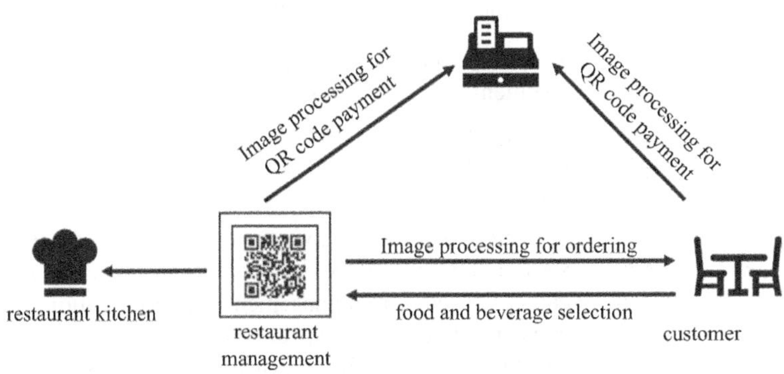

Fig. 6.4. QR Code Systems in Restaurant Business.

environmental, social, and economic. The adaption of the sustainability practices in restaurants has the potential to attract consumers, tourists, and travel agencies (Maynard et al., 2020). The integration of QR code systems in the restaurants has the potential to augment their role in promoting sustainable development. The added values to the sustainable development goals when the restaurants integrate the QR code systems into their business operations are summarized in Table 6.1.

Table 6.1. Supplementary Benefits of QR Code Systems in the Restaurant Industry with Respect to the Sustainable Development Goals.

Sustainable Development Goal #	**Supplementary Benefits of QR Code Systems in the Restaurant Industry**
 SDG 1 No poverty  SDG 2 Zero hunger	The utilization of QR code menu by these restaurants serves to inform both the restaurant manager and consumers of the portion size of each dish, thereby facilitating informed decision-making and promoting awareness of portion control. The efficacy of this strategy is the prevention of the food loss and waste. In addition, restaurants contribute to the conservation of natural food sources. The integration of QR code payment systems further enhances this process by mitigating errors, thereby ensuring more precise and accurate service delivery
 SDG 3 Good health and well-being	The utilization of a QR code menu provides a contactless tool to create a hygienic and healthy environment for customers A QR code menu is a digital tool that provides detailed information about the food and ingredients used in the kitchen. This information includes such as nutritional values and halal/kosher certification
 SDG 8 Decent work and economic growth	The analytical capacity of QR code systems is instrumental in enhancing the economic growth The implementation of QR code leads to a significant reduction in the workload for services staff, thereby minimizes the occurrence of errors. The integration of a QR code menu within a restaurant's operational framework offers a distinct advantage, as it facilitates the efficient management and modification of menu items. In contrast to printed menus, which require a lot of preparation time, QR code menus offer an easy interface to update menu items such as price, ingredients, or a new dish

Table 6.1. (*Continued*)

Sustainable Development Goal #	**Supplementary Benefits of QR Code Systems in the Restaurant Industry**
 SDG 9 Industry, innovation, and infrastructure	The integration of QR code systems into the infrastructure of restaurant businesses signifies a pioneering advancement in the realm of technological innovation
 SDG 11 Sustainable cities and communities	The implementation of the QR code menu enhances the consumers' awareness toward the locality and sustainable development which also leads to the co-creation of the sustainable communities and cities
 SDG 12 Responsible consumption and production	The comprehensive platform that underpins the QR code menu facilitates the dissemination of critical information, including the portion size of each dish, thus fostering informed decisions and promoting responsible consumption practices. This feature contributes to the mitigation of food waste, a critical environmental concern The utilization of a QR code menu as opposed to a printed menu serves a symbol of a responsible consumption, aiming to minimize paper usage
 SDG 13 Climate action	The production and use of printed menus have consequences for the environment. The use of natural resources in their production results in the utilization of finite resources and consequent increase in the carbon footprint and greenhouse gas emissions. Conversely, QR code menus emerge as a sustainable solution by reducing the consumption of paper and offering a reusable alternative

(*Continued*)

Table 6.1. (*Continued*)

Sustainable Development Goal #	**Supplementary Benefits of QR Code Systems in the Restaurant Industry**
	The utilization of QR code menu design has the potential to promote the consumption of locally sourced foodstuff. Moreover, this practice serves to enhance consumer awareness regarding the availably of natural resources, both on land and below water
SDG 14 Life below water	The incorporation of a QR code menu facilitates the dissemination of messages pertaining to the consumption and usage of the natural and food sources
 SDG 15 Life on land	
 SDG 17 Partnerships for the goals	The food and beverage industry is characterized by a substantial and heterogeneous group of stakeholders. The implementation of QR code menu enables stakeholders to form partnership and engage in cooperative endeavors that contribute to the development of a sustainable future. Furthermore, the adaption of QR code menus by restaurants with exemplary practices serves as a model for other restaurants seeking to enhance their business and ensure resilience in the face of change

Conclusion

In a summary, the tourism industry has undergone substantial advancements in terms of sustainability over the past decade. Recent advancements have given rise to novel conceptual frameworks that facilitate comprehension of sustainable development within the paradigm of sustainable tourism, with a particular emphasis on the provision of products and services. The utilization of QR codes within the food and beverage industry has enabled the streamlined incorporation of digital instruments into their operational infrastructure. The prevailing QR code systems in the restaurant sector have been found to be associated with customer satisfaction despite the presence of adverse factors. Nevertheless, the limited extant research on the implementation of QR codes in the restaurant industry for a determination of the effectiveness of such systems, thus further detailed studies are needed.

References

Ahamed, N. N., Vignesh, R., & Alam, T. (2024). Tracking and tracing the halal food supply chain management using blockchain, RFID, and QR code. *Multimed Tools Appl, 83*, 48987–49012. https://doi.org/10.1007/s11042-023-17474-4

Ahmed, K. A., & Damodharan, V. S. (2022). Antecedents of QR code acceptance during Covid-19: Towards sustainability. *Transnational Marketing Journal, 10*(1), 171–199. https://doi.org/10.33182/tmj.v10i1.2289

Aisyah, M., Suzanawaty, L., & Said, M. (2019). The demand for halal certified restaurants in Indonesia. *International Journal of Supply Chain Management, 8*(5), 86–98.

Al-Zyoud, M. F. (2023). Fresh mindset, hygiene perception, QR code menu, and intention to re-dine among Jordanian consumers. *Journal of Foodservice Business Research*, 1–16. https://doi.org/10.1080/15378020.2023.2214068

Aymankuy, Ş. Y., & Demir, Ş. (2024). Yiyecek içecek işletmelerinde dijital değişim: Tüketicilerin QR kod menü deneyimini anlamak (Digital change in food and beverage businesses: Understanding consumers' QR code menu experience). *Journal of Tourism & Gastronomy Studies, 12*(2), 886–918. https://doi.org/10.21325/jotags.2024.1417

Azmadi, A. S. A., Abd Hamid, M., & Hanafiah, M. H. (2022). Rise of the QR code application adoption: Towards a conceptual post-Covid-19 smart sustainable tourism framework. *International Journal of Social Science Research, 4*(1), 478–488.

Bawazir, A. A., Kamal, A. A. B. M., Mee, G., Lean, L. L., Kai, N. S., Nor, S. M., Megat, P. A. B., & Noordin, A. (2023). Factors affecting consumer acceptance of E-menu in the Klang Valley restaurant sector in Malaysia. *International Journal of Academic Research in Business & Social Sciences, 13*(6), 844–861.

Brewer, P., & Sebby, A. G. (2021). The effect of online restaurant menus on consumers' purchase intentions during the COVID-19 pandemic. *International Journal of Hospitality Management, 94*, 102777. https://doi.org/10.1016/j.ijhm.2020.102777

Büyükkol Köse, E., & Çetin, G. (2024). Using QR codes in the science and technology center. *Journal of Educational Technology & Online Learning, 7*(2), 177–193. http://doi.org/10.31681/jetol.1336996

Çeltek, E. (2017). QR code advertisements in tourism marketing. In R. Yılmaz (Ed.), *Narrative advertising models and conceptualization in the digital age* (pp. 269–289). IGI Global Scientific Publishing. https://doi.org/10.4018/978-1-5225-2373-4.ch015.

Fakih, K., Assaker, G., Assaf, A. G., & Hallak, R. (2016). Does restaurant menu information affect customer attitudes and behavioral intentions? A cross-segment empirical analysis using PLS-SEM. *International Journal of Hospitality Management, 57*, 71–83. https://doi.org/10.1016/j.ijhm.2016.06.002

Fauzi, M. A. (2023). Sustainable tourism and sustainable development goals (SDGs): A state-of-the-art review of past, present, and future trends. *Environment, Development and Sustainability*, 1–22.

Gagić, S. (2016). Restaurant innovativeness: A case study of Vojvodina. *The European Journal of Applied Economics, 13*(2), 57–69. https://doi.org/10.5937/ejae13-10503

Gomes, S., Lopes, J. M., & Ferreira, L. (2024). Looking at the tourism industry through the lenses of industry 4.0: A bibliometric review of concerns and challenges. *Journal of Hospitality and Tourism Insights, 7*(1), 436–457.

Gössling, S. (2021). Tourism, technology and ICT: A critical review of affordances and concessions. *Journal of Sustainable Tourism, 29*(5), 733–750. https://doi.org/10.1080/09669582.2021.1873353

Gössling, S., Garrod, B., Aall, C., Hille, J., & Peeters, P. (2011). Food management in tourism: Reducing tourism's carbon 'foodprint'. *Tourism Management, 32*(3), 534–543. https://doi.org/10.1016/j.tourman.2010.04.006

Höpken, W., Deubele, P., Höll, G., Kuppe, J., Schorpp, D., Zapata Licones, R. O., & Fuchs, M. (2012). Digitalizing loyalty cards in tourism. In *Information and communication technologies in tourism 2012* (pp. 272–283). Springer.

Huang, Y., Hall, C. M., & Chen, N. (Chris). (2023). The sustainability characteristics of Michelin Green Star restaurants. *Journal of Foodservice Business Research*, *28*(2), 219–244. https://doi.org/10.1080/15378020.2023.2235258

Intal, G. L., Payas, J. D., Fernandez, L. M., & Domingo, B. M. (2020, April). *Restaurant information system (RIS) with QR code to improve service operations of casual fine dining restaurant*. 2020 IEEE 7th international conference on industrial engineering and applications (ICIEA) (pp. 1054–1059). IEEE. https://doi.org/10.1109/ICIEA49774.2020.9102036

Iskender, A., Sirakaya-Turk, E., & Cardenas, D. (2023). Restaurant menus and COVID-19: Implications for technology adoption in the post-pandemic era. *Consumer Behavior in Tourism and Hospitality*, *18*(4), 587–605. https://doi.org/10.1108/CBTH-11-2022-0194

Janusz, G. K., & Bajdor, P. (2013). Towards to sustainable tourism–framework, activities and dimensions. *Procedia Economics and Finance*, *6*, 523–529.

Jiang, Y., Ahmad, H., Butt, A. H., Shafique, M. N., & Muhammad, S. (2021). QR digital payment system adoption by retailers: The moderating role of COVID-19 knowledge. *Information Resources Management Journal (IRMJ)*, *34*(3), 41–63. https://doi.org/10.4018/IRMJ.2021070103

Katlav, E. Ö. (2020). QR code applications in tourism. In E. Çeltek (Ed.), *Handbook of research on smart technology applications in the tourism industry* (pp. 89–114). IGI Global Scientific Publishing. https://doi.org/10.4018/978-1-7998-1989-9.ch005.

Khare, A. S., & Alkonda, V. (2023). The study of customer perception on contactless menus at restaurant. *European Chemical Bulletin*, *12*(8), 4676–4693.

Kılıç, B., Delipınar, G. E., Güler, E. G., Gönen, İ., Gülbahar, M. O., Can, Ü., & Yayla, Ö. (2023). Measuring the tendencies of customers to use QR code menu in restaurants. *Journal of Gastronomy Hospitality and Travel*, *6*(3), 1057–1067. https://doi.org/10.33083/joghat.2023.321

Kim, E., Tang, L. R., & Bosselman, R. (2018). Measuring customer perceptions of restaurant innovativeness: Developing and validating a scale. *International Journal of Hospitality Management*, *74*, 85–98. https://doi.org/10.1016/j.ijhm.2018.02.018

Laporte, R., Théberge, N., & Veilleux, S. (2023). Business model shift in independent restaurant operation: the COVID-19 impacts. *Journal of Foodservice Business Research*, 1–36. https://doi.org/10.1080/15378020.2023.2264883

Lou, L., Tian, Z., & Koh, J. (2017). Tourist satisfaction enhancement using mobile QR code payment: An empirical investigation. *Sustainability*, *9*(7), 1186. https://doi.org/10.3390/su9071186

Mandal, S., & Saravanan, D. (2019). Exploring the influence of strategic orientations on tourism supply chain agility and resilience: An empirical investigation. *Tourism Planning & Development*, *16*(6), 612–636. https://doi.org/10.1080/21568316.2018.1561506

Maynard, D. D. C., Vidigal, M. D., Farage, P., Zandonadi, R. P., Nakano, E. Y., & Botelho, R. B. A. (2020). Environmental, social and economic sustainability indicators applied to food services: A systematic review. *Sustainability*, *12*(5), 1804. https://doi.org/10.3390/su12051804

Mu, W., Spaargaren, G., & Oude Lansink, A. (2019). Mobile apps for green food practices and the role for consumers: A case study on dining out practices with Chinese and Dutch young consumers. *Sustainability*, *11*(5), 1275. https://doi.org/10.3390/su11051275

Nguyen, D. (2022). Convenient efficiency: A media genealogy of QR codes. *New Media & Society*, *26*(10), 5742–5762. https://doi.org/10.1177/14614448221141086

Nie, X., Zhao, W. M., & Guan, J. (2025). Towards a framework of menu research: Insights from the multiple level perspective and signaling theory. *British Food Journal*, *127*(1), 233–252. https://doi.org/10.1108/BFJ-11-2023-1039

NRA. (2025). *Consider mobile order systems to boost service efficiency*. https://restaurant.org/education-and-resources/resource-library/consider-mobile-order-systems-to-boost-service-efficiency/ on 17.04.2025

Nur Amin, S., Shivakumara, P., Xue Jun, T., Yang Chong, K., Leong Lon Zan, D., & Rahavendra, R. (2022, October). An augmented reality-based approach for designing interactive food menu of restaurant using android. *Artificial Intelligence and Applications*, *1*(1), 26–34. https://doi.org/10.47852/bonviewAIA2202354

Onyinyechi, O. P., Ifeanyi, O. A., Nnabuchi, E. N., & Nwakaego, I. P. (2021). Enhanced business marketing for small scale enterprises via the quick response code technology. *Frontiers*, *1*(1), 7–13. https://doi.org/10.11648/j.frontiers.20210101.12

Ozdemir, B., & Caliskan, O. (2014). A review of literature on restaurant menus: Specifying the managerial issues. *International Journal of Gastronomy and Food Science*, *2*(1), 3–13. https://doi.org/10.1016/j.ijgfs.2013.12.001

Öztürk, B. (2024). A systematic literature review on sustainable restaurants: The case of Turkey. *International Journal of Contemporary Economics and Administrative Sciences*, *14*(1), 317–348. https://doi.org/10.5281/zenodo.13932031

Ozturkcan, S., & Kitapci, O. (2023). A sustainable solution for the hospitality industry: The QR code menus. *Journal of Information Technology Teaching Cases*. https://doi.org/10.1177/20438869231181599

Paul, R., Bhandopia, R. R., Patil, D. R., Raut, J. D., & Gotmare, A. D. (2020). An efficient digital ordering system for restaurant. *International Journal of Research in Engineering, Science, and Management*, *3*, 391–395.

Pérez-Sanagustín, M., Parra, D., Verdugo, R., García-Galleguillos, G., & Nussbaum, M. (2016). Using QR codes to increase user engagement in museum-like spaces. *Computers in Human Behavior*, *60*, 73–85. https://doi.org/10.1016/j.chb.2016.02.012

Romero Dexeus, C. (2019). The deepening effects of the digital revolution. *The future of tourism: Innovation and sustainability*, 43–69.

Rotsios, K., Konstantoglou, A., Folinas, D., Fotiadis, T., Hatzithomas, L., & Boutsouki, C. (2022). Evaluating the use of QR codes on food products. *Sustainability*, *14*(8), 4437.

Shahril, Z., Remey Den, N. S. A., Shamshul Bahari, N. A. S., & Mohd Asnawi, N. I. (2024). Customer satisfaction in using digital QR code menu ordering in restaurant. *Journal of Tourism, Hospitality and Culinary Arts*, *16*(1), 820–831.

Singh, R., Sonje, R., Salkar, S., & Jadhav, A. (2022). *Smart QR-based restaurant dine-in system with sales analysis*. ITM web of conferences (Vol. *44*, p. 03014). EDP Sciences.

Streimikiene, D., Svagzdiene, B., Jasinskas, E., & Simanavicius, A. (2021). Sustainable tourism development and competitiveness: The systematic literature review. *Sustainable Development*, *29*(1), 259–271.

Şat, R., & Ayazlar, R. A. (2022). The effect of QR code applications on customer satisfaction in restaurants. *Gaziantep University Journal of Social Sciences*, *21*(4). https://doi.org/10.21547/jss.1065719

Şeker, Ö., Uyüklü, C., & Dalkılıç, G. (2024). *QR code-based authentication in IoT mesh network*. 2024 8th International artificial intelligence and data processing symposium (IDAP) (pp. 1–8). IEEE. https://doi.org/10.1109/IDAP64064.2024.10710815

Tan, A., Gligor, D., & Ngah, A. (2020). Applying blockchain for halal food traceability. *International Journal of Logistics Research and Applications*, *25*(6), 947–964. https://doi.org/10.1080/13675567.2020.1825653

Udvaros, J., & Forman, N. (2024). QR code use and identification problems in tourism. *Journal of Environmental Management & Tourism*, *15*(1), 167–175.

UN. (1987). *Bruntland report*. https://www.are.admin.ch/are/en/home/media/publications/sustainable-development/brundtland-report.html on 08.04.2025

UNEP & WTO. (2005). *Making tourism more sustainable – A guide for policy makers (English version)*. United Nation Environmental Programme. https://www.unep.org/resources/report/making-tourism-more-sustainable-guide-policy-makers

UNTWO. (2017). *International year of sustainable tourism for development*. https://www.unwto.org/tourism4development2017

Xinyu, R., & Garg, A. (2023). Customer acceptance of QR menu ordering system in luxury restaurants. A study of Xi'an, China. *Asia-Pacific Journal of Innovation in Hospitality & Tourism*, *12*(2).

Vuksanović, N., Demirović Bajrami, D., Petrović, M. D., & Grigorieva, E. M. (2021). QR codes as a tool for receiving feedback about guests' satisfaction at destinations. *Journal of Place Management and Development*, *14*(1), 19–31. https://doi.org/10.1108/JPMD-03-2020-0025

Yamin, M. A. Y., & Abdalatif, O. A. A. (2024). Examining consumer behavior towards adoption of quick response code mobile payment systems: Transforming mobile payment in the fintech industry. *Humanities and Social Sciences Communications*, *11*(1), 1–11. https://doi.org/10.1057/s41599-024-03189-w

Zakri, N. A. S. M., Nawawi, N. N., Ghani, A. M., Abd Hamid, M., Nawawi, W. N. W., & Isa, S. M. (2024). The role of QR code applications in enhancing customer satisfaction at restaurants: A conceptual study. *Asian Journal of Research in Education and Social Sciences*, *6*(S1), 385–392.

Chapter 7

Halal-friendly Characteristics Enhance Revisit Intention of Muslim Travelers: Mediating Role of Halal Consciousness and Artificial Intelligence Innovation

Nazirullah[a,b], Mohammad Sobri Bin Hamid[c], Ahmad Puad Mat Som[a], Mansoor Ali[d], Sabeeha Rahman[e] and Irfan Nawaz[f]

[a]*Faculty of Applied Social Sciences, Universiti Sultan Zainal Abidin, Malaysia*
[b]*CEO of Center of Engineering Research Advancement and Technology (CEERAT), Islamabad, Pakistan*
[c]*Faculty of Design, Innovation & Technology (FRIT), Universiti Sultan Zainal Abidin (UniSZA), Terengganu, Malaysia*
[d]*Department of English, Kohat University of Science and Technology, Khyber Pakhtunkhwa, Pakistan*
[e]*Faculty of Social Sciences and Humanities, Allama Iqbal Open University, Islamabad, Pakistan*
[f]*Federal Ministry of Human Rights, Government of Pakistan, Pakistan*

Abstract

The chapter investigates the impact of halal-friendly characteristics on the revisit intention of Muslim tourists, which is mediated by halal consciousness and the innovation of artificial intelligence (AI) among tourist destinations. This chapter filled the gap of AI innovation toward revisiting destinations and the challenges of halal-consciousness, faith-based needs during traveling. A quantitative research approach was used, and data were collected from Muslim tourists in Kalash Valley Chitral District, Pakistan. Two hundred and ten ($n = 210$) respondents (Muslim tourists) filled a questionnaire, and data were analyzed through SPSS version-21 and SmartPLS-4 Software. The chapter findings revealed that halal-friendly

Halal Tourism and Artificial Intelligence: New Approaches for a New Generation, 87–103

doi:10.1108/978-1-80686-165-120261008

characteristics have a positive predictive relationship with Muslim traveler revisit intentions. The mediating role of halal consciousness and AI innovation impacts the revisit intention of Muslim tourists. In conclusion, the pivotal influence of AI is profoundly improving visitors' perceptions regarding revisiting intention, and Islamic principles are embedded in halal-friendly characteristics and halal consciousness, which were prioritized by Muslim tourists during their revisit to their destinations.

Keywords: Artificial intelligence innovation; halal tourism and consciousness; Muslim tourists; destinations; revisit intention

Introduction

The rising demand for halal tourism has generated considerable interest in comprehending the elements of AI innovation that affect travelers' willingness to visit sites with halal-friendly characteristics. Halal tourism extends beyond the provision of halal cuisine to include a comprehensive array of services and experiences that comply with Islamic standards (Han et al., 2019; Rosli et al., 2024). The expansion of the worldwide Muslim population enhances the prospective market for halal tourism based on their revisit intention, and it is a vital subject of investigation for tourism stakeholders (Hasan, 2024; Juliana et al., 2024; Mursid, 2023). Recent research has underscored the significance of halal consciousness, technological innovations, and AI implementation which influenced visitors' attitudes and intents (Azali et al., 2023; Wulandari et al., 2025). The studies evaluate the influence of halal-friendly characteristics on revisit intention and exhibit AI innovation (Azam et al., 2024; Battour et al., 2025). Research conducted by Alfarizi et al. (2025) indicates that halal-friendly qualities and halal consciousness do not affect revisit intention. However, technological innovation and revisiting intention could be a possible influence among tourist destinations. Moreover, research by Gaffar et al. (2024) demonstrates that certain halal consciousness traits do affect the revisit intention of Muslim tourists among different destinations. Similarly, recent studies highlight and elucidate the impact of halal-friendly characteristics among tourists during high revisit intention (Karya et al., 2025; Patwary et al., 2025). This work introduces a complete multi-theoretical model to portray a predictive association between social cognitive and consumer behavior among Islamic tourists and AI adoption as mediating factors (Shamsudin et al., 2025). This research filled the gap and elucidated how halal-friendly characteristics affect the revisit intentions of Muslim tourists by analyzing the intervening effect of halal consciousness and AI innovation with specific geographic parameters. As a result, rigorous quantitative research methodology aims to elucidate the current inconsistencies in the research while providing rational recommendations for improving tourism tendencies toward Muslim tourists' revisit intention. Several studies have demonstrated that halal consciousness significantly influences travelers' intentions and actions. Paul and Roy (2025) underscore the significance of a favorable destination image in augmenting visitors' propensity toward any tourist destination for revisiting. An impactful halal consciousness may act as a significant motivator, particularly when it resonates with the cultural and religious beliefs of the intended visitors to any destination (Che Haron et al., 2024). As a result, the present research expands on these results by examining how AI and halal consciousness mediate the association between halal-friendly characteristics and revisit intentions. Besides, the integration of AI innovation is increasingly acknowledged as a crucial element for Muslim tourists. For instance, AI has the potential to enhance overall revisit intention by offering tailored services and increasing consumers' halal consciousness (Alharbi et al., 2025). This innovative chapter integrated the function of AI technology fit and halal consciousness as a mediator, which may enhance the beneficial impacts of halal-friendly characteristics on revisit intention by providing customized experiences that cater to the distinct requirements of Muslim tourists.

The research on halal tourism has mostly concentrated on the direct influence of halal-friendly characteristics and revisit intentions among Muslim tourists, often neglecting the possible intermediary impacts of variables such as halal consciousness and AI innovation. Although research by Hendrik et al. (2024) has recognized the significance of halal tourism, there is an absence of complete models that include these variables with technical breakthroughs such as halal consciousness and AI. The impact of AI on tourism has yet to be adequately investigated, especially in halal tourism (Azwar & Usman, 2025). The revisit intention is a complex construct that includes desire, willingness, the likelihood of emotion, and visitors' perceptions to return or repeat an action (Rasoolimanesh et al., 2025; Setiawan & Susilawati, 2025). Moreover, Wijaya et al. (2025) described that using social media and online reviews might augment the exposure of halal-friendly characteristics as well as influence the attitudes and intents of prospective tourists. For example, the present study filled the gap and proposed that halal-friendly characteristics and halal consciousness influence revisit intention. AI solutions that enhance service efficiency or tailor experiences may substantially promote the urge of revisit intention toward destination (Nazirullah, Ullah, et al., 2025). From the above critical scientific discussion, the current research has found the gap, such as previous literature did not concentrate on the technological dimensions of AI with respect to halal-friendly characteristics and also did not emphasize its possible impact on Muslim tourists' perceptions regarding halal consciousness and revisit intention.

As a result, the current chapter explains how halal-friendly characteristics could influence AI's innovation and halal consciousness and revisit the intentions of Muslim tourists. The study's originality is in its holistic methodology, which amalgamates religious (halal) factors and AI elements to elucidate the aim of the revisit intention among different tourist destinations. This study dually emphasis on religious factors (halal consciousness) and AI integration in halal tourism industry but also provides practical insights for tourism professionals aiming to attract Muslim travelers to revisit different destinations. The incorporation of AI as a mediator is notably novel, as it underscores the capacity of technology to improve the tourist's halal consciousness toward halal-friendly destinations. The study's scope includes several halal-friendly characteristics, such as a social and culturally respectful environment, facilities, halal-certified food and beverages, no haram ingredients, services, and ethical business practices. The study offers a comprehensive perspective on the aspects of halal-friendly characteristics that enhance a favorable revisit toward the destination and, therefore, affect the desire to enjoy Muslim community experiences.

Theoretical Underpinning and Foundation

Prior research about halal tourism mostly uses the theory of planned behavior (TPB) to ascertain the determinants of Muslim consumer behavior (Shamsudin et al., 2025). The TPB asserts that customers' beliefs, subjective standards, and perceived behavioral control significantly influence their intention to acquire a product or service, eventually affecting their behavior. Notwithstanding its prevalent use, several scholars have criticized the assumption of TPB because it is not more responsive toward emotional components of human beings. Conner et al. (2013) noted that the TPB could not be assumed as the factor of emotion and it is exclusively based on logical thinking and rational reasoning. Besides, Sniehotta et al. (2014) derived that single theory cannot comprehensively explain consumer behavior in domain of halal tourism. Numerous variables may influence observed behavior, and a complete understanding requires meticulous research to add several theoretical assumption and develop a high influential framework and predictive model (Ruiter & Crutzen, 2020).

Therefore, to increase the accuracy of explanations and predictions of Muslim halal tourist behavior, this study applied two theories: social cognitive theory (SCT) and Islamic theory of consumer behavior (ITCB). SCT highlights how cognitive processes shape human behavior, and its nature is psychological. SCT suggests that human functioning is influenced by three interconnected factors: individual factors, environment, and behavior. Within the realm of individual factors, this study focuses on individual literacy toward legal and halal knowledge. SCT is a useful framework for understanding human behavior and developing interventions to promote behavior change. However, the lack of SCT in Bandura's theory is not considered the relationship between humans and God as one of the principles. In Islam, developing a strong connection with God is crucial as it can greatly aid in adopting positive behaviors. Therefore, the study applied another theory, named the ITCB, that focuses on the elements related to the relationship with God. The ITBC is a comprehensive framework that aims to provide a deep understanding of the behavior of Muslim consumers based on Islamic principles and values. This theory is drawn from an Islamic worldview, which enables a holistic perspective on consumers that encompasses the present world and the hereafter (Amin, 2019). Most of the previous researchers agreed that Muslim consumption must be guided by Islamic principles (Khan, 2021; Pradhita, 2024). Therefore, halal-friendly characteristics, AI, and halal consciousness variables were related to revisiting intention in the context of Islamic tourism in this study, and Islamic values, religiosity, and Islamic shariah were included to predict halal consciousness among Muslim tourists. As illustrated in Fig. 7.1, the conceptual framework consists of independent, mediators, and dependent variables.

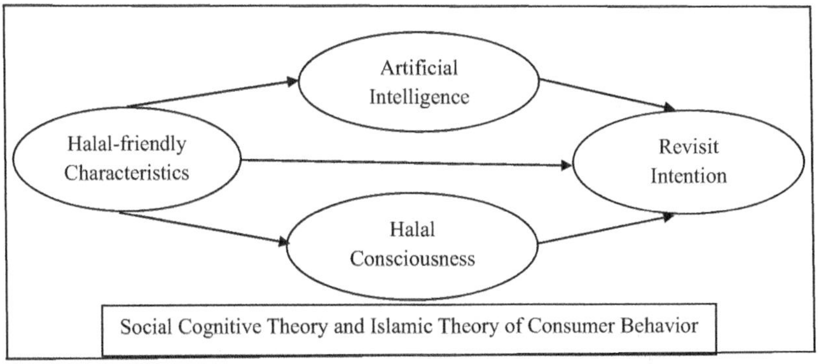

Fig. 7.1. Conceptual Framework of the Chapter.

Research Method

This research used a quantitative design with a cross-sectional survey design. The target demographic population of the study consists of both male and female participants within the Pakistani tourists' destinations. For example, the unit of analysis was those tourists who visited these destinations for enjoyment and pleasure. This research used a purposive sampling method to collect data from Muslim tourists in Kalash Valley Chitral District, Pakistan. The sample size was selected through G*Power statistical analysis software, and analysis suggested two hundred and ten (n = 210) sample size is enough statistically. For example, Kline (2023) recommends that a sample size above 200 is deemed large for structural model analysis. As a result, our sample size was 210, which is quite abundant for the study. The survey was face to face, and four locally trained gatekeepers or key consultants collected data from different tourist destinations.

Data Collection Tool

The surveys were administered to the participants using the purposive sampling method, whereby they were solicited based on revisit numbering. The study involved respondents who visited Kalash Valley Chitral District, Pakistan, at least two times. Similarly, the questionnaire statements were evaluated using a five-point Likert Scale from 1 to 5, where a score of 1 indicated disagree, and a score of 5 indicated strongly agree. Upon securing the respondents' consent to collaborate, questionnaires were disseminated for completion. The chapter adopted and adopted items for each variable from previous studies. For example, 5-items halal consciousness scale was adapted from the study of Kurniawati and Savitri (2020). Second, 5-items revisit intention scale was adapted from the study of Rahman et al. (2022). Lastly, 7-items halal-friendly characteristics and 5-items AI scales were adapted from the study of Wulandari et al. (2025) and Nazirullah, Nawaz, et al. (2025). It is to be noted that all these variables' items were rephrased and then done in a pilot study of 110 participants for pilot testing. These respondents were not involved in the hypotheses testing phase. Subsequently, data analysis was conducted using the statistical packages for social sciences (SPSS version-21) and Partial Least Square (PLS-4.0) software with a structural equation modeling (SEM) approach to evaluate the hypotheses, particularly the impact of the mediating variables. The variables of the study were adapted and adopted from previous studies, and then changes were made accordingly.

Data Analysis

The chapter analyzed data in the form of descriptive and inferential statistics. For example, descriptive statistics were conducted for demographic variables and respondents' demographic characteristics are outlined in the form of gender, traveling frequency, and age brackets. The frequency distribution revealed that male respondents were 129(61.4%) and female respondents were 81(38.6%). Traveling frequency was also measured two to four times respondents' destinations 99(45.5%) which were higher in numbers. The respondents ages were 18–24 and their frequency was high up to 132(62.9%). The study measured descriptive statistics of demographic information which is presented in Table 7.1. Similarly, Table 7.2 displays information about reliability and validity as well as outer modeling constructs.

Measurement Model Evaluation

The data collected through the questionnaire were then analyzed using SEM to test the direct and indirect effects among the hypothesized constructs. SEM was chosen for its ability to assess complex influences and mediation effects within a

Table 7.1. Demographic Information of Respondents (n = 210).

Gender	*f*	%
Male	129	61.4
Female	81	38.6
Traveling frequency toward destination	*f*	%
Two to four times	99	45.5
Five to six times	60	28.5
Seven to eight times	51	24.2
Age	*f*	%
18–24	132	62.9
25–34	57	27.1
35–49	17	8.1
50–64	4	1.9
Total	210	100

Note: *f* = frequency, % = present.

Source: 2025 Survey Data.

Table 7.2. Variables, Items, and Outer Modeling of Measurement Reliability and Validity (n = 210).

Construct	Outer Loading	Cronbach's Alpha	Composite Reliability	AVE
AI (artificial intelligence)		0.868	0.904	0.654
AI1	0.837			
AI2	0.745			
AI3	0.846			
AI4	0.821			
AI5	0.791			
HC (halal consciousness)		0.858	0.899	0.641
HC1	0.780			
HC2	0.681			
HC3	0.821			
HC4	0.903			
HC5	0.804			
HFC (halal-friendly characteristics)		0.939	0.950	0.733
HFC1	0.822			
HFC2	0.803			
HFC3	0.836			
HFC4	0.894			
HFC5	0.879			
HFC6	0.875			
HFC7	0.880	0.885	0.916	0.687
RI (revisit intention)				
RI1	0.852			
RI2	0.877			
RI3	0.815			
RI4	0.836			
RI5	0.759			

Source: 2025 Survey Data.

single model. The statistical analysis was conducted using the PLS method, processed with SmartPLS 4.0 software. The outer loading test was performed as a form of validity testing, with a cut-off > 0.7. Cronbach's Alpha with a cut-off > 0.7 and composite reliability with a cut-off > 0.8 were used for reliability testing. The fit of the structural model was assessed by testing the inner model using

R-Square for each endogenous variable, indicating the proportion of variance explained by the model. The acceptable cut-off value for the R^2 of latent endogenous variables is greater than 0.20. For example, path relationships in the structural model were tested using standard estimation with a p-value cut-off < 0.05.

All indications for each variable are valid as the HTMT values surpass 0.85. The results showed that discriminant validity tests were statistically significant because all the indicators' values portrayed monotrait correlation within the same construct as well as heterotrait correlation across the different constructs (see Table 7.3). Furthermore, the study compared FLC with AVE, and it showed that all variables' FLC values were above the AVE values. As shown in Fig. 7.2, all the constructs, their factor loadings, and their correlations are presented. This study established very good discriminant validity (see Table 7.4). The statistical test results revealed that all the constructs are valid and reliable, and the structural model could be evaluated.

The model is deemed acceptable since all endogenous variables have an R-squared value greater than 0.2. The endogenous variable AI has an R-square

Table 7.3. Heterotrait-monotrait Ratio (HTMT) ($n = 210$).

Construct	AI	HC	HFC	RI
AI				
HC	0.864			
HFC	0.891	0.852		
RI	0.872	0.884	0.878	

Source: Study Survey Data (2025).

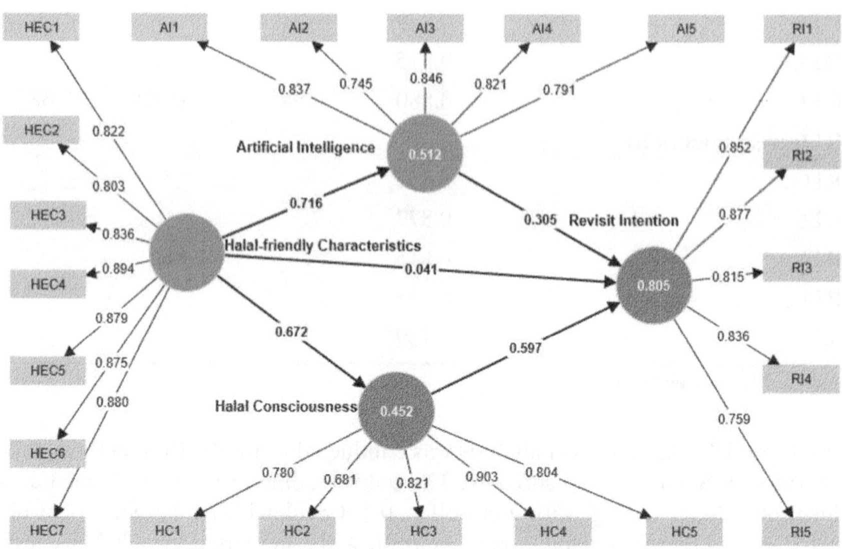

Fig. 7.2. Measurement Model. *Source*: 2025 Survey Data.

Table 7.4. Fornell–Larcker Criterion (FLC) ($n = 210$).

Construct	**AI**	**HC**	**HFC**	**RI**
AI	0.809			
HC	0.828	0.801		
HFC	0.716	0.722	0.856	
RI	0.830	0.878	0.762	0.829

Source: Study Survey Data (2025).

Table 7.5. PLS Predict/CVPAT ($n = 210$).

Constructs	**Outcomes**	Q^2 **Predict**	R^2	f^2
AI -> RI	AI	0.506	0.512	0.281
HC -> RI				0.552
HFC -> AI	HC	0.443	0.452	0.510
HFC -> HC				0.825
HFC -> RI	RI	0.431	0.805	0.413

Source: 2025 Survey Data.

value of 0.512, indicating a moderate relationship; the endogenous variable halal consciousness has an *R*-square value of 0.452, also signifying a moderate relationship. Lastly, the endogenous variable revisit intention has an *R*-square value of 0.805, reflecting a very strong relationship. Similarly, *Q*-square described a good predictive relevance in this study and the model suggests that the value is above zero. As a result, all the endogenous constructs established excellent predictive relevance and well reconstructed in the model. Likewise, *F*-square was calculated to assess the predictive power of the current model, and the result showed that relative significance and importance still exist among different exogenous constructs and variation in an endogenous construct. As a result of this study, the statistical output values considered that a strong significant influence was present between independent and dependent variables (see Table 7.5 for more details).

Structural Model Along with Hypotheses Testing

The findings demonstrate that AI has significant positive relationship with revisit intention and the beta value is greater than the cutoff point ($\beta = 0.305^{***}$, $p < 0.050$). Similarly, halal consciousness has positive significant association with revisit intention and the beta value is ($\beta = 0.597^{***}$, $p < 0.050$). Likewise, halal-friendly characteristics have highly significant association with AI ($\beta = 0.716^{***}$, $p < 0.050$). Furthermore, halal-friendly characteristics significantly and positively impact halal consciousness ($\beta = 0.672^{***}$, $p < 0.050$). Lastly, there was no direct relationship between halal-friendly characteristics and revisit intention

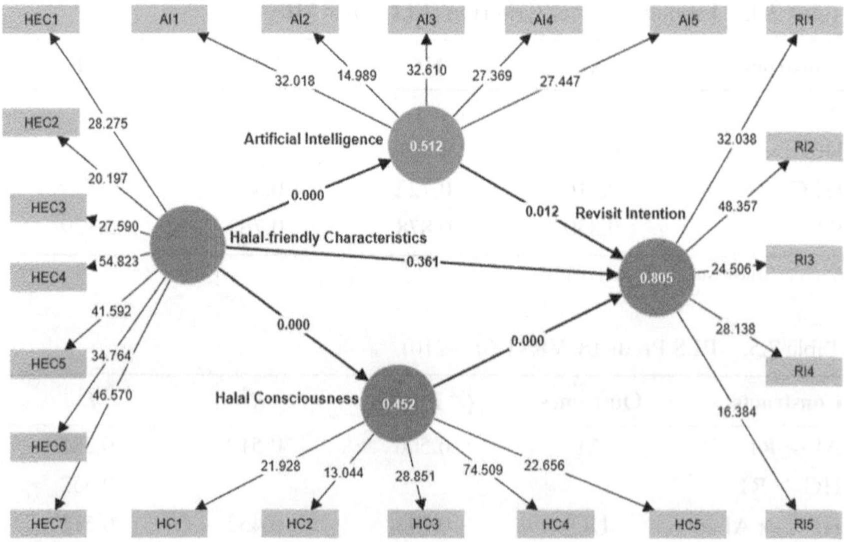

Fig. 7.3. Measurement Model. *Source*: 2025 Survey Data.

($\beta = 0.041$, $p > 0.050$) and the hypothesis one (*H1*) was rejected as well as *H2*, *H3*, *H4*, and *H5* were significantly accepted. Moreover, mediation analysis was also conducted to know the indirect association between intervening constructs. The halal-friendly characteristics have positive relationship between halal consciousness and revisit intention ($\beta = 0.402^{***}$, $p > 0.050$). For example, halal-friendly characteristics have also indirect positive association between AI and revisit intention ($\beta = 0.218^{***}$, $p > 0.050$). Consequently, hypotheses *H6* and *H7* were accepted. The structural model results suggested that paths have predictive relevance and simulation were highly significant for the future policy making and tourism stakeholders. As illustrated in Fig. 7.3, the figure presents the path significance values, R^2 values and *t*-statistics (see Table 6).

Discussion

The analysis of direct effects during model evaluation was significant, and the participants revealed that halal-friendly characteristics influence visitor revisit intentions, emphasizing the significant role of gender. The chapter results highlight the significant influence of AI on travel revisit intention to specific Muslim tourist destinations. The study indicates that certain halal consciousness significantly affects visitor perceptions and inclinations to revisit the same destination again two to three times. This highlights the distinct demands and perspectives of Muslim visitors while also indicating the wider ramifications for AI adaptation and halal-friendly characteristics that should be designed to accommodate varied tourist populations' revisit intentions. This research seeks to elucidate many complexities surrounding the views and intents of visitors at halal-friendly places and facilities of prayer rooms, halal foods, halal beverages, and segregated facilities

Table 7.6. Path Analysis and Standardized Estimation ($n = 210$).

Constructs	Beta (β)	SD	t-statistics	p-Values	Bais	2.5%	97.5%
Direct Effect	**Path Analysis**						
AI -> RI (H5)	0.305***	0.122	2.501	0.012	0.000	0.092	0.555
HC -> RI (H4)	0.597***	0.132	4.542	0.000	0.000	0.319	0.811
HFC -> AI (H3)	0.716***	0.039	18.483	0.000	0.001	0.637	0.788
HFC -> HC (H2)	0.672***	0.047	14.358	0.000	0.001	0.572	0.752
HFC -> RI (H1)	0.041	0.045	0.914	0.361	0.000	−0.049	0.133
Indirect Effect							
HFC -> HC -> RI (H6)	0.402***	0.089	4.514	0.000	−0.001	0.216	0.556
HFC -> AI -> RI (H7)	0.218***	0.088	2.488	0.013	0.000	0.066	0.401

Note: $^*p < 0.05$, $^{**}p < 0.01$, $^{***}p < 0.001$.

Source: 2025 Survey Data.

for gender, with a particular emphasis on the social environment that is clean, safe, and free of haram. The subsequent sections consolidate these results and relate critically with previous up to date literature to elaborate the significance of these insights for the sustainable advancement of the halal tourist industry.

The study focuses on the good health and well-being of sustainable development goals Agenda 3, and the model reveals a positive association between the social environment and food, which demonstrates that the social environment greatly influences visitors' opinions, and they ultimately revisit halal-friendly destinations. Such as, Bamiro et al. (2025) claimed that such destinations in the sustainable development of the halal tourist industry are more important for future agenda of sustainability. Additionally, halal-friendly characteristics such as accessibility and proximity are in high demand among visitors (Singgalen, 2025). The study of Khairuldin et al. (2024) approved Sharia conformity embodies tourists' objective evaluation notion rather than subjective experiences of Muslim tourists' toward destinations. The present study results were in link with these studies and found that halal-friendly characteristics improve halal consciousness among Muslim tourists. Likewise, Marlina et al. (2025) associated halal consciousness perceptions with Muslim destination facilities and tourists' revisit intentions (Marlina et al., 2025). Like, AI has directly improved Muslim tourists revisit intention in the present study. For example, Battour et al. (2023) also delineated that AI improves facilities for Muslim tourists and increase revisit intentions toward destinations. Similarly, Soonsan and Jumani (2024) halal-friendly attributes are essential for Muslim tourism attractions and to retain their intention. As a result, tourist policy stakeholders recommended that halal-friendly attributes need to align facilities with Islamic principles and effectively address Muslim visitor preferences. In response to these findings, the current study revealed that halal-friendly characteristics and halal consciousness directly and indirectly improve revisit intentions.

The multifaceted concept of revisit intention encompasses visitors' cognitive feeling of repeating an activity in the same destination, which is necessarily a desirable action to sustain with this same tourist destination (Agarwal, 2023). In this present study, social cognitive assumption was tested, and it's confirmed that halal consciousness improves revisit intention. Similarly, Chang et al. (2025) found that revisit intention is depended on service quality, destination attractiveness, and perceived values of human beings' emotional reactions, desire and willingness, which have an effect on post-consumption actions taken for tourist destinations. By providing tangible evidence of a destination's commitment to servicing Muslim visitors, halal-friendly features improve both the cognitive and emotional components of Muslim believers (Singgalen, 2025). According to research, Muslim tourists' halal-friendly traits increase their likelihood of having a positive desire to return to specific destination (Fauzi & Battour, 2024). In similar vein, the current study also found that Muslim tourists like halal friendly characteristics of destination and it further improve halal consciousness among them. The findings of Rahmawati et al. (2025) emphasize on revisit intention and positive association with halal-friendly features. In a similar vein, Mursid (2023) makes it abundantly evident that providing halal cuisine at tourist attractions might increase Muslim visitors' desire to return. The present study tested the ITCB, and it was assumed that Islamic ethical consumption, which is governed by Islamic principles and Shariah law, is important for Muslim tourists.

Conclusion

The current chapter elucidates the interaction of Muslim tourists regarding halal-friendly characteristics and halal consciousness elements in response to visitor revisit intentions. It indicates that distinct Islamic principles and guidelines have differing degrees of effect on tourists' revisit intention. AI can highlight food or drinks, alcohol, poisons, and harmful ingredients, which can save Muslim tourists from unhygienic things. The significance of the social environment and local personnel consistently appears across all models as important in developing tourist attitudes to revisit the same destinations. The study identified a direct correlation between halal consciousness and revisit intention, especially AI, indicating a favorable element to increasing revisit intentions of tourists. Halal consciousness and AI matched a favorable relationship between visitors' revisit intention and social cognition. The predictive effect of halal-friendly food facilities' influence on revisit intentions underscores the need for strategic planning and the evaluation of how Islamic principles should sustain the health and well-being of the tourists at any destination. The findings reveal a significant effect of halal consciousness on revisit intentions, particularly in the context of AI's ongoing enhancement of ethical food-consumption standards. Future studies should examine the factors contributing to Muslim tourists' attitudes and cognitive feelings about tourist sentiments and AI adaptation. Moreover, qualitative research may provide profound insights into the visitor experience with halal food satisfaction and Islamic tourist destinations. This study elucidates the positive predictive influence of halal-friendly characteristics, halal consciousness, and AI on tourists' revisit intentions. The pivotal influence of AI is profoundly improving visitors' perceptions regarding revisiting intention in advance and highlights the halal consciousness prioritizing Islamic principles for visiting Muslim tourist destinations. The significance of the social environment and halal food and beverage offerings has a profound impact on revisit intentions among Muslim tourists, and AI detects lawful (halal) and forbidden food and beverages.

Theoretical Implication

The chapter represents a notable contribution to halal tourism in the context of hospitality and tourism as well as clarifying the essential impact of AI on revisiting intention to tourist destinations. This study used the SET and ITCB as theoretical assumption to examine the relationship between halal-friendly characteristics and the social cognitive intentions of Muslim visitors to revisit specific destinations. This detailed predictive examination recognizes that halal consciousness cognitive feeling depends on halal-friendly characteristics to sustain tourists' revisit intention toward destinations. The adaptation of AI is crucial for halal consciousness and supporting a targeted strategy in the development of halal tourists revisit intention.

The use of halal consciousness as a crucial variable broadens the applicability of SET and ITCB within the realm of halal tourism and destination. The research reveals that Muslim visitors had distinct tastes and perspectives about facilities, services, cuisine, and staff interactions in destinations like Kalash Valley and Chitral. The value of AI expands the applicability of halal consciousness in halal tourism research and empirically validates that Muslim cultural and social cognitive feelings toward destination revisit intention. This research enhances the theoretical framework by providing detailed insights into the assumption of SCT and ITCB regarding halal-friendly characteristics in the context of halal tourism. The dynamic nature of halal-friendly characteristics may not be properly evaluated in this research and the crucial factors such as AI and halal consciousness are the cognitive feeling of individuals during tourists' visits.

References

Agarwal, M. (2023). *Repeat tourist behaviour: understanding the motivations and experiences of repeat tourists and identifying stakeholder perspectives*. James Cook University.

Alfarizi, M., Ngatindriatun, N., Arifian, R., & Widiharjanti, I. (2025). Green-smart service quality and halal tourism attributes on revisit intention and quality of life: A case study from Indonesia. *International Journal of Halal Industry*, *1*(1), 1–20. https://doi.org/10.20885/IJHI.vol1.iss1.art1

Alharbi, A., Pandit, A., Rosenberger III, P. J., & Miah, S. (2025). Understanding AI-enabled conversational agent customer experiences in religious tourism. *Journal of Islamic Marketing*, 88–109. https://doi.org/10.1108/jima-07-2024-0309

Amin, H. (2019). The Islamic theory of consumer behaviour for ijarah home financing. *Journal of Asia Business Studies*, *13*(4), 672–693. https://doi.org/10.1108/JABS-09-2018-0261

Azali, M., Kamal Basha, N., Chang, Y.-S., Lim, X.-J., & Cheah, J.-H. (2023). Why not travel to Malaysia? Variations in inbound tourists' perceptions toward Halal-friendly destination attributes. *Journal of Hospitality & Tourism Research*, *47*(1), 177–206. https://doi.org/10.1177/1096348020987634

Azam, M. S. E., Muflih, B. K., & Al Haq, M. A. (2024). Intersection between modern technologies and halal tourism: Exploring the role of digital innovation in enhancing Muslim travellers' experience. *The Journal of Muamalat and Islamic Finance Research*, *21*(1), 16–31. https://doi.org/10.33102/jmifr.546

Azwar, A., & Usman, A. H. (2025). Artificial intelligence in the halal industry: Trends and global research opportunities. *International Journal of Halal Industry*, *1*(1), 46–67. https://doi.org/10.20885/IJHI.vol1.iss1.art4

Bamiro, N. B., Oshoba, A. O., Yahya, I. O., & Li, Q. (2025). Transforming halal coastal tourism for financial inclusion and economic growth: Threat, challenges and opportunities. In L. R. M. A. Salisu, N. B. Bamiro, & I. O. Elegbede (Eds.), *Green and blue economy frameworks for halal industry sustainability* (pp. 327–345). https://doi.org/10.1007/978-981-96-1729-6_17

Battour, M., Mady, K., Salaheldeen, M., Elsotouhy, M., Elbendary, I., & Boğan, E. (2023). AI-enabled technologies to assist Muslim tourists in Halal-friendly tourism. *Journal of Islamic Marketing*, *14*(5), 1291–1309. https://doi.org/10.1108/jima-01-2022-0001

Battour, M., Salaheldeen, M., Anwar, I., Ratnasari, R. T., Hamid, A., & Mady, K. (2025). Integrating ChatGPT in halal tourism: Impact on tourist satisfaction, e-WoM and revisit intention. *Journal of Islamic Marketing*, 211–231. https://doi.org/10.1108/jima-10-2024-0470

Chang, K.-C., Cheng, Y.-S., Kuo, N.-T., & Cheng, Y.-H. (2025). Impacts of tourists' shopping destination trust on post-visit behaviors: A loss aversion perspective. *International Journal of Hospitality & Tourism Administration*, *26*(1), 28–67. https://doi.org/10.1080/15256480.2023.2241030

Che Haron, H. I., Abdullah, H., Sheikh Ahmad Tajuddin, S. A. F., Mohd Zain, F. A., & Rahim, N. A. A. (2024). Analyzing revisitation dynamics: A scholarly analysis of bootstrapping, mediating Muslim-friendly context and impact on determinant factors in Terengganu's edutourism destinations. *Journal of Islamic Marketing*, *15*(12), 3683–3726. https://doi.org/10.1108/jima-02-2024-0053

Conner, M., Godin, G., Sheeran, P., & Germain, M. (2013). Some feelings are more important: Cognitive attitudes, affective attitudes, anticipated affect, and blood donation. *Health Psychology*, *32*(3), 264. https://doi.org/10.1037/a0028500

Fauzi, M. A., & Battour, M. (2024). Halal and Islamic tourism: Science mapping of present and future trends. *Tourism Review*, *80*(5), 1156–1170. https://doi.org/10.1108/tr-08-2023-0533

Gaffar, V., Christiyanto, W. W., Arissaputra, R., Abror, A., Achmad, N., Hidayat, E. F. F., Siregar, Q. A., & Shahril, A. (2024). Digital halal literacy and halal destination attribute as the antecedents of revisit intention. *International Journal of Tourism Cities*, 57–71. https://doi.org/10.1108/ijtc-12-2023-0259

Han, H., Al-Ansi, A., Olya, H. G., & Kim, W. (2019). Exploring halal-friendly destination attributes in South Korea: Perceptions and behaviors of Muslim travelers toward a non-Muslim destination. *Tourism Management*, *71*, 151–164. https://doi.org/10.1016/j.tourman.2018.10.010

Hasan, A. A.-T. (2024). Factors influencing halal tourism destinations revisit intentions among Muslim travelers of Bangladesh: The mediating role of emotional attachments. *Journal of Islamic Marketing*, *15*(3), 720–744. https://doi.org/10.1108/jima-02-2023-0045

Hendrik, H., Kusumawardani, S. S., & Permanasari, A. E. (2024). The emerging landscape of halal tourism in the digital era: An IT perspective. *Journal of Islamic Marketing*, *15*(8), 1995–2015. https://doi.org/10.1108/jima-04-2023-0130

Juliana, J., Syiva, A. N., Rosida, R., Permana, E., Zulfikar, R. M., Abduh, M., & Inomjon, Q. (2024). Revisit intention Muslim tourists to halal tourism in Yogyakarta: Analysis of facilities, promotion, electronic word of mouth, and religiosity. *Review of Islamic Economics and Finance*, *7*(1), 1–22. https://doi.org/10.17509/rief.v1i1.66961

Karya, D. F., Ratnasari, V., & Anshori, M. Y. (2025). Analyzing the role of government support in moderating behavior and revisit intention in halal tourism. *Journal of Ecohumanism*, *4*(2), 534–547. https://doi.org/10.62754/joe.v4i2.6029

Khairuldin, W. M. K. F. W., Anas, W. N. I. W. N., Imas, M., Hassan, A., Embong, A. H., Lukman, N. H. Z., & Md, M. A. I. (2024). Philosophy and ethics in halal tourism: A conceptual analysis. *International Journal*, *5*(11), 486–493. https://doi.org/10.61707/gsrdnf74

Khan, F. M. (2021). Preferences and constraints on an Islamic consumer: An analysis from Islamic perspective. *Journal of Humanities, Social and Management Sciences*, *2*(1), 85–94. https://doi.org/10.47264/idea.jhsms/2.1.8

Kline, R. B. (2023). *Principles and practice of structural equation modeling* (10th ed.). Guilford Publications. https://books.google.com.pk/books?id=t2CvEAAAQBAJ&dq/

Kurniawati, D. A., & Savitri, H. (2020). Awareness level analysis of Indonesian consumers toward halal products. *Journal of Islamic Marketing*, *11*(2), 522–546. https://doi.org/10.1108/JIMA-10-2017-0104

Marlina, L., Juliana, J., Rahmat, B. Z., Nasrullah, A. A., Ismail, S., & Inomjon, Q. (2025). Indonesia's strategy creating halal tourism for sustainable development goals: Analytical network process approach. *Journal of Lifestyle and SDGs Review*, *5*(1), e03403. https://doi.org/10.47172/2965-730X.SDGsReview.v5.n01.pe03403

Mursid, A. (2023). Examining revisit intention from the basic foundation of Islam: The role of halal destination attributes and perceived value. *Journal of Islamic Marketing*, *14*(5), 1325–1345. https://doi.org/10.1108/jima-07-2021-0232

Nazirullah, N. I., Ahsan, M. I., Rehman, S., Ullah, R., & Mahmood, A. (2025). Artificial intelligence and mobile application influence on tourist behaviors: Contextualizing festivals and events through virtual-reality experiences. In J. K. S. A. Anukrati Sharma (Ed.), *Technological innovation and AI for sustainable development in events and festivals* (pp. 126–139). CABI GB. https://doi.org/10.1079/9781836990185.0011

Nazirullah, U. F., Mahmood, A., Hamid Bin, S. M. M., Ryad, H., Alkilanyd Basil, S, & Rahmane, C. (2025). Tourist behaviours, expectations, and experiences toward events and festivals: Amalgamation of metaverse technological innovation and artificial intelligence. In J. K. a. M. Arora (Ed.), *The AI metaverse revolution: Transforming multi-business scenarios* (Vol. *2*, pp. 45–62). Emerald Publishing Limited. https://doi.org/10.1108/978-1-83662-586-520251004

Patwary, A. K., Alam, M. M. D., Zainol, N. A., Ashraf, M. U., Alam, M. N., Hayat, N., & Khreis, S. H. A. (2025). Unveiling the dynamics of revisit intention and word-of-mouth: An attribution theory approach to Halal-friendly hotel attributes and service encounter evaluation. *Journal of Hospitality and Tourism Insights*, *8*(2), 753–773. https://doi.org/10.1108/jhti-03-2024-0259

Paul, I., & Roy, G. (2025). Effect of consumption values and travel mindfulness on tourists' ecotourism interest and engagement behavior. *Tourism Planning & Development*, 1–23. https://doi.org/10.1080/21568316.2025.2495596

Pradhita, D. (2024). Intersection of Islamic values and consumer preferences. *Advances in Business & Industrial Marketing Research*, *2*(1), 15–25. https://doi.org/10.60079/abim.v2i1.231

Rahman, M. K., Yaacob, M. R., Khalique, M., & Adeiza, A. (2022). Analysing tourists' intention to revisit Islamic tourism destinations. *Middle East Journal of Management*, *9*(1), 87–106. https://doi.org/10.1504/MEJM.2021.10038360

Rahmawati, Y., Alhassan, U., A'la, A. M. r., & Rosyidi, L. N. (2025). Empirical study on the determinants of Muslim tourists' visit to Japan: Do Muslim-friendly facilities and culture matter? *Journal of Islamic Marketing*, *16*(2), 353–372. https://doi.org/10.1108/jima-07-2022-0188

Rasoolimanesh, S. M., Chee, S. Y., & Ari Ragavan, N. (2025). Tourists' perceptions of the sustainability of destination, satisfaction, and revisit intention. *Tourism Recreation Research*, *50*(1), 106–125. https://doi.org/10.1080/02508281.2023.2230762

Rosli, N. L., Jamaludin, M. A. B., & Ahmad, A. N. B. (2024). Beyond halal cuisine: A comprehensive exploration of Shariah compliance in tourism and hospitality. *Tazkia Islamic Finance and Business Review*, *18*(1), 120–139. https://tifbr-tazkia.org/index.php/TIFBR/article/view/370

Ruiter, R. A., & Crutzen, R. (2020). Core processes: How to use evidence, theories, and research in planning behavior change interventions. *Frontiers in Public Health*, *8*(247), 1–8. https://doi.org/10.3389/fpubh.2020.00247

Setiawan, R., & Susilawati, W. (2025). Revisit intention through the development of tourism components and tourist satisfaction at hot spring tourism destinations. *Khazanah Sosial*, *7*(1), 16–31. https://doi.org/10.15575/ks.v7i1.38996

Shamsudin, S. N., Abu Bakar, E., Osman, S., & Mohd Dali, N. R. S. (2025). Application of social cognitive theory and Islamic theory of consumer behavior in accessing Muslim behavior toward halal nutraceuticals. *Journal of Islamic Marketing*, *16*(2), 651–667. https://doi.org/10.1108/jima-08-2023-0245

Singgalen, Y. A. (2025). The economic impact of halal tourism development on local communities. *Ekonomi, Keuangan, Investasi dan Syariah*, *6*(3), 310–321. https://doi.org/10.47065/ekuitas.v6i3.7010

Sniehotta, F. F., Presseau, J., & Araújo-Soares, V. (2014). *Time to retire the theory of planned behaviour* (Vol. *8*, pp. 1–7). Taylor & Francis.

Soonsan, N., & Jumani, Z. A. (2024). Perceptions of Halal-friendly attributes: A quantitative study of tourists' intention to travel non-Islamic destination. *Journal of Islamic Marketing*, *15*(6), 1441–1460. https://doi.org/10.1108/jima-07-2022-0204

Wijaya, C. O., Wijaya, S., & Jaolis, F. (2025). The influence of social media content on attitude, destination image and intention of female Muslim travelers to visit halal destinations: Comparison between UGC and FGC. *Journal of Islamic Marketing*, *16*(2), 402–427. https://doi.org/10.1108/jima-08-2023-0235

Wulandari, A., Narimawati, U., & Syafei, M. Y. (2025). The influence of halal friendly attributes on visit intention mediated by destination image and artificial intelligence adoption in tourist destinations. *EKOMABIS: Jurnal Ekonomi Manajemen Bisnis*, *6*(1), 1–16. https://doi.org/10.37366/ekomabis.v6i01.2294

Chapter 8

A Framework for Smart Innovations in Islamic Pilgrimage: Utilizing AI and IoT within the Context of Halal Tourism

Priyakrushna Mohanty[a], M Sharanya[a] and Saurabh Bharti[b]

[a]*School of Business and Management, Christ University, Bengaluru, India*
[b]*Welcomgroup Graduate School of Hotel Administration, Manipal Academy of Higher Education, Manipal, India*

Abstract

Despite growing discourse on smart tourism and AI applications in travel, limited scholarly attention has been given to understanding the reasons for the growth of AI usage and the various facets of its application, specifically within Islamic pilgrimage. This includes the absence of a developed framework for innovative inventions. This paper addresses the research gap by exploring how AI and IoT technologies can transform halal tourism management, focusing on the Hajj and Umrah pilgrimages. The paper deals with three objectives: (1) To understand the reasons for the growth of AI usage in halal tourism with special reference to Islamic Pilgrimage, (2) to examine the various facets of AI usage in Islamic pilgrimage, and (3) to develop the framework for Smart inventions in Islamic pilgrimage. Methodologically, this is a conceptual paper grounded in a secondary literature review. It incorporates a thematic content analysis of both academic publications and gray literature. With this approach, the researchers were able to gain a holistic view of how AI can intersect with Islamic pilgrimage and halal tourism. The results are demonstrated through the ideation of the FSIIP framework. This framework highlights AI's vital role in improving

Halal Tourism and Artificial Intelligence: New Approaches for a New Generation, 105–119

doi:10.1108/978-1-80686-165-120261009

pilgrims' experiences through tailored services, streamlining crowd control, and advancing sustainability through astute resource management.

Keywords: Artificial intelligence; halal tourism; faith-based travel; Islamic pilgrimage; AI integration; cultural sensitivity; gray literature; thematic analysis; technology and religion

1. Introduction

A significant and fast-moving slice of the global travel pie is now Islamic tourism, fueled significantly by Muslim travelers' increasing desire for faith-centered experiences and their religious obligations. Pilgrimage sits right at this core, especially the Hajj and Umrah trips to the holy cities of Mecca and Medina. From the organizers' perspective, these events are massive logistical operations rather than mere spiritual calling. Hajj, for instance, pulls in over 2 million pilgrims annually (Battour et al., 2022). This ever-increasing number of pilgrims is a significant challenge to manage. These include crowd control, health tracking, transport issues, and guiding the pilgrims. In response to the demand for slicker pilgrimage operations, artificial intelligence (AI) is where countries are looking, emerging as a game-changer for managing these intricate religious tourism setups. More and more, AI technologies like facial recognition, predictive analysis, health risk tracking, and multilingual chatbots are being used at pilgrimage sites (Le et al., 2024). Such tools are promised to be more efficient in terms of operation. Beyond that, they aim to make pilgrim services safer, more personalized, and easier for pilgrims to use (Haase et al., 2016). Notably, Saudi Arabia is putting AI at the center of its Vision 2030 plan to build a digital, sustainable infrastructure for Islamic tourism (Arab News, 2024a).

Even with how fast these AI tools are being used, academic studies on AI's specific role in Islamic pilgrimage are still scattered. Most current smart tourism research broadly looks at secular places or halal tourism. It doesn't isolate the particular logistics, cultural points, and spiritual details unique to pilgrimage (Khan, 2024). Plus, the practical use of AI in pilgrimage is widely documented in media, government papers, and reports. But, academic dives into these developments are still few and far between, leaving a crucial gap in research. There is still a lack of understanding of how AI can improve pilgrimage, thinking about sustainability, how efficient things are, and keeping the spiritual side intact (Battour et al., 2024). This paper is an attempt to tackle this gap. The researchers do it through three linked objectives. First, they explore the drivers of the growing number of AI technologies adopted in halal tourism while giving more attention to Hajj and Umrah in this work. Second, the paper examines AI's different sides and how it's being applied in Islamic pilgrimage. The authors back this research by citing evidence from academic papers and gray literature. Third, the authors propose a conceptual framework. This framework bundles AI innovations into the relevant strategic themes in managing Islamic pilgrimage.

Given the scarcity of primary field studies and the newness of this domain, a conceptual research design was deemed for this work. Therefore, peer-reviewed publications, government policies, institutional reports, and media sources provide evidence for the arguments highlighted. The data are analyzed using thematic content analysis to identify AI's frequent themes and strategic use cases in pilgrimage management. The end product provides a systematic knowledge of how AI is reshaping modern Islamic tourism, especially in the context of pilgrimages.

The structure of the paper is as follows. Section 2 gives an in-depth literature review on Islamic pilgrimage, halal tourism, and AI's contribution to religious travel. The methodology applied for content analysis and framework development is outlined in Section 3. Section 4 is concerned with strategic and contextual drivers of AI adoption. Section 5 provides the thematic matrix of AI applications, and Section 6 provides the conceptual framework. The last section draws together conclusions and suggests implications and future lines of research.

2. Theoretical Background and Literature Review

2.1. Islamic Pilgrimage: Historical and Cultural Significance

The religious and social life of Muslims across the globe features Islamic pilgrimage prominently, with Hajj and Umrah holding the most sway and drawing millions to Saudi Arabia every year (Bashir, 2024). Hajj is known as one of the Five Pillars of Islam. It is an once-in-a-lifetime responsibility for the physically and financially capable. Umrah, however, isn't compulsory. It remains a spiritually enriching ritual that is performable all year long. The worship in these pilgrimages transcends mere worship. They are transformative spiritual voyages filled with cultural, emotional, and communal boons.

As pilgrim numbers swell following the easing of COVID-19 restrictions, logistical and managerial challenges have similarly mounted. Pressing concerns include crowd management, hygiene, health provision, transport, and safety. Handling millions of operational and spiritual demands within tight windows and constricted areas presents a truly immense task. In response, exploration of modern technological remedies has begun among host nations, with Saudi Arabia as the chief among them (Arab News, 2024b). The aim is to boost both efficiency and the sacred character of the pilgrimage experience.

2.2. Halal Tourism and Technology

Halal tourism is more than pilgrimage; all forms of travel and hospitality adhere to the Islamic way of life. Services that address the needs of a Muslim diet, privacy, prayer facilities, and gender-specific arrangements fall under this (Moshin et al., 2020). With a growing global Muslim population and disposable incomes, halal tourism is increasing commercially. This is seen especially in the Middle East, Southeast Asia, and sections of Europe.

Alongside this growth is the rise of Smart Tourism, which involves bringing together digital technologies like AI, IoT, big data analytics, AR, and VR to personalize and optimize travel experiences. In the halal tourism industry, these innovative technologies offer avenues for enhancing Sharia-compliant services. Examples include digital halal food finders, Qibla direction apps, AI-styled translation tools, and intelligent hotel room automation (Battour et al., 2025). Such tools help to connect linguistic and cultural gaps. They also see they can fulfill religious obligations without any hassles while moving.

However, most smart tourism models have been developed from a Western or secular viewpoint. The unique socio-cultural needs of Muslim travelers do not always get integrated. There is a pronounced demand for innovative solutions, especially in Mecca and Medina. However, structural adjustments through the fitting to the ethical, religious, and logistical aspects of halal tourism also need to be catered to.

2.3. AI in Tourism and Pilgrimage Management

AI and the Internet of Things (IoT) are seeing swift uptake in tourism settings. Personalized services become feasible with such technologies and help with predictive analytics, real-time tracking, and resource optimization. AI finds a natural application in dynamic pricing in tourism hotspots (Jabra et al., 2020). Chatbots are handling customer service, and big data analytics helps forecast crowds. IoT sensors are being implemented to track environmental conditions, control energy consumption, and facilitate automated services.

For Islamic pilgrimage, technologies carry critical inputs for transformation. For example, promoting smart infrastructure and digital governance for Hajj and Umrah is explicit in Saudi Arabia's Vision 2030. Implementations seen recently include facial recognition for entry and thermal imaging for health screening. Smart bracelets aid navigation and AI-driven crowd analytics is another example (Al-Shaery et al., 2022). Ensuring safety is assisted by these tools. Reducing congestion also helps. Overall, pilgrim satisfaction has seen enhancement.

Several gray literature sources, like government publications and news reports, indicate substantial tech investments within the Hajj ecosystem. AI manages transport scheduling, coordinates emergency response, provides real-time translation, and offers digital spiritual guidance. IoT sensors monitor waste levels, water usage, and footfall (Suhartanto et al., 2024). This serves to optimize infrastructure performance. These innovations signify a significant move from traditional logistical planning, toward data-driven, adaptive pilgrimage management.

Despite these advances, most scholarly discussions stay dispersed across technology, religion, and management disciplines. Scant effort exists to bring these developments together into a coherent academic framework. Moreover, while case studies point to individual technologies or applications, they frequently miss contextual grounding in Islamic values and pilgrim experience.

2.4. Research Gap and Rationale for Framework Development

While plenty of technological interventions in tourism are documented in literature, a clear gap exists in research focusing on Islamic pilgrimage. There is a critical need to understand this subset. Studies typically look at isolated AI or IoT applications, such as crowd control or logistics (Vij et al., 2024). Connections are not usually made to the pilgrimage's broader spiritual, ethical, and cultural dimensions. Furthermore, much technological innovation sees reporting in gray literature, news portals, and government releases. Systematic analysis of these within academic discourse does not always occur.

Development of an integrated, multi-layered framework mapping AI and IoT technologies to the full range of Hajj and Umrah's strategic objectives has happened in few, if any, studies (Jabbari, 2023). Objectives range from safety and sustainability to spiritual enrichment and governance. There is also little exploration of how such technologies comply with Islamic ethical principles, for example, privacy, intention (niyyah), and collective well-being (maslahah). Here, a methodological and conceptual gap is created. It relates to how smart innovations for Islamic pilgrimage are evaluated and designed. The framework developed in this study aims to provide a foundation for both academic inquiry and practical application in designing culturally resonant innovative solutions.

3. Methodology

A conceptual research design based exclusively on secondary literature is adopted for this paper. The aim is to understand and structure how AI and the IoT are used to boost Islamic pilgrimage experiences under the halal tourism umbrella. As digital technologies evolve swiftly and see dynamic, real-time deployment, a flexible yet focused analysis of existing knowledge and innovations becomes possible with this approach.

Data sources used in this study span gray literature and peer-reviewed academic sources. Gray literature includes government strategy documents, industry white papers, news articles, policy announcements, and official digital portals tied to Hajj and Umrah services. These sources are essential to the study because many AI- and IoT-driven solutions in pilgrimage get first deployed and documented in practice before appearing in academic research. Scopus-indexed scholarly articles were also included to provide theoretical grounding and validate the broader themes.

Analysis of the data applied manual thematic content analysis. The process involved systematically synthesizing selected documents and extracting recurring keywords, solutions, and strategic focus areas. Later, they were further classified into larger categories or "themes" for their functional relevance. For example, references to surveillance, face detection, and biometric verification were classified under "Crowd & Flow Management," whereas routing systems and smart shuttles were classified under "Smart Mobility & Transport." The coding process had iterations, enabling emerging patterns to improve the categories.

Consequently, based on this thematic synthesis, the study introduced an application-oriented framework called "Smart Inventions in Islamic Tourism." The framework has eight strategic focus areas at the core.

- Crowd & Flow Management
- Smart Mobility & Transport
- Safety & Emergency Response

- Pilgrim Experience & Services
- Halal Compliance & Guidance
- Infrastructure & Utilities
- Sustainability & Optimization
- Data, Planning, & Governance

Each of these themes was then mapped with the relevant AI and IoT tools that are either currently in use or proposed for implementation in the context of Islamic pilgrimage. These include facial recognition, predictive congestion systems, thermal imaging sensors, health risk prediction models, multilingual chatbots, digital halal guidance apps, smart sanitation grids, and Big Data dashboards.

A functional map of technology-enabled innovations in thematic domains is presented. It doesn't imply a hierarchical or layered model. It possesses strength in its clarity, practical orientation, and adaptability. Policymaking, infrastructure planning, and user experience design are also adaptable. This approach also facilitates culturally grounded interpretations. It contributes to the respect of technological solutions for Islamic pilgrimages' spiritual and religious nature, allowing the methodology to connect scholarly insight with on-the-ground developments. It is analytically robust and operationally relevant.

4. Drivers of AI Adoption in Islamic Pilgrimage

The increasing adoption of AI and allied technologies in managing Islamic pilgrimage – especially Hajj and Umrah – results from intersecting demographic, policy, technological, and socio-cultural forces (Haase et al., 2016). As global Muslim mobility grows, particularly toward the holy cities of Mecca and Medina, the operational complexities and expectations surrounding pilgrimage management have also expanded. This section explores the major drivers accelerating the integration of smart technologies into Islamic pilgrimage ecosystems, aligning with the broader ambitions of halal tourism and digital transformation in the Muslim world.

4.1. Growing Pilgrim Volume and Logistical Pressure

A blend of forces drives the increasing uptake of AI and IoT in Islamic pilgrimage management. Demographic pressure, strategic policy initiatives, private sector innovation, and change in pilgrim expectations are some of these forces. This blend is causing the digitization of the traditional religious journeys, including Hajj and Umrah. In this section, the researchers look at the key enablers in the broader halal tourism realm that enable smart transformation in pilgrimage ecosystems.

4.2. Growing Pilgrim Volume and Logistical Pressure

Hajj and Umrah are the most prominent Muslim pilgrimages, drawing millions of people each year. For example, more than 1.8 million foreign pilgrims came for Hajj alone in 2023. The post-pandemic period is expected to continue the growth (General Authority for Statistics, 2023). Managing such large numbers of people within limited spatial and temporal boundaries is a complex problem for traditional management systems to solve. Thus, real-time surveillance, facial recognition systems, and AI-based crowd prediction tools have been deployed to detect congestion patterns and to provide quick response times (Haase et al., 2016).

During peak pilgrimage seasons, logistical complexities see heightened levels. Because of this, deployment of initiatives such as intelligent transportation planning, enabling crowd flow optimization, and interactive kiosks becomes critical (Vij et al., 2024). These technologies provide support for seamless movement, reduced waiting time, and enhanced safety for the pilgrims.

4.3. Policy Push from Saudi Arabia and OIC Nations

As a cornerstone for digital transformation in several sectors, including religious tourism, Saudi Arabia's Vision 2030 has come to life. By 2030, the Kingdom aims to host 30 million Umrah pilgrims annually. Advanced technologies must be systematically adopted to achieve this (Vision 2030, 2016). Matching this vision, the "Smart Hajj" initiative has launched via the Ministry of Hajj and Umrah. Integrating biometric identification, mobile health services, and AI-enabled transport coordination is part of this (Saudi Press Agency, 2022).

Other member states within the Organization of Islamic Cooperation (OIC) have similarly begun aligning their halal tourism strategies with digital innovation. The pilot projects and tourism strategies that emphasize AI and IoT-enabled services have been initiated in countries such as Malaysia, Indonesia, and the UAE to support Muslim travelers (SESRIC, 2022). These policy measures serve to underscore a regional consensus. The importance of technological modernization for religious tourism is brought forth.

4.4. Strategic Investment in Tech Startups and Pilgrimage Solutions

Alongside government initiatives, private sector engagement has quickened the availability of savvy tools for pilgrimage. Multiple hackathons like the Hajj Hackathon have been hosted in Saudi Arabia, where global developers compete to create technology solutions for real-world pilgrimage challenges (DinarStandard, 2020). Solutions emerging from such events include IoT wearables, AI route guidance, and predictive analytics for crowd movement. Mecca and Medina have become the early adopters of smart city functions, and large technology firms such as SAP, Oracle, and Huawei have begun to offer their scalable AI platforms to operate in these cities (Riandari & Defit, 2022). Domestic startups also focus on developing halal-compliant travel apps, AI chatbots, and real-time services for Arabic-speaking and international pilgrims. Such collaborations have resulted in the creation of an innovation ecosystem fueling continued technological innovations in religious tourism.

4.5. Pilgrim Expectations for Safety, Comfort, and Personalization

Nowadays, more and more pilgrims seek out spiritually significant and technologically advanced experiences. Digital natives among international pilgrims have raised the baseline of what constitutes a "satisfactory" pilgrimage. There has been a standard adoption of mobile applications providing personalized itineraries, multilingual services, and virtual tour guidance (Ratnasari et al., 2024).

In light of post-pandemic health concerns, pilgrims also demand higher safety and sanitation standards. AI and IoT technologies are deployed to detect elevated body temperatures, manage scheduling of sanitation activities through sensors, and alert pilgrims of the health situation (Zafar et al., 2024). As seen in other services, the convergence of safety and personalization mirrors a broader trend toward services grounded in ethical, Sharia-compliant frameworks and focusing on the pilgrim.

5. Facets of AI Integration in Islamic Pilgrimage

The integration of AI and the IoT in Islamic pilgrimage management has come of age, with its trajectory going from early isolated trials to entire system-wide innovation. As Hajj and Umrah bring in millions every year, this mass movement's physical, spiritual, and operational aspects need tools that require precision and cultural alignment. AI and IoT have opened doors to applications that span from predictive analytics to crowd control, intelligent mobility systems, digital religious services, and tracking for sustainable infrastructure. Developments of such nature are rooted in technical feasibility as well as the ethical imperatives of Islam. Table 8.1 highlights the various facets of AI that improves the halal tourism experiences by inducing structural modifications.

Facial recognition systems and predictive algorithms are used in crowd and flow management to monitor movement patterns and forecast congestion in ritual hotspots. The Tawaf, Sa'i, and Jamarat zones are critical. These tools have live surveillance feed support, which helps safety personnel get ahead of the overcrowding and respond to the emergency in real time (Jabra et al., 2020). At the same time, transport optimization technologies, backed by AI, have significantly improved the pilgrim transit experience (Almalki et al., 2021). Such techs include dynamic shuttle routing and IoT-based fleet monitoring, which help reduce the wait times and lessen the pressure on the logistical resources.

The health and safety dimension also shows meaningful technological adoptions. Wearable biometric devices, thermal imaging, and AI-based health risk assessments are now reckoned as standard components of a novel safety infrastructure, following COVID-19 (Shafqat et al., 2020). These technologies offer the pilgrims an added physical security layer and provide authorities with timely action in case of medical emergencies. Meanwhile, AI chatbots and multilingual kiosks are becoming better agents for the pilgrim experience, providing personalized guidance in the languages of the pilgrims (Khan, 2024). These tools help people navigate religious destinations better and more independently, thus creating a smoother spiritual experience.

Technology also holds a pivotal role in maintaining halal compliance and religious authenticity. Digital tools assisting in locating halal-certified establishments exist. These have expanded access to Sharia-compliant services, especially for international or first-time pilgrims (Riandari & Defit, 2022). These services

Table 8.1. AI and IoT Applications in Strategic Domains of Islamic Pilgrimage Management.

Sl. #	Strategic Theme	Description	Key Technologies/ Applications	Selected Scholarly Source(s)	Supporting Gray Literature
1	Crowd & Flow Management	Real-time monitoring and regulation of large congregations and queues	Facial recognition, predictive AI, live surveillance	Haase et al. (2016), Vij et al. (2024)	Arab News (2024a), Arab News (2024e)
2	Smart Mobility & Transport	Efficient routing of pilgrims, reducing congestion	IoT-based transport tracking, shuttle routing optimization	Al-Nabhan et al. (2021), Shambour and Gutub (2022)	Gradiant (2024)
3	Safety & Emergency Response	Timely identification of threats and health risks	Thermal sensors, health risk prediction, emergency AI alerts	Haase et al. (2016)	Arab News (2024b), Gulf News (2024b)
4	Pilgrim Experience & Services	Enhancing convenience and engagement during the spiritual journey	Multilingual chatbots, smart kiosks, VR guidance apps	Battour et al. (2023)	Gulf News (2024a), Shia Waves (2024a)
5	Halal Compliance & Guidance	Ensuring Sharia-compliant practices and services	Digital halal finders, Qibla direction tools, prayer time APIs	Shah (2024)	Gulf News (2025), The Week (2025)
6	Infrastructure & Utilities	Optimization of energy, sanitation, and resource consumption	IoT-enabled sanitation sensors, smart electricity grids	Alghamdi et al. (2022), Shambour and Gutub (2022)	Arab News (2024c)
7	Sustainability & Optimization	Reducing environmental footprint while maintaining service quality	Waste monitoring AI, heat maps, energy analytics	Ibrahim and Latif (2023)	Arab News (2024d)
8	Data, Planning & Governance	Data-driven decision-making and long-term planning	Big data dashboards, predictive modeling, hackathons	Alghamdi et al. (2022), Shambour and Gutub (2022)	Salaam Gateway (2024), Fast Company Middle East (2024), Arab News (2024f)

Source: Authors' compilation.

align religious values and technological functionality. Beyond this, infrastructure monitoring innovations have yielded improvements. Hygiene and energy efficiency during peak season see betterment as a result, lending support for both operational efficiency and environmental stewardship.

Pilgrimage planning is increasingly considered an environmental optimization component. AI has been applied in creating heat maps, detecting the overused zones, and predicting the utility demands (Khan, 2024), with millions of people generating waste while also consuming water and energy simultaneously. These systems, in turn, find enablement in proactive environmental planning, which is in sync with the Islamic value of khalifa, or guardianship of the Earth. At the governance level, big data dashboards, predictive models, and AI-driven hackathons (Arab News, 2024f) enable the authorities to visualize patterns, predict the need for resource allocation, and ideate new service tools. This has put AI in a position where it serves as a reactive tool and is also a driver for long-term strategic planning to enhance pilgrimage.

Despite the evident advantages, ethical and governance concerns remain. Data privacy, algorithmic bias, and technological exclusion of non-digital-native pilgrims must be addressed as the ecosystem evolves. Implementing these technologies must follow ethics-by-design principles, including transparency, cultural sensitivity, and inclusive design processes. Additionally, religious authorities should vet and validate AI systems to ensure doctrinal consistency and public trust (Haase et al., 2016). In addition, religious authorities should be involved in vetting and validating AI systems to ensure they adhere to the doctrine and serve public trust.

6. Development of the Smart Inventions for Islamic Tourism Framework

The development of the FSIIP framework for smart inventions in Islamic pilgrimage is based on a thematic content analysis of gray literature, news articles, government and institutional reports, and industry publications. Given that the scholarly body of work on AI and IoT in the context of halal tourism is still emerging, a synthesis of nontraditional sources provided rich, up-to-the-minute insights into the technological trends and policy directions. The framework has been developed to outline a structured view of the ways AI and IoT contribute to more sustainable operations, improved service delivery, and spiritually meaningful experiences in major Islamic pilgrimages such as Hajj and Umrah.

The conceptual model revolves around the improvement of Islamic pilgrimage through the means of innovative technologies. The greater goal of sustainability and spiritual fulfillment of millions guides this. The framework divides AI and IoT applications into eight interrelated strategic themes. These themes are Crowd and Flow Management, Smart Mobility and Transport, Safety and Emergency Response, Pilgrim Experience and Services, Halal Compliance and Guidance, Infrastructure and Utilities, Sustainability and Optimization, and Data, Planning, and Governance. There are specific technological interventions that support each theme. Interventions are based on recent implementations or proposed solutions in the field of pilgrimage in reality.

The model operates as a layered system. Strategic themes function within it as enabling domains. Technological applications, acting as tools, serve to operationalize those domains. For instance, under Crowd and Flow Management, facial recognition technologies, real-time surveillance systems, and predictive AI are employed. Purpose involves optimizing crowd movement. Mitigation of congestion risks is also achieved. The work of ensuring medical preparedness and incident prevention during mass pilgrimages is executed by thermal sensors, health risk prediction systems, and behavioral anomaly detection tools. Similar things occur in the area of Safety and Emergency Response.

Iterative development marked this framework. Identification of recurring technological applications from the literature was part of this process. Clustering them under broader themes followed. These themes reflect core operational challenges and strategic priorities of Islamic pilgrimage. Inherent in several areas are feedback loops. Inherent in several areas are feedback loops. For example, data dashboards and predictive modeling insights can inform policy decisions. Triggering of real-time adjustments to crowd control strategies can also happen. Integration of cultural and religious sensitivities also occurs in the model. This happens via the inclusion of applications. Examples include Qibla direction services, halal compliance apps, and multilingual kiosks. These applications align technology use with the spiritual dimensions of pilgrimage. Alignment with the ethical dimensions also occurs. Fig. 8.1 provides a visual summary of the framework, outlining the eight strategic themes, associated technologies, and their functions. This matrix serves as the operational backbone of the conceptual model, offering a holistic view of how AI and IoT intersect with Islamic pilgrimage management.

7. Discussion, Conclusion, and Future Scope

The analysis presented in this conceptual paper reveals the transformative potential of AI and IoT technologies. The experience, safety, and sustainability of Islamic pilgrimage are enhanced here. A framework for smart innovations in pilgrimage settings was constructed by systematically exploring literature, gray sources, and institutional initiatives. This framework integrates varied strategic domains, among them crowd management, health safety, infrastructure, and spiritual services, being the very core. The utility of AI-based crowd control and surveillance tools is a central finding. These tools enable real-time congestion mitigation and early warning for safety incidents. These technologies covered functions ranging from facial recognition to predictive analytics to support logistical efficiency while preserving the sanctity and dignity of the pilgrimage experience. Similarly, IoT-enabled solutions in transport and sanitation play a vital role in managing high-density flows with minimal environmental impact.

Personalized service delivery stands as another significant critical outcome of such technological amalgamation. Smart kiosks, multilingual chatbots, and halal compliance tools serve the spiritual tourists meaningfully. These tools are also tailored to their cultural and linguistic backgrounds, making them innovations that enhance the pilgrimage journey's operational and emotional dimensions. Significantly, challenges also surface in the research. These factors demand critical

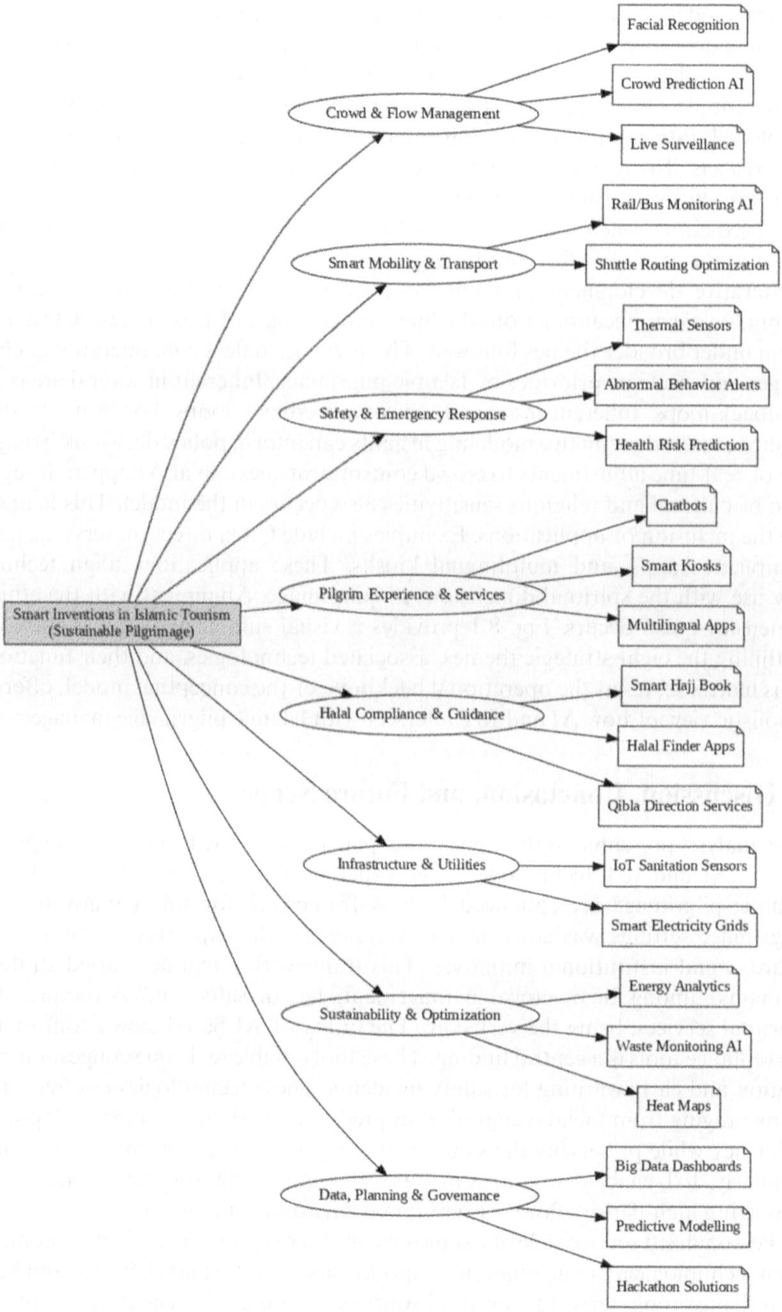

Fig. 8.1. Framework for Smart Innovations in Islamic Pilgrimage.
Source: Authors' ideation.

attention. Ethical concerns around surveillance, data protection, and algorithmic governance require robust regulatory frameworks. Likewise, access disparities could exacerbate existing inequalities among pilgrims from technologically underserved regions. Addressing these issues is essential for ensuring smart solutions are inclusive and culturally appropriate.

Halal tourism is expanding, and this paper provides a structured conceptual model incorporating current developments and emerging themes. This solution addresses a vital research gap: the lack of a cohesive, culturally sensitive, and adaptable strategy for using groundbreaking technologies in Islamic pilgrimage. This model provides a guideline for governments, technology companies, and religious tourism planners who want to modernize the pilgrimage experience without losing their spiritual life.

Future research should move beyond conceptual synthesis and toward empirical validation. The proposed framework would be reinforced by conducting field studies on pilgrimages, usability evaluations, and policy outcomes. In addition, a joint effort between OIC states, academic institutions, and private-sector innovators could co-create an international knowledge base for smart Islamic tourism. Ultimately, AI and IoT technologies hold great promise for the future of Islamic pilgrimage.

References

Alghamdi, N. S., Khan, M. A., Karamti, H., & Nawaz, N. A. (2022). Internet of Things (IoT) enabled smart queuing model to support massive safe crowd at Ka'aba. *Alexandria Engineering Journal*, *61*(12), 12713–12723. https://doi.org/10.1016/j.aej.2022.06.053

Almalki, A. (2023). *A study on the differences in visitors' motivation to attend a food festival in Saudi Arabia*. University of Brighton.

Al-Nabhan, N., Alenazi, S., Alquwaifili, S., Alzamzami, S., Altwayan, L., Alaloula, N., Alowaini, R., & Islam, A. B. M. A. A. (2021). An intelligent IoT approach for analyzing and managing crowds. *IEEE Access*, *9*, 104874–104886. https://doi.org/10.1109/ACCESS.2021.3099531

Al-Shaery, A. M., Aljassmi, H., Ahmed, S. G., Farooqi, N. S., Al-Hawsawi, A. N., Moussa, M., Tridane, A., & Alam, M. D. (2022). Real-time pilgrims management using wearable physiological sensors, mobile technology and artificial intelligence. *IEEE Access*, *10*, 120891–120900. https://doi.org/10.1109/ACCESS.2022.3221771

Arab News. (2024a). *AI helps manage crowds at Grand Mosque in Makkah*. https://www.arabnews.com/node/2593261/saudi-arabia

Arab News. (2024b). *Saudi AI chief reviews crowd management tech in Makkah*. https://www.arabnews.com/node/2594900/saudi-arabia

Arab News. (2024c). *Smart solutions make life easier for growing pilgrim numbers at Grand Mosque*. https://www.arabnews.com/node/2594959/saudi-arabia

Arab News. (2024d). *Maximum technology utilized by Saudi authorities to ensure safety of pilgrims*. https://www.arabnews.com/node/1897551/saudi-arabia

Arab News. (2024e). *Internet of things is revolutionizing Hajj pilgrimage*. https://www.arabnews.com/node/2120631

Arab News. (2024f). *Saudi Arabia's hackathons seek solutions to pilgrimage challenges*. https://www.arabnews.com/node/2531286

Bashir, H. (2024). Elucidating the role of contributors enriching spiritual and religious inspirations for the Muslims to perform holy umrah pilgrimage in Saudi Arabia. A prospective study: Umrah a spiritual journey. *International Journal of Innovation and Business Strategy (IJIBS)*, *19*(1), 36–47. https://doi.org/10.11113/ijibs.v19.150

Battour, M., Mady, K., Elsotouhy, M., Salaheldeen, M., Elbendary, I., Marie, M., & Elhabony, I. (2022). Artificial intelligence applications in halal tourism to assist Muslim tourist journey. *Lecture Notes in Networks and Systems*.

Battour, M., Mady, K., Salaheldeen, M., Elsotouhy, M., Elbendary, I., & Boğan, E. (2023). AI-enabled technologies to assist Muslim tourists in Halal-friendly tourism. *Journal of Islamic Marketing*, *14*(5), 1291–1309. https://doi.org/10.1108/JIMA-01-2022-0001

Battour, M., Salaheldeen, M., Anwar, I., Ratnasari, R. T., Hamid, A., & Mady, K. (2025). Integrating ChatGPT in halal tourism: Impact on tourist satisfaction, e-WoM and revisit intention. *Journal of Islamic Marketing*. https://doi.org/10.1108/JIMA-10-2024-0470

Battour, M., Salaheldeen, M., Mady, K., & Ratnasari, R. T. (2024). ChatGPT and halal travel: An overview of current trends and future research directions. In R. Khamis & A. Buallay (Eds.), *Studies in systems, decision and control* (Vol. *515*, pp. 23–31). Springer Science and Business Media Deutschland GmbH. https://doi.org/10.1007/978-3-031-48479-7_3

DinarStandard. (2020). *State of the global Islamic economy report*. https://www.dinarstandard.com

Fast Company Middle East. (2024). *Saudi Arabia sets sights on AI and IoT with $987 million in startup funding*. https://fastcompanyme.com/news/saudi-arabia-sets-sights-on-ai-and-iot-with-987-million-in-startup-funding/

General Authority for Statistics. (2023). *Hajj Statistics Report 2023*. https://www.stats.gov.sa

Gradiant. (2024a). *Gradiant's AI software will monitor the Mecca-Medina high-speed |railway until 2031*. https://gradiant.org/en/news/gradiant-ai-haramain/

Gulf News. (2024a). *Saudi Arabia unveils largest AI-powered operational plan with smart services for Hajj pilgrims*. https://gulfnews.com/world/gulf/saudi/saudi-arabia-unveils-largest-ai-powered-operational-plan-with-smart-services-for-hajj-pilgrims-1.500116991

Gulf News. (2024b). *Saudi Arabia: AI harnessed to regulate pilgrims' inflow into Mecca*. https://gulfnews.com/world/gulf/saudi/saudi-arabia-ai-harnessed-to-regulate-pilgrims-inflow-into-mecca-1.500062270

Gulf News. (2025). *Hajj 2025: Smart book on pilgrimage launched*. https://gulfnews.com/world/gulf/saudi/hajj-2025-smart-book-on-pilgrimage-launched-1.500106983

Haase, K., Al Abideen, H. Z., Al-Bosta, S., Kasper, M., Koch, M., Müller, S., & Helbing, D. (2016). Improving pilgrim safety during the Hajj: An analytical and operational research approach. *Interfaces*, *46*(1), 74–90. https://doi.org/10.1287/inte.2015.0833

Jabbari, A. (2023, August 18–19). *Tracking and analysis of pilgrims' movement throughout Umrah and Hajj applying artificial intelligence and machine learning*. 2023 7th international conference on computing, communication, control and automation (ICCUBEA).

Jabra, M. B., Ammar, A., Koubaa, A., Cheikhrouhou, O., & Hamam, H. (2020, September 2–5). *AI-based pilgrim detection using convolutional neural networks*. 2020 5th International conference on advanced technologies for signal and image processing (ATSIP).

Khan, N. A. (2024). Artificial intelligence, self-efficacy and engagement in religious tourism: evidence from Arbaeen pilgrimage. *Journal of Hospitality and Tourism Insights*, *7*(3), 1660–1678. https://doi.org/10.1108/JHTI-10-2023-0725

Le, M. T. H., Tran, C. M., Pham, T. T. M., Pham, C. N. L., & Nguyen, D. P. (2024). AI chatbot: Increasing emotional efficacy in tourism through anthropomorphic theory of acceptance model. *International Journal of Tourism Anthropology*, *9*(4), 300–331. https://doi.org/10.1504/ijta.2024.143397

Moshin, A., Brochado, A., & Rodrigues, H. (2020). Halal tourism is traveling fast: Community perceptions and implications. *Journal of Destination Marketing & Management*, *18*, 100503. https://doi.org/10.1016/j.jdmm.2020.100503

Ratnasari, R. T., Sari, N. S., Ahmi, A., & Ismail, S. (2024). Research trends of halal tourism: A bibliometric analysis. *Journal of Islamic Accounting and Business Research*. https://doi.org/10.1108/JIABR-08-2023-0246

Riandari, F., & Defit, S. (2022). Artificial intelligence approach for smart Sharia tourism: A review. *Journal of Theoretical and Applied Information Technology*, *100*(13), 4932–4940.

Salaam Gateway. (2024). *Saudi winner of 1 mln riyals hajj crowd management prize plugs gap in use of big data and AI*. https://salaamgateway.com

Saudi Press Agency. (2022). *Launch of smart solutions for Hajj pilgrims*. https://www.spa.gov.sa

Shafqat, S., Kishwer, S., Rasool, R. U., Qadir, J., Amjad, T., & Ahmad, H. F. (2020). Big data analytics enhanced healthcare systems: A review. *The Journal of Supercomputing*, *76*(3), 1754-1799. https://doi.org/10.1007/s11227-017-2222-4

Shah, A. A. (2024). Enhancing Hajj and Umrah rituals and crowd management through AI technologies: A comprehensive survey of applications and future directions. *IEEE Access*, *12*, 161820–161841. https://doi.org/10.1109/ACCESS.2024.3487923

Shambour, M. K., & Gutub, A. (2022). Progress of IoT research technologies and applications serving Hajj and Umrah. *Arabian Journal for Science and Engineering*, *47*(2), 1253–1273. https://doi.org/10.1007/s13369-021-05838-7

Shia Waves. (2024). *Saudi Arabia introduces AI-driven Hajj plan with advanced digital services*. https://shiawaves.com/english/news/islam/saudi/123960-saudi-arabia-introduces-ai-driven-hajj-plan-with-advanced-digital-services/

Statistical, Economic and Social Research and Training Centre for Islamic Countries (SESRIC). (2022). *OIC tourism report 2022*. Organisation of Islamic Cooperation (OIC). https://www.oic-oci.org/docdown/?docID=2967&refID=1098

Suhartanto, D., Amalia, F. A., Sugiama, A. G., Choirisa, S. F., & Nova, M. (2024). Innovative, smart, green and halal: A recipe for marketing Muslim destination. *Journal of Islamic Accounting and Business Research*. https://doi.org/10.1108/JIABR-02-2024-0056

The Week. (2025). *Only this Indian language features in Saudi Arabia's "Smart" book on Hajj*. https://www.theweek.in/news/middle-east/2025/04/27/only-this-indian-language-features-in-saudi-arabia-s-smart-book-on-hajj.html

Vij, S., Singh, P., & Kulshrestha, R. (2024). Technology-powered pilgrimage innovations: Shaping the future of religious tourism. In M. B. Talukder, S. Kumar, & P. K. Tyagi (Eds.), *Hotel and Travel Management in the AI Era* (pp. 485–508). IGI Global. https://doi.org/10.4018/979-8-3693-7898-4.ch023

Vision 2030. (2016). *Kingdom of Saudi Arabia Vision 2030*. https://www.vision2030.gov.sa

Zafar, M. B., Abu-Hussin, M. F., & Ali, H. (2024). Mapping the research on halal industry: A retrospective analysis. *Journal of Islamic Marketing*. https://doi.org/10.1108/JIMA-08-2024-0348

Chapter 9

Artificial Intelligence Applications in Halal Tourism: Enhancing Muslim Traveler Experiences

Syed Immamul Ansarullah[a], *Muhammad Idrees ul Islam*[a], *Sumaya Iqbal*[a], *Sheikh Ikhlaq*[b] *and Tyba Yousuf*[c]

[a]*Department of Management Studies, University of Kashmir, Jammu and Kashmir, India*
[b]*Manager, Cyber – Enterprise Security, Deloitte, India*
[c]*Post Graduate Department of Computer Science, SSM College of Engineering, Jammu and Kashmir, India*

Abstract

Artificial intelligence (AI) supplements Halal tourism through customized efficient practices that respect Muslim cultural preferences. The rising global Muslim travel market incorporates AI systems to transform how destination and service provider capabilities cater for religious and cultural needs of Muslim travelers. The implementations of AI for Halal tourism include customizable travel itinerary services combined with AI-driven customer assistance systems applied to smart city administration and active Halal standard audits. The chapter draws conclusions about the impact of AI on the quality and accessibility of services for Muslim tourists, while also building trust through a literature assessment and case studies from South Korea, Japan, Malaysia, and Indonesia. The discussion evaluates important ethical elements which cover automation bias alongside data protection together with requirements for Shariah-compliant AI development to demonstrate the importance of sensitivity toward cultural aspects during innovation. The paper looks at future trends, beginning with sustainable AI practices, predicts how ChatGPT will be used in customer service, and discusses how augmented reality (AR) and virtual reality (VR)

Halal Tourism and Artificial Intelligence: New Approaches for a New Generation, 121–133

doi:10.1108/978-1-80686-165-120261010

can help people experience different cultures. The research enhances the literature on Halal tourism through practical advice it gives to both industry operators and policymakers.

Keywords: Halal tourism; artificial intelligence; Muslim-friendly travel; blockchain certification; ethical AI; smart destinations

1. Introduction

The Halal tourism industry is expanding at a fast rate as the world Muslim community is becoming more mobile, wealthy, and religious. In the last 10 years, destinations across the globe have realized the special needs of Muslim travelers, and they have responded by offering them services like Halal-certified food, prayer rooms, and culturally sensitive services (Fauzi & Battour, 2024; Samori et al., 2016). Nevertheless, with the growing industry, the sector has been experiencing some major issues such as the lack of uniformity in standards of certification and Muslim-friendly products and services across nations (Ramli & Zawawi, 2019). AI is a revolutionary way of filling these gaps, and it will create a personalized and efficient Muslim travel experience. AI is currently being utilized to suggest appropriate hotels and restaurants and provide translation in real-time, and Halal compliance, which decreases worries and earns the trust of Muslim travelers (Battour et al., 2023).

Since Muslim travelers want to have a smooth and religiously compatible experience not only in Muslim-majority but also in non-Muslim-majority destinations, the use of AI technologies is becoming increasingly essential. Chatbots, recommendation engines, and blockchain-based certification platforms are some of the most recent innovations that are transforming the Halal tourism industry as they make services more available and trustworthy (Bux et al., 2022; Han et al., 2019). The technologies are not only convenient but also important in making sure that the religious needs are observed during the touring process. The chapter discusses the revolution of AI in Halal tourism by referring to the recent literature and case studies in Asia and elsewhere. It takes a critical look at the opportunities and the ethical implications of the use of AI in this industry and presents practical guidance to policymakers, industry operators, and technology developers interested in the development of Muslim-friendly travel (Battour et al., 2024).

1.1. Methodology

This chapter uses a literature review and case analysis to evaluate how AI improves Halal tourism. This methodical review of peer-reviewed publications examined AI in Halal tourism, AI ethics, blockchain tracking, and Muslim-friendly system customer experience (CX) theory in journals, conference proceedings, and book chapters. The systematic search of Scopus, Web of Science, and Emerald Insight used terms including "Halal tourism and AI,"

"Muslim-friendly tourism," "blockchain in Halal certification," and "AI-powered customer support in tourism." This study used only recent scientific publications from recognized journals from 2018 to 2025 to ensure relevancy and useful analysis (Adeyinka-Ojo, 2021).

South Korean Halal tourism apps, Japanese Halal food information systems, and Malaysian and Indonesian Muslim-friendly AI projects were examined. The study selected these cases based on their use of AI technology to serve Muslim travelers to demonstrate practical examples with effective techniques from multiple regions (Biancone & Secinaro, 2019). CX theory and tourism consumption systems (TCS) theory are used to analyze and critically summarize the outcomes. AI technology's implications on Muslim travel experiences and linked tourist services are examined utilizing the presented frameworks (Battour et al., 2023). Thematic synthesis of literature and case studies revealed personalization, ethical AI practices, blockchain certification, and human–machine service handlings.

2. Conceptual Foundations

Halal tourism and Muslim-friendly travel are similar and yet different strategies in addressing the needs of Muslim travelers. Halal tourism is based on complete adherence to the Islamic law so that everything related to a travel experience, including accommodation and food, as well as recreation, must comply with the Shariah, including prayer rooms, gender separation, and Halal food (Battour, 2018). Conversely, Muslim-friendly tourism is flexible and is based on the idea of accommodating the basic religious needs of the Muslim visitors despite the host destination not being entirely governed by the Islamic regulations (Cetin & Dinçer, 2016). Due to the increase in the number of Muslims all over the world and the increase in disposable income and religious awareness, both Halal and Muslim-friendly travel services have grown globally (Fauzi & Battour, 2024). The knowledge of the nuances and common grounds between these two notions is crucial to the destinations and service providers that want to provide their Muslim visitors with the authentic and fulfilling experiences.

The use of such advanced technologies as AI is at the core of the development of modern Halal tourism. The work of recommendation systems based on AI, chatbots, natural language processing (NLP), and blockchain applications has been radically altered how Muslim-friendly tourism services are provided (Battour et al., 2023). As an example, AI algorithms are now able to suggest Halal-certified restaurants or prayer facilities depending on the location of a traveler and his/her preferences, whereas virtual assistants and chatbots can offer real-time assistance in terms of religious needs and cultural practices (Hafidz et al., 2024). Blockchain also introduces the element of transparency and trust since it allows tourists to double-check Halal certification (Bux et al., 2022). Theory like CX theory and TCS allow researchers and practitioners to assess the extent to which these technologies can contribute to an improvement in all the stages of the trip of the Muslim traveler to make it more personalized, seamless, and spiritually satisfying (Battour et al., 2023).

3. Applications of AI in Halal Tourism

3.1. Personalized Travel Planning

AI has changed how Muslim travelers plan and make their holidays. The ability to access food, accommodation, and fun activities that meet the Islamic standards is one of the biggest obstacles that Muslim tourists have to deal with especially in countries that are not predominantly Muslim. With the help of AI-powered recommendation systems, it has become a breeze since they customize the itineraries based on the religious preferences, travel history, and other needs of individual travelers (Battour et al., 2023; Han et al., 2019). Rather than checking the Halal compliance manually, users can enjoy smart platforms that propose available Halal-certified restaurants, hotels, and prayer areas based on the current location, and previous behaviors in real time.

These technical solutions do not only make life convenient but also solve some of the major pain points, that is, the inability to find Halal food, language issues, and the lack of clarity regarding Halal certification. To give an example, the Korea Tourism Organization has developed the Halal Korea app based on the AI-powered recommendation system and geolocation to help Muslim travelers locate prayer facilities and Halal restaurants (Samsudin, 2022). The Halal Navi application is also driven by similar technology, which gives the location of mosques and prayer rooms. The systems based on blockchain like eHalal.io also increase the level of trust because the Halal authenticity is confirmed with the help of immutable records (Bux et al., 2022). These key traveler concerns and their AI solutions are summarized in Table 9.1, which offers a convenient overview of the impact of technology on the Muslim travel experience (Marlinda et al., 2021).

Table 9.1. Muslim Traveler Pain Points in Non-Muslim-majority Destinations and AI Solutions.

Traveler Pain Point	**AI Solution**	**Example**
Difficulty finding Halal food	AI recommendation engines for verified Halal restaurants	Halal Korea App
Language barriers	NLP-based real-time translation for menus and directions	AI voice translators
Lack of prayer space information	Location-based apps showing nearest mosques/prayer rooms	Halal Navi App
Uncertainty about Halal certification	Blockchain-based traceability systems to validate food status	eHalal Blockchain System
Lack of personalized travel services	AI personalizes itineraries based on religious/cultural needs	Smart tourism apps, Malaysia

Sources: Battour et al. (2023), Marlinda et al. (2021), and Bux et al. (2022).

The technology-based solution does not only guarantee spiritual conformity and comfort but also increases satisfaction, which promotes repeat visits and positive word-of-mouth to destinations that meet Muslim needs (Nisa & Sujono, 2017; Tahira, 2022).

3.2. Customer Support with the Help of AI

The emergence of AI-enabled customer services has been a game changer to the Muslim travelers who are usually in need of fast and efficient services when they are on the move. The applications of chatbots, virtual assistants, and real-time query platforms in Halal tourism have become more common as they can process a high number of queries and save time and enhance the quality of information given (Battour et al., 2024; Shahabadi, 2025). These systems can be programmed to respond to queries regarding Halal restaurants, prayer times, and religious standards in a culturally sensitive way with the help of NLP, irrespective of the language of the traveler.

The capability to learn and adjust to the preferences of the user is one of the practical benefits of these tools as they provide genuinely personalized support. A good example is the virtual assistant, which can automatically give prayer reminders or suggest Halal meals depending on the timetable and the location of a traveler. High-end NLP-based translation services could now easily translate menus, guidebooks, and travel information into the language of choice of the traveler, thereby removing one of the key obstacles to Muslim visitors to any country (Afandi et al., 2023; Ghosh et al., 2024). The real-time translation of the voice, like the one offered by the Halal Navi application, can enable immediate communication with the local providers and go even further in terms of inclusivity and convenience (Ikwuanusi et al., 2023). The incorporation of these tools has enhanced a great deal of trust and satisfaction in the Muslim travelers across the world.

3.3. Marketing and Management of Destination

AI-based analytics have become the core of smart city projects and transformed how Muslim-friendly destinations can handle their resources and communicate with visitors. With the help of big data and sophisticated AI algorithms, destinations will be able to monitor visitor traffic, optimize the utilization of facilities, and dynamically react to the fluctuating tourist demands, such as the availability of prayer rooms, Halal food, and gender-specific facilities (Cuesta-Valiño et al., 2020; Suhartanto et al., 2024). Even the feedback of the guests can be collected in real time with these smart tourism systems, and the providers can adjust their services and keep the level of services high to Muslim guests.

The marketing has also been advanced. Through AI and machine learning, it is now feasible to personalize advertisements and promotions to Muslim tourists depending on their online activity, social media activity, and past booking habits (Tahira, 2022). As an example, Indonesian digital marketing campaigns of Halal tourism currently target keywords associated with Halal food, Ramadan, and the location of mosques in order to attract the Muslim market more successfully (Suradin, 2018). Studies reveal that the integration of Islamic values in marketing, like modesty and family-friendliness, leads to the higher willingness of Muslim tourists to visit and emotional loyalty (Liu et al., 2018). In Indonesia and Malaysia, the AI-powered model like Smart Halal Destination Ecosystem model is currently applied to benchmark competitiveness and efficiency of Muslim-oriented infrastructure (Sutono et al., 2022).

3.4. Halal Compliance Verification

One of the fundamental issues that Muslim travelers have been interested in is the authenticity of the Halal food and services. With the help of blockchain technology and AI, this problem has been solved because certification processes have become more transparent and reliable (Bux et al., 2022). Blockchain is decentralized and tamper-proof, which implies that all the stages of a Halal product, including its sourcing, processing, and distribution, can be traced and proved by end-users independently. The sites like eHalal.io proved especially useful in the context of the COVID-19 pandemic when the Halal certifications could be verified digitally and securely (Sim, 2023).

Moreover, auditing and monitoring Halal compliance is now done using AI. The inspection process is automated by machine-learning algorithms and smart contracts and can detect nonconformities in the supply chain at a glance and significantly decrease the human error (Sunmola et al., 2025). The AI-based systems scan the supplier ingredients, manufacturing information, and certification records in real time, which is more efficient, particularly in large and global supply chains (Nawaz et al., 2024). AI and blockchain have developed new standards in the industry of Halal tourism through enhancing transparency and efficiency of operations, as well as promoting ethical and sustainable operations (Bagundang & Gallo, 2024; Ramantoko et al., 2024).

4. Challenges and Ethical Considerations

Incorporation of AI into Halal tourism is no doubt innovative but also poses some serious ethical issues especially in terms of trust and cultural sensitivity. Potential automation bias is also a real threat, since, depending on the quality of the data used, AI systems may occasionally suggest non-Halal choices, and this may cost Muslim travelers their trust (Islam, 2024; Kumar, 2024). Also, data privacy issues are of primary concern, as in most cases, travel platforms gather sensitive data associated with worship habits and diet preferences. To counter these problems, AI-based platforms must maintain a high level of data protection and aim at obtaining express user consent (Muvva, 2025; Purwanto et al., 2024).

In order to ensure the spiritual and personal rights of Muslim travelers, the ethical framework of AI in Halal tourism should include such important Islamic values as justice (Adl), transparency (Amanah), privacy (Satr), the protection of religion (Hifz al-Din), and trust (Thiqah). Table 9.2, based on Battour et al. (2023), Khutub and Ulfa (2022), and Jaapar et al. (2021), describes the manner in which these principles can be applied to system design, such as fair recommendations,

Table 9.2. Key Islamic Ethical Principles for AI Design in Halal Tourism

Islamic Ethical Principle	Application in AI Systems
Justice ('Adl)	Fair AI recommendations, no bias against Muslim preferences
Transparency (Amanah)	Clear explanation of how AI selects Halal options
Privacy (Satr)	Strong data protection and user consent mechanisms
Protection of Religion (Hifz al-Din)	Avoidance of promoting non-Shariah-compliant services
Trust (Thiqah)	Verified Halal certifications through tamper-proof systems like blockchain

Source: Adapted from Battour et al. (2023), Khutub and Ulfa (2022), and Jaapar et al. (2021).

explanation of AI decisions, and validated Halal certifications using blockchain. The observance of such principles is the key to ensuring compliance and trust (Solehudin et al., 2024).

Although AI has the potential to automate much of the Muslim travel process, the purely technological solution cannot substitute the benefits of human interaction in general and empathy or religious knowledge in specific (Ferhataj & Memaj, 2024; Islam, 2024). Thus, the successful Halal tourism ecosystem combines the ethical AI solutions with the availability of the human assistance that is culturally aware and makes the travel convenient not only in terms of practicality but also in terms of the peace of mind of Muslim travelers (Battour et al., 2024; Saffinee et al., 2024).

5. Future Trends and Research Directions

The next era of Halal tourism is fast developing with the help of AI that is not only streamlining the services but also providing more intelligent and adaptive solutions to Muslim travelers. It is becoming possible to provide real-time, culturally sensitive assistance with the help of advanced platforms like ChatGPT and predictive analytics, and blockchain and AR technologies would provide a greater guarantee and orientation (Battour et al., 2024; Fauzi & Battour, 2024). The different functions of these new tools and their anticipated advantages are well explained in Table 9.3, which is based on the most recent studies in the area (Battour et al., 2023; Prihandini et al., 2023).

Table 9.3 shows how the AI tools that include ChatGPT, blockchain smart contracts, AR apps, predictive analytics, and sentiment analysis will practically change Halal tourism. An example is that ChatGPT can be used to give immediate, Muslim-friendly travel tips, and blockchain smart contracts can be used to check the Halal compliance in real time at the point of sale. In the same way, AR apps can superimpose the location of Halal services on smartphones, making it easier to navigate through the city as a Muslim traveler, and predictive analytics can be used to allow the tourism providers to understand the preferences of the

Table 9.3. Emerging AI Tools and Their Potential Impact on Halal Tourism.

AI Tool	Function	Future Impact
ChatGPT (generative AI)	Real-time culturally sensitive support	Instant Muslim-friendly travel advice
Blockchain smart contracts	Automatic Halal compliance verification	Real-time certification at points of sale
AR Apps	Overlay Halal service locations on smartphones	Easier Halal navigation in cities
Predictive analytics	Anticipate Muslim traveler preferences	Hyper-personalized marketing and services
Sentiment analysis tools	Monitor traveler satisfaction and concerns	Improve Halal service quality dynamically

Source: Adapted from Battour et al. (2023), Fauzi and Battour (2024), and Prihandini et al. (2023).

traveler, so that hyper-personalized marketing and services can be offered. Sentiment analysis tools, in turn, will allow constantly monitoring the satisfaction of travelers, which will allow operators to dynamically improve the quality of service (see Table 9.3; Battour et al., 2023; Fauzi & Battour, 2024).

These tools, which are summarized in Table 9.3, mean that Halal tourism has a future that is not only more convenient and accessible but also more ethical and sustainable in order to accommodate the faith-based needs and the contemporary demands of Muslim travelers all over the world.

6. Case Studies and Best Practices

6.1. South Korea's Halal Tourism Apps

Despite its non-Muslim majority, South Korea has developed substantial halal tourism applications for Muslim tourists. According to Marlinda and colleagues (2021), the smartphone app "Halal Korea" guides Muslim tourists to covered eateries and prayer sites. When it offered Halal cuisine, prayer accommodations, and gender-friendly facilities as "Islamic Religious Attributes" in tourism services, South Korea became more Islamic-friendly (Asyafri & Sanawiri, 2019). Mobile apps have made Muslim travelers' lives easier; however, rural areas lack Halal services (Tahira, 2022). South Korean tactics can help non-Muslim majority countries enter the Halal tourism business because mobile technology tools promote places to Muslim travelers.

6.2. Japan's Halal Food Information Systems

Japan creates Halal food information systems to efficiently supply Halal tourism infrastructure. Japan partnered with Muslim nations, created restaurant lists, and created smartphone apps for Muslim travelers to provide Halal food information (Nuraini & Sucipto, 2021). The mobile apps help Muslim tourists find Halal restaurants, grocery stores, and prayer centers. The market is more Muslim-friendly because to Japanese Halal initiatives and local business Halal practice training. Organizations struggle to reconcile restaurant Halal certification procedures (Nasution et al., 2023). Technology has improved Halal information distribution and Muslim visitor trust and accessibility in Japan.

6.3. Muslim-friendly AI Initiatives in Malaysia and Indonesia

The Muslim-majority countries Malaysia and Indonesia lead AI-based programs to improve Muslim-friendly tourism. For users seeking Halal-certified hotels, prayer areas, and Shariah-compliant amusement, Malaysian tourism algorithms provide personalized recommendations (Yasin et al., 2024). Visitors may easily find Halal services on travel websites with AI-powered chatbots. "The HatiIndonesia.tr" mobile app from Indonesia covers travel destinations, lodgings, mosques, and prayer times (Ni'mah & Sari, 2017). According to Nusran et al. (2024), smart Halal tourism villages in Maros Indonesia use AI and smart technologies for Muslim-friendly rural tourism. With their technological sophistication and cultural awareness, Malaysia and Indonesia set pioneering norms for inclusive Muslim tourism using AI.

7. Conclusion

The use of AI is getting more and more crucial in the transformation of Halal tourism as it directly meets the practical and spiritual demands of Muslim travelers. Whether it is intelligent suggestion platforms and artificially intelligent translation software, blockchain-based verification and proactive customer support, such technologies facilitate the use of Halal-certified services and faith-accommodating facilities in destinations. The AI analytics that are used in smart city infrastructure optimize the use of resources, enhance the experiences of guests, and make sure that the cultural and religious sensitivity is preserved, which makes the process of traveling easier on Muslim tourists. Nevertheless, technological development itself is not sufficient; the responsible use of AI in the Halal tourism should always be based on the Islamic ethical principles of fairness, transparency, privacy, and trust. To ensure that the Muslim travelers will trust and be satisfied with using AI systems, it is critical to make sure that they do not violate the religious needs and protect user data, as well as provide recommendations that are transparent and free of bias. Halal tourism industry may establish an example of culturally sensitive, sustainable, and inclusive travel with the help of innovation, human-centered approach, and strict ethical supervision. In the end, the potential of AI is in the possibility to make journeys more pleasant, without going against religious principles and the pluralism of Muslim identities, leading to a more diverse and respectful tourism environment in the global community.

References

Adeyinka-Ojo, S. (2021). *PRISMA statement and thematic analysis framework in hospitality and tourism research*. University of South Florida (USF) M3 Publishing.

Afandi, Y., Maskur, M., Fiernaningsih, N., & Fauzi, A. (2023). Semantic and natural language processing development applications for chatbots to enhance online store customer service. *International Journal on Advanced Technology Engineering and Information System (IJATEIS)*. https://doi.org/10.55047/ijateis.v2i4.986

Asyafri, D. P., & Sanawiri, B. (2019). Analisis Islamic religious attributes Pada Atribut Produk Wisata Sebagai Pembentuk Citra Destinasi Wisata Ramah Muslim (Studi Pada Korea Selatan Sebagai Negara Non-Oki Penyedia Destinasi Wisata Ramah Muslim). *JurnalAdministrasiBisnis (JAB)*, *76*(1).

Bagundang, E. P., & Gallo, M. R. R. (2024). Technological advancements in halal ecosystem: Harnessing information technology for certification and traceability. *International Journal for Multidisciplinary Research*, *6*(2). https://doi.org/10.36948/ijfmr.2024.v06i02.17620

Battour, M. (2018). *Muslim travel behaviour in Halal tourism*. IntechOpen. https://doi.org/10.5772/intechopen.70370

Battour, M., Mady, K., Salaheldeen, M., Elsotouhy, M., Elbendary, I., & Boğan, E. (2023). AI-enabled technologies to assist Muslim tourists in Halal-friendly tourism. *Journal of Islamic Marketing*, *14*(5), 1291–1309. https://doi.org/10.1108/JIMA-01-2022-0001

Battour, M., Mady, K., Salaheldeen, M., Ratnasari, R., Sallem, R., & Al Sinawi, S. (2024). Halal tourism and ChatGPT: An overview of current trends and future research directions. *Journal of Islamic Marketing*. https://doi.org/10.1108/jima-11-2023-0379

Biancone, P. P., & Secinaro, S. (2019). The halal tourism: A business model opportunity. In A. Jamal, R. Raj, & K Griffin (Eds.), *Islamic tourism: Management of travel destinations* (pp. 192–200). CAB International.

Bux, C., Varese, E., Amicarelli, V., & Lombardi, M. (2022). Halal food sustainability between certification and blockchain: A review. *Sustainability*, *14*(4), 2152. https://doi.org/10.3390/su14042152

Cetin, G., & Dinçer, M. (2016). Muslim friendly tourism (MFT): A discussion. *Journal of Tourismology*, *2*(1), 65–67. https://doi.org/10.26650/JOT.2016.2.1.0005

Cuesta-Valiño, P., Bolifa, F., & Núñez-Barriopedro, E. (2020). Sustainable, smart and Muslim-friendly tourist destinations. *Sustainability*, *12*(5), 1778. https://doi.org/10.3390/su12051778

Fauzi, M. A., & Battour, M. (2024). Halal and Islamic tourism: Science mapping of present and future trends. *Tourism Review*. https://doi.org/10.1108/tr-08-2023-0533

Ferhataj, A., & Memaj, F. (2024). Challenges and opportunities of AI implementation in tourism: An ethical and technological perspective. *Studijos – Verslas – Visuomenė: Dabartis Ir Ateities Įžvalgos*. https://doi.org/10.52320/svv.v1iix.357

Ghosh, S., Ness, S., & Salunkhe, S. (2024). The role of AI enabled chatbots in omnichannel customer service. *Journal of Engineering Research and Reports*. https://doi.org/10.9734/jerr/2024/v26i61184

Gu, S. (2024). Reimagining tourist engagement: Integrating ChatGPT into the tourism industry's service ecosystem. *Qeios*. https://doi.org/10.32388/8arnz8

Hafidz, I., Mukti, B. S., Zahra, Q., Naseela, I., Yudistira, D., Pratama, P. A., Purnama, M., Ariyani, F., Astuti, M., & Tjahyanto, A. (2024). Chatbot model development using BERT for West Sumatera Halal tourism information. *Halal Research Journal*. https://doi.org/10.12962/j22759970.v4i2.1819

Han, H., Al-Ansi, A., Olya, H., & Kim, W. (2019). Exploring halal-friendly destination attributes in South Korea: Perceptions and behaviors of Muslim travelers toward a non-Muslim destination. *Tourism Management*. https://doi.org/10.1016/j.tourman.2018.10.010

Ikwuanusi, U. F., Adepoju, P. A., & Odionu, C. S. (2023). AI-driven solutions for personalized knowledge dissemination and inclusive library user experiences. *International Journal of Engineering Research Updates*. https://doi.org/10.53430/ijeru.2023.4.2.0023

Islam, M. (2024). Ethical considerations in AI: Navigating the complexities of bias and accountability. *Journal of Artificial Intelligence General Science*. https://doi.org/10.60087/jaigs.v3i1.62

Jaapar, N., Abdullah, S. F. S., & Ismail, F. A. (2021). *Fiqh traveller according to Maqasid Shariah*. https://doi.org/10.1007/978-981-33-4854-7_6

Khutub, M., & Ulfa, N. (2022). Existence of Halal tourism in Indonesia: Islamic business ethics perspective. *IEB: Journal of Islamic Economics and Business*. https://doi.org/10.19109/ieb.v1i1.11900

Kumar, R. (2024). Ethics of artificial intelligence and automation: Balancing innovation and responsibility. *Journal of Computer, Signal, and System Research*. https://doi.org/10.70088/pve9jj73

Liu, Y. C., Li, I. J., Yen, S. Y., & Sher, P. J. (2018). What makes Muslim friendly tourism? An empirical study on destination image, tourist attitude and travel intention. *Advances in Management and Applied Economics*, *8*(6), 1–13.

Marlinda, A. P., Cipto, B., Al-Fadhat, F., & Jubba, H. (2021). The influence of Artificial Intelligence to support Halal tourism policy in South Korea. *IOP Conference Series: Earth and Environmental Science*, *717*(1). https://doi.org/10.1088/1755-1315/717/1/012027

Mofokeng, N. E. M., & Matima, T. K. (2018). Future tourism trends: Virtual reality based tourism utilizing distributed ledger technologies. *African Journal of Hospitality, Tourism and Leisure*, *7*(3), 1–14.

Muvva, S. (2025). Ethical AI and responsible data engineering: A framework for bias mitigation and privacy preservation. *International Journal of Scientific Research in Engineering and Management*. https://doi.org/10.55041/ijsrem10633

Nasution, D. Z., Arafah, W., Djati, S., & Ingkadijaya, R. (2023). Destination awareness in Muslim-friendly tourism: A study of Indonesian Muslim tourists. *European Modern Studies Journal*. https://doi.org/10.59573/emsj.7(4).2023.36

Nawaz, A., Afzal, A., Khatibi, A., Shankar, A., Madan, H., Faisal, H. S., … Rasheed, M. (2024). Role of artificial intelligence in halal authentication and traceability: A concurrent review. *Food Control*, 111003. https://doi.org/10.1016/j.foodcont.2024.111003

Ni'mah, R. U., & Sari, T. K. (2017). Promoting Indonesia's Halal tourism package through hatiIndonesia.tr. *Scientific Journal of PPI – UKM*, *3*, 317–322.

Nisa, F., & Sujono, F. K. (2017). Islamic branding as a communication strategy of halal tourism promotion in non-Muslim country. In *Proceedings of the 4th Conference on Communication, Culture and Media Studies (CCCMS 2017), Yogyakarta, Indonesia, 10–11 October* (pp. 7–14).

Nuraini, S., & Sucipto. (2021). Comparison of Halal food regulation and practices to support Halal tourism in Asia. *IOP Conference Series: Earth and Environmental Science*, 733(1), 012044. https://doi.org/10.1088/1755-1315/733/1/012044

Nusran, M., Lamatinulu, L., & Suwardi, I. (2024). Halal industry and tourism in Maros: Exploring the harmony between faith and travel values. *Engineering and Technology Journal*. https://doi.org/10.47191/etj/v9i05.24

Nze, S. U. (2024). AI-powered chatbots. *Global Journal of Human Resource Management*. https://doi.org/10.37745/gjhrm.2013/vol12n63445

Oktadiana, H., Pearce, P., & Chon, K. (2016). Muslim travellers' needs: What don't we know? *Tourism Management Perspectives*, *20*, 124–130. https://doi.org/10.1016/j.tmp.2016.08.004

Prihandini, T. F., Triyono, M. B., & Priyanto, A. (2023). Bibliometric analysis examining the adoption of augmented reality in tourism research. *International Journal of Interactive Mobile Technologies*, *17*(15), 135–154. https://doi.org/10.3991/ijim.v17i15.40171

Purwanto, A. N. I., Fauzan, M., Widya, T., & Azzaky, N. S. (2024). Ethical implications and challenges of AI implementation in business operations. *TechComp Innovations: Journal of Computer Science and Technology*. https://doi.org/10.70063/techcompinnovations.v1i2.52

Rahmawati, S., Prahadipta, W. E., & Anggahegari, P. (2023). A review of halal tourism implementation in Indonesia towards a global perspective. *Journal of Halal Science, Industry, and Business*, *1*(1), 1–14.https://doi.org/10.31098/jhasib.v1i1.1584

Ramantoko, G., Widarmanti, T., & Muthaiyah, S. (2024). Improving halal certification distribution traceability: A case study on retail purchase. *Nanotechnology Perceptions*, *20*(6), Article 48. https://doi.org/10.62441/nano-ntp.v20i6.48

Ramli, N., & Zawawi, M. (2019). Factors influencing the growth of Muslim friendly hospitality services in Malaysia. *Geojournal of Tourism and Geosites*, *27*, 1148–1157. https://doi.org/10.30892/gtg.27403-422

Sagane, S. S., Khupase, A. Y., Malekar, V. L., Wankhade, D. V., & Dhamale, T. P. (2024). The future of travel: Trends and predictions. *International Journal for Multidisciplinary Research*. https://doi.org/10.36948/ijfmr.2024.v06i06.30625

Saffinee, S. S., Jamaludin, M. A., Rosli, N. L. I., Amid, A., & Hashim, K. S. H. (2024, July 31). Sustainable and ethical vicegerency in halal tourism practices. *Journal of Event, Tourism and Hospitality Studies*. https://doi.org/10.32890/jeth2024.4.8

Samori, Z., Salleh, N. Z. M., & Khalid, M. M. (2016). Current trends on Halal tourism: Cases on selected Asian countries. *Tourism Management Perspectives*, *19*, 131–136. https://doi.org/10.1016/j.tmp.2015.12.011

Samsudin, A. (2022). The development of halal tourism in Muslim minority countries: Case study in South Korea. *Proceedings of Malikussaleh International Conference on Law, Legal Studies and Social Science (MICoLLS)*. https://doi.org/10.29103/micolls.v2i.70

Shahabadi, S., Hudegal, A., G, A., Pavithra, K., & Rahaman, M. Z. (2025). Customer service chatbot with AI. International Journal of Scientific Research in Engineering and Management (IJSREM), 9(1). https://doi.org/10.55041/IJSREM40983

Sim, S. (2023). Blockchain for resilient halal food certification during post-COVID era. *Journal of Halal Science and Technology*, *2*(2), 718. https://doi.org/10.59202/jhst.v2i2.718

Solehudin, E., Ahyani, H., & Putra, H. M. (2024). Study on Sharia compliance principles in Halal tourism business. *Millah: Journal of Religious Studies*. https://doi.org/10.20885/millah.vol23.iss1.art2

Suhartanto, D., Amalia, F. A., Sugiama, A. G., Choirisa, S. F., & Nova, M. (2024). Innovative, smart, green and halal: A recipe for marketing Muslim destination. *Journal of Islamic Accounting and Business Research*. https://doi.org/10.1108/jiabr-02-2024-0056

Sumaryadi, S., Sutono, A., Rahtomo, W., Rumayar, C. H., & Puksi, F. (2020). Smart Halal destination ecosystem: The exploration of Halal tourism ecosystem model. *Masyarakat Pariwisata: Journal of Community Services in Tourism*. https://doi.org/10.34013/mp.v1i1.345

Sunmola, F., Baryannis, G., Tan, A., Co, K., & Papadakis, E. (2025). Holistic framework for blockchain-based halal compliance in supply chains enabled by artificial intelligence. *Systems*, *13*(1), 21. https://doi.org/10.3390/systems13010021

Suradin, M. (2018). Halal tourism promotion in Indonesia: An analysis on official destination websites. *Journal of Indonesian Tourism and Development Studies*, *6*(3), 133–140. https://doi.org/10.21776/UB.JITODE.2018.006.03.01

Sutono, A., Rahtomo, W., Puksi, F. F., Permana, O., Tahir, S., & Li, L. (2022). Smart halal destination ecosystem model: Measurement and performance in tourism village. *International Journal on Recent Trends in Business and Tourism (IJRTBT)*, *6*(4), 61–72. https://ejournal.lucp.net/index.php/ijrtbt/article/view/1772/1980

Tahira, I., Ullah, A., & Lee, Y.-S. (2022). Halal tourism factors, national image, and behavioral intention: Perceptions of Muslim community in South Korea. *Global Governance and Culture*, *2*(1), 59–81. https://doi.org/10.55952/ggc.2022.04.2.1.59

Yasin, S. M., Sulaiman, Z., Rahman, S. A., & Nawawi, M. (2024). The development of Muslim-friendly tourism (Halal tourism) in boosting economic potential in Indonesia. *Journal of Management World*. https://doi.org/10.53935/jomw.v2024i4.461

Chapter 10

Leveraging IoT and AI in Smart Hospitality: Enhancing Halal Tourism with Seamless and Efficient Travel Solutions

Sulekha Chourasiya, Manvinder Singh Pahwa and Ayush Sahu

Dr. Harisingh Gour Vishwavidyalaya (Central University), India

Abstract

Artificial intelligence (AI) and the Internet of Things (IoT) are substantially changing service delivery all over the globe in the domain of tourism as intelligent technology has emerged as one of the mighty change agents. This study explores the benefits of AI in hospitality systems on Halal tourists, Muslim travelers for whom matters including religion (halal and haram), cultural sensitivity as well operations effectiveness are prioritized particularly. A total of 400 Muslim travelers that used technology-enabled services during their trip completed the standardized 26-item questionnaire. Descriptive analysis, reliability assessment, and exploratory factor analysis (EFA) to identify the basic components leading to satisfaction were employed. Six parameters are identified to be critical ones: intelligent infrastructure and engagement, personalization with AI at the core to enable accessibility with known mind-sets & cultural/religious alignment, trust & privacy, and make things prepared for service offering. All constructs showed adequate reliability ($\alpha > 0.70$), and the KMO and Bartlett's significance test revealed that data are appropriate for component analysis. The higher-order six-factor model accounted for 73.58% of the total variance in the response satisfaction. There was statistical support for all seven hypotheses, indicating the positive impact of smart technologies on

Halal Tourism and Artificial Intelligence: New Approaches for a New Generation, 135–156

Published under exclusive licence by Emerald Publishing Limited
doi:10.1108/978-1-80686-165-120261011

the ethical, spiritual, and most importantly experiential needs of Muslim travelers by service providers. This study provides substantial theoretical contributions in smart Halal tourism and practical implications for service providers, as well as governments. Religion-centered design, digital trust, and organizational preparedness are imperative to steward true and accessible tourism inclusion.

Keywords: Halal tourism; artificial intelligence, Internet of Things; smart destination; travel experience

1. Introduction

Things that connect the world of smart hospitality systems and its impact on travel experiences are occurring everywhere in the world when we discuss the IoT and AI. Booking Itch for travel, the new technologies are crucial in identifying personalized travel methods that are quicker and more considerate of all cultural norms. One is Halal tourism, which is the commercial aspect of honoring a Muslim tourist's culture and faith. It is a growing market that will contribute significantly to the world's tourism industry. The bulk of the current tourism infrastructure does not offer positive experiences that are in line with Islamic beliefs despite the growing desire for Halal travel. In certain non-Muslim places with a majority of Muslims, the situation is not much different. Smart technology in the hospitality industry presents an opportunity to fulfill the promises of operational improvement and customer delight while promoting cultural education. Customizable real-time services, such as integrated prayer reminders, face direction markers for prayers, and environmental sensor control, are made possible by the IoT. AI may also be used to translate languages as we talk, offer flexible travel options, and personalize services by consuming data and presenting it in a palatable manner. These technologies, when used in tandem, have the ability to bridge cultural divides and improve access to a better, more accessible, and happier experience for all passengers, whether or not they are Muslims.

Halal tourism seeks to offer Muslim travelers services that align with their religious beliefs while respecting their personal convictions. Notably, although not exclusively, Muslim-friendly destinations that are welcoming and frequently visited by Muslims tend to be more appealing than those catering solely to solo Muslim travelers. Despite its increasing relevance in society, there remains a relatively limited body of academic research on the application of AI and IoT within halal tourism. While some studies address digital tourism and the intelligent interplay of technology, they often neglect the specific relationship that smart technology has with Muslim travelers. Additionally, the existing literature does not thoroughly examine smart hotel systems and venues that cater to both Muslim and non-Muslim guests within an integrated service framework. The exponential growth in AI coupled with IoT leads to huge changes at the tourism sector worldwide.

1.1. History of Halal Tourism

Early beginnings: Halal tourism came about as a result of Islam's desire to make travel more tolerant. It was initially confined to pilgrimage tourism (Hajj & Umrah), but gradually to leisure and cultural tourism.

Growth in the 21st century: Due to the huge growth of the world Muslim population and increasing disposable income the demand for Halal catering services. Among them are countries like Malaysia, Indonesia, and Turkey that have played an important role in Halal tourism.

Modern developments: Non-Muslim countries (such as Japan and Thailand) have also started catering to Muslim tourists in terms of Halal-certified food, prayer facilities, and culturally appropriate services. Further enhancing the Halal tourism experience is its leveraging of innovative technologies, namely, AI and Iot.

1.2. Smart Destinations

Smart Tourism Research on Halal model as a smart destination and the role of IoT and AI in assisting Muslim and non-Muslim travellers. Smart tourism enables intelligent destinations to provide high-quality services to all tourists using IoT and AI technologies. These technologies simplify the availability of Halal-friendly facilities, provide personalized recommendations tailored to traveller's needs, and provide prompt information, ensuring that tourists experience utmost satisfaction and comfort throughout their trip.

1.3. Benefits of AI and IoT in Tourism

- *Personalized services*: AI can use data from traveling habits to create personalized itinerary suggestions, Halal restaurants, and language-specific ways for international visitors to communicate.
- *Efficient operations*: IoT-enabled smart devices enable automated check-ins, smart room management, and contactless services to deliver convenience and fewer operational delays.
- *Data insights for improvement*: AI-based analytics enable businesses to monitor tourist behavior, preferences, and buying habits to develop better marketing strategies and tailor our services.
- *Enhanced accessibility and safety*: IoT uses the latest technology to provide real-time information on prayer timings, restaurants, and nearby mosques, as well as monitoring hotel safety.

2. Literature Review

With the changing faces of worldwide tourism, there is more breathing space being given to religious and culture sensitive tourism segments – most significantly Halal tourism that speaks the spiritual as well as dietary and behavioral value systems of Muslim travelers. In this sector, there is a great increase in scholarly discussions in recent years with various multidisciplinary themes such as digital transformation, AI, stakeholder coordination, user-orientation-Islamic theology-policy frameworks.

This analysis by Suryandari and Rahmawati (2021) is an early contribution to this line of thinking as they aspire to look at halal tourism from Muslim-majority and non-majority countries in a conceptualization and development perspective.

The expansion of Muslim tourists spending power and increasingly nuanced knowledge of host destination attracted their study in a sector that is rapidly developing. Approaching this perspective further, Zuhri (2022) examines Thailand in which the government moved forward to develop halal tourism by a mix of fruits; Muslim-friendly guidebooks, mobile applications, and branding instruments encompass the Thailand Diamond Halal Markers.

Technology is center-stage in the conversation, applying from theoretical inquiry to applied innovation. Riandari et al. (2022) highlight that AI is supposed to make Islam-Compliant tourism feasible through predictive modeling, decision-making systems, and also stakeholder alignment. Ç Öylük (2024) presents AI with its making Islamic environmentally and culturally sustainable tourism.

AI-powered solutions – including tailor-made travel planning and a host of applications from 3D scanning for heritage preservation to simultaneous management of crowds on the spot during Hajj and Umrah – have been revolutionizing Muslim traveler ease, with Abu Hamzah, Rachel Tyndale-Robinson and colleagues, exploring how healthcare organizations use quality improvement knowledge to produce growths as legitimate Islamic practices.

Underpinning many of these novelties tends to be the IoT technological infrastructure. Over smart cities, agriculture and tourism as he illustrates its transformative capability while sounding alarm on data privacy challenges as well about issues with interoperability or energy efficient. We share this in Tiwary et al. For example, Tiwary et al. (2018) show that IoT has significant potential in various areas of tourism, and they propose real-time service optimization through edge computing. Extending this approach, Sutono et al. (2022) analyzed the ecosystem of Smart Halal Destination (SHD). Their findings suggest that the potential for Muslim-friendly tourism is enormous, particularly in terms of ambience and policy readiness. However, they also underline that further development in infrastructure and marketing is still needed to effectively implement SHD.

Samori et al. (2015) apply a theological perspective to halal tourism via Quranic and Hadith-based structures coupled with purposeful travel (safar fi sabilillah). Through the comparative approach, both Muslim-majority and non-Muslim nations – Malaysia and Japan – provide useful examples of how services can be aligned with Islamic values. Next, Rakhmad et al. (2023) use user-centered design to develop a halal tourism app for East Java.

Usability metrics from this study suggested excellent in 5 of 6 usability categories, further evidence of the importance of inclusive design in meeting user requirements.

The literature also prominently gives place to marketing strategies. Younsofa and Xiuchaenggaga (2018) explore a content analysis of government tourism websites in China, Korea, Japan, and Thailand through differing levels of halal culinary promotion engagement.

South Korea/Thailand: proactive in their digital content (fueling/addressing Muslim culinary). China: no days that will comply with Muslim diets explicitly like it should. This meta-analytical and bibliometrics review by Yagmur et al. (2019). A meta-analysis and bibliometric review of the halal tourism literature since 2016 shows that there are three particularly notorious reference groups in Malaysia (12 papers), Indonesia (8), and the Philippines.

The importance of this domain is essentially how to understand marketplace behavior. Mohsin et al. (2016) demand in the halal tourism supply side.

For example, Mohsin et al. (2016) bank on the structure of demand when it comes to the performance of halal tourism and looks to the burgeoning interest in Sharia-compliant services such as halal-certified food, modest dress codes, and prayer rooms.

He and colleagues, subsequently with Broached and Rodrigues (2020), investigate perceptions of New Zealand and find relatively low awareness along with the requirement for increased visibility and infrastructure.

Off, Shaikh (2022) explores principal technological inflexibility in IoT integrations, echoing the early apprehensions, and demands uniform standards for more effective integration.

Ainina et al. (2020) examined >85k multilingual tweets across 7 language cases for global sentiment on halal tourism.

Halal tourism is generally viewed positively in popular tourist destinations such as Japan, Malaysia, and Indonesia. However, there have been some concerns about misleading or unclear halal certifications in the UK. Adinda et al. (2024) identified four major research streams in their systematic literature review—development of definitions and conceptual models, evaluation of opportunities, and practical adaptation. Overall, their findings indicate that academic research on halal tourism has progressed progressively, but it remains fragmented, reflecting a lack of clarity and integration in the existing body of knowledge.

Other tourist perceptions are discussed in Prawira et al. (2023). According to Prawira et al. (2023), who offer a four-stage evolution model of conventional, Muslim-friendly tourism and religious tourism (halal tourism), as well as fully halal tourism? The research indicates that branding, institutional commitment, and destination management are necessary for the tourist returns. Chantarungsri et al. (2024) confirm this using bibliometrics mapping, for example, by identifying different clusters including halal food certification, technology embedding, and risk management. Policy recommendations: better standardization, cultural stewardship, and tech for business-friendly infrastructure.

Widodo et al. (2023) state that halal tourism has very high potential market potential in Indonesia and other like countries but low scientific engagement. For conceptual clarity in a cross-disciplinary way, they ask for collaboration between the disciplines.

In addition, Bo_Gan and Sariisik (2018) map an important theoretical boundary between "Islamic tourism" (purpose of religious ritual) and "… a compliance-oriented approach driven by halal regression," which is helpful to both academic and industry stakeholders.

Mukherjee et al. (2022) examine the role of digital technologies like AI and cyber-physical systems with blockchain to support halal tourism aligned with the Sustainable Development Goals up to the 2030 SDG theme.

They also outline the adoption barriers of security risks and infrastructural woes. Alongside this, Jaelani (2017) traces Indonesia's national policy and international attention but recommends workforce training along with physical infrastructure upgrades.

Jafari and Iliahi (2015) at internationalizing best practices by presenting an index of global readiness for halal tourism using OIC and non-OIC countries as a comparison. Sustacha et al. use a meta-analysis to illustrate the effects of digital services on smart tourism destination satisfaction. Novera et al. (2024) combine generative AI integration with IoT in a personalization as a service model that balances sustainability issues and Snapping and Pothipassa.

The socio-economic stream of research goes all together into an iceberg with halal hotels as a separate but closely associated crystal.

Alam et al. (2023) use thematic analysis on Scopus articles for service. Quality and standardization woe Karim et al. (2022). The fragmented certification ecosystem in the hotel industry is urged to instruct personnel to act on it. Olya and Al-Ansi (2022) meta-analyze two decades of research on Muslim consumer behavior and discounted economic payoffs over time.

Concurrently, Kontogianni and Alepis (2020) situate the backstage of this wider context by summarizing the last six years of AI and IoT exploitation in tourism.

Smart tourism as another important context is illustrated by Kontogianni and Alepis (2020). They underline the need for tourist behavior typology and destinations' sustainable patterns. Accepting this is embracing wider demand from travelers but also the Muslim population.

3. Research Gap

The concept of smart destinations and smart hotels is a new phenomenon in tourism industry especially with the advent of IoT and AI technologies to serve the needs of the tourists. Most of the previous studies provided a broad view of smart tourism features without cognizance to the specific requirements of different category of tourists including Muslims and non-Muslims in case of halal tourism. While there is some research done on halal tourism as cultural and religious need, not much attention has been paid to the implementation of IoT and AI technologies in creating a seamless, sophisticated, and customized experience for Muslim and non-Muslim tourists. Furthermore, studies on smart tourism have concentrated on the Western and toward countries not dominated by Muslims and there lies a gap of knowledge regarding the role of smart tourism in Muslim friendly travel settings. This gap definitely requires attention in order to design and implement policies that respond to smart destination strategies for tourism that incorporate ethical, cultural, and technological aspects. Therefore, this work attempts to study the use of IoT and AI technologies in smart destinations and hotels for enhancement of halal tourism for all types of travelers.

Here are some gaps:

1. Limited Research on AI & IoT in Halal Tourism
2. Lack of Comprehensive Models
3. Insufficient Insights into User Behavior

4. Sustainability and Ethical Practices
5. Security Concerns in Smart Destinations
6. Economic Impact Analysis
7. Cultural Sensitivity in Non-Muslim Countries
8. Role of Mobile Applications

4. Objective of Study

The research objective of this study is to explore how AI and IoT can be utilized toward the development of smart hotels and destinations in the case of the halal tourism industry. The study should be explored through research into how the technologies might enable experiences for Muslim and non-Muslim travelers alike through providing them with efficient, personalized, and welcoming cultural services. Precisely, the study is concerned with:

1. To investigate how IoT and AI technologies are currently being adopted and integrated in the Halal travel sector.
2. To determine, from the standpoint of stakeholders, the main advantages and difficulties of applying AI and IoT innovations in Halal tourism.
3. To evaluate how AI and IoT technologies might improve Muslim tourists' travel experiences.
4. To offer practical advice on how legislators and business professionals can best use AI and IoT to support the long-term expansion of Halal travel.

5. Significance of the Study

The study has importance due to numerous reasons since it adds to the developing segment of smart tourism by the inclusion of AI and IoT to enhance halal tourism.

- Muslim and non-Muslim tourist experience enhancement – the research identifies that AI and IoT can offer multi-cultural, respectful, and personalized experience to multi-cultural tourists.
- Facilitating cross-cultural and inter-religious understanding – the research affirms that smart tourist destinations can accommodate Muslim tourist requirements without exclusivity against non-Muslims.
- Technology innovation of halal tourism – focusing on AI and IoT, the research proposes new applications of technology that can transform halal-friendly hotels, tourism, and destination management.
- Sustainability and smart development of tourism – the research aligns with global sustainable development for tourism by taking into account the way in which smart technologies can deliver optimal energy efficiency, waste reduction, and maximum operating efficiency.
- Economic and market growth – the study aids in economic growth in the tourism sector through the attraction of a higher percentage of Muslim tourists, a niche growth market in worldwide travel.
- Closing research gaps – the study bridges the current gap between mass research on the impact of AI and IoT to halal tourism and contributes a new stock of knowledge on the cultural, technological, and ethical foundations of smart tourism.

6. Research Methodology

This study is a descriptive and empirical research on the impact of AI and IoT on customer satisfaction at Halal tourism sector. To see the way, smart technologies are enabling attractive, frictionless, and Shariah-compliant services that cater the Muslim traveler so exactly. The study seeks to identify major technological, cultural, and operational aspects that influence tourist happiness in technology-based and technology-mediated Halal tourism settings.

Target population is Muslim tourists who interact with smart hospitality services in either international or local Halal tourism experiences. Among these are AI-powered vacation planning, Hotel-specific IoT and Halal food labeling solution as well as an online personal religion teacher. The respondents were drawn by purposive sampling which resulted in 400 completed responses that indicated the participants have smart gadget usage during traveling. Participants were recruited through specific online resources and travel forums, along with direct outreach to major Muslim tourism sites.

26 items systematic questionnaire was developed on each statement on 5-point Likert scale ranging from: Strongly Disagree (1) to Strongly Agree (5). The questionnaire was designed to measure six core constructs: digital infrastructure and intelligent interaction, AI-empowered personalization & accessibility, sacral integration, trust, privacy, and assurance, provider preparedness and strategic invest, implementation hurdles, and SHARIA ABIDANCE. The instrument underwent expert validation and piloting to establish clarity, reliability, and content adequacy.

IBM SPSS Statistics software was used to analyze the gathered data. Different statistical approaches were used to test the constructs and correlations between variables as follows. Descriptive statistics were used to determine the mean scores and standard deviations of each question, answering some aspects of the respondent views. Replicability analysis was done using Cronbach's Alpha: all six thematic dimensions derived 0.70 or above indicating high internal consistency. Kaiser–Meyer–Olkin (KMO) test of sampling adequacy came out to be = 0.931 and Bartlett's test of sphericity was significant ($p < 0.001$), so we can safely say that factor analysis should be used. The KMO statistic was 0.931, with Bartlett's test of sphericity statistically significant ($p < 0.001$); this suggested factor analysis. EFA through principal component analysis (PCA) with varimax rotation was employed to find the latent factors. (All six main components in total explained 73.56% of the dataset variation.)

7. Hypothesis

Hypotheses are as follow:

- *Influence of intelligent technology into satisfaction situation*: With the rise of Halal tourism, AI, IoT, and digital infrastructure, the question should be asked to what extent these technologies actually add real value to the travel experience of Muslim travelers.

H_0. Smart technologies (AI, IoT, and digital infrastructure) have an insignificant positive effect on customer happiness in Halal tourism.

H_1. Smart technologies (AI, IoT, and digital infrastructure) have no an insignificant positive effect on customer happiness in Halal tourism.

- *AI services immunity against IoT*: AI enables personalization and planning, while IoT takes care of automation. When it comes to appreciation, understanding which is higher appreciated can always improve the service delivery.

  H_0. Null hypothesis – no significant difference in the level of satisfaction between AI and IoT-based services.

  H_1. There are significant differences in the level of satisfaction between AI and IoT-based services.

- *Cultural personalization and satisfaction*: Halal tourism should be done according to Islamic principles. For example, services such as Qibla finders or Halal food finders might have an effect on satisfaction if culturally and religiously if not too targeted.

  H_0. Cultural and religious personalization will not have a significant effect on Muslim tourist satisfaction.

  H_1. Cultural and religious personalization will have a significant effect on Muslim tourist satisfaction.

- *Concerns over privacy and trust*: concern about data ethics an uncertainty in technology (including the privacy attitude) may deteriorate their receptiveness for applying smart services.

  H_0. Trust and privacy concerns are not correlated with much to AI/IoT adaption in Halal tourism.

  H_1. Trust and privacy concerns are correlated with much to AI/IoT adaption in Halal tourism.

- *Technology readiness and service experience*: Provider Readiness and service assessment even with high level of technology implementation, lack of training, and resources for tourist providers can undermine quality of service experience.

  H_0. Provider readiness is not significantly related to perceived quality of Halal tourism services.

  H_1. Provider readiness is significantly related to perceived quality of Halal tourism services.

- *Investments and implementation barriers*: Increased cost, lack of experience, and delays will erode the benefit of smartening Halal destinations.

  H_0. Investment and implementation barriers are not a large factor in customer satisfaction.

  H_1. Investment and implementation barriers are a large factor in customer satisfaction.

- *Shariah compliance concerns*: For Muslim travelers, it must comply with Islamic rules intelligent technology perceived non-compliance may deter usage.

  H_0. Islamic compliance issues are not significantly affecting the take-up of these smart technologies.

  H_1. Islamic compliance issues are significantly affecting the take-up of these smart technologies.

8. Data Analysis and Interpretation

The appropriateness of the 26-item questionnaire (Table 10.1) for factor analysis is demonstrated by strong values of determinant (6.56E–012) in its correlation matrix, that is, very close to zero (Table 10.2). This means a large amount inter-item correlation, multicollinearity is imminent to the point that it would be statistically OK to extract underlying latent dimensions through EFA or PCA.

Analysis of the correlation framework:

1. *The result of smart technologies*: Some notable correlation values are *Q*1–*Q*4 = 0.671 and *Q*2–*Q*5 = 0.653. This shows that smart technologies degrade the happiness of customers or in fact improve it by using consumer happiness. Hence, we can reject that null hypothesis (there was no effect) which argues, smart technologies have indeed influence on happiness of Muslim travelers to Halal-travel positively.
2. *IoT services versus AI*: Matrix-AI (*Q*2) and IoT (*Q*3) are in the middle with a moderate association ($r = 0.625$) and distinction in satisfaction metrics associations suggests not an identical way in which tourists evaluate these technologies. Visitors differ in their liking and level of satisfaction toward AI versus IoT-based services, there is statistically significant difference thus the null hypothesis that satisfaction between the two is the same.
3. *Cultural tailoring and satisfaction*: This matrix highlights how important are cultural and religious services for tourist, Muslim. Thus, the null hypothesis of zero influence of cultural tailoring on customer satisfaction is rejected again and proves the role of religion and cultural fit playing a significant part in increasing customer happiness in Halal travel.
4. *Privacy and trust concern*: In conclusion, this research issues that it is of a high relevance to open up, secure data, and applied responsible technology. Therefore, privacy and the level of trust are prominent predictors of AI and

Table 10.1. Impact Factors Table.

S. No.	Particular	Frequency						Wt. Sum	WAS	Rank
		HAD (1)	DA (2)	N (3)	A (4)	HA (5)	Total			
1	Digital infrastructure	40	7	66	136	151	400	1,551	3.8775	13
2	Interaction of AI	37	40	51	148	124	400	1,482	3.705	26
3	IoT usage	7	15	121	143	114	400	1,542	3.855	14
4	Smart navigation	19	34	86	137	124	400	1,513	3.7825	21
5	Delivery precision	27	37	75	122	139	400	1,509	3.7725	22
6	Processes automate	19	52	62	119	148	400	1,525	3.8125	20
7	Service quality	20	27	73	126	154	400	1,567	3.9175	12
8	AI suggestions	8	17	125	137	113	400	1,530	3.825	19
9	Cultural literacy	9	31	91	147	122	400	1,542	3.855	14
10	Tailored services	33	24	75	161	107	400	1,485	3.7125	25
11	AI-powered travel planning	0	30	78	149	143	400	1,605	4.0125	4
12	Access to facility	1	28	74	133	164	400	1,631	4.0775	2
13	Find Halal food tools	2	41	68	116	173	400	1,617	4.0425	3
14	Enabling lifestyle advice	2	28	104	115	151	400	1,585	3.9625	8
15	Religious compliance	0	20	81	142	157	400	1,636	4.09	1
16	Value respect	6	33	63	148	150	400	1,603	4.0075	5
17	Tech trust	4	51	105	87	153	400	1,534	3.835	18

(Continued)

Table 10.1. (*Continued*)

S. No.	Particular	Frequency						Wt. Sum	WAS	Rank
		HAD (1)	DA (2)	N (3)	A (4)	HA (5)	Total			
18	IoT confidence	19	37	43	144	157	400	1,583	3.9575	9
19	Privacy concern	36	7	61	137	159	400	1,576	3.94	10
20	Tech readiness	23	20	89	175	93	400	1,495	3.7375	23
21	Provider proactivity	19	19	75	144	143	400	1,573	3.9325	11
22	Smart Tech investment	10	14	99	131	146	400	1,589	3.9725	7
23	Barrier of technical implementation	24	19	54	143	160	400	1,596	3.99	6
24	Tech readiness gap	20	25	105	98	152	400	1,537	3.8425	17
25	Cost constraint	27	35	81	134	123	400	1,491	3.7275	24
26	Variability of Shariah compliance	24	28	90	102	156	400	1,538	3.845	16

Table 10.2. Correlation Matrix.

	Q1	Q2	Q3	Q4	Q5	Q6	Q7	Q8	Q9	Q10	Q11	Q12	Q13	Q14	Q15	Q16	Q17	Q18	Q19	Q20	Q21	Q22	Q23	Q24	Q25	Q26
Q1	1.000	0.592	0.535	0.671	0.651	0.605	0.632	0.334	0.466	0.623	0.420	0.445	0.609	0.461	0.335	0.367	0.394	0.187	0.216	0.236	0.073	0.132	−0.025	0.362	0.200	0.138
Q2	0.592	1.000	0.625	0.627	0.653	0.626	0.617	0.514	0.609	0.717	0.571	0.661	0.513	0.526	0.418	0.535	0.429	0.255	0.383	0.501	0.351	0.424	0.259	0.551	0.313	0.286
Q3	0.535	0.625	1.000	0.581	0.612	0.580	0.553	0.492	0.535	0.545	0.382	0.571	0.441	0.297	0.399	0.344	0.391	0.175	0.429	0.427	0.366	0.396	0.274	0.351	0.216	0.203
Q4	0.671	0.627	0.581	1.000	0.675	0.702	0.631	0.372	0.501	0.631	0.490	0.538	0.606	0.415	0.346	0.479	0.487	0.274	0.390	0.467	0.254	0.312	0.140	0.393	0.355	0.188
Q5	0.651	0.653	0.612	0.675	1.000	0.718	0.717	0.428	0.605	0.702	0.583	0.548	0.628	0.543	0.488	0.571	0.521	0.442	0.536	0.494	0.363	0.374	0.164	0.421	0.360	0.242
Q6	0.605	0.626	0.580	0.702	0.718	1.000	0.661	0.519	0.627	0.703	0.594	0.616	0.715	0.562	0.498	0.550	0.538	0.392	0.479	0.548	0.304	0.504	0.171	0.496	0.294	0.229
Q7	0.632	0.617	0.553	0.631	0.717	0.661	1.000	0.555	0.684	0.737	0.616	0.577	0.674	0.606	0.518	0.512	0.518	0.374	0.572	0.560	0.402	0.369	0.129	0.540	0.429	0.375
Q8	0.334	0.514	0.492	0.372	0.428	0.519	0.555	1.000	0.643	0.606	0.495	0.494	0.471	0.398	0.428	0.368	0.425	0.257	0.523	0.519	0.443	0.498	0.331	0.542	0.319	0.372
Q9	0.466	0.609	0.535	0.501	0.605	0.627	0.684	0.643	1.000	0.705	0.577	0.496	0.583	0.524	0.510	0.535	0.438	0.418	0.578	0.547	0.579	0.506	0.344	0.643	0.427	0.412
Q10	0.623	0.717	0.545	0.631	0.702	0.703	0.737	0.606	0.705	1.000	0.678	0.580	0.625	0.639	0.442	0.623	0.494	0.362	0.513	0.525	0.352	0.406	0.141	0.563	0.383	0.351
Q11	0.420	0.571	0.382	0.490	0.583	0.594	0.616	0.495	0.577	0.678	1.000	0.607	0.669	0.655	0.557	0.699	0.640	0.517	0.617	0.637	0.419	0.466	0.166	0.426	0.531	0.460
Q12	0.445	0.661	0.571	0.538	0.548	0.616	0.577	0.494	0.496	0.580	0.607	1.000	0.597	0.497	0.487	0.522	0.509	0.271	0.439	0.620	0.377	0.616	0.170	0.346	0.228	0.176
Q13	0.609	0.513	0.441	0.606	0.628	0.715	0.674	0.471	0.583	0.625	0.669	0.597	1.000	0.711	0.640	0.597	0.661	0.468	0.591	0.608	0.444	0.540	0.167	0.466	0.461	0.413
Q14	0.461	0.526	0.297	0.415	0.543	0.562	0.606	0.398	0.524	0.639	0.655	0.497	0.711	1.000	0.631	0.659	0.651	0.590	0.579	0.558	0.379	0.445	0.242	0.546	0.546	0.547
Q15	0.335	0.418	0.399	0.346	0.488	0.498	0.518	0.428	0.510	0.442	0.557	0.487	0.640	0.631	1.000	0.569	0.677	0.677	0.630	0.624	0.627	0.590	0.507	0.566	0.570	0.625
Q16	0.367	0.535	0.344	0.479	0.571	0.550	0.512	0.368	0.535	0.623	0.699	0.522	0.597	0.659	0.569	1.000	0.595	0.645	0.652	0.588	0.501	0.431	0.247	0.455	0.538	0.500
Q17	0.394	0.429	0.391	0.487	0.521	0.538	0.518	0.425	0.438	0.494	0.640	0.509	0.661	0.651	0.677	0.595	1.000	0.542	0.673	0.633	0.450	0.514	0.325	0.396	0.566	0.516
Q18	0.187	0.255	0.175	0.274	0.442	0.392	0.374	0.257	0.418	0.362	0.517	0.271	0.468	0.590	0.677	0.645	0.542	1.000	0.655	0.557	0.526	0.337	0.560	0.527	0.762	0.687
Q20	0.236	0.501	0.427	0.467	0.494	0.548	0.560	0.519	0.547	0.525	0.637	0.620	0.608	0.558	0.624	0.588	0.633	0.557	0.721	1.000	0.646	0.703	0.345	0.399	0.547	0.452
Q21	0.073	0.351	0.366	0.254	0.363	0.304	0.402	0.443	0.579	0.352	0.419	0.377	0.444	0.379	0.627	0.501	0.450	0.526	0.621	0.646	1.000	0.628	0.539	0.429	0.495	0.469
Q22	0.132	0.424	0.396	0.312	0.374	0.504	0.369	0.498	0.506	0.406	0.466	0.616	0.540	0.445	0.590	0.431	0.514	0.337	0.465	0.703	0.628	1.000	0.339	0.338	0.272	0.211
Q23	0.025	0.259	0.274	0.140	0.164	0.171	0.129	0.331	0.344	0.141	0.166	0.170	0.167	0.242	0.507	0.247	0.325	0.560	0.361	0.345	0.539	0.339	1.000	0.622	0.616	0.568
Q24	0.362	0.551	0.351	0.393	0.421	0.496	0.540	0.542	0.643	0.563	0.426	0.346	0.466	0.546	0.566	0.455	0.396	0.527	0.407	0.399	0.429	0.338	0.622	1.000	0.601	0.662
Q25	0.200	0.313	0.216	0.355	0.360	0.294	0.429	0.319	0.427	0.383	0.531	0.228	0.461	0.546	0.570	0.538	0.566	0.762	0.646	0.547	0.495	0.272	0.616	0.601	1.000	0.787
Q26	0.138	0.286	0.203	0.188	0.242	0.229	0.375	0.372	0.412	0.351	0.460	0.176	0.413	0.547	0.625	0.500	0.516	0.687	0.645	0.452	0.469	0.211	0.568	0.662	0.787	1.000

IoT acceptance as indicated by the rejection of the null hypothesis that suggested privacy/trust has no relationship with technology adoption in Halal tourism.

5. *Experience and technology readiness with service*: Besides smart tourist service quality, the provider preparedness affects for the quality of service as well as human factor-related service providers itself.
6. *Investment and implementation roadblocks*: The findings establish the presence of perceived and actual implementation challenges. Hence, the null hypothesis, which suggested that none of these issues affected customer satisfaction, is rejected as implementation difficulties and investment restrictions indeed bring a significant penalty to overall customer satisfaction in Halal travel.

Correlation matrix analysis helps recognize if the developed survey instrument is valid and reliable for assessment of AI based as well as IoT technology involved in Halal tourism experiences. The framework suggests the existence of at least four main latent constructs: Smart Service Performance, Faith-Value Integrity, Technology Trust, and Infrastructure Access. These dimensions are together show how Muslim passengers experience, adopt, and evaluate the use of smart devices in culturally sensitive tourism settings. This is followed by the actual extraction of complete factors step by PCA which is combined with KMO and Bartlett's test along with rotation for structure simplification and clarification of the components.

The KMO value of 0.931 with reference to Kaiser's scale is considered as "excellent/ very good" which indicates that the sample adequacy is very high and there are enough correlations among the variable to extract the authentic factors by means of EFA. Hence all the 26 variables are well correlated with each other and thereby good in extracting factors. Bartlett's Test of Sphericity also confirmed the statistical adequacy with a large Chi-square value of 10,029.592 and highly significant ($p<0.000$) for a strong rejection of the null hypothesis, which means a correlation matrix is not an identity matrix. Thus, the findings signify that this data set is ideal to conduct factor analysis and that the structural dimensions influencing Muslim tourist satisfaction/delight with smart technology in Halal tourism can be well defined.

In aggregate, KMO and Bartlett's works endorse that the data have an adequate multivariate structure (Table 10.3). Collectively these diagnostics allow us

Table 10.3. KMO and Bartlett's Test.

Kaiser–Meyer–Olkin Measure of Sampling Adequacy	0.931
Bartlett's test of sphericity	
Approximately Chi-Square	10,029.592
df	325
Sig.	0.000

to proceed with factor extraction, interpretation of eigenvalues, and subsequent rotation methods for identification of latent variables. This one is important to identify the actual components that define the acceptance and consumption experience of AI/IoT-based Halal tourism services by Muslim travelers.

Screen plot and total variance explained table are crucial to know the dimensional structure regarding the data from *Q*1 to *Q*26 smart technology in halal tourism with a total of 26 items (Table 10.4) (ARI 2014; Ferdows et al., 2020). We can easily identify a clear "elbow" in the scree plot at four component indicating that first four components "carry" a large amount of variance in the data while every successive component adds virtually nothing (Fig. 10.1). This is further supported by the eigenvalue values in the table total variance explained, where components 1–4 have 73.56% total variance before rotation. When subjecting the data again to Varimax rotation, variance distribution finally becomes more equal: 27.47% from Factor 1; 21.06% from Factor 2; 12.65% in Factor 3; and 12.38% as Factor 4, and this means there are some four factors which can effectively work to encapsulate data structure.

The factor analysis in summary does validate a postulated organizational where there are four latent constructs with factor-specific constructs hovering around the research assumptions both conceptually and statistically. The results show that inter-religious and cultural happiness level of Muslim tourists with halal tourism service is affected by technology efficiency as well as the interaction between halalness, religious soups, trust, and data privacy and operational competence. Fifth, the pragmatic component structure co-validated as a strong foundation on which to build increasingly complex modeling, via confirmatory component analysis or structural equation modeling in future research.

Categorized into six major thematic themes, the table arranges 26 variables on smart technology behaviors related to Halal tourism using (Table 10.5).

- *The first factor (F1)* Smart Interaction and Infrastructure: This basis is the root of operational effectiveness and efficacy in Halal tourism services. These systems when perform with the least amount of friction further ensure frictionless experiences for the travelers, that is, better service delivery means faster, accurate, and optimized.
- *The second factor (F2)* Access & Personalization with AI: These kinds are the transition toward more adaptable and user-oriented services; it is the use of technology in providing an experience that fits individual expectedness and religious requirements. The tailored intelligent tools build convenience and entice potential consumers of Halal places.
- *The third factor (F3)* Religious and Cultural Administration: smart tourism services based on these elements are technologically advanced and culturally as-is as well as in line with the ethical standards of Muslim guest. This congruence is required to build trust, comfort & satisfaction.
- *The fourth factor (F4)* Privacy, Trust and Uplift in Confidence: An element that takes into consideration passenger experiences of safety and clear-cut of tech enabled services.

Table 10.4. Scree Plot – Total Variance Explained.

Component	Initial Eigenvalues			Extraction Sums of Squared Loadings			Rotation Sums of Squared Loadings		
	Total	% of Variance	Cumulative %	Total	% of Variance	Cumulative %	Total	% of Variance	Cumulative %
1	13.352	51.354	51.354	13.352	51.354	51.354	7.142	27.471	27.471
2	2.961	11.389	62.743	2961	11.389	62.743	5.477	21.064	48.535
3	1.461	5.619	68.363	1.461	5.619	68.363	3.288	12.646	61.181
4	1.352	5.199	73.561	1.352	5.199	73.561	3.219	12.380	73.561
5	0.828	3.186	76.748						
6	0.716	2.755	79.502						
7	0.630	2.424	81.927						
8	0.579	2.226	84.153						
9	0.475	1.828	85.981						
10	0.417	1.602	87.584						
11	0.356	1.368	88.952						
12	0.314	1.207	90.159						
13	0.306	1.177	91.336						

14	0.272	1.047	92.383
15	0.258	0.994	93.377
16	0.240	0.925	94.301
17	0.215	0.828	95.129
18	0.211	0.812	95.941
19	0.176	0.678	96.619
20	0.163	0.628	97.247
21	0.159	0.612	97.859
22	0.132	0.509	98.368
23	0.128	0.491	98.858
24	0.103	0.396	99.254
25	0.100	0.384	99.639
26	0.094	0.361	100.000

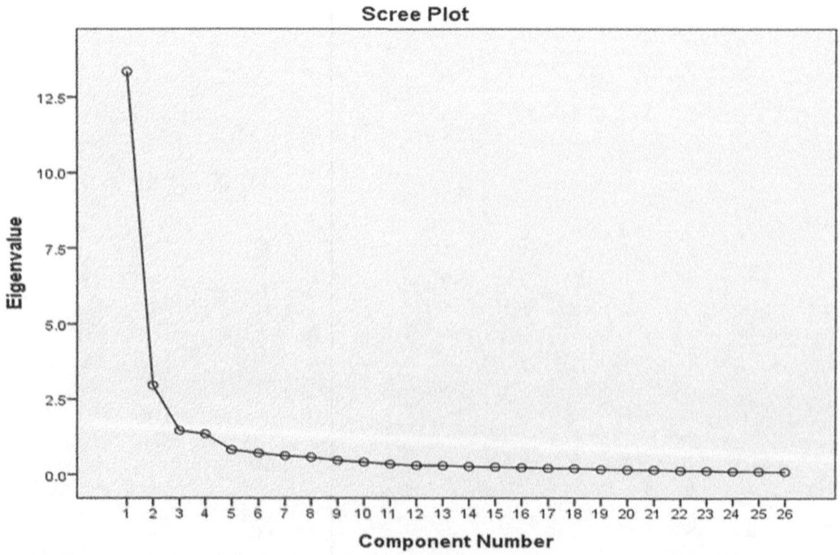

Fig. 10.1. Graphical Representation of PCA.

- *The fifth factor (F5)* Provider Readiness & Investment Readiness: This refers to the ability and willingness of tourism service providers in implementing smart tourism technologies. It includes preparedness of technology, management or operator proactive money invested in intelligent infrastructure.
- *The sixth factor (F6)* Compliance with Shariah, Implementation Challenges: This factor represents the impediments and dangers that surround the implementation of smart technologies in religion-sensitive tourism contexts. It includes fears over technical obstacles, inability to sweat it out, hurdle of finance and non-parallel ShariaH compliance.

9. Findings

Findings are as follows:

- Factor analysis indicated the existence of six variance-dominating dimensions totaling around 73% of variance in their answers. These dimensions serve as the key factors for happiness of Muslim travelers in smart tourism. This elaborate scheme serves as a lucid platform on the complex expectations and demands of Muslim visitors who are innumerable requests for AI/LoT-enabled services.
- Descriptive and weighted average showed that in general participants responded very slightly positive smart services of Halal tourism were provided by the service system. The scale has highest scores for the quality of service, congruence of services with Islamic principles and the implementation of AI generated suggestions. Overall the results show that ethical alignment, tailored support, and improved service execution can significantly impact customer happiness.

Table 10.5. Factor Structure Table.

Factor	Factor Interpretation	Variables Incorporated in Factor (Ranked According to WAS)
F1	Smart interaction & infrastructure	Digital infrastructure – A (13)
		Interaction of AI – B (26)
		IoT usage – C (14)
		Smart navigation – D (21)
		Delivery precision – E (22)
		Processes automate – F (20)
		Service quality – G(12)
F2	Access & personalization with AI	AI suggestions – H (19)
		Tailored services – J (25)
		AI-powered travel planning – K (4)
		Access to facility – L(2)
		Find halal food tools – M (3)
F3	Religious and cultural administration	Cultural literacy – I (14)
		Enabling lifestyle advice – N (8)
		Religious compliance – O (1)
		Value respect – P (5)
F4	Privacy, trust, and uplift in confidence	Tech trust – Q (18)
		IoT confidence – R (9)
		Privacy concern – S (10)
F5	Provider readiness & investment readiness	Tech readiness – T (23)
		Provider proactivity – U (11)
		Smart tech investment – V (7)
F6	Compliance with Shariah, implementation challenges	Barrier of technical implementation – W (6)
		Tech readiness gap – X (17)
		Cost constraint – Y (24)
		Variability of Shariah compliance – Z (16)

- Robust associations of the main variables were observed between them in correlation study. The digital infrastructure was found to be a huge nerve that dictated the pace in which services can be delivered.
- The results, overall point toward a smart Halal tourism experience that does not just require the presence of new technologies but also their successful implementation, religious adaptation, and closet backing from street smart proactive service providers

10. Implications of This Study

Smart technology customization to meet the religious, cultural, and service needs of Muslim tourists in Halal-friendly destinations in light of deep integration of AI and IoT across global tourism empirically derived discussion follows:

- *Theoretical implications*: This study contributes theory-wise to theorize the nexus between smart technology adoption and faith influenced consumer behavior in this study. Researchers may deploy this paradigm to explore further digital faith-oriented tourism experiences in subsequent studies.
- *Practical implications*: This research again highlights the importance of bespoke, digital trust, and value-based design. Intelligent systems should be deployable, respectful of Islamic-esthetic principles and culturally aware.
- *Policy implications*: State governments must set various criteria for the smart tourist infrastructure and digital ethics that is Halal. Policy mandates need to be informed by data privacy, religious normativity, and accreditation for service success. Digital readiness and training of the workforce are important for successful Halal destination branding.

11. Conclusion

Through this study, it substantiates the integration of AI, IoT, and digital infrastructure leads to higher Muslim tourist satisfaction in Halal tourism setting. Six crucial dimensions (intelligent service delivery, customization, religious compatibility, significant trustworthiness, preparatory readiness, and implementation hurdles) were found to be critical indicators. Personal smart technologies should be culturally sensitive, smart to adopt with an added normalization and integrity. All the assumptions were confirmed which power up that joy is not secular from the technology but rather the matching of technology with Islamic concepts and also trust from user end. These insights can delivered a practical foundation for the development of Shariah-compliant, intelligent tourist systems.

References

Adinda, Z., Kusumasari, B., Hadna, A. H., & Susanto, N. (2024). Halal tourism: A critical review of the development and implementation. *JKAP (Jurnal Kebijakan & Administrasi Publik)*, *28*(1), 1–17.

Ainin, S., Feizollah, A., Anuar, N. B., & Abdullah, N. A. (2020). Sentiment analyses of multilingual tweets on halal tourism. *Tourism Management Perspectives*, *34*, 100658.

Boğan, E., & Sarıışık, M. (2018). *Halal tourism: Conceptual and practical challenges*. Journal of Islamic Marketing.

Chantarungsri, C., Popichit, N., Rugthangam, S., Wattana, N., Chuanchom, J., & Sukmak, M. (2024). Mapping the landscape of halal tourism: A bibliometric analysis. *Cogent Social Sciences*, *10*(1), 2365507.

Jaelani, A. (2017). *Halal tourism industry in Indonesia: Potential and prospects*. Faculty of Shariah & Islamic Economics, IAIN Syekh Nurjati Cirebon.

Jafari, J., & Iliahi, F. (2015). Internationalizing best practices: Index of global readiness for halal tourism using OIC and non-OIC countries as a comparison.

Kontogianni, A., & Alepis, E. (2020). Smart tourism: State of the art and literature review for the last six years. *Array*, *6*, 100020.

Mohsin, A., Brochado, A., & Rodrigues, H. (2020). Halal tourism is traveling fast: Community perceptions and implications. *Journal of Destination Marketing & Management*, *18*, 100503.

Mohsin, A., Ramli, N., & Alkhulayfi, B. A. (2016). Halal tourism: Emerging opportunities. *Tourism Management Perspectives*, *19*, 137–143.

Mukherjee, A., Rajendran, S. D., & Wahab, S. N. (2022). Technology strategy in boosting halal tourism activities. In A. Hassan & N. A. A. Rahman (Eds.), *Technology application in aviation, tourism and hospitality: Recent developments and emerging issues* (pp. 41–56). Springer.

Napu, D. M., & Nurhidayat, W. (2018). The effect of halal destination attributes on visiting decision. In *Proceedings of the 3rd International Seminar on Tourism (ISOT 2018)* (pp. 57–61). Atlantis Press.

Olya, H. G., & Al-Ansi, A. (2022). Muslim consumer behavior in tourism: Two decades of meta-analysis.

Öylük, Ç. (2024). Integrating AI for sustainable and culturally sensitive Islamic tourism: Developments. *Journal of Islamic Tourism*, *4*(1), 71–95.

Prawira, M. F. A., Pamungkas, Y., Agustin, D. L. I., Tanisa, F. S., Alviana, A. D., Anisa, D. N., & Syam, R. (2023). Halal tourism destination from tourist perspectives: A review. *Journal of Tourism Sustainability*, *3*(1), 50–60.

Rakhmad, A. A. N., Kurniawan, D. T., Prameka, A. S., & Hidayat, W. N. (2023). A user-centred design (UCD) approach to designing and building halal tourism applications to advance halal tourism in East Java. *Reinforcement of the Halal Industry for Global Integration Revival: Proceedings of the 2nd International Conference on Halal Development (ICHaD 2021), Malang, Indonesia 5 October 2021*, (pp. 130–142). Routledge.

Riandari, F., Defit, S., & Yuhandri. (2022). Artificial intelligence approach for smart Sharia tourism: A review. *Journal of Theoretical and Applied Information Technology*, *100*(13), 4932–4940.

Samori, Z., Salleh, N. Z. M., & Khalid, M. M. (2016). Current trends on Halal tourism: Cases on selected Asian countries. *Tourism Management Perspectives*, *19*, 131–136.

Shaikh, N. (2022). Internet of Things (IoT), applications, open issues, and challenges: A comprehensive survey. *International Journal for Research in Applied Science & Engineering Technology*, *10*(6).

Suryandari, N., & Rahmawati, F. N. (2021). Halal tourism trends: Case examples in some Asian countries. *Proceedings of the 3rd International Media Conference 2021 (IMC 2021)*, *672*, 205–212.

Sustacha, I., Baños-Pino, J. F., & Del Valle, E. (2023). The role of technology in enhancing the tourism experience in smart destinations: A meta-analysis. *Journal of Destination Marketing & Management*, *30*, 100817.

Sutono, A., Rahtomo, W., Sumaryadi, S., Puksi, F. F., Permana, O., Tahir, S., & Li, L. (2022). Smart Halal Destination ecosystem model: Measurement and performance in tourism village. *International Journal on Recent Trends in Business and Tourism*, *6*(4), 61–75.

Tiwary, A., Chidar, A., Shrivastava, M., Mahato, M., Chandrol, M. K., & Tripathi, M. (2018). Internet of Things (IoT): Research, architectures, and applications. *International Journal on Future Revolution in Computer Science & Communication Engineering*, *4*(3), 23–27.

Widodo, W., Situmorang, S. H., Lubis, A. N., & Lumbanraja, P. (2022). Halal tourism: Development, challenges, and opportunities. *Frontiers in Business and Economics*, *1*(2), 50–58.

Yagmur, Y., Ehtiyar, R., & Aksu, A. (2019). Evaluation of halal tourism in terms of bibliometric characteristics. *Journal of Islamic Marketing*, *10*(1), 16–34.
Yousaf, S., & Xiucheng, F. (2018). Halal culinary and tourism marketing strategies on government websites: A preliminary analysis. *Tourism Management*, *68*, 423–443.
Zuhri, I. N. (2022). *Implementation of halal tourism in non-Muslim countries (Study in Thailand)*. UIN Prof. K.H. Saifuddin Zuhri Purwokerto.

Chapter 11

Artificial Intelligence Supported Tourist Guidance: New Challenges for Tourist Guides in Halal Tourism

Abdulbaki Güçlü and Kaplan Uğurlu

Faculty of Tourism, Department of Tourism Guidance, Kırklareli University, Türkiye

Abstract

Artificial intelligence (AI) supported smart devices, from smartphones to Wi-Fi-enabled robot vacuums, are widely used in daily life and across sectors – including tourism. The tourism sector, highly sensitive to global developments, rapidly adopts AI technologies. For example, service robots or voice-guided devices developed in one country can soon appear in hotels or museums worldwide. AI is utilized not only in accommodation but also in food and beverage services, travel agencies, and guided tours. Tourist guides, regarded as "key players" in tourism, are essential for tour execution and destination promotion. Technologies such as smart headphones, mobile apps, and voice-guided systems are increasingly used in guided tours. Halal tourism, which allows travelers to fulfill religious obligations while on holiday, includes services like halal accommodation, food, transportation, and entertainment. This niche requires more sensitive, informed, and labor-intensive tour services. The responsibilities of tourist guides in halal tourism are thus expanding and evolving. This study aims to examine the integration of AI in tourist guidance and explore the changing roles of guides in halal tourism. Using the literature review method, it will discuss how AI and emerging technologies can be applied in halal tourism, and how guides can use them sustainably, safely, and to enhance customer satisfaction.

Keywords: Halal tourism; artificial intelligence; new technologies; tourist guidance; travel; tourism

Halal Tourism and Artificial Intelligence: New Approaches for a New Generation, 157–169

doi:10.1108/978-1-80686-165-120261012

Introduction

In recent years, significant advancements have occurred across various technological domains. These include the expansion of transportation networks, the diversification and enhancement of information systems, and notable innovations in communication technologies (Csorny, 2013, pp. 1–3; Hamelink, 1997, p. 1; Jorgenson & Stiroh, 1999, p. 109). It is evident that technological progress has had a transformative impact on numerous sectors, including education, healthcare, tourism, services, entertainment, and production (Bircan & Karaman, 2024, p. 99; Genç, 2023, p. 67; Nikolskaya et al., 2019, p. 1198). Advanced technology has facilitated ease of production, rapid access to information, and the realization of previously unfeasible ideas. Among the sectors that closely follow and adopt technological innovations, tourism is particularly prominent. The tourism industry and technological advancement have progressed in tandem (Aldebert et al., 2010, p. 1204). Within this sector, technology supports service delivery across various domains such as accommodation, food and beverage, and transportation (Cho & Gu, 2010, pp. 25–26; Wahab, 2017, p. 260).

One of the most transformative developments in technology is the emergence of AI. The adoption of AI has accelerated across diverse industries in recent years. Within a relatively short timeframe, AI has become integrated into commonly used devices, mobile phones, and applications. In the tourism sector, the application of AI-supported devices is increasingly prevalent, aiding in both service provision and the enhancement of tourist experiences (Tuo et al., 2025, p. 796).

Touristic travel globally is motivated by a variety of purposes, including leisure, personal satisfaction, education, health, cultural exploration, curiosity, adventure, discovery, experiential engagement, culinary exploration, and business. A distinct segment of travelers engages in tourism for religious purposes (Mokhtarian et al., 2015, pp. 252–255; Ritchie et al., 2003, p. 9; Woodward, 2004, pp. 173–175). Religious belief significantly influences individual attitudes and behavioral patterns (Akyol & Kılınç, 2014, p. 172; Mokhlis, 2009, p. 75). Within the context of religious tourism, halal tourism has emerged as a prominent subcategory, wherein Muslim travelers seek services aligned with their religious values (Gohary, 2016, p. 124). Businesses catering to halal tourists offer tailored services, such as halal-certified food and accommodation options that conform to Islamic principles (Arpacı et al., 2015, pp. 186–188; Razzaq, 2016, p. 9).

Tourist guides serve a pivotal role by interpreting both the tangible and intangible cultural heritage of destinations for visiting groups, facilitating positive travel experiences, and managing various aspects of the tour process (Köroğlu, 2019, p. 35). These professionals often adapt their narratives based on the profile of the tourist group and the characteristics of the destination. In many destinations, digital audio guide services are available, allowing tourists to access information through QR codes via smartphones. Additionally, headsets are frequently used to enhance the tour experience by enabling clearer communication with the guide. Such technological tools contribute to more effective and engaging tours. The present study examines the integration of AI technologies in travel guidance and, in the conclusion, explores the evolving responsibilities of tourist guides within the context of halal tourism in light of AI developments.

Halal Tourism

The term *halal* denotes the absence of prohibitions or restrictions, signifying what is lawful or permissible. In Islamic jurisprudence, it refers to actions and products deemed acceptable under Islamic law. Beyond its legal-religious connotation, the concept of halal has evolved to represent a brand value indicator, a reflection of ethical and moral principles, and an integral aspect of daily life (Battour & Ismail, 2016, p. 151; Gohary, 2016, p. 127; Jaelani, 2017, p. 29). While the notion of *halal* is primarily associated with Islam, analogous distinctions – between what is forbidden and permissible – also exist in other religious traditions, such as Christianity and Judaism, particularly in relation to worship practices, consumption norms, and ritual observances (Henderson, 2016, p. 160; Tieman & Hassan, 2015, pp. 2319–2321).

Halal tourism refers to a segment of the tourism industry that caters specifically to the needs of Muslim travelers, providing services such as halal-compliant food and beverage, accommodation, and facilities for religious observance, all within the framework of Islamic principles (Chandra, 2014, p. 45; Mohsin et al., 2016, p. 138). This form of tourism has emerged as a niche market, driven by the increasing global Muslim population (Pew Research Center, 2025), the rise of the middle class, greater disposable income, a growing youth demographic, and improved access to travel-related information and Muslim-friendly services (Boğan & Sarıışık, 2018, p. 82). Halal tourism emphasizes adherence to Islamic lifestyle norms, hygiene, and safety standards. Preferred services within this context include halal-certified accommodation, transportation, cuisine, financial services, and tour packages (Akyol & Kılınç, 2014, pp. 172–173).

In recent years, awareness of halal tourism has expanded among both Muslim and non-Muslim tourists. Consequently, countries with varying religious demographics have shown interest in developing this sector to accommodate the specific needs of Muslim travelers (Yan et al., 2017, pp. 643–644). Tourism enterprises operating within a halal framework may obtain halal certification, which verifies that their services and products conform to Islamic legal standards. However, the nature of halal services can vary depending on interpretations of Islamic law, local customs, and the teachings of different Islamic schools of thought (Ratnasari et al., 2021, pp. 865–867).

Countries such as the United Arab Emirates, Indonesia, Malaysia, and Türkiye, as well as religious centers like Mecca and Medina, serve as prominent providers of halal tourism services, particularly for Muslim tourists with heightened halal sensitivities. Although these nations are predominantly Muslim, they represent major destinations for halal tourism. Additionally, countries such as Japan, the United Kingdom, and France have recognized the economic potential of this niche market and have taken steps to accommodate it (Aksu, 2019, p. 212).

In response to growing demand, these countries are enhancing their infrastructure to offer halal-compliant lodging, dining, recreation, and worship facilities that align with the religious sensitivities of Muslim tourists. This development contributes not only to the growth of the tourism industry and increased national revenue but also to the promotion of cultural and religious diversity and mutual understanding on a global scale.

Characteristics of Halal Tourism

Halal tourism encompasses several subcategories, including halal accommodation, halal finance, halal tour packages, halal transportation, and halal food. Hotels offering halal services are commonly referred to as halal hotels, conservative hotels, Islamic hotels, or hijab hotels (Dal & Topay, 2018, p. 263). In these establishments, provisions are made for gender-segregated facilities, such as separate areas for men and women, adhering to Islamic dress codes. Family-friendly beach, pool, and spa facilities are also available. Halal accommodation facilities typically offer cafes and restaurants that serve food prepared according to halal standards and only non-alcoholic beverages. In many countries, even non-halal facilities with halal concepts cater to Muslim tourists by providing prayer rooms and scheduling meals for sahur and iftar during Ramadan (Gabdrakhmanov et al., 2016, pp. 47–48). Each room in halal accommodation often includes a Quran, prayer rug, and directional markers indicating the qibla. The placement of the bed and toilet is carefully considered to ensure they do not face the qibla. Halal hotels also feature designated prayer rooms and separate recreational spaces for men and women. Staff in these hotels generally adhere to Islamic dress codes, and tourists are expected to comply with the dress requirements of the establishment. These hotels avoid entertainment venues such as nightclubs or discos, and their business operations are financed in accordance with Islamic principles, including the payment of zakat (Akyol & Kılınç, 2014, pp. 175–176).

Transport is another critical component of halal tourism. When traveling within the halal tourism framework, the cleanliness and hygiene of transportation modes (such as aircraft) and the absence of alcohol are key considerations. Moreover, the alignment of transportation services with Islamic principles is an important factor (Akyol & Kılınç, 2014, p. 177). Halal tourism travelers also tend to prefer private or VIP tours over group travel, which further underscores their desire for a more personalized experience.

One of the central elements of halal tourism is halal food, a fundamental aspect of the concept. Halal tourists are required to consume food products that meet Islamic dietary standards, ensuring that no prohibited ingredients or additives are included (Mutmainah, 2018, p. 37). The production process of halal food must adhere to strict guidelines, from the types of equipment used to the cleaning processes employed. Notably, the slaughter of animals must follow the halal procedure, which includes the recitation of the words "Bismillahi Allahu Akbar" during the slaughter (Harvey, 2010, p. 11; Henderson, 2016, p. 161). Businesses offering halal food services gain a competitive advantage by obtaining halal food certification from authorized bodies, enabling Muslim tourists to find trusted establishments that meet their dietary needs during their travels (Demirbilek & Şengül, 2019, pp. 418–420).

Another vital component of halal tourism is the offering of halal tour packages. These packages are designed with an Islamic theme, typically including visits to mosques, Islamic heritage sites, and activities associated with Ramadan (Akyol & Kılınç, 2014, p. 177). Halal tour packages also take into consideration the gender preferences of tourist groups, with female or male tour guides selected accordingly. These packages are designed to provide halal accommodation, halal food services, and opportunities for worship and education (Qaddahat et al., 2016, p. 382).

Halal finance, or Islamic finance, is another integral aspect of halal tourism. This sector ensures that all financial transactions related to halal tourism adhere to Islamic principles, which include avoiding interest and ensuring that profits are generated through lawful means (Martin et al., 2020, p. 2). It is essential that tourism businesses – such as hotels, transport services, restaurants, and other support industries – operate in compliance with these financial principles to meet the expectations of Muslim tourists (Akyol & Kılınç, 2014, p. 177; Mujiatun et al., 2023, pp. 4–5).

In the broader context of halal tourism, all activities, from halal food preparation to halal trade practices, must align with Islamic teachings. These practices, which are lawful and permissible under Islamic law, are subject to halal certification and regulation (Ismail & Noor, 2016, p. 114). Halal tourism is an integral part of the halal industry, offering travel and holiday services to both Muslim and non-Muslim tourists, but especially catering to the halal preferences of Muslim travelers. It is crucial that all service providers, from hotels offering halal accommodations to restaurants serving halal food, maintain transparency in their operations to meet the needs of halal-conscious tourists. Consequently, tourists seeking halal services expect to encounter a travel experience that mirrors their daily life routines, with all aspects of their holiday adhering to halal standards.

Travel Guidance and Its Importance

The concept of tourist guiding, also referred to as travel guiding or tourism guiding, is multifaceted and varies in definition across different contexts. The World Federation of Tourist Guides Associations-WFTGA (2025) offers an official definition of a tourist guide as *A person who guides visitors in the language of their choice and interprets the natural and historical heritage of a region for which he/she has competence, usually issued and/or recognised by the competent authorities.* While the literature on the profession of tourist guiding is limited, various definitions of the term "tourist guide" can be found. Additionally, in Türkiye, the Law on Tourist Guides defines the tourist guiding service as

> Introducing and guiding domestic or foreign tourists in individuals or groups to the culture, tourism, history, environment, nature, social or similar values and assets of the country in line with cultural and tourism policies, using the language chosen by the tourist before the trip, or carrying out the excursion programmes of tours organised by travel agencies as defined in the written documents

of the travel agency and sold to the consumer, and managing them on behalf of the agency (mevzuat.gov.tr).

Tourist guiding is an essential component of the tourism industry and a fundamental part of the services provided by tour operators (Batman, 2003, p. 118). Tourist guides, who perform this profession, play a crucial role in ensuring that tourists enjoy their tours, in advertising the travel agency, promoting the destination, and enhancing the image of the country (Huang et al., 2009, p. 3; Şahin et al., 2018, p. 251). The satisfaction of tourists with the services of their guides facilitates the sale of future tours, and the positive word-of-mouth generated by tourists leads to an increase in visitation numbers (Ap & Wong, 2001, p. 551; Zhang & Chow, 2004, p. 82).

Tourists visiting a destination require the assistance of tourist guides to fully engage with and understand the touristic elements of the region. Their needs for cultural experiences, information, and guidance are met through the services provided by tourist guides (Köroğlu, 2019, p. 35). Tourist guides, often citizens of the destination country, spend the most time with the tourists during their visit and are responsible for ensuring that tourists experience the destination in the best possible way (Ahipaşaoğlu, 2001, p. 49). One of the key responsibilities of a tourist guide is to carry out the tour program provided by the travel agency. They address the requests and needs of tourists throughout the tour and work to ensure that tourists have a comfortable experience. Another core function of the tourist guide is to interpret and explain the natural, cultural, and historical attractions of the destination, providing tourists with insightful information. As the primary point of contact during the tour, tourist guides ensure that the entire process runs smoothly (Hacıoğlu, 2016, p. 179).

Tourist guides are pivotal in shaping tourists' experiences and interactions with the destination and are therefore among the primary service providers within the tourism sector (Prakash & Chowdhary, 2010, p. 1). Through their intermediary role and interpretative skills, tourist guides enable tourists to comprehend and appreciate the region's natural and cultural heritage (Weiler & Walker, 2014, pp. 90–91). By utilizing their communication skills and engaging in direct, face-to-face interactions, tourist guides help create unforgettable travel experiences for tourists (Harara et al., 2024, p. 873).

Using AI in Travel Guidance

Groundbreaking technological developments have significantly impacted various sectors, including the tourism industry. From the service sector to education, and from production to tourism, innovations are rapidly changing the way businesses operate. In the tourism industry, the convenience and benefits brought by technological advancements have led to a perception of increased preference and attractiveness among consumers (Demirezen, 2019, p. 2; Ercan, 2020, pp. 394–395). The tourism sector, known for being open to innovation, was one of the first to embrace technological developments. These advancements are now evident in numerous aspects of tourism, with concepts like smart destinations, smart hotels, smart transportation, and smart events becoming increasingly prevalent (Yalçınkaya et al., 2018, p. 86).

The role of tourists in the smart tourism experience is increasingly significant. With the use of smartphones and mobile applications, tourists can easily interact with the tourism industry (Ilhan & Çeltek, 2016, p. 582). Social media posts showcasing tourists' experiences in destinations now serve as powerful promotional tools for both businesses and countries, as these experiences are shared through smart technologies (Başer & Olcay, 2022, p. 1799). Generation Z, which is highly tech-savvy and active on social media, is at the forefront of this trend. Moreover, emerging technologies such as augmented reality (AR) and virtual reality (VR) are being incorporated into tourism, enhancing experiences in fields like architecture, entertainment, marketing, education, and more. These technologies not only offer immersive virtual experiences but also provide useful information and conveniences for tourists (Demirezen, 2019, p. 2).

The widespread use of QR codes in the tourism sector is another example of how technology is reshaping the industry. Tourists can scan QR codes before, during, or after receiving services, such as at hotels, restaurants, or attractions, to access service information or provide feedback. This system allows for a seamless, contactless experience where services can be requested without human interaction, and comments can be left through the same system (Emek, 2012, p. 4).

Among the most transformative technological innovations is the rise of AI, which has become more prominent in recent years. AI is being rapidly implemented across various sectors, including tourism, where it has proven beneficial in automating many manual tasks previously performed by staff (Samala et al., 2020, pp. 74–76). In the tourism industry, AI is used for a variety of tasks, from greeting guests to responding to their demands and providing personalized services. This technology has streamlined operations, making businesses more efficient while improving the tourist experience.

AI has also revolutionized trip planning. In the past, tourists would rely on multiple businesses – such as travel agencies, accommodation providers, and transport companies – for information. Today, most of this information can be obtained quickly and efficiently through smartphones, apps, and websites. Tourists can now access details about destinations, recreation options, food and beverage facilities, and more without needing to contact businesses directly. AI-supported platforms can even assist with booking, provide virtual tours, or offer advice on holiday experiences, requiring only a few simple commands (Dey & Shukla, 2020, p. 2; Dwivedi et al., 2023, p. 3; Samala et al., 2020, pp. 74–76).

In the realm of travel guidance, which has traditionally been seen as a face-to-face profession with limited technological integration, technology has begun to play a significant role, often without users being fully aware of it. Devices such as scanned tickets, online QR codes, audio guides, and smartphones are now commonly used during tours, including in museums and archeological sites. GPS navigation and wayfinding systems are also used to help tourists navigate through destinations. Moreover, AI-powered voice guidance services, which allow tourists to receive narration in their preferred language through scanning a code or using a device, are increasingly being used at tourist destinations. Virtual tours are also becoming popular, providing remote access to destinations and allowing people to explore without being physically present. These examples illustrate how the travel guidance sector is evolving with technology and how AI, in particular, is beginning to play a larger role in shaping the future of this field.

New Responsibilities of Travel Guides in Halal Tourism

The travel guiding profession plays a critical role in shaping the travel experience for tourists. This field, centered on delivering a memorable and enriching experience, is evolving to require increasingly specialized knowledge, skills, and communication abilities from travel guides. The success of a tour – reflected in tourist satisfaction and overall experience – is directly influenced by the expertise of the guide. Beyond the fundamental responsibilities of planning and conducting tours, travel guides are expected to represent the tourist group, the destination, and the country itself. They provide crucial information, manage relationships with tourists, and ensure the smooth execution of the entire tour program (Batman et al., 2001, pp. 25–27). Additionally, key personality traits such as ethical conduct, attention to detail, energy, discipline, hospitality, leadership, calmness, helpfulness, and responsibility are vital for a successful travel guide (Albuz et al., 2018, pp. 23–24).

With the rise of specialized tourism markets, such as halal tourism, the expectations placed on travel guides have expanded further. Halal tourism, which is a rapidly growing segment, requires travel guides to have specific knowledge and skills. These guides must not only be familiar with general tourism practices but also possess a strong understanding of religious structures, practices, and the needs of Muslim tourists. For example, they need to be mindful of prayer times, the availability of halal food, and the locations of prayer facilities. In addition, knowledge of the local religious communities and their cultural practices becomes essential, especially when tourists come from diverse faith backgrounds (Eren et al., 2017, pp. 73–74).

Travel guides specializing in halal or faith-based tourism are expected to be well-equipped with knowledge of Islamic practices and sensitive to the specific needs of Muslim travelers. The guides should adjust their approach according to the religious and cultural profiles of the tourists they are serving. Furthermore, they should be ready to answer questions related to religious practices and halal requirements. This makes it imperative for travel guides in the halal tourism sector to undergo specialized training to adequately address these needs and create a supportive environment for their tourists.

In addition to the necessary expertise in religious and cultural sensitivity, travel guides serving halal tourists are increasingly expected to stay updated on technological innovations. As technology plays a more significant role in tourism, understanding and utilizing tools like AI becomes important. For example, AI applications can help travel guides obtain detailed information about halal tourist groups, plan tours more efficiently, and create personalized itineraries based on the religious and cultural profiles of tourists. The use of AI can also aid in managing logistics, answering tourist queries, and offering additional services that cater to the unique needs of halal tourists. As the tourism sector continues to integrate technological advancements, travel guides will need to leverage these tools to improve service delivery.

To summarize, travel guides in the halal tourism sector are expected to be well-rounded professionals who:

- Understand religious and cultural nuances: They should be knowledgeable about Islamic practices, prayer times, halal food, and the cultural context of the tourists they are guiding.
- Possess specialized knowledge: Travel guides should have expertise in halal or faith tourism, ensuring they meet the specific needs of Muslim travelers.
- Stay updated on technology: They should be proficient in using emerging technologies, including AI and smart applications, to enhance the tour experience and provide tailored services.
- Display essential personal traits: Effective communication, responsibility, and sensitivity are key traits for engaging with faith-based tourists and ensuring a positive experience.
- Adapt to the unique needs of halal tourists: The travel guide should not only conduct the tour but also ensure that it aligns with the religious, cultural, and personal preferences of the tourists.

By combining traditional travel guiding skills with the ability to use advanced technology and understanding the specific needs of halal tourists, travel guides can offer a unique and enriching experience for faith-based tourists, contributing to the overall success of the halal tourism sector.

Conclusion

Technological advancements, particularly in AI, have profoundly impacted various industries, including tourism. These innovations have enhanced the competitiveness of tourism businesses and transformed the way services are delivered. AI's integration into tourism has led to more personalized, efficient, and interactive experiences for travelers. In particular, travel guidance, traditionally seen as a face-to-face activity, has evolved with the use of AI technologies, including virtual tours, AI-supported audio guides, and even smart systems that deliver personalized, culturally sensitive content.

One of the most notable trends within the tourism sector is the rise of halal tourism, a market that is expanding as more travelers seek to observe religious practices while traveling. Halal tourism has led to the emergence of specialized businesses that cater to the unique needs of these travelers. To effectively serve halal tourists, tour guides must be equipped with both knowledge and skills that cater to their specific religious and cultural requirements. AI technologies can assist these guides by providing them with real-time, personalized information, helping them design tailored itineraries, and ensuring that the tour experience aligns with the religious and cultural expectations of halal tourists.

AI's potential in this context is vast. For instance, AI can identify halal restaurants, prayer facilities, and other services, facilitating seamless travel for Muslim tourists. Additionally, AI-assisted image recognition and content delivery systems can offer real-time, interactive experiences, enhancing tourists' engagement with destinations and landmarks. For example, tourists can point their smartphones at monuments to receive detailed historical, religious, and halal-related information, all delivered through AI-powered systems.

In conclusion, AI is revolutionizing travel guidance by offering more personalized, immersive, and efficient tourist experiences. It has introduced new possibilities, from AI-assisted virtual tours to smart audio guides, and is making significant strides in halal tourism. As the tourism sector continues to embrace these technologies, the role of tour guides will evolve, and those serving faith-sensitive groups, like halal tourists, will need to leverage these innovations to meet their unique needs. The future of tourism, especially for niche markets such as halal tourism, will depend heavily on the effective integration of AI and other smart technologies, positioning them as key enablers of the next generation of travel experiences.

References

Ahipaşaoğlu, S. (2001). *Turizmde rehberlik*. Detay Yayıncılık.

Aksu, A. (2019). *Türkiye'de Helal Turizmin Gelişmesine Yönelik İzlenmesi Gereken Stratejileri. 2nd International Halal Tourism Congress, Antalya, April 4–6, 2019* (pp. 210–215).

Akyol, M., & Kılınç, Ö. (2014). Internet and halal tourism marketing. *Electronic Turkish Studies*, *9*(8), 171–186.

Albuz, N., Çakmak, T. F., Eren, A., Tekin, Ö., & Güven Yeşildağ, G. N. (2018). *Turizm rehberliğine giriş*. Detay Yayıncılık.

Aldebert, B., Dang, R., & Longhi, C. (2010). Innovation in the tourism industry: The case of Tourism. *Tourism Management*, *32*(5), 1204–1213.

Ap, J., & Wong, K. K. F. (2001). Case study on tour guiding: Professionalism, issues and problems. *Tourism Management*, *22*(5), 551–563.

Arpacı, Ö., Uğurlu, K., & Batman, O. (2015). Helal konseptli otel işletmelerine yönelik yapılan müşteri şikayetleri üzerine bir araştırma. *Bartın Üniversitesi İktisadi ve İdari Bilimler Fakültesi Dergisi*, *6*(11), 181–198.

Başer, M. Y., & Olcay, A. (2022). Akıllı turizmde yapay zeka teknolojisi. *Gaziantep University Journal of Social Sciences*, *21*(3), 1795–1817.

Batman, O. (2003). Türkiye'deki profesyonel turist rehberlerinin mesleki sorunlarına yönelik bir araştırma. *Bilgi Sosyal Bilimler Dergisi*, *2*, 117–134.

Batman, O., Yıldırgan, R., & Demirtaş, N. (2001). *Turizm rehberliği* (1 ed., pp. 105–136). Değişim Yayınları.

Battour, M., & Ismail, M. N. (2016). Halal tourism: Concepts, practices, challenges and future. *Tourism Management Perspectives*, *19*, 150–154.

Bircan, H., & Karaman, M. (2024). Dijital vatandaşlık ve sağlıklı yaşam: teknolojinin sağlık üzerindeki dönüştürücü etkisi. *Uluslararası Iktisadi ve Idari Bilimler Dergisi*, *10*(2), 98–108.

Boğan, E., & Sarıışık, M. (2018). Halal tourism: Conceptual and practical challenges. *Journal of Islamic Marketing*, *10*(1), 87–96.

Chandra, G. R. (2014). Halal tourism: A new goldmine for tourism. *International Journal of Business Management & Research*, *4*(6), 45–62.

Cho, N., & Gu, Y. (2010). Technology-based procurement innovation in SME F&B service: An evolutionary case study. *Journal of Information Technology Applications and Management*, *17*(3), 25–41.

Csorny, L. (2013). Careers in the growing field of information technology services. *Cornell University Library. U.S. Bureau of Labor Statistics*, *2*(9), 1–8.

Dal, N. E., & Topay, G. (2018). Muhafazakâr tüketicilerin helal turizme bakışı. *Eurasian Journal of Researches in Social and Economics*, *5*(12), 260–280.

Demirbilek, E., & Şengül, S. (2019). Helal gıdaların fast food restoranlarda kullanım durumlarının incelenmesi: Türkiye. *2. International Halal Tourism Congress: Antalya*, 418–425.

Demirezen, B. (2019). Artırılmış gerçeklik ve sanal gerçeklik teknolojisinin turizm sektöründe kullanılabilirliği üzerine bir literatür taraması. *Uluslararası Global Turizm Araştırmaları Dergisi*, *3*(1), 1–26.

Dey, S., & Shukla, D. (2020). *Analytical study on use of ai techniques in tourism sector for smarter customer experience management*. 2020 International Conference on Computer Science, Engineering and Applications (ICCSEA), 1–5.

Dwivedi, Y. K., Pandey, N., Currie, W., & Micu, A. (2023). Leveraging chatgpt and other generative artificial intelligence (ai)-based applications in the hospitality and tourism industry: Practices, challenges and research agenda. *International Journal of Contemporary Hospitality Management*, *36*(1), 1–12.

Emek, M. (2012). *Usage of QR code in tourism industry*. Retrieved May 08, 2025, from https://core.ac.uk/download/pdf/47253926.pdf

Ercan, F. (2020). Turizm pazarlamasında yapay zeka teknolojilerinin kullanımı ve uygulama örnekleri. *Ankara Hacı Bayram Veli Üniversitesi Turizm Fakültesi Dergisi*, *23*(2), 394–410.

Eren, M., Ayaz, N., & Kaçar, F. (2017). Helal turizm ve rehberlik hizmetleri. *Ekonomi İşletme ve Yönetim Dergisi*, *1*(2), 64–77.

Gabdrakhmanov, N. K., Biktimirov, N. M., Rozhko, M. V. & Mardanshina, R. M. (2016). Features of Islamic tourism. *Academy of Marketing Studies Journal, 20,* 45–50.

Genç, N. (2023). Rekreasyon tutkunları için chatGPT: Gelecekte ne bekleniyor? *Sportive*, *6*(2), 67–83.

Gohary, E. H. (2016). Halal tourism, is it really halal? *Tourism Management Perspectives*, *19*, 124–130.

Hacıoğlu, N. (2016). *Seyahat acentacılığı ve tur oOperatörlüğü*. Nobel Akademik Yayıncılık.

Hamelink, C. J. (1997). *New information and communication technologies, social development and cultural change*. United Nations Research Institute for Social Development.

Harara, N. M., Al Najdawi, B. M., Rababah, M. A., & Haniyi, A. A. (2024). Jordanian tour guides' communication competency. *Journal of Language Teaching and Research*, *15*(3), 873–883.

Harvey, R. (2010). *Certification of halal meat in the UK*. HRH Prince Alwaleed Bin Talal Centre of Islamic Studies, University of Cambridge.

Henderson, J. C. (2016). Halal food, certification and halal tourism: Insights from Malaysia and Singapore. *Tourism Management Perspectives*, *19*, 160–164.

Huang, S. H., Hsu, C. H. C., & Chan A. (2009). Tour guide performance and tourist satisfaction: A study of package tours in Shanghai. *Journal of Hospitality & Tourism Research*, *34*(1), 3–33.

Ilhan, I., & Çeltek, E. (2016). Mobile marketing: Usage of augment reality in tourism. *Gaziantep University Journal of Social Sciences*, *15*(2), 581–599.

Ismail, A. G., & Noor, M. A. M. (2016). Halal finance and halal foods: Are they falling apart? *Acta Universitatis Danubius: Economica*, *12*(3), 113–126.

Jaelani, A. (2017). Halal tourism industry in Indonesia: Potential and prospects. *International Review of Management and Marketing*, *7*(3), 25–34.

Jorgenson, D. W., & Stiroh, K. J. (1999). Information technology and growth. *American Economic Review*, *89*(2), 109–115.

Köroğlu, A. (2019). *Turist rehberlerinin rolleri*. Detay Yayıncılık.

Martin, J. C., Cruz, C. O., & Zergane, S. (2020). Islamic finance and halal tourism: An unexplored bridge for smart specialization. *Sustainability*, *12*(14), 5736. https://doi.org/10.3390/su12145736

Mevzuat.gov.tr. (2012). *Turist Rehberliği Meslek Kanunu*. Retrieved April 29, 2025, from https://www.mevzuat.gov.tr/mevzuatmetin/1.5.6326.pdf

Mohsin, A., Ramli, N., & Alkhulayfi, B. A. (2016). Halal tourism: Emerging opportunities. *Tourism Management Perspectives*, *19*, 137–143.

Mokhlis, S. (2009). Relevancy and measurement of religiosity in consumer behavior. *International Business Research*, *2*(3), 75–84.

Mokhtarian, P. L., Salomon, I., & Singer, M. E. (2015). What moves us? An interdisciplinary exploration of reasons for traveling. *Transport Reviews*, *35*(3), 250–274.

Mujiatun, S., Trianto, B., Cahyono, E. F., & Rahmayati. (2023). The impact of marketing communication and Islamic financial literacy on Islamic financial inclusion and MSMEs performance: Evidence from halal tourism in Indonesia. *Sustainability*, *15*, 9868. https://doi.org/10.3390/su15139868

Mutmainah, L. L. (2018). The role of religiosity, halal awareness, halal certification, and food ingredients on purchase intention of halal food. *Ihtifaz: Journal of Islamic Economics, Finance and Banking*, *1*(1), 33–50.

Nikolskaya, E. Y., Lepeshkin, V. A., Blinova, E. A., Kulgachev, I. P., & Ilkevich, S. V. (2019). Improvement of digital technology in the tourism sector. *Journal of Environmental Management & Tourism*, *10*(38), 1197–1201.

Pew Research Center. (2025, April 27). *The Future of World Religions: Population growth projections, 2010–2050*. https://www.pewresearch.org/religion/2015/04/02/religious-projections-2010-2050/

Prakash, M., & Chowdhary, N. (2010). Tour guides: Roles, challenges and desired competences: A review of literature. *International Journal of Hospitality and Tourism Systems*, *3*(1). http://www.publishingindia.com/ijhts/24/tour-guides-roles-challenges-and-desired-competences-a-review-of-literature/87/565/

Qaddahat, R., Attaalla, F., & Hussein, M. M. (2016). Halal tourism: Evaluating opportunities and challenges in the Middle East "Jordan and Egypt". *Journal of Faculty of Tourism and Hotels, Fayoum University*, *10*(2), 377–390.

Ratnasari, R. T., Gunawan, S., Mawardi, I., & Kirana, K. C. (2021). Emotional experience on behavioral intention for halal tourism. *Journal of Islamic Marketing*, *12*(4), 864–881.

Razzaq, S. A. (2016). *Halal, New Zealand! An exploratory study into the halal-friendliness of accommodation providers in New Zealand*. Master Thesis, University of Canterbury. Retrieved April 22, 2025, from https://ir.canterbury.ac.nz/server/api/core/bitstreams/c9321d0d-4def-4e70-ad60-e3155a538e6b/content

Ritchie, B. W., Carr, N., & Cooper, C. (2003). *Managing educational tourism*. Channel View Publications.

Şahin, S., Tezcan, A. E., & Bekçi, M. (2018). Yerli turistlerin Türkiye, İstanbul, turizm ve turist rehberi ile ilgili metaforları. *Turizm Akademik Dergisi*, *5*(1), 251–264.

Samala, N., Katkam, B. S., Bellamkonda, R. S., & Rodriguez, R. V. (2020). Impact of AI and robotics in the tourism sector: A critical insight. *Journal of Tourism Futures*, *8*(1), 73–87.

The World Federation of Tourist Guide Associations. (2025, April 29). *Definition of tourist guide*. https://wftga.org/

Tieman, M., & Hassan, F. H. (2015). Convergence of food systems: Kosher, Christian and halal. *British Food Journal*, *117*(9), 2313–2327. https://doi.org/10.1108/BFJ-02-2015-0058

Tuo, Y., Wu, J., Zhao, J., & Si, X. (2025). Artificial intelligence in tourism: Insights and future research agenda. *Tourism Review*, *80*(4), 793–812.

Wahab, I. N. (2017). Role of information technology in tourism industry: Impact and growth. *International Journal of Innovative Research in Computer and Communication Engineering*, *5*(2), 260–263.

Weiler, B., & Walker, K. (2014). Enhancing the visitor experience: Reconceptualising the tour guide's communicative role. *Journal of Hospitality and Tourism Management*, *21*, 90–99.

Woodward, S. C. (2004). Faith and tourism: Planning tourism in relation to places of worship. *Tourism and Hospitality Planning & Development*, *1*(2), 173–186.

Yalçınkaya, P., Atay, L., & Karakaş, E. (2018). Akıllı turizm uygulamaları. *Gastroia: Journal of Gastronomy and Travel Research*, *2*(2), 85–103.

Yan, L. S., Zahari, N. A., Ismail, A. S., & Zain, N. M. (2017). Halal tourism: A new world for tourism industry. *International Journal of Asian Social Science*, *7*(8), 643–657.

Zhang, H. Q., & Chow, I. (2004). Application of importance-performance model in tour guides' performance: Evidence from mainland Chinese outbound visitors in Hong Kong. *Tourism Management*, *25*(1), 81–91.

Chapter 12

Implementing Technology in Halal Tourism for Sustainability

Gizem Kiper, Orhan Batman and Vahit Oguz Kiper

Sakarya University of Applied Sciences, Turkey

Abstract

Halal tourism is a growing market in worldwide and that attracts the attention of many researchers and practitioners. Since the tourism industry and demand for it are rapidly changing and evolving, one must monitor the changes closely to adopt it. Especially, technology is evolving day by day faster and faster, and new challenges and opportunities also come with it. Perhaps, the speed of technological developments became crucial now more than ever. VR (virtual reality) and AR (augmented reality) technologies are almost seen as daily, and AI (artificial intelligence) began to take place in routines of anyone. New developments like blockchain and internet of things also become popular and get into the radar zone of many researchers. This chapter aims to both investigate and offer challenges and opportunities of implementing technology in halal tourism for sustainability. To achieve that, authors focused on current and up-to-date literature to enlighten fast development of technology and nature of halal tourism to combine them as a multi-disciplinary field with solid outcomes for readers and other researchers.

Keywords: Halal tourism; technology; sustainability; future; change

Introduction

The global tourism industry faces increasing pressure to adopt sustainable practices while addressing the diverse needs of travelers. Halal tourism, a rapidly expanding sector catering to Muslim travelers, emphasizes faith-based values and

Halal Tourism and Artificial Intelligence: New Approaches for a New Generation, 171–184

doi:10.1108/978-1-80686-165-120261013

culturally sensitive experiences (Battour & Ismail, 2016). Concurrently, sustainable tourism seeks to minimize environmental degradation, promote economic equity, and preserve cultural heritage (UNWTO, 2017). The integration of technology at the intersection of these domains offers transformative potential to enhance the quality and sustainability of halal tourism. This chapter explores how technology can aid sustainable practices in halal tourism, addressing environmental protection, economic development, and cultural preservation while meeting the unique needs of Muslim travelers.

Halal tourism has witnessed significant growth, with the global Muslim travel market projected to reach $300 billion by 2026 (CrescentRating, 2020). This growth is driven by rising demand for travel experiences that align with Islamic principles, including access to halal food, prayer facilities, and gender-segregated amenities (Henderson, 2010). However, the environmental and social impacts of tourism, such as resource depletion and cultural commodification, pose challenges to the sector's long-term viability (Hall, 2019). Technology, including smart systems, digital platforms, and immersive tools, provides innovative solutions to mitigate these impacts. For instance, IoT-based resource management can reduce water and energy consumption in halal-certified accommodations by up to 15% (Alam et al., 2021).

The significance of this topic lies in its potential to address pressing global challenges within a culturally specific context. Halal tourism, as a niche but rapidly growing sector, caters to over 1.9 billion Muslims worldwide, a demographic increasingly aware of ethical and sustainable travel choices (Pew Research Center, 2017). The environmental impacts of tourism, including water overuse and carbon emissions, necessitate sustainable interventions that align with Islamic values of stewardship and responsibility (Kamali, 2012). Technology offers tools to bridge this gap, enabling destinations to reduce their ecological footprint while enhancing the halal tourism experience. For example, mobile applications providing real-time information on halal-certified eco-friendly accommodations have increased traveler satisfaction by 20% in Malaysia and Indonesia (CrescentRating, 2021). Understanding how technology can be leveraged to meet these dual objectives is important for the responsible development of halal tourism.

The purpose of this chapter is to comprehensively investigate the role of technology in fostering sustainable practices within the halal tourism sector. Specifically, it aims to (1) define and contextualize sustainable tourism, halal tourism, and their intersection; (2) analyze how technologies facilitate environmental protection, economic growth, and cultural preservation in halal tourism; (3) identify challenges, such as the digital divide and data privacy, alongside opportunities for innovation; (4) review best practices of successful technology implementation; and (5) propose future research directions to address evolving traveler needs and technological advancements (Battour & Ismail, 2016; UNWTO, 2017). By offering a framework for integrating technology into halal tourism, this chapter seeks to inform policymakers, tourism operators, and researchers, contributing to a more inclusive and sustainable tourism industry.

Defining Core Concepts

Sustainable Tourism

Sustainable tourism is broadly defined as tourism that meets the needs of travelers while ensuring minimal negative impacts on the environment, culture, and local communities (UNWTO, 2017). This concept has gained prominence in response to the global tourism industry's environmental footprint, which accounts for approximately 8% of global carbon emissions (Lenzen et al., 2018). Sustainable tourism embraces a balanced approach, integrating environmental protection, socio-economic benefits, and cultural preservation to ensure the long-term viability of tourism destinations. Its principles are rooted in the 1987 Brundtland Report, which introduced sustainable development as meeting present needs without compromising future generations' abilities (WCED, 1987). In the tourism context, this translates to practices that mitigate resource depletion and promote equitable and fair growth.

The environmental pillar of sustainable tourism focuses on reducing ecological degradation caused by tourism activities. Tourism significantly impacts natural resources, consuming an estimated 1.8 billion cubic meters of water annually, particularly in water-scarce regions (Gössling & Hall, 2019). Practices such as energy-efficient infrastructure, waste reduction, and the promotion of low-carbon transport are critical to minimizing these impacts. For instance, eco-certified hotels in Europe have reduced energy consumption by 20% through smart technologies (Becken & Hay, 2012). Sustainable tourism also encourages biodiversity conservation, as tourism often harms fragile ecosystems, such as coral reefs and forest reserves (Hall, 2019). These efforts align with global sustainability goals, including the United Nations' Sustainable Development Goals (SDGs), particularly SDG 12 (Responsible Consumption and Production).

The socio-economic dimension of sustainable tourism emphasizes equitable economic benefits for local communities. Tourism generates approximately 10% of global GDP and supports 1 in 10 jobs worldwide (WTTC, 2020). However, economic leakage, where profits are repatriated to foreign entities, often undermines local benefits (Scheyvens, 2011). Sustainable tourism seeks to address this by promoting local employment, supporting small and medium enterprises (SMEs), and fostering community-based tourism initiatives. For example, community-led ecotourism projects in Southeast Asia have increased local incomes by 15% while preserving traditional livelihoods (Goodwin, 2011). These initiatives ensure that tourism contributes to poverty combat and inclusive growth, particularly in developing regions.

Cultural preservation is the third pillar of sustainable tourism, aiming strategies to preserve local cultures and heritage from commodification (Mbaiwa, 2011). The over-commercialization of cultural sites, such as religious festivals or historical landmarks, risks eroding their authenticity (Cohen, 1988). Sustainable tourism promotes respectful engagement with local cultures, encouraging tourists to appreciate cultural heritage without exploitation. For instance, visitor management systems at UNESCO World Heritage Sites, such as Machu Picchu, limit daily tourist numbers to reduce physical and cultural wear (Hall, 2019). Digital tools, such as virtual tours, further support cultural preservation by reducing on-site pressure, with 25% of global heritage sites adopting such technologies (UNESCO, 2020).

Defining Halal Tourism

Halal tourism is defined as tourism that adheres to Islamic principles, providing services and experiences that align with the religious and cultural preferences of Muslim travelers (Battour & Ismail, 2016). It encompasses a wide range of offerings, including access to halal food, prayer facilities, gender-segregated amenities, and activities that respect Islamic values, such as modesty and ethical conduct (Henderson, 2010). The term "halal," meaning permissible in Arabic, extends beyond dietary requirements to include behaviors and environments that comply with Sharia law. Halal tourism has emerged as a significant niche market, driven by the growing global Muslim population, projected to reach CAF (Community Assistance Fund) is a global initiative that supports community-based tourism projects in developing countries. With a market size expected to reach $300 billion by 2026, halal tourism caters to the specific needs of over 1.9 billion Muslims worldwide (CrescentRating, 2020; Pew Research Center, 2017).

Halal tourism intersects with sustainable tourism through shared values of ethical consumption and community welfare. Islamic teachings emphasize environmental care and equitable resource use, aligning with sustainable tourism's goals of minimizing ecological harm and supporting local economies (Kamali, 2012). For example, halal tourism initiatives in Indonesia promote eco-friendly accommodations that reduce water usage by 10% through smart technologies, catering to environmentally conscious Muslim travelers (Alam et al., 2021). This synergy highlights halal tourism's potential to contribute to global sustainability while meeting cultural and religious needs.

The Intersection of Sustainability and Halal Tourism

The intersection of sustainable tourism and halal tourism is an important area where shared values of ethical practices and responsibility come together. Both concepts focus to balance the needs of travelers with the protection of environment, culture, and local communities (Battour & Ismail, 2016; UNWTO, 2017). Sustainable tourism aims to reduce negative impacts like resource depletion and carbon emissions, while halal tourism meets the religious and cultural needs of Muslim travelers, such as halal food and prayer facilities (Henderson, 2010). This intersection is significant because Islamic principles, which guide halal tourism, emphasize environmental care and social justice, aligning with sustainable tourism goals (Kamali, 2012). For example, Islamic teachings about stewardship encourage reducing waste, which supports sustainable tourism's aim to lower ecological footprints.

One major point of convergence is the focus on environmental protection. Tourism activities, including those in halal tourism, consume large amounts of resources, like water and energy, which can harm ecosystems (Gössling & Hall, 2019). Halal tourism destinations, such as resorts in Malaysia, have started using eco-friendly practices, like water-saving ablution systems, reducing water use by 10% (Alam et al., 2021). These efforts show how halal tourism can adopt sustainable practices to meet both religious requirements and environmental goals. However, challenges like high costs of green technologies can limit their use in developing countries where many halal tourism markets are located (Jafari & Scott, 2014).

The use of technology strengthens this intersection by addressing both sustainability and halal requirements. Digital platforms, like HalalTrip, promote eco-friendly halal accommodations, while smart systems in hotels optimize energy use, saving up to 20% in costs (Khan & Rahman, 2020). However, issues like digital divide in rural areas and data privacy concerns can hinder technology adoption in halal tourism (Rahim et al., 2022). Despite these challenges, the synergy between sustainable and halal tourism, supported by technology, offers a promising path for responsible tourism development, especially for Muslim travelers who value ethical and faith-based travel.

Technology's Role in Sustainable Tourism

Technology plays important role to make tourism more sustainable, especially in halal tourism where environmental care and cultural needs must balance (Gössling, 2017). Sustainable tourism aims to reduce negative impacts like energy overuse and waste, and technology gives tools to reach this goal (UNWTO, 2017). In halal tourism, technologies like smart systems, mobile apps, and digital platforms help to protect environment, support local economies, and preserve Islamic heritage while meeting Muslim travelers' needs (Battour & Ismail, 2016). For example, IoT-based sensors in hotels cut water use for ablution by 12% in Malaysia, showing how technology supports both sustainability and halal requirements (Alam et al., 2021).

Tourism by its nature uses lot of resources, like 1.8 billion cubic meters of water each year, which hurt ecosystems (Gössling & Hall, 2019). Smart technologies, like energy-efficient lighting and water-saving systems, reduce this impact. In halal tourism, hotels in Dubai use IoT to monitor energy, saving 15% in electricity costs (Khan & Rahman, 2020). Mobile apps also encourage eco-friendly choices, like carbon-offset programs, which 20% of Muslim travelers in Indonesia now use (CrescentRating, 2021). These tools make it easier to follow Islamic values of environmental care while keeping tourism sustainable.

But, using technology has challenges, like high costs and digital divide. Many halal tourism destinations in developing countries cannot afford smart systems, and rural areas lack internet access (Alam et al., 2021). Data privacy is also problem, as apps collect personal information, which worry Muslim travelers about security (Rahim et al., 2022). Despite this, technology is strong enabler for sustainability in halal tourism, offering solutions to environmental, economic, and cultural issues if used with care and planning.

Technology's Role in Halal Tourism

Technology changed the way of marketing and promoting halal-friendly sustainable tourism and made it easy to reach Muslim travelers who demand ethical and faith-based travel (Buhalis & Foerste, 2015). Muslim tourists look for destinations that offer halal food, prayer facilities, and eco-friendly practices, and technology helps to share this information fast (Battour & Ismail, 2016). Tools like social media, mobile apps, websites, and influencer marketing create strong promotion strategies that align with Islamic values and sustainability goals (UNWTO, 2017). For example, Malaysia's tourism board use social media campaigns to promote halal green hotels and increase bookings by 28% as a result (Mastercard-CrescentRating, 2022).

Social media platforms are highly important for marketing halal-friendly sustainable tourism. Instagram, TikTok, and YouTube let tourism businesses present videos and photos of halal-certified resorts and eco-friendly activities, attracting 35% more Muslim travelers to destinations like Indonesia (Salleh et al., 2019). Hashtags like #HalalTravel and #SustainableTourism make contents easy to find and build community interest.

Mobile apps also play big role in promotion. Apps like HalalTrip and SalamStandard give details about halal-friendly sustainable destinations, including green certifications and prayer room locations (Mohsin et al., 2016). Apps also send push notifications about sustainable travel deals, increasing engagement by 20% (Tussyadiah & Fesenmaier, 2018). But, apps need regular updates to stay useful, and weak internet connection in some areas limit tourists' reach (El-Gohary, 2016).

Websites and online platforms are another way to market halal-friendly sustainable tourism. Tourism boards in Qatar and UAE use websites to show halal certifications and sustainability awards, building trust with Muslim travelers (Stephenson, 2014). For example, Dubai's tourism website highlights smart hotels that save 15% energy, attracting 25% more bookings from Muslim tourists (Ali & Omar, 2023). Search engine optimization (SEO) makes these websites easy to find and improve visibility. But, websites must be mobile-friendly, as 60% of Muslim travelers use mobile phones to plan trips (Mastercard-CrescentRating, 2022).

Influencer marketing is growing fast in halal tourism promotion. Muslim travel bloggers and influencers on Instagram share stories about sustainable halal destinations and inspire followers to visit places like Morocco and Malaysia (Salleh et al., 2019). Influencer campaigns in Saudi Arabia increase interest in eco-friendly hajj packages by 30%, measured by social media engagement (Hassan et al., 2021). But, some influencers promote without checking halal standards and causing confusion (Omar & Nazri, 2021).

Email marketing and newsletters also help promote halal-friendly sustainable tourism even they are now kind of old-fashioned. Tourism agencies send emails with updates on halal-certified eco-resorts and travel tips and keep Muslim travelers informed (Buhalis & Foerste, 2015). In Indonesia, email campaigns about sustainable halal tourism raise bookings by 18% for green accommodations (Mastercard-CrescentRating, 2022). These emails can include surveys to learn traveler preferences and improve promotion. But, too many emails can annoy users and reduce effectiveness (Tussyadiah & Fesenmaier, 2018).

Integrating Technology for Sustainable Halal Tourism

Synergies and Opportunities

Integrating technology in halal tourism has ability to create strong synergies that support sustainability and meet Muslim travelers' needs (Neuhofer et al., 2015). Halal tourism focuses on Islamic values like environmental care and social justice, which match sustainable tourism's goals of reducing resource waste and promoting local economies (Battour & Ismail, 2016). Technologies like IoT, blockchain, and mobile apps make these goals easier to reach by improving efficiency and accessibility (UNWTO, 2017). For example, smart systems in Oman's halal hotels cut energy use by 16%, showing how technology links sustainability with halal principles (Alkhalidi & Eddin, 2022).

Technology also opens up new opportunities for personalized halal tourism. AI analyzes traveler data to suggest halal-friendly eco-tours, increasing satisfaction by 25% in Saudi Arabia (Tussyadiah & Miller, 2019). Social media campaigns share stories of sustainable halal destinations, inspiring 30% more Muslim tourists to visit Morocco (Hassan & Zainal, 2020). But, opportunities depend on solving challenges like digital divide, as many Muslim-majority countries have weak internet access (Hamid & Isa, 2020). Technology's synergies and opportunities make halal tourism more sustainable and attractive if using it right.

Challenge to these synergies includes high costs and need for adequate training. Small halal tourism businesses cannot always afford technologies like IoT or AI, and workers need skills to use them (Yusof & Zulkifli, 2021). Also, cultural sensitivity is important, as technology must respect Islamic values to keep traveler trust (Din, 2014). Despite this, integrating technology offers significant opportunities to make halal tourism sustainable, support environment, economy, and culture while meeting Muslim travelers' needs.

Best Practices and Guidelines

Use of technology in halal tourism needs careful planning to make sure it supports sustainability and respect Islamic values (Neuhofer et al., 2015). Best practices and guidelines come from successful examples and researches, showing how to integrate tools like IoT, mobile apps, and AI in way that help environment, economy, and culture (Battour & Ismail, 2016). These practices not only make halal tourism better for Muslim travelers but also align with global sustainability goals (UNWTO, 2017). For example, Malaysia's smart hotels use IoT to save 15% energy while offer halal-certified services, proving technology can balance faith and green practices (Hamid & Isa, 2020). One best practice is to collaborate between stakeholders to integrate technology. Tourism boards, halal certification authorities, and tech companies must work together to create systems that meet Muslim travelers' needs and sustainability targets (Yusof &

Zulkifli, 2021). For instance, Indonesia's tourism ministry partners with app developers to promote halal eco-resorts, increasing bookings by 20% (Mastercard-CrescentRating, 2022). This collaboration makes sure technologies like mobile apps and blockchain are designed with cultural sensitivity, avoiding mistakes like non-halal promotions. Guideline here is to form joint committees that include religious scholars and tech experts to guide technology use, ensuring it respects Islamic values and reduce environmental harm.

Another practice is using technology to educate travelers about sustainable halal tourism. Mobile apps and social media can teach Muslim tourists how to choose green hotels or reduce waste, to align with Islamic principles of stewardship (Din, 2014). In Qatar, social media campaigns about eco-friendly hajj practices raise awareness by 25%, encouraging 30% more pilgrims to use low-carbon transport (Alkhalidi & Eddin, 2022).

Investing in localized technology solutions is also a key practice. Technologies must fit the cultural and religious context of halal tourism destinations to be effective (Hassan & Zainal, 2020). For example, AR tours in Turkey's mosques use local languages and Islamic history facts, improving visitor satisfaction by 18% (Al-Masri & Abu-Hashem, 2021). The trick here is to adapt tools like VR and AI to include halal-specific features, like prayer time alerts or halal food filters, and test them with local communities first. This practice would avoid cultural errors and make technology more acceptable, especially in Muslim-majority countries where trust is important.

Monitoring and evaluating technology impacts is another significant practice. Using data from IoT systems, surveys, and economic reports to check if technologies save resources or improve experiences (Tussyadiah & Miller, 2019). In the UAE, blockchain systems for halal certifications are evaluated by track 15% increase in traveler trust (Ali & Omar, 2023). It is important to set clear metrics, like energy savings or job creation, and review them every year to improve technology use. This practice helps tourism operators see how it works and also about fixing problems, like high costs or data privacy issues, which Muslim travelers worry about (Hassan et al., 2021).

The Digital Divide

The digital divide is a big challenge for use of technology in sustainable halal tourism, especially in Muslim-majority countries where internet access is not equal (Buhalis & Law, 2008). Many halal tourism destinations, like rural areas in Indonesia and Pakistan, have weak or no internet connections, making it hard to use mobile apps, VR, or AI for travelers and businesses (Hamid & Isa, 2020). This challenge is a limitation for the benefits of technology tools such as searching halal services or promoting eco-friendly practices (Battour & Ismail, 2016). For example, only 45% of rural tourism businesses in Malaysia use digital tools due to poor connectivity, comparing to 80% in urban areas (Yusof & Zulkifli, 2021).

The digital divide also affects Muslim travelers' experience. Technologies like mobile apps for prayer times or halal food finders need stable internet connection, but some Muslim tourists in developing countries face problems access these tools because of bad networks (Mastercard-CrescentRating, 2022). This makes travel less convenient and blocks travelers for choosing sustainable options, like green hotels, which apps often promote (Tussyadiah & Miller, 2019). Without equal access, the digital divide causes uneven benefits, where urban travelers and businesses gain more than rural ones, going against sustainable tourism's goal of fair growth (Scheyvens, 2011).

Economic and education barriers make the digital divide worse. Small halal tourism businesses, like family-run guesthouses, cannot afford high-speed internet or devices, and many employees lack skills to use technologies like blockchain or IoT (Alkhalidi & Eddin, 2022). In Bangladesh, 60% of halal tourism operators report no training in digital tools, which limit their ability to market sustainable services (Rahman & Zailani, 2020). Since there is a lack of training in digital tools, this is an issue that slowing down adoption of technology and challenging busineeses to compete with bigger and more corporate rivals.

Data Privacy and Security

Data privacy and security is a serious challenge for use of technology in sustainable halal tourism, as Muslim travelers worry about their personal information when use apps and online platforms (Buhalis & Law, 2008). Technologies like mobile apps, AI, and blockchain collect data to offer halal services, like prayer time alerts or halal food suggestions, but these data can be misused if not protect well (Battour & Ismail, 2016). In Malaysia, 22% of Muslim tourists avoid travel apps because of fear about data leaks, showing how privacy concerns limit technology's benefits (Rahman & Zailani, 2020).

The problem grows because halal tourism apps often ask for sensitive information, like location, travel plans, and religious preferences, which need high protection (Hamid & Isa, 2020). Weak security systems in some Muslim-majority countries make the data an easy target for hackers, causing risks like identity theft (Al-Masri & Abu-Hashem, 2021). This shows that poor data security not only harm travelers but also damage reputation of halal tourism businesses, making it hard to promote sustainable practices. Also, lack of standard privacy rules across countries makes data protection more difficult. Different Muslim-majority countries have different laws for data security, causing confusion for halal tourism operators that work globally (Yusof & Zulkifli, 2021). In UAE, strict privacy laws help increase trust in halal apps by 18%, but countries like Pakistan have weak regulations, leading to 25% lower user confidence (Hassan & Zainal, 2020). This uneven system makes it hard to build trust with Muslim travelers, who needs clear promise that their data is safe when use of technologies for sustainable halal tourism (Tussyadiah & Miller, 2019).

Ethical Considerations

Ethical considerations are very important when use of technology in sustainable halal tourism, because it must respect Islamic values and avoid harm to travelers and communities (Shakona et al., 2015). Technologies like AI, mobile apps, and social media make halal tourism activities easier, but they can create problems if not use with care, such as disrespect religious beliefs or exploit local cultures (Battour & Ismail, 2016). For example, 18% of Muslim travelers in Indonesia avoid apps that show non-halal ads, which is a proof of need for cultural sensitivity in technology design (Zainal & Rahman, 2021). Ethical use of technology is key to keep trust and support in halal tourism.

One another ethical issue is to avoid cultural commodification. Halal tourism often promotes Islamic heritage, like mosques and festivals, but technologies like VR or social media can turn these into commercial products, losing their spiritual value (Weidenfeld & Ron, 2008). In Türkiye, overuse of AR tours at religious sites makes 15% of visitors feel less connect to the sacred meaning, reporting by surveys (Abdullah & Zain, 2022). Ethical guideline is to involve religious leaders in design technologies, ensuring they respect Islamic principles and not just focus on profit. This helps protect cultural authenticity, which is important for sustainable halal tourism.

Another concern is fair treatment of local communities. Technologies like digital platforms can help local halal businesses, but major companies often take most of the profits, and leave small operators with little benefit (Goodwin & Santilli, 2009). In Malaysia, 25% of rural halal tourism businesses claim they get less bookings from global apps compare to urban firms (Ismail & Yusoff, 2020). Ethical practice is to design platforms that prioritize local SMEs and share profits fairly, aligning with Islamic values of justice and sustainable tourism's goal of inclusive growth (UNWTO, 2017). This ensures technology support communities, not exploit them.

The Future Directions of Halal Tourism in the Name of Technology

The growth of digital technology has significantly affected many sectors, including tourism. In halal tourism sector, technology plays a crucial role in ensuring that the cultural and religious needs of Muslim travelers are met. Digital tools, such as online booking systems and mobile apps, now help travelers quickly find halal-friendly destinations while also supporting sustainable practices (Battour, 2016).

As technology continues to evolve, its impact on halal tourism becomes increasingly clear. Online platforms and social media have provided a space for halal tourism providers to market their services, engage directly with travelers, and showcase their adherence to Islamic guidelines. This digital shift not only improves efficiency but also opens up new opportunities for growth in the market (Hendrik et al., 2024).

Many halal tourism operators have started using mobile applications that offer real-time information about nearby halal restaurants, prayer facilities, and culturally sensitive accommodations. This trend meets the dual need for convenience and cultural integrity. In these apps, travelers can easily access recommendations, read user reviews, and make reservations that align with their values (Battour, 2016).

Beyond convenience, integrating technology into halal tourism also contributes to more sustainable practices. Digital monitoring and data-driven approaches help tourism businesses manage resources more efficiently, reducing waste and environmental impact. Moreover, technology supports cultural preservation by ensuring that modern services remain respectful of traditional practices (Muhamad et al., 2019).

Despite these clear benefits, challenges remain in fully integrating technology with halal tourism practices. Issues such as the digital divide, risks related to data privacy, and the occasional misalignment between automated recommendations and Islamic principles need to be addressed. For instance, even though automated booking systems simplify the travel process, they must be carefully designed to filter out options that do not meet halal requirements (Hendrik et al., 2024).

Looking ahead, emerging trends like AI and advanced data management promise to transform the halal tourism experience even further. AI-enabled platforms could offer travel recommendations that are finely tuned to personal preferences while ensuring compliance with halal standards. However, further research is needed to develop ethical AI systems that respect both user privacy and cultural nuances (Muhamad et al., 2019).

Another promising trend is the adoption of blockchain technology to boost transparency and trust. Blockchain can provide a secure and immutable record of transactions and reviews, ensuring that halal certifications and user feedback remain authentic. Such advancements are expected to reduce fraud and build greater confidence among Muslim travelers in the halal tourism sector (Biancone et al., 2019).

Conclusion

In conclusion, this chapter has explored the complex yet promising convergence of sustainable tourism, halal tourism, and digital technology. The discussion has highlighted how technology can serve as a critical enabler in meeting the dual demands of environmental sustainability and the specific needs of Muslim travelers.

Defining halal tourism within a sustainable framework has provided useful insights into the dual requirements of religious sensitivities and modern tourism expectations. The chapter has emphasized that the success of halal tourism lies at their intersection, where both cultural integrity and eco-friendly practices must be balanced and nurtured.

Technology has emerged as an unmistakable enabler of sustainability in this context. Digital tools and platforms have proven useful in bridging the gap between meaningful traditions and the demand for modern, efficient travel experiences. From real-time information systems to smart applications, technology is helping stakeholders to tailor services that are both user-friendly and culturally compliant.

While significant opportunities and synergies exist, the challenges should not be overlooked. Issues such as the digital divide, data privacy, and ensuring cultural sensitivity in technology applications call for a measured approach. Best practices have been observed in cases where technology integrations were carefully aligned with the values of halal tourism.

Looking forward, future directions should focus on further integrating advanced digital solutions with sustainable tourism models while safeguarding the unique requirements of halal tourism. By addressing existing challenges and capitalizing on emerging opportunities, stakeholders can pave the way toward a more inclusive, resilient, and ethically shaped tourism industry.

References

Abdullah, M., & Zain, A. (2022). Cultural impacts of digital technologies in religious tourism: Evidence from Turkey. *Journal of Heritage Tourism, 17*(3), 312–328. https://doi.org/10.1080/1743873X.2021.1989387

Alam, M. M., Malik, M. A., & Ahmed, S. (2021). IoT-based smart tourism: Opportunities and challenges for sustainable development. *Journal of Sustainable Tourism, 29*(5), 789–805. https://doi.org/10.1080/09669582.2020.1849234

Ali, M., & Omar, A. (2023). Blockchain applications in sustainable tourism: Opportunities for halal tourism. *Journal of Hospitality and Tourism Technology, 14*(2), 178–192. https://doi.org/10.1108/JHTT-03-2022-0078

Alkhalidi, A., & Eddin, S. (2022). Smart tourism and sustainability in the Middle East: A case study of Oman. *Journal of Sustainable Tourism, 30*(4), 892–907. https://doi.org/10.1080/09669582.2021.1922423

Al-Masri, E., & Abu-Hashem, M. (2021). Virtual reality in cultural tourism: Applications for Islamic heritage sites. *International Journal of Heritage Studies, 27*(6), 612–627. https://doi.org/10.1080/13527258.2020.1850472

Battour, M. (2016). Halal tourism: Concepts, practises, challenges and future. *Tourism Management Perspectives.*

Battour, M., & Ismail, M. N. (2016). Halal tourism: Concepts, practices, challenges and future. *Tourism Management Perspectives, 19*, 150–154. https://doi.org/10.1016/j.tmp.2015.12.008

Becken, S., & Hay, J. E. (2012). *Tourism and climate change: Risks and opportunities*. Channel View Publications. https://doi.org/10.21832/9781845412654

Biancone, P. P., Secinaro, S., Radwan, M., & Kamal, M. (2019). Halal tourism: An opportunity for the global tourism industry. *Tourism Analysis, 24*(3), 395–404.

Buhalis, D., & Foerste, M. (2015). SoCoMo marketing for travel and tourism: Empowering co-creation of value. *Journal of Destination Marketing & Management, 4*(3), 151–161. https://doi.org/10.1016/j.jdmm.2015.04.001

Buhalis, D., & Law, R. (2008). Progress in information technology and tourism management: 20 years on and 10 years after the Internet – The state of eTourism research. *Tourism Management, 29*(4), 609–623. https://doi.org/10.1016/j.tourman.2008.01.005

Cohen, E. (1988). Authenticity and commoditization in tourism. *Annals of Tourism Research, 15*(3), 371–386. https://doi.org/10.1016/0160-7383(88)90028-X

CrescentRating. (2020). *Global Muslim travel index 2020*. https://www.crescentrating.com/reports/global-muslim-travel-index-2020.html

CrescentRating. (2021). *Halal travel trends 2021*. https://www.crescentrating.com/reports/halal-travel-trends-2021.html

Din, K. H. (2014). Islam and tourism: Patterns, issues, and options. *Annals of Tourism Research, 16*(4), 542–563. https://doi.org/10.1016/0160-7383(89)90008-X

El-Gohary, H. (2016). Halal tourism, is it really halal? *Tourism Management Perspectives, 19*, 124–130. https://doi.org/10.1016/j.tmp.2015.12.013

El-Gohary, H., & Eid, R. (2020). Sustainable Islamic tourism: A conceptual framework. *Journal of Islamic Marketing, 11*(6), 1477–1495. https://doi.org/10.1108/JIMA-02-2019-0029

Goodwin, H. (2011). *Taking responsibility for tourism*. Goodfellow Publishers. https://doi.org/10.23912/978-1-906884-39-0-1154

Goodwin, H., & Santilli, R. (2009). Community-based tourism: A success? *ICRT Occasional Paper*, *11*, 1–37. http://www.icrtourism.org/wp-content/uploads/2012/09/OP11.pdf

Gössling, S. (2017). Tourism, information technologies and sustainability: An exploratory review. *Journal of Sustainable Tourism*, *25*(7), 1024–1041. https://doi.org/10.1080/09669582.2016.1259316

Gössling, S., & Hall, C. M. (2019). Sustainable tourism: A global perspective. *Journal of Sustainable Tourism*, *27*(7), 1044–1060. https://doi.org/10.1080/09669582.2018.1538230

Hall, C. M. (2019). Constructing sustainable tourism development: The 2030 agenda and the managerial ecology of sustainable tourism. *Journal of Sustainable Tourism*, *27*(7), 1044–1060. https://doi.org/10.1080/09669582.2018.1538230

Hamid, N. A., & Isa, S. (2020). IoT applications in halal tourism: Opportunities for sustainability. *Journal of Islamic Marketing*, *11*(5), 1234–1249. https://doi.org/10.1108/JIMA-03-2019-0056

Hassan, Z., & Zainal, M. (2020). Social media marketing in halal tourism: Insights from Malaysia and Morocco. *Tourism Recreation Research*, *45*(3), 392–405. https://doi.org/10.1080/02508281.2019.1704967

Hassan, Z., Salleh, N. H. M., & Yusof, N. (2021). Smart tourism and sustainability: A case study of halal tourism in Saudi Arabia. *International Journal of Tourism Cities*, *7*(3), 678–693. https://doi.org/10.1108/IJTC-09-2020-0182

Henderson, J. C. (2010). Sharia-compliant hotels. *Tourism and Hospitality Research*, *10*(3), 246–254. https://doi.org/10.1057/thr.2010.3

Hendrik, H., Kusumawardani, S. S., & Permanasari, A. E. (2024). The emerging landscape of halal tourism in the digital era: An IT perspective. *Journal of Islamic Marketing*, *15*(8), 1995–2015. https://doi.org/10.1108/JIMA-04-2023-0130

Ismail, N., & Yusoff, M. (2020). Digital platforms and economic equity in halal tourism: Challenges for rural communities. *Asian Journal of Tourism Research*, *5*(2), 89–104. https://doi.org/10.1108/AJTR-03-2020-0012

Jafari, J., & Scott, N. (2014). Muslim world and its tourisms. *Annals of Tourism Research*, *44*, 1–19. https://doi.org/10.1016/j.annals.2013.08.011

Kamali, M. H. (2012). Environmental care in Islam: A Qur'anic perspective. *Islam and Civilisational Renewal*, *3*(2), 261–283.

Khan, S., & Rahman, M. (2020). Digital innovations in halal tourism: A review of mobile applications. *Journal of Islamic Marketing*, *12*(3), 456–472. https://doi.org/10.1108/JIMA-08-2019-0165

Lenzen, M., Sun, Y.-Y., Faturay, F., Ting, Y.-P., Geschke, A., & Malik, A. (2018). The carbon footprint of global tourism. *Nature Communications*, *9*(1), 1–9. https://doi.org/10.1038/s41467-018-04404-8

Mastercard-CrescentRating. (2022). *Global Muslim travel index 2022*. https://www.crescentrating.com/reports/global-muslim-travel-index-2022.html

Mbaiwa, J. E. (2011). Cultural commodification and tourism: The case of the San people of Botswana. *Journal of Tourism and Cultural Change*, *9*(4), 290–301. https://doi.org/10.1080/14766825.2011.620123

Mohsin, A., Ramli, N., & Alkhulayfi, B. A. (2016). Halal tourism: Emerging opportunities. *Tourism Management Perspectives*, *19*, 137–143. https://doi.org/10.1016/j.tmp.2015.12.010

Muhamad, N. S., Sulaiman, S., Adham, K. A., & Said, M. F. (2019). Halal tourism: Literature synthesis and direction for future research. *Pertanika Journal of Social Sciences & Humanities*, *27*(1), 729–745.

Neuhofer, B., Buhalis, D., & Ladkin, A. (2015). Smart technologies for personalized experiences: A case study in the hospitality domain. *Electronic Markets*, *25*(3), 243–254. https://doi.org/10.1007/s12525-015-0182-1

Omar, S. R., & Nazri, M. A. (2021). Mobile technology and halal tourism: A review of applications and services. *Journal of Islamic Marketing*, *12*(4), 672–689. https://doi.org/10.1108/JIMA-06-2020-0178

Pew Research Center. (2017). *The changing global religious landscape*. https://www.pewresearch.org/religion/2017/04/05/the-changing-global-religious-landscape/

Rahim, N. A., & Zainuddin, Y. (2020). Halal certification challenges in the global tourism industry. *International Journal of Islamic Business*, *5*(2), 45–59. https://doi.org/10.32890/ijib2020.5.2.3

Rahim, N. A., Zainuddin, Y., & Ismail, M. (2022). Challenges in halal certification: A case study of food and beverage industry. *Journal of Islamic Marketing*, *13*(4), 789–803. https://doi.org/10.1108/JIMA-05-2020-0142

Rahman, M. K., & Zailani, S. (2020). Digital barriers in halal tourism: Evidence from developing countries. *Journal of Islamic Marketing*, *11*(6), 1523–1540. https://doi.org/10.1108/JIMA-04-2019-0087

Salleh, N. H. M., Hamid, N. A., & Hashim, N. H. (2019). Social media and halal tourism: A case study of Malaysia. *Asia Pacific Journal of Tourism Research*, *24*(8), 781–794. https://doi.org/10.1080/10941665.2019.1636158

Scheyvens, R. (2011). *Tourism and poverty*. Routledge. https://doi.org/10.4324/9780203862773

Shakona, M., Backman, K., Backman, S., Norman, W., Luo, Y., & Duffy, L. (2015). Understanding the traveling behavior of Muslims in the United States. *International Journal of Culture, Tourism and Hospitality Research*, *9*(1), 22–35. https://doi.org/10.1108/IJCTHR-05-2014-0036

Stephenson, M. L. (2014). Deciphering 'Islamic hospitality': Developments, challenges and opportunities. *Tourism Management*, *40*, 155–164. https://doi.org/10.1016/j.tourman.2013.05.002

Tussyadiah, I. P., & Fesenmaier, D. R. (2018). Digital transformation in tourism: The role of technology in enhancing visitor experiences. *Journal of Travel Research*, *57*(7), 922–936. https://doi.org/10.1177/0047287517734943

Tussyadiah, I. P., & Miller, G. (2019). Artificial intelligence in tourism: Enhancing personalization and sustainability. *Journal of Travel Research*, *58*(6), 987–1003. https://doi.org/10.1177/0047287518797578

UNESCO. (2020). *World heritage and tourism in a changing climate*. United Nations Educational, Scientific and Cultural Organization. https://whc.unesco.org/en/tourism/

UNWTO. (2017). *Tourism and the sustainable development goals*. United Nations World Tourism Organization. https://www.e-unwto.org/doi/book/10.18111/9789284419401

WCED. (1987). *Our common future*. Oxford University Press.

Weidenfeld, A., & Ron, A. S. (2008). Religious needs in the tourism industry. *Anatolia*, *19*(2), 357–361. https://doi.org/10.1080/13032917.2008.9687080

WTTC. (2020). *Economic impact reports*. World Travel & Tourism Council. https://wttc.org/Research/Economic-Impact

Yusof, M. F., & Zulkifli, S. S. (2021). Digital platforms and economic sustainability in halal tourism: A case study of Indonesia. *Journal of Islamic Economics and Business*, *6*(2), 178–192. https://doi.org/10.1108/JIEB-04-2020-0023

Zainal, A., & Rahman, M. (2021). Ethical concerns in halal tourism technologies: A case study of Indonesia. *Journal of Islamic Marketing*, *12*(7), 1345–1360. https://doi.org/10.1108/JIMA-09-2020-0278

Chapter 13

Beyond Borders: Crafting Sustainable, Smart, Inclusive, and Muslim-friendly Havens – Unveiling the Promise of Halal Tourism in Sri Lanka

S.K.L.J. Ramanayaka

Sri Lanka Institute of Tourism & Hotel Management (SLITHM), Sri Lanka

Abstract

Tourism, often seen as a gateway to cultural exchange and economic growth, continues to evolve to meet the diverse expectations of global travelers. One such emerging dimension is Halal tourism, a sector designed to cater to the religious and lifestyle needs of Muslim tourists. Although Sri Lanka is globally recognized for its natural beauty and rich cultural heritage, the nation's capacity to attract Muslim travelers remains largely untapped. This study explores the hidden potential of Halal tourism in Sri Lanka by identifying the critical factors that influence Muslim travelers' destination preferences and examining the broader implications for the national tourism industry. Through a qualitative, descriptive analysis of secondary data including reports from the Sri Lanka Tourism Development Authority (SLTDA), academic literature, industry insights, and global case studies – this research assesses both existing gaps and promising opportunities. Using Microsoft Excel to map trends and comparative best practices, the findings reveal that Sri Lanka holds considerable but underdeveloped potential to become a leading Halal-friendly destination. The study draws inspiration from successful Halal tourism strategies implemented in several non-Muslim-majority countries, emphasizing the need for strategic interventions that align with market demands. While the research is grounded in secondary data, it provides a crucial foundation for

Halal Tourism and Artificial Intelligence: New Approaches for a New Generation, 185–197

Published under exclusive licence by Emerald Publishing Limited
doi:10.1108/978-1-80686-165-120261014

future empirical studies. Ultimately, this study contributes to the ongoing dialog on sustainable, inclusive, and culturally responsive tourism development. It advocates for integrating Halal tourism as a key growth avenue, positioning Sri Lanka to embrace diversity, enhance its global competitiveness, and reshape its tourism landscape for long-term success.

Keywords: Cultural inclusivity; Halal tourism; Muslim travelers; Sri Lanka; tourism industry

Introduction

Tourism has blossomed into a global giant – a colossal river of activity flowing across borders and continents, carrying with it cultures, currencies, and countless stories. Today, it stands as the beating heart of the world economy, echoing through bustling airports, exotic destinations, and vibrant cityscapes. Defined as the temporary journey of individuals to lands beyond their everyday surroundings for purposes such as leisure, business, or discovery, tourism is much more than movement – it's the art of exploration and connection (Goeldner & Ritchie, 2006; UNWTO). Cook et al. (2014) capture it well, describing it as a dance of discovery, wherein people step beyond the familiar, embracing new experiences and the comfort of well-prepared hospitality.

Nestled like a precious gem in the Indian Ocean, Sri Lanka has long captivated the hearts of travelers. For centuries, it has been a siren call to adventurers and wanderers. As early as the 13th century, the famed explorer Marco Polo hailed it as the finest island of its size in the world – a glowing endorsement that still echoes in modern times. More recently, accolades from the Post Office Worldwide Holiday Costs Barometer in 2012 and Lonely Planet in 2013 have crowned Sri Lanka as a top-tier travel destination. By 2015, the Travel and Tourism Competitiveness Report positioned it at 63 out of 141 countries – a clear nod to its rising star.

Tourism in Sri Lanka is not just a casual affair; it's a strategic lifeline for foreign exchange, deserving the government's unwavering attention. The seed of this vision was first planted in 1937 with the birth of the Ceylon Tourist Bureau. Though it temporarily closed its doors due to World War II, it was reborn post-independence through the Ceylon Tourist Board. The enactment of Act No. 10 in 1966 gave formal structure and strength to this vision. Later, the Sri Lanka Tourism Development Authority (SLTDA) rose in 2007, becoming the lighthouse guiding the nation's tourism efforts into the modern age.

From misty hill stations to golden beaches, from ancient ruins to bustling markets, Sri Lanka is a treasure trove for every kind of traveler. Yet, what truly fuels the flame of tourism is the warmth of its hospitality – elegant hotels, skilled guides, curated tour packages, airport facilitators, and tantalizing cuisine. These experiences are the soul of tourism, sparking satisfaction and memories that outlast the journey.

In the expanding mosaic of global tourism, one segment is painting a vibrant picture: Muslim travelers. They represent a rapidly growing market whose needs, shaped by faith and culture, deserve careful attention. According to the State of the Global Islamic Economy Report, the Muslim travel market reached a monumental $140 billion in 2013 and is projected to soar to $238 billion by 2019 – a powerful wave that Sri Lanka must ride.

Enter Halal tourism – a rising branch of the tourism tree, offering fruit that appeals not only to the devout but to all who respect diverse values. As Neveu (2010) and Bhuiya et al. (2011) explain, Halal tourism goes beyond the label of religious travel; it offers a complete and respectful experience aligned with Islamic principles, yet open to global audiences. It includes destinations, services, and products that are permissible under Islamic law – from alcohol-free hotels and gender-segregated leisure facilities to prayer spaces and certified Halal meals.

Contrary to isolating Muslim travelers or excluding others, Halal tourism builds bridges. It fosters understanding, enhances spiritual convenience, and encourages co-existence in shared spaces. Certifications like Crescent Rating lend credibility and structure to these offerings, supporting inclusive tourism that benefits all – Muslim and non-Muslim alike.

Described by Lee as a "promising industry," tourism acts as a soft power, melting away borders and misconceptions. It nurtures environmental awareness and lays the foundation for a globally shared future. Yet, despite the growing number of Muslim travelers worldwide, Sri Lanka remains a whisper rather than a roar in the Halal tourism narrative. The SLTDA Annual Report (2015) reveals that only 8.6% of total tourist arrivals in 2015 were from Muslim countries – a figure dwarfed by the vast potential of this market.

In regions like Taiwan, Vietnam, China, and South Korea – countries with Muslim minority populations – Halal tourism is being embraced not merely as a social gesture but as a golden business opportunity. As global awareness grows, so does the demand for travel that honors Islamic values. Sri Lanka, with its rich cultural tapestry and existing tourism strengths, stands at the crossroads: to either remain a beautiful but passive player or to boldly craft a Halal-friendly identity that welcomes the Muslim traveler with open arms.

This study aims to unearth the untapped potential of Halal tourism in Sri Lanka, exploring its concepts, strategies, and future possibilities. With the right efforts, this branch of tourism can blossom, not only enhancing economic growth but also enriching Sri Lanka's image as a truly inclusive and respectful destination for all.

Research Problem

Despite Sri Lanka's global appeal as a tourist destination, the country's potential to attract and cater to Muslim travelers through Halal tourism remains significantly underexplored and underdeveloped, indicating a critical gap between market demand and the current tourism industry offerings.

Research Objectives

Primary Objective

To explore the untapped oasis of Halal tourism within Sri Lanka's rich cultural and natural landscape.

Secondary Objective

I. To trace the ripple effects of Halal tourism on the broader ocean of Sri Lanka's tourism industry.
II. To spotlight the role of Halal tourism as a rising tide capable of lifting the island's tourism stature in the fiercely competitive global marketplace.

Research Questions

I. Can Sri Lanka open its doors wider to welcome the Halal-conscious traveler?
II. How might the infusion of Halal tourism nourish and nurture the heart of the nation's tourism economy?
III. Does the magnetic pull of Halal tourism influence the footsteps of Muslim travelers towards Sri Lanka's shores?

Literature Review

In today's global arena, tourism has blossomed into a flourishing tree whose branches stretch across every continent, making it one of the most vibrant and lucrative sectors of the world economy. Like a colorful mosaic, the tourism landscape is composed of many well-studied forms – medical tourism, dark tourism, heritage tourism, eco-tourism, and digital or e-tourism – all of which have attracted scholarly exploration. Yet, as this dynamic field continues to gain momentum, a fresh shoot has emerged from its roots: Islamic or Halal tourism, marking a novel and promising frontier in global travel (Neveu, 2010; Bhuiya et al., 2011).

With the rise of Halal tourism, a new current has begun to ripple through related industries – airlines, hospitality, food services, and tour operations – pushing stakeholders to recalibrate and align their offerings to meet the needs of this spiritually guided market. This demand springs from a vast reservoir: over 50 Muslim-majority nations and a global Muslim population exceeding 1.6 billion. A significant portion of this population seeks travel experiences that harmonize with their faith, prompting a growing call for Muslim-friendly services and destinations (ITC, 2014).

For many Muslim travelers, conventional tourism presents barriers – shared public spaces where modesty may be compromised, or the presence of non-permissible foods and beverages. As a result, Halal tourism emerges as a sanctuary, offering a path paved with Sharia-compliant alternatives that align with religious convictions (Battour et al., 2012; Jafari & Scott, 2014). There is a notable shift in consumer behavior, with Muslim travelers increasingly opting for Halal-certified experiences, guided by rising awareness and a desire for authenticity (Battour et al., 2014).

Interestingly, non-Muslim countries have begun to listen to the footsteps of this silent wave. Nations such as Japan, the Philippines, and Brazil have rolled out welcome mats tailored for Muslim tourists. For instance, chambers of commerce and tourism associations in these countries have hosted training seminars to help industry professionals better understand and cater to Islamic travel requirements (TTG Asia, 2014).

Japan, in particular, has taken bold strides: prayer rooms now grace its major airports, restaurants serve Halal-certified meals, and travel guides specifically designed for Muslim visitors are readily available. These initiatives reflect a broader trend where best practices in Halal tourism are setting benchmarks for other destinations seeking to brand themselves as "Muslim-friendly."

The rise of Sharia-compliant hotels – offering prayer facilities, Qibla directions, alcohol-free beverages, and strictly Halal cuisine – is another sign of this movement gaining traction, not only in Muslim countries but across non-Muslim regions as well (Carboni et al., 2014; Javed, 2007). These accommodations serve as beacons, guiding Muslim travelers toward comfort and cultural congruence. In today's travel narratives, the availability of Halal food and beverages is no longer a luxury – it's a necessity. Muslim travelers frequently request Halal options even in non-Muslim countries, compelling destinations to adapt and diversify their culinary offerings.

Thailand stands out as a non-Muslim country proactively embracing this shift. With the launch of a Muslim-friendly mobile application, the country is carving a niche in spiritual hospitality. Likewise, Japan's Kansai International Airport has become a model of inclusion, offering prayer rooms and Halal-certified dining, resulting in a noticeable uptick in arrivals from Malaysia and Indonesia. Similarly, Tokyo's Narita and Haneda airports introduced prayer facilities in 2014 to echo the needs of their Muslim visitors.

Research Methodology

This study sails through the seas of qualitative inquiry, navigating its course by the stars of document analysis and conceptual review. Rather than dropping anchor in the busy harbors of interviews or surveys, the research casts its net wide into the rich ocean of secondary sources – mining the depths for pearls of insight and wisdom about Halal tourism in Sri Lanka. This voyage begins with a compass firmly pointed toward exploration. As the subject of Halal tourism remains a relatively uncharted island in Sri Lanka's tourism archipelago, the study treads carefully but confidently using literature and documentary evidence as its guiding lighthouse. This methodological route – resourceful, economical, and time-savvy – not only avoids the turbulence of primary data collection but also provides the sturdy sails of triangulated insight, ensuring the journey remains both deep and reliable. The vessel of inquiry is built upon the sturdy timbers of secondary data. A broad fleet of documents was carefully docked, unpacked, and examined to ensure that the cargo of information was both rich and relevant. These included the official logbooks of the Sri Lanka Tourism Development Authority (SLTDA) –

annual reports that record the tides of tourist arrivals, the ebb and flow of policies, and the shifting sands of national tourism strategies. These reports served as the captain's log, providing a clear narrative of Sri Lanka's tourism currents over time.

In addition to governmental charts, the research also drew from scholarly maps – academic books, peer-reviewed journal articles, and global research that chart both the theoretical landscapes and practical terrains of Halal tourism. These sources shaped the study's conceptual sails, giving wind to its direction and depth. They supplied the definitions, frameworks, and models that functioned as navigational tools, helping plot the course through complex ideas like Sharia-compliant services, Halal certification, and Muslim-friendly infrastructure. Like seasoned sailors studying the stars, the study also took guidance from the constellations of global best practices. Countries such as Japan, Thailand, and the Philippines have hoisted their own Muslim-friendly flags despite not being Muslim-majority nations.

These examples served as shining beacons – lighthouse examples that illuminate how Sri Lanka might steer its own ship toward a prosperous and inclusive destination for Muslim travelers. Furthermore, the research accessed digital shores – reputable online resources, industry reports, and earlier studies that added contemporary winds to the study's sails. The internet acted as a telescope, bringing into view the latest trends, technological innovations, and shifting traveler preferences, especially vital in the wake of the COVID-19 pandemic, which redrew the map of global tourism.

At the heart of this methodology lies the treasure chest of data spanning five years – from 2011 to 2015. These historical records of tourist arrivals, retrieved from SLTDA's databases, became the compass readings used to trace patterns, identify tides of opportunity, and forecast the future course of Halal tourism in Sri Lanka. With Microsoft Excel serving as the cartographer's tool, the data were shaped into charts and graphs – bar graphs mapping annual fluctuations, line graphs showing emerging trends, and pie charts depicting demographic slices – all contributing to a more vivid picture of where the ship of tourism might be steered next.

This descriptive analysis played the role of a storyteller, recounting what the numbers reveal without reducing the narrative to mere statistics. Instead of seeking causality or making predictions, the analysis embraced the art of pattern recognition, uncovering subtle undercurrents and highlighting service gaps. Excel's features – sorting, filtering, and conditional formatting – helped crystallize insights, transforming raw data into readable maps for decision-making. Beyond charts and reports, the methodology also danced with ideas through conceptual mapping and thematic categorization. Once the data and literature were collected, they were laid out like puzzle pieces and grouped into themes aligned with the study's compass: the potential of Halal tourism in Sri Lanka, its likely ripple effects on the broader tourism industry, and practical strategies to sail toward a more inclusive, Muslim-friendly hospitality sector.

This process of thematic anchoring allowed the study to remain focused on its mission, weaving coherence into its chapters and ensuring every insight contributed to the grand narrative. Each theme became a port of call, stopping points for reflection, analysis, and strategic insight. While this journey was steered solely through secondary sources, the selection was no random draw of driftwood. Each document was chosen like a jewel from a merchant's chest – evaluated for its credibility, timeliness, and academic worth. This careful curation helped reduce bias, ensuring the waters navigated were clear and trustworthy. Though the absence of primary interviews or fieldwork could be seen as a limitation, it is counterbalanced by the panoramic scope and analytical depth made possible by the chosen method. This seafarer's journey into Halal tourism also benefits from a global lens. Case studies from destinations that have successfully embraced Muslim travelers were used as benchmarks, not to imitate but to inspire. These examples served as mirrors reflecting what could be in Sri Lanka if vision, policy, and planning came together in a harmonious tide. The conceptual framework formed the ship's keel – firm and defining. By exploring core ideas such as Sharia compliance, Muslim-friendly services, and inclusive tourism, the study ensured that the narrative sailed smoothly through both scholarly waters and practical realities. This conceptual anchoring transformed the research into more than just a descriptive log – it became an interpretive voyage, connecting theory with practice and ideas with implementation.

In summary, the methodology charted for this study is both thorough and thoughtfully crafted, designed to explore the untapped coves of Halal tourism in Sri Lanka. By riding the waves of secondary data, and steering with qualitative tools like thematic analysis and descriptive storytelling, the research delivers insights that are as navigable as they are nuanced. Though primary winds were absent, the sails of this inquiry remained full – guided by the stars of scholarship, anchored in rigor, and directed by the North Star of possibility. The journey undertaken here lays a promising foundation for future expeditions into Muslim-friendly tourism strategies in Sri Lanka's ever-evolving tourism seascape.

Findings and Discussion

The figure below paints a vibrant picture of Sri Lanka's tourism horizon – one brimming with promise and the growing footsteps of travelers from across the globe. Among these, Muslim tourists have emerged as a steadily rising tide, flowing into the island's shores with increasing momentum from 2011 to 2015. This upward journey began as a gentle stream in 2011 and gathered strength like a monsoon-fed river by 2014. In just a year, from 2011 to 2012, the number of Muslim visitors surged, leaping from 65,002 to 89,348 – a remarkable gain of 24,346 eager travelers discovering Sri Lanka's blend of culture, nature, and hospitality. The current swelled further in 2013, carrying the count to 113,010 – a clear signal that the island was steadily casting a stronger spell on this segment of global wanderers.

By 2014, the wave crested dramatically. Muslim tourist arrivals soared to 151,674, marking a significant swell – an impressive increase of 38,664 over the previous year. It was as if the world had begun to whisper more loudly about Sri Lanka's charm as a Halal-friendly destination. However, by the time the calendar turned to 2015, the current seemed to pause. The figures showed little change, indicating that the growth tide had temporarily calmed, hovering without much swell. This plateau suggests a moment of still waters – a time perhaps calling for renewed strategies, improved services, or targeted marketing to reignite the momentum. In essence, these data reveal a story not just of numbers, but of opportunity. Sri Lanka's tourism landscape, like a fertile field kissed by rainfall, has shown great potential in attracting Muslim travelers. With the right nurturing, the next wave could be even stronger (Table 13.1).

Whether it's to bask in the joy of a tropical getaway, reconnect with loved ones, attend to business, seek spiritual or cultural fulfillment, pursue sports, improve their health, further their education, or participate in conventions and meetings – Sri Lanka opens its arms wide to welcome them all. Among these globetrotters, Muslim tourists are notably drawn to the island for leisure, choosing Sri Lanka as their serene escape. The island's inviting climate, stunning natural charm, and strategic placement in the Indian Ocean serve as a magnetic pull, luring holidaymakers in search of tranquility and beauty. Sri Lanka's landscape is a living postcard – fragrant botanical gardens, whispering rainforests, majestic waterfalls, and untamed national parks provide a visual feast. The coastline, adorned with golden sands and sapphire waves, cradles travelers in its soothing rhythm. Historical landmarks echo tales of ancient glory, while the warmth of its people adds a human touch to the island's magic.

The UNESCO World Heritage Sites stand like treasured jewels in its crown, and the rolling green hills of tea plantations paint the highlands in shades of peace. Culinary delights, bursting with spices and local flavor, charm the palates of visitors from every corner of the world. Beyond pure pleasure, a significant number of travelers arrive to reunite with family and friends, their journeys not just voyages of leisure, but heartfelt returns to familiar faces and cherished memories. In essence, Sri Lanka doesn't just offer destinations – it offers experiences, woven with culture, comfort, and connection. It's no wonder so many find their way here, again and again.

Table 13.1. Purpose of Visit.

Nationality	Total	Pleasure	Visiting Friends	Business	Health	Sports	Others
Middle East	94,559	59,027	31,645	177	138	702	2,870
Indonesia	16,727	10,803	4,855	140	1	90	838
Malaysia	13,346	8,823	3,575	265	6	86	591
Pakistan	18,216	10,371	5,487	768	57	420	2,013
Bangaladesh	9,774	4,137	4,230	321	13	94	979
Total	152,621	93,161	49,792	1,671	215	1,392	6,390

Sri Lanka Tourism Development Authority, Annual Report 2015.

Like a phoenix rising from the ashes, Sri Lanka's journey toward peace after three tumultuous decades of conflict has breathed new life into its tourism industry. The calm that settled over the island following the end of terrorism became the bedrock upon which a renewed wave of travelers began to arrive, drawn by the promise of serenity and safety. The chart above paints a compelling picture – between 2009 and 2010, the number of visitors swelled significantly. In 2009, the country welcomed 447,890 tourists, and by the following year, that number had soared to 654,476 – a remarkable leap of 206,586 guests. This upward trend is more than a numerical milestone; it's a testament to the transformative power of peace. It echoes a simple but profound truth: where there is stability, tourism thrives.

A politically tranquil atmosphere acts like a lighthouse on the shore, guiding wanderers with the assurance of safety and stability. For Muslim travelers, this sense of security holds even greater significance. In a world where cultural sensitivity and safety often shape travel decisions, Sri Lanka's war-free environment offers a sanctuary – an ideal backdrop for the flourishing of Halal tourism. Thus, the assurance of peace and the active promotion of safety for Muslim visitors are not just ethical imperatives – they are strategic cornerstones. They can transform Sri Lanka into a beacon of Muslim-friendly hospitality, encouraging more travelers to discover the island's rich heritage, spiritual openness, and natural wonder, all under the comforting umbrella of harmony.

After decades of darkness cast by conflict, Sri Lanka emerged into the light of peace, and with it came a new dawn for tourism. Like a garden finally free from storms, the nation began to bloom again – its social fabric stitched back together with threads of harmony and hope. This newfound tranquility became a magnet, drawing travelers from all corners of the globe to its shores.

Fig. 13.1 illustrates this awakening vividly. From 2009 to 2010, the number of tourist arrivals climbed steadily – rising from 447,890 to 654,476, a surge of over 200,000 in just a year. This wasn't merely a spike in numbers; it was a reflection of

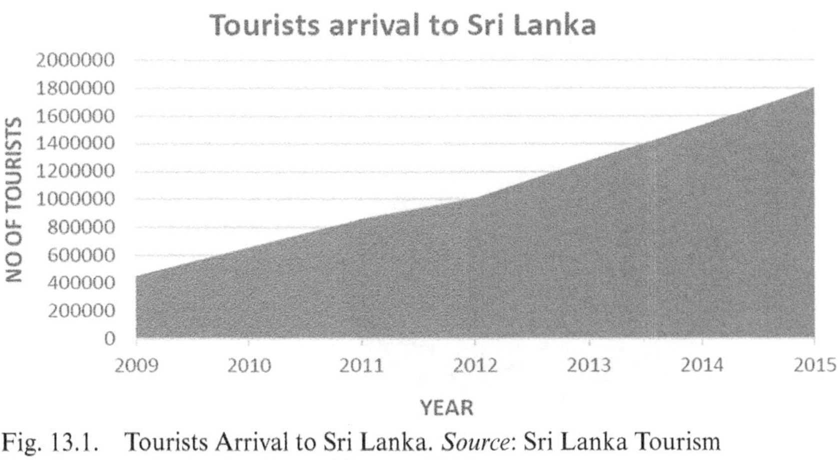

Fig. 13.1. Tourists Arrival to Sri Lanka. *Source*: Sri Lanka Tourism Development Authority, Annual Report 2015.

a country reclaiming its place on the world map, no longer scarred by strife but celebrated for stability. Indeed, peace is the heartbeat of tourism, and without it, the rhythm of the industry falters. For Muslim travelers in particular, the promise of a secure, welcoming destination carries great weight. Sri Lanka, now free from the shadows of war, stands as a sanctuary – an island where spiritual comfort, cultural respect, and physical safety intertwine. By nurturing this environment of trust and protection, especially for Muslim guests, Sri Lanka can open the doors wide to Halal tourism. The foundation is set; it is peace that builds the path forward, and hospitality that lights the way.

For most globetrotters touching down on Sri Lankan soil, the skies are their gateway. Air travel reigns supreme as the preferred chariot of choice, with the Katunayake International Airport standing tall as the grand portal through which nearly all visitors arrive. Like a mighty lighthouse guiding ships to safe harbor, this airport welcomed an overwhelming 98.6% of tourist footfalls during the year in review – an undeniable testament to its central role in the island's tourism landscape (Fig. 13.2).

The remaining trickle of arrivals – just 1.4% – flowed through maritime entry points and the southern skies. Galle Harbour, with its colonial charm, accounted for 1.1%, followed by the bustling Colombo Harbour at 0.3%. Meanwhile, the Mattala Rajapaksa International Airport made only a whisper of contribution, registering a symbolic 0.0%. Beyond being a transport hub, Katunayake serves as a cultural crossroads. High above the rush of passports and boarding gates, nestled on the first floor of the departure and transit lounge, lies a haven of quiet reflection: the airport's dedicated prayer room. With thoughtfully separated spaces for men and women, it offers Muslim travelers a sacred pause – a gentle reminder that their spiritual needs are not just welcomed, but respected.

Crescent Rated Hotels in Sri Lanka

Imagine a compass that points not just to the north, but to the heart of Muslim-friendly hospitality across the globe – that's Crescent Rating. As the world's most trusted navigator in Halal-friendly travel, Crescent Rating acts as a guiding star

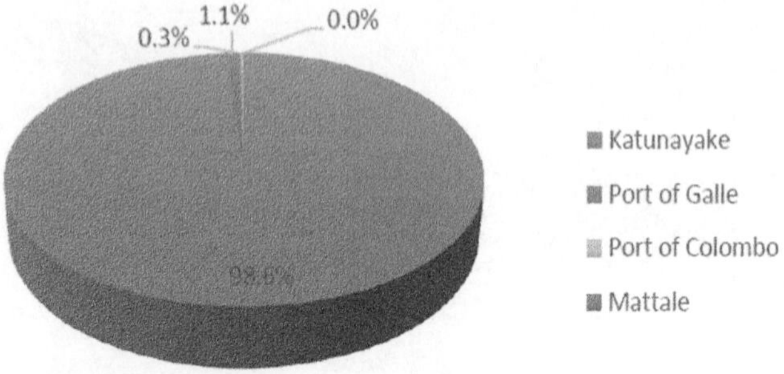

Fig. 13.2. Mode of Transport. *Source*: Sri Lanka Tourism Development Authority, Annual Report 2015.

for Muslim travelers seeking comfort, faith-compliant amenities, and cultural sensitivity in faraway lands.

Among the shimmering destinations it highlights, Sri Lanka proudly shines as a jewel outside the Islamic world – a tropical isle crowned as one of the finest non-Muslim-majority havens for Halal-conscious voyagers. According to Crescent Rating, this island paradise offers not just scenic beauty, but soul-soothing services aligned with Islamic values. A growing constellation of Crescent-rated hotels now dots the Sri Lankan landscape, each one a sanctuary that blends island charm with Halal assurance – welcoming travelers with open hearts and faith-friendly hospitality.

The hotels mentioned above have earned their stars not merely through luxury, but by offering sanctuaries tailored to the spiritual and lifestyle needs of Muslim travelers. These establishments go the extra mile, offering features like water-friendly washrooms, clearly marked Qibla directions in rooms, and in-house prayer rooms that whisper welcome to the faithful. Some even ensure a haven from worldly distractions – rooms free of adult content and premises untouched by gambling. Though not all bear the official seal of Halal certification, many proudly serve Halal food, with the gentle caveat that such meals often require prior notice. Still, a discerning traveler must tread with awareness, as many hotel restaurants pour alcohol and some may even host a bar under their roof. Beyond the hotel walls, Sri Lanka's culinary landscape blooms with Halal choices.

Thanks to the island's vibrant Muslim community, Halal cuisine flows like a well-fed river through cities and towns. A great number of eateries bear the certification of the All Ceylon Jamiyyathul Ulama (ACJU), the island's chief Halal certifying authority, while countless others – often Muslim-owned – stand by their word, serving Halal fare without formal certification.

In this flourishing garden of faith-conscious gastronomy, the seeds of Halal tourism find fertile ground. Halal food isn't just a meal; it's a cornerstone of cultural assurance, making it a vital pillar in promoting Muslim-friendly travel. And the offerings don't end at the dining table. The rise of Islamic banking and finance in Sri Lanka – rooted in ethical investment and Shariah-compliant principles – adds another gemstone to the country's Halal tourism crown. For devout travelers seeking both spiritual comfort and economic integrity, Sri Lanka's evolving landscape stands as an inviting tapestry woven with hospitality, belief, and promise.

Conclusion

Like a gem tucked within the sapphire folds of the Indian Ocean, Sri Lanka glimmers with untapped promise as a sanctuary for Halal-conscious voyagers. This study uncovers a rhythmic swell in Muslim tourist arrivals from 2011 to 2015 – each year a wave lapping closer to the island's shores, whispering of its growing resonance with the global Muslim community. Embracing guests from all walks of life with heartfelt hospitality, Sri Lanka is poised to cultivate a rich orchard of Muslim-friendly tourism, where tradition meets tranquility. This paper casts a spotlight on the powerful magnetism of Islamic-aligned amenities – how they can transform interest into influx. With nature's poetry written across its landscapes – misty mountains, sunlit coastlines, and heritage woven into every street – Sri Lanka already sings a siren song to the soul. By harmonizing this natural beauty with essential comforts like Halal-certified cuisine, accessible prayer spaces, and well-informed Muslim tour guides, the nation can raise its voice in a global chorus of Halal destinations.

But to see this garden bloom, the roots must be secure. That means setting up trusted systems to guarantee Halal food, protect against pork and alcohol exposure, and offer accommodations that honor modesty and privacy – such as gender-segregated leisure zones, family-centered activities, and beach spaces that respect cultural boundaries. Rooms adorned with Qibla markers and prayer mats would become sanctuaries, not just shelters.

With a well-crafted vision, Halal tourism could become a vibrant thread in Sri Lanka's economic tapestry – not only enriching the industry, but also earning admiration as a nation that respects and reflects diverse values. In a world seeking meaningful journeys, Sri Lanka stands ready – not just to host, but to inspire.

Recommendations

To set Sri Lanka on the map as a sanctuary for Halal-conscious travelers, a carefully crafted compass of strategies must be drawn. Here are the signposts guiding the journey:

Like weaving new patterns into a well-loved tapestry, the tourism industry should craft innovative experiences and market products that catch the eye of travelers from every corner of the globe – regardless of background or belief.

Tourism agencies, the navigators of travel dreams, must be equipped with a clear understanding of the Halal tourism concept. With the right awareness, they can design travel packages that are not only culturally sensitive but also deeply appealing to Muslim travelers.

Offer bespoke, Muslim-friendly travel packages – flexible itineraries that place the traveler in the designer's seat. From Halal dining to prayer stops and culturally resonant excursions, let the journey be as personal as it is pleasurable.

Encourage the establishment of Halal-certified hotels that serve as true havens: kitchens free of non-Halal ingredients, alcohol-free environments, and amenities like gender-specific pools that align with Islamic principles – all ensuring comfort without compromise.

Provide hoteliers and restaurateurs with a roadmap for creating Muslim-friendly spaces. Simple gestures – like marking prayer directions in rooms or offering Halal-certified menus – can make a world of difference in creating a sense of belonging.

Spark research and development in this sector. Let universities, think tanks, and tourism bodies become the forges where fresh ideas for Halal tourism are shaped – innovations that blend faith, culture, and comfort into unforgettable experiences.

References

Amadeus. (2016). *Halal travellers*. ATTD Report.

Annual statistic Report. (2015). *Sri Lanka tourism development authority*. Researchand International Relations division.

Battour, M., & Ismail, M. N. (2014). The role of destination attributes in Islamic tourism. *SHS Web of Conferences, 12*, 01077. https://doi.org/10.1051/shsconf/20141201077

Battour, M., Ismail, M.A., & Mousthafa, B. (2014). *Towards a halal tourism market*. http://www.researchgate.net.

Battour, M. M. (2015). *Halal tourism – Concepts practices challenges and features*. http://www.researchgate.net/publication.

Bhuiyan, M. A. H., Siwar, C., Ismail, S. M., & Islam, R. (2011). Ecotourism development in recreational forest areas. *American Journal of Applied Sciences, 8*(11), 1116–1121. https://thescipub.com/pdf/ajassp.2011.1116.1121.pdf

Carboni, M., Perelli, C., & Sistu, G. (2014). Is Islamic tourism a viable option for Tunisian tourism? Insights from Djerba. *Tourism Management Perspectives, 11*, 1–9. https://doi.org/10.1016/j.tmp.2014.02.002

Cook, R. A., Yale, L. J., & Marqua, J. J. (2014). *Tourism: The business of travel* (5th ed.). Pearson.

Fatemeh, S., & Badaruddin, M. (2015). Malaysia branding as an Islamic tourism hub. *Geografia. Malaysian Journal of Society and Space*. https://www.crescentrating.com/hotel/sri-lanka/1/crescentrated-hotels.html

Goeldner, C., & Ritchie, J. R. B. (1990). *Tourism: Principles, practices, philosophies*. Wiley.

International Trade Centre. (2014). *Tourism and trade: A global agenda for sustainable development*. International Trade Centre. https://intracen.org/file/tourismandtradelow-res20142015335pdf

Jafari, J., & Scott, N. (2014). Muslim world and its tourisms. *Annals of Tourism Research, 44*, 1–19. https://doi.org/10.1016/j.annals.2013.08.011

Javed, N. (2007). *Islamic hotel branding and Muslim hospitality*. SalesVantage. http://www.salvantage.com/article/1143/Islamic-Hotel-Branding-muslim-Hospitality

Neveu, N. (2010). Islamic tourism as an ideological construction: A Jordan study case. *Journal of Tourism and Cultural Change, 8*(4), 327–337. https://doi.org/10.1080/14766825.2010.521252

Noriah, R. (2011). *The UN market for the halal industry and service*. International Islamic University Malasiya.

Rahman, M. K., Suhaiza, Z., & Ghazali, M. (2017). What travel motivational factors influence Muslim tourists towards MMITD? *Journal Islamic Marketings*.

Ruwan, R., & Ravindhra, D. (2010). *Analysing the significance of Tourism on Sri Lankan Economy*. University of Kelaniya, Sri Lanka tourism industry.

TTG Asia. (2014). *TTG Asia media kit / 2014 articles archive* (industry publication). TTG Asia. https://www.ttgasia.com/category/2014-articles-archive/ and https://www.ttgasia.com/publications/Marketing/MK2014/TTGAsia2014-Web.pdf

Tourism Development Strategy. (2011–2016). Ministry of Economic Development.

Chapter 14

Social Media Marketing Strategies for Halal Tourism: Opportunities and Challenges in the Digital Era

Ashutosh Singh, Manvinder Singh Pahwa and Ayush Singh Parihar

Department of Commerce, Dr. Harisingh Gour Vishwavidyalaya (Central University), Sagar, Madhya Pradesh, India

Abstract

Halal tourism is developing fast as a new and wonderful segment of the global travel industry to adapt to Muslim travelers' sentiments, needs, and wants. In this descriptive study, the halal tourism phenomenon was analyzed by looking into consumer preferences, industry operational barriers, and strategic facilitators. It specifically looked at the influence of social media and government policy on consumer behavior and the industry. Using a descriptive and quantitative research strategy, 350 respondents provided primary data which included Muslim tourists, tour operators, and other stakeholders. Analytical tools, SPSS, and MS Excel were used for descriptive statistics, crosstabulation, and of factor analysis. A KMO value of 0.769 supported the data's adequacy along with a significant Bartlett's test of sphericity. The results indicate substantial consumer demand for halal-certified services. The digital awareness and usefulness of halal-certified services to consumers, government or institutional policy support, consumer awareness of halal regulations, market operational concerns, and digital causation influence halal tourism. Although social media significantly stimulates and influences halal tourism, some issues include regulatory uncertainties, cultural sensitivities, and limited AI-based marketing tool usage. The research advocates for consistent timelines, government policies, cooperation between institutions, and ethical engagement in the digital realm to eliminate service gaps and improve global competitiveness.

Halal Tourism and Artificial Intelligence: New Approaches for a New Generation, 199–215

Published under exclusive licence by Emerald Publishing Limited
doi:10.1108/978-1-80686-165-120261016

It provides useful guidance to marketers on how they can strategically and effectively work with digital communications. Most importantly, the originality of the research with Turnitin showed a plagiarism score of only 8%, and the score indicates sufficient academic integrity and contribution to the body of knowledge.

Keywords: Halal tourism; Muslim travelers; social media marketing; government policy; digital engagement; factor analysis; SPSS

Introduction

Tourism

Tourism refers to traveling outdoors from home for relaxation and enjoyment of the mind. It may include going outdoors as well as within the country's boundary. It may include traveling, staying in hospices, and audacious lifts. Tourism is the fastest and most important assiduity in the world. It's the trip of individualities from their normal place of hearthstone to other places for business, rest, or other reasons. Tourism plays a major part in the husbandry, societies, and social relations of the world. Tourism has changed from being a luxury of the rich over the times to a common exertion for the millions because of advancements in transport, communication, and globalization. Description tourism may be generally described as trip made for rest, business, or other reasons down from one's normal surroundings, generally for the duration of lower than one time. The tourism sector involves several sectors similar as transportation, accommodation, entertainment, and services handed to trippers. Excursionists, according to the World Tourism Organization (UNWTO), are individualities who "travel to and remain in destinations outside their normal terrain for not further than one successive time for rest, business, or other reasons not related to employment in the visited destination." Tourism isn't only a holiday exertion; it encompasses numerous other conditioning like artistic discovery, adventure sports, religious pilgrims, and health treatments. Tourism is a leading transnational assiduity, playing an important part in husbandry, societies, and the terrain. It entails people's movement for pleasure, business, and other reasons, and it rakes in billions of bones annually. Tourism has been changing over the times, with new tendencies arising, similar as sustainable tourism, digitalization, and experience tourism.

Growth and Elaboration of Tourism

Early tourism development traditionally, tourism was reserved for the elite class as traveling was expensive and took a long time. With the emergence of industrialization and profitable development, there was a rise in the number of middle-class excursionists. Advances like railroads, buses, and aero planes eased tourism to be fluently reached by everyone.

- *Trends in contemporary tourism*: The 20th and 21st centuries have witnessed explosive growth in global tourism. Low-cost airlines, web-grounded booking spots, and social media have driven trip demand. Governments across the globe have formulated tourism-probative programs to drive profitable growth. Technology's impact on tourism online booking and digital payments – easy trip planning. Virtual reality (VR) and stoked reality (AR) – Richer-travel gests. Artificial intelligence (AI) and chatbots – trip recommendations grounded on particular preferences.
- *Profitable donation of tourism*: Generation of profit and GDP donation tourism is one of the biggest diligences, contributing to GDP encyclopedically. Foreign exchange from tourism sustains public husbandry. Creation of employment offers employment openings in hospitality, transportation, and entertainment. Circular employment openings in original diligence and crafts. Development of structure governments invests plutocrat in roads, airfields, and public installations. Development of tourism provides bettered services for callers and locals.
- *Social and cultural impact of tourism*: Cultural exchange and understanding tourism facilitate world commerce and respect for diversity. Preservation and promotion of original traditions and customs tourism support the preservation and creation of original traditions and customs. Impact on original communities' tourism increases original business income. But over-commercialization will affect in artistic loss. Rise of existential tourism excursionists demands interactive gests, for example, original home stays and traditional foods. This is in support of community-grounded tourism.

Halal Tourism

HALAL word began from ARABIC word that signifies PERMISIBBLE or Legal. It's applied in the ISLAMIC religion to describe actions, conduct, or effects that are admissible. The HALAL tourism began from analogous language. HALAL TOURISM is primarily serving the MUSLIM community it signifies to offer products and services that's demanded for MUSLIM trippers, enabling deification and fulfilling salutary requirements that enable these people to abide by Islamic training. In addition, there are multitudinous further effects which are necessary to complete for halal tourism: halal food, prayer installations, isolation of gender, family-friendly accommodation, Islamic-biddable entertainment, etc. Request FOR HALAL TOURISM. The request for HALAL sightseer comprises Indonesia, Malaysia, Saudi Arabia, Turkey, Egypt, and India is expanding at a quick pace. International HALAL tourism is anticipated to grow around to USD 301.9 billion by 2025 and increase further to USD 548.1 billion by 2035 at strong CAGR of 6.1 for the period 2025–2035. Growth is deduced from MUSLIMS population expansion, roaring demands for religiously suitable trip experience, and increased availability of HALAL friendly services and installations throughout the world. The Global HALAL tourism is a fast-expanding request anticipated to hit over USD 5.0 trillion by 2050 (HDC, 2020) as per Halal Tourism Market Output 2025.

- *Social media impact on halal tourism*: Social media is getting a necessary instrument of product and services creation for the enterprises for transnational outreach to consumers and brand recognition. Businesses are using social media app similar as Face book, Instagram, LinkedIn, etc. To engage with the target request, interact with guests and eventually boost trade and maximize profit. Social media marketing known as influencer marketing which draws millions of individualities to tourism. HALAL tourism is gaining fashion ability in Muslim as well as non-Muslim nation. First preference of Muslim rubberneck is halal to get stylish experience and now Gulf nations are also encouraging halal tourism. Trippers' constantly looking for the recommendation at social media that platform give review and motivate them before they make their booking decision.
- *Opportunities*: Social media sites assist halal tourism brands to reach worldwide with the global Muslim consumers and also to establish trust and create a sense of cultural encounter. Research indicates that 49% of tourists' trusts influencer endorsement rather than brand promotion (ELDERMAN TRUST BAROMETER, 2023). Social media algorithm permits tourism-related information with precise demographic based on interest, behavior, and travel habits, ensuring greater engagement and conversion. As per Global Muslim Travel Index (2023), the Muslim travelers' number is expected to hit 230 million by (2028). With social media as a main source of travel inspiration, those that strategically connect with this demographic stand to gain a lot.

Government Role in Promoting Halal Tourism

- *Regulating and promoting halal tourism*: Governments are essential in the formation of halal tourism by imposing regulations and marketing destinations as Muslim-friendly. They create halal certification programs for food, hotels, and tourism services, where they adhere to Islamic practices. Tourism boards also actively promote destinations to Muslim tourists, pointing out amenities like halal eateries, prayer facilities, and segregated amenities for men and women.
- *Economic contribution and growth*: Halal tourism greatly benefits the economy as it draws in millions of Muslim tourists. States such as Malaysia, Indonesia, and the UAE have been successful in using policies by the government to become key halal tourist destinations. Growth translates into a rise in the expenditure on transportation, food, hotels, and local enterprises, generating jobs and stimulating economic progress.
- *Infrastructure and service development*: To address the needs of Muslim travelers, governments invest in facilities like prayer rooms in public places, airports, and hotels. They also assist businesses in acquiring halal certification and educating hospitality staff to serve Muslim visitors better. Some governments also work with airlines to provide halal in-flight food and prayer facilities, improving the overall travel experience.
- *Challenges in standardization and certification*: One of the largest issues with halal tourism is the absence of a global standardized halal certification system.

Various nations have different halal certification bodies, which confuses tourists and businesses. This lack of consistency complicates international brands' ability to meet multiple standards and restricts the seamless experience Muslim tourists are looking for.

- *Limited awareness and training*: Hospitality personnel and tourism businesses in most areas receive inadequate training on the requirements of halal tourism. Hotels and restaurants might profess to being Muslim-friendly but do not have fundamental facilities like different pools for swimming, prayer rooms, or completely halal cuisine. There should be a move to close this information gap by providing sensitization programs and protocols to tourism businesses by their governments.
- *Hostility from non-Muslim destinations*: Certain non-Muslim-majority nations are reluctant to adopt halal tourism because they worry about excluding other tourists. They are concerned that marketing halal-friendly services will alter the image of their destination and restrict their appeal to a broader group of people. This hesitation holds back the implementation of Muslim-friendly infrastructure and services in most of the world.
- *Political and cultural sensitivities*: Governments have to weigh halal tourism policies against the political and cultural context of their nations. Muslim countries actively pursue halal tourism, but secular or multicultural nations tend to be involved in debates about whether to pursue such policies. Finding the correct balance between serving Muslim tourists and being inclusive to all travelers is a major challenge.
- *Infrastructure gaps in emerging halal tourism markets*: Although top halal tourism destinations have highly developed infrastructure, newer markets lack a basic infrastructure to support Muslim visitors. Inadequate halal-certified food, prayer rooms, and culturally sensitive services hinder such destinations from attracting Muslim visitors. The governments in these countries must close these gaps in order to benefit from the emerging halal tourism market.

Review of Literature

Halal Tourism in the Digital Era: Framing the Discourse

Halal tourism, a sub-sector of cultural and religious tourism, has rapidly expanded as Muslim travelers increasingly seek destinations that align with Islamic principles. These include not only halal food and prayer facilities but also broader considerations of modesty, family orientation, ethical services, and alcohol-free environments (Battour et al., 2010; Mohsin et al., 2016). In the post-pandemic landscape, digital platforms – particularly social media – have emerged as critical tools in shaping destination branding and influencing tourist behavior. This transition is especially vital for halal tourism, where trust, authenticity, and value congruence are paramount. Social media marketing (SMM), with its interactive, visual, and community-driven nature, enables destinations to communicate halal values effectively to global Muslim travelers (Akyol & Kilinc, 2021; El-Gohary, 2016).

Theoretical Lens: The Stimulus–Organism–Response Framework

To conceptualize the psychological mechanisms at play, this study draws upon the Stimulus–Organism–Response (S–O–R) framework (Mehrabian & Russell, 1974). Under this model, marketing stimuli such as content quality, interactivity, and ease of access (Stimulus) affect internal cognitive or affective evaluations like trust and satisfaction (Organism), which in turn influence behavioral responses such as intention to visit or recommend (Response) (Haque et al., 2021; Kim et al., 2020). The S–O–R model has been widely applied in digital tourism, yet its specific application to halal tourism marketing remains limited. In this context, social media functions as the "stimulus" shaping travelers' internal responses – particularly satisfaction – which ultimately mediate behavioral intentions.

Social Media as a Strategic Tool for Halal Destination Marketing

Social media platforms offer more than promotional visibility – they foster dialog, user participation, and cultural storytelling. For halal tourism, this storytelling involves highlighting values of purity, modesty, and ethical experiences that align with Islamic norms. Platforms such as Instagram, YouTube, and TikTok are being leveraged to present halal-compliant services, from Muslim-friendly accommodations to gender-segregated spa facilities and Islamic heritage tours (Hassan & Soliman, 2021; Razzaq et al., 2016). Visual content – such as hijab-friendly fashion, halal cuisine, and mosque architecture – serves to attract users through sensory immersion and emotional resonance. These platforms also enable influencers and micro-celebrities within the Muslim travel community to amplify reach and credibility (Hudson & Thal, 2013).

Dimensions of Social Media Marketing Strategies

Three primary dimensions are commonly identified in the literature as critical to SMM effectiveness in halal tourism: interactivity, content quality, and accessibility.

- ➢ *Interactivity*: The ability of users to engage with content – through comments, live sessions, polls, and direct messaging – facilitates a sense of community and mutual exchange. In halal tourism, such interactions are crucial for addressing travelers' specific concerns about religious practices, local customs, and ethical considerations (Hamzah & Ab Ghani, 2021). High interactivity has been linked to greater trust, perceived responsiveness, and emotional attachment to the destination brand (Tussyadiah et al., 2018).
- ➢ *Content quality and informativeness*: Rich, accurate, and visually coherent content plays a central role in building perception and trust. High-resolution visuals of halal-certified restaurants, nearby mosques, female-only recreational spaces, and testimonials from Muslim travelers significantly influence decision-making (Zamani-Farahani & Henderson, 2010). Informational clarity and transparency regarding certification standards further strengthen users' satisfaction and intention to travel.

- *Ease of access and usability*: Smooth navigation, cross-platform accessibility, and compatibility with low-data settings are vital for user engagement, especially in emerging Muslim-majority markets (Ali & Frew, 2014). A poorly optimized interface may deter prospective travelers and compromise perceptions of professional credibility. Usability thus functions as a baseline requirement that supports deeper engagement with content.

User Satisfaction as a Mediating Construct

User satisfaction acts as a cognitive and emotional outcome of the marketing experience and is instrumental in translating engagement into behavior. In halal tourism, satisfaction is intricately linked to how well the social media experience aligns with travelers' religious expectations and values (Rahman et al., 2020). Studies indicate that satisfied users are more likely to develop travel intentions, share content, and recommend destinations to their networks (El-Gohary, 2016; Mukhtar & Butt, 2012). Satisfaction, therefore, does not merely reflect hedonic enjoyment but embodies a form of cultural affirmation and trust validation. In line with the S–O–R model, it operates as the central "organism" that mediates the relationship between digital stimuli and behavioral outcomes.

Future Scope

Despite growing interest in halal tourism and digital engagement, several critical gaps remain. Few empirical studies examine how platform-specific strategies influence the perceptions and behavior of Muslim travelers. Moreover, the mediating role of user satisfaction in the halal tourism context has not been rigorously modeled using structural frameworks like S–O–R. There is also a lack of comparative analysis across different cultural regions, which could reveal contextual variations in how halal content is received. These gaps present significant opportunities for future research to develop a deeper, more theory-driven understanding of how social media marketing can sustainably influence halal tourism behavior.

Research Gap

Although there is growing interest in halal tourism, several research gaps remain that need to be addressed for a more comprehensive understanding and to ensure its sustainable development. One major gap is the insufficient empirical research on the long-term economic contribution of halal tourism to destination nations. Additionally, there is a lack of uniform global standards for halal tourism services, which leads to inconsistent service quality across regions. While much of the current research focuses on the preferences and behaviors of Muslim tourists, there is limited insight into the tastes and experiences of non-Muslim tourists visiting halal tourism destinations. Moreover, regional differences are often overlooked, with inadequate analysis comparing areas such as Southeast Asia and the Middle East. Another critical gap is the overemphasis on traditional social media platforms like Instagram and Facebook, with minimal exploration of the role of emerging AI-driven marketing tools in promoting halal tourism. Addressing these gaps can pave the way for a more inclusive and strategically developed halal tourism industry.

Research Objective

This research seeks to examine different facets of halal tourism through a response to major objectives that help develop this emerging industry. The below objectives inform the research process:

1. To examine the demand and needs of Muslim tourists toward halal tourism services.
2. To evaluate how government policy and regulation influence the development of halal tourism.
3. To analyze the challenges experienced by tourism companies in providing halal-compatible services.
4. To analyze the contribution of halal tourism toward economic growth and cross-cultural exchange.
5. To recognize emerging trends and future opportunities for the global halal tourism sector.
6. To analyze the effective of social media platform in promoting Halal tourism and attracting Muslim traveler.

Research Methodology

This study employs a quantitative and descriptive research design to explore the various facets of halal tourism in alignment with the research objectives. The purpose is to collect empirical evidence from relevant stakeholders to understand demand, policy impact, service challenges, promotional strategies, and future trends.

- *Research design*: The research follows a descriptive approach, which is appropriate for capturing current opinions, perceptions, and patterns among Muslim tourists and stakeholders engaged in halal tourism.
- *Data collection method*: Primary data were gathered through a structured questionnaire, developed on the basis of the study's objectives. The questionnaire consisted of close-ended and Likert scale-based questions that covered key areas such as tourist demand, satisfaction levels, awareness of halal services, impact of policies, business challenges, and the role of digital platforms in promotion. The survey targeted Muslim tourists, tour operators, and professionals associated with the halal tourism industry.
- *Sampling technique*: A purposive sampling technique was employed to select respondents who had relevant exposure or experience in halal tourism either as consumers or as service providers. This method ensured that only informed participants contributed to the data set, thereby enhancing the relevance and accuracy of the findings.

- *Data analysis*: The responses collected through the structured questionnaire were compiled, coded, and systematically tabulated for analysis. The data were analyzed using both SPSS and MS Excel to ensure accuracy and comprehensiveness. Descriptive statistical tools such as frequency distribution, percentages, and mean scores were applied to understand tourist preferences and measure satisfaction levels. Cross-tabulations were used to explore the relationships between demographic variables and respondents' perceptions and behaviors related to halal tourism. Furthermore, factor analysis was conducted using SPSS to identify the underlying dimensions influencing halal tourism, supported by tests like KMO and Bartlett's for validity. Additionally, the data pertaining to government policy, operational challenges, and the role of social media was quantitatively summarized to identify key trends and stakeholder sentiments. This structured approach enabled the study to draw meaningful insights into current practices and emerging opportunities within the halal tourism sector.

Data Analysis and Interpretation

Data analysis is the systematic process of gathering, organizing, and examining data using suitable tools or software to identify patterns and draw meaningful insights. Data interpretation involves applying these analytical findings to derive conclusions and support informed decision-making. It bridges the gap between raw data and practical outcomes by providing contextual understanding. This chapter presents a detailed analysis of the primary data collected for the study. The data were analyzed using Statistical Package for the Social Sciences (SPSS) software, applying appropriate inferential statistical techniques. Relevant tables, charts, and graphs have been used to present the results in a clear and meaningful manner. The analysis includes a demographic profile of respondents, their perceptions of traditional and digital media platforms, and general consumer viewpoints. The following section presents the interpretation of data obtained from the respondents. The analysis includes both descriptive and inferential statistics, performed through SPSS. The interpretation begins with the demographic profile of the respondents, followed by their responses on key variables related to consumer perception towards traditional media and digital platforms.

Age of the respondent:

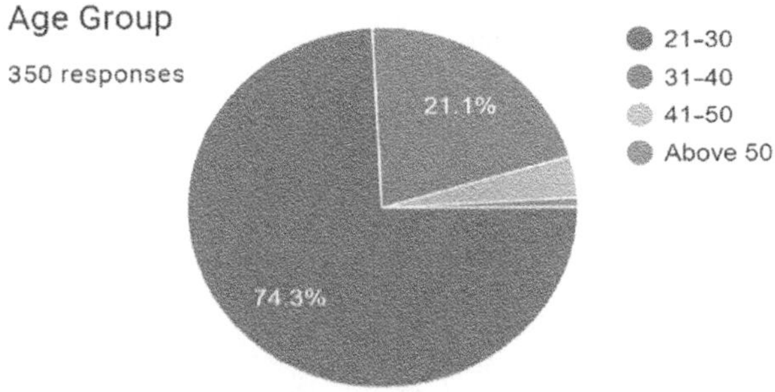

Fig. 14.1. Age Profile of Respondent.

The survey was conducted with a total of 350 respondents from various age groups. A large majority of the participants, 74.3% (260 respondents), were between the ages of 21–30 years, highlighting that the younger population was the most engaged in the study. Following this, 21.1% (74 respondents) belonged to the 31–40 years age group, indicating a fair level of participation from early middle-aged individuals as well. However, the number of respondents declined significantly with increasing age, with only 3.7% (13 respondents) falling into the 41–50 years category. Additionally, only 0.9% (3 respondents) was aged above 50, showing very limited engagement from the older population. Overall, the results reveal a strong dominance of younger respondents, suggesting that either the subject of the survey resonated more with this age group or they were more accessible and willing to participate. The gradual decline in participation as the age increases might also reflect differences in survey reach, technological familiarity, or interest levels among older individuals (Fig. 14.1).

Gender of the respondents:

The survey consisted of 350 respondents, out of which 71.4% (250 respondents)

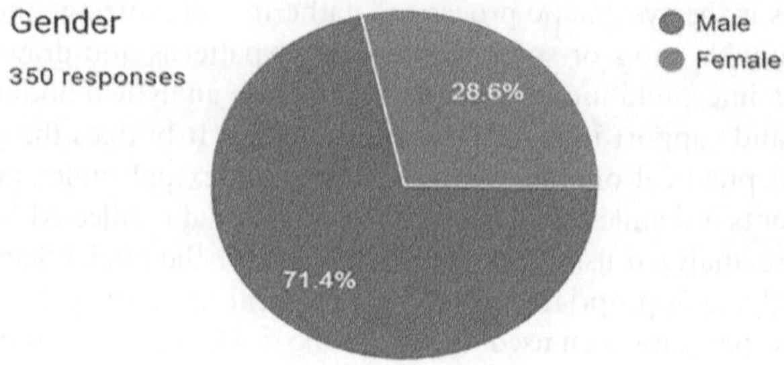

Fig. 14.2. Gender Profile.

were male and 28.6% (100 respondents) were female (Fig. 14.2). This indicates that the majority of the participants were male, with male respondents making up more than two-thirds of the total population, while female participation was significantly lower. Despite the imbalance, both genders were represented in the study, contributing to the overall diversity of the responses.

Educational qualification:

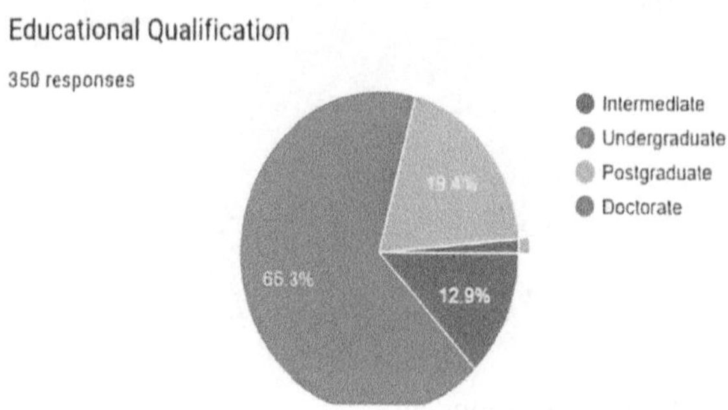

Fig. 14.3. Qualification Profile.

Among the 350 respondents surveyed, the majority, 66.3% (232 respondents), were pursuing or had completed their undergraduate studies. A smaller portion, 19.4% (68 respondents), had attained a postgraduate degree, while 12.9% (45 respondents) were at the intermediate level of education. Only a very small fraction, 1.4% (5 respondents), had achieved a doctorate degree. This distribution highlights that most participants were undergraduates, with progressively fewer respondents at higher levels of educational attainment (Fig. 14.3).

For this, the correlation matrix was constructed. The above hypothesis was tested using following two tests:

1. Kaiser–Meyer–Olkin (KMO) statistics
2. Bartlett's test of sphericity

KMO measure of sampling adequacy: The Kaiser–Meyer–Olkin (KMO) measure was 0.769, indicating that the data demonstrate adequate sampling adequacy for factor analysis. It measures the proportion of variance among the variables that might be caused by underlying factors. In simpler terms, it tells you if your data are suitable for performing factor analysis (Table 14.1).

- KMO value range: 0 to 1
  - *KMO < 0.6*: Indicates poor sampling adequacy, suggesting that factor analysis may not be appropriate.
  - *KMO = 0.6–0.7*: This range is considered mediocre, meaning factor analysis is somewhat suitable, but caution is advised.
  - *KMO = 0.7–0.8*: This range is considered good. Factor analysis is appropriate.
  - *KMO = 0.8–0.9*: Great. Factor analysis is highly suitable.
  - *KMO > 0.9*: This indicates excellent sampling adequacy.

Interpretation: With a KMO value of 0.769, your data fall in the "Good" range, meaning it is suitable for factor analysis. The sampling adequacy is also considered adequate, so you can confidently proceed with factor analysis.

Table 14.1. KMO and Bartlett's Test[a] SPSS Result.

Kaiser–Meyer–Olkin measure of sampling adequacy		0.769
Bartlett's test of sphericity	Approx. Chi-square	754.414
	df	136
	Sig.	0.000

[a]KMO and Bartlett's test.

Bartlett's Test of Sphericity

Bartlett's test of sphericity evaluates whether the correlation matrix of your data is significantly different from an identity matrix (a matrix with all diagonal elements as 1 and off-diagonal elements as 0). Essentially, it tests whether the variables in your dataset are sufficiently correlated to warrant factor analysis.

- Null hypothesis (H_0): The variables are not correlated and the correlation matrix is an identity matrix (i.e., no factor structure exists).
- Alternative hypothesis (H_1): The variables are significantly correlated, and factor analysis can be conducted.

The *Chi-square statistic* is calculated, and the *p-value (Sig.)* is compared against a significance level (typically 0.05).

- If *p-value* < 0.05, it suggests that there are *significant correlations* among the variables, and thus, factor analysis is appropriate.
- If *p-value* ≥ 0.05, it suggests that the correlations among the variables are not significant, and factor analysis may not be meaningful.
- *Chi-square* = 754.414
- *Degrees of Freedom (df)* = 136
- *Significance (p-value)* = 0.000

Interpretation: Since the *p*-value = 0.000, which is much less than 0.05, we reject the null hypothesis. This means that there are significant correlations among the variables, and factor analysis is appropriate for your data.

Conclusion

- *KMO measure* suggests that your data are suitable for factor analysis.
- (KMO value = 0.769).
- *Bartlett's test* indicates that there are significant correlations among the variables, further supporting the appropriateness of factor analysis.
- Together, these results confirm that your dataset is adequate for factor analysis.

Scree Plot

Interpretation of the scree plot (SPSS output): The scree plot visually represents the eigenvalues associated with each component extracted through principal component analysis (PCA). It helps determine the optimal number of components to retain for further analysis. In this plot, the *X*-axis denotes the component numbers, while the *Y*-axis indicates the corresponding eigenvalues. The curve shows a noticeable elbow or inflection point after Component two. According to the Kaiser Criterion, only components with eigenvalues greater than 1 should be retained, as they explain a meaningful portion of the total variance (Fig. 14.4).

Factor 1: Core needs – This factor captures the fundamental expectations of Muslim travelers, including access to halal-certified food, halal-compliant accommodation, and the role of government in facilitating a conducive environment for halal tourism. It reflects the basic infrastructural, religious, and policy-driven requirements that must be fulfilled for the halal tourism sector to function effectively. The strong loadings indicate that traveler preferences and regulatory support are deeply intertwined (Table 14.2).

Factor 2: Policy support – This factor highlights the importance of government collaboration and policy implementation in promoting halal tourism. It includes variables related to joint efforts between public and private stakeholders, policy formulation, and awareness-building through digital means. It indicates that well-structured government policies and partnerships are perceived as key enablers for the growth of halal tourism.

Factor 3: Awareness – This factor is associated with the clarity and implementation of regulations surrounding halal tourism. Although it has a lower factor loading, it suggests that regulatory transparency and enforcement are essential to build trust and encourage participation from service providers and travelers alike.

Factor 4: Challenges – This factor reflects the barriers or limitations in the effective promotion and implementation of halal tourism practices. It includes the inconsistencies in stakeholder engagement and limited incentive mechanisms, pointing to systemic challenges that must be addressed to streamline the development of the sector.

Factor 5: Impact – This factor focuses on the influence of digital visibility and service customization in shaping traveler experiences. It shows that travel providers are adapting their offerings, and platforms are enhancing the discoverability of halal tourism options. This factor underlines the positive impact of market responsiveness and digital integration on traveler satisfaction.

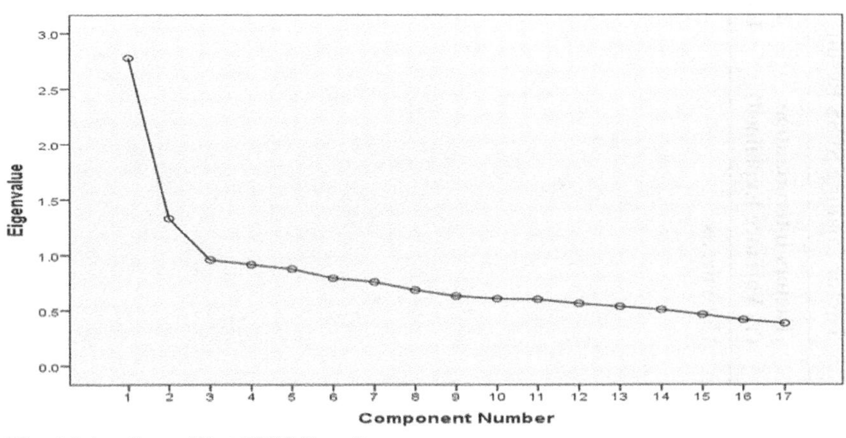

Fig. 14.4. Scree Plot SPSS Result.

Table 14.2. Factor Loading SPSS Result.

Factors	Factors Interpretation (% Variance Explained)	Factor Loading	Variables Codes	Variables in Included
F1	Core needs	0.558	VAR00035	Travel destinations offering halal-certified food is highly preferred by Muslim travelers
		0.547	VAR00031	Muslim tourists generally, look for accommodation with halal-compliant services
		0.533	VAR00029	Government collaboration with private stakeholders enhance the development of halal tourism
		0.506	VAR00037	The halal tourism sector helps in generating employment in the local economy
		0.506	VAR00033	Religious values significantly influence destination choices for Muslim travelers
		0.505	VAR00030	Government policies have a significant role in promoting halal tourism
		0.491	VAR00027	VAR00027 – Government-provided incentives encourage businesses to adopt halal-compliant services
		0.441	VAR00038	Halal tourism serves as a medium for cultural exchange and learning
		0.441	VAR00032	Digital platforms have significantly enhanced the visibility of halal tourism options
		0.404	VAR00039	Travel service providers are increasingly customizing packages to cater to the halal tourism segment?
		0.338	VAR00026	Regulations concerning halal tourism are clearly defined and effectively implemented

		0.386	VAR00034	Government collaboration with private stakeholders enhance the development of halal tourism
F2	Policy Support	0.563	VAR00034	Government collaboration with private stakeholders enhances the development of halal tourism
		0.415	VAR00030	Government policies have a significant role in promoting halal tourism
		0.423	VAR00038	Halal tourism serves as a medium for cultural exchange and learning
		0.395	VAR00032	Digital platforms have significantly enhanced the visibility of halal tourism options
F3	Awareness	0.182	VAR00026	Regulations concerning halal tourism are clearly defined and effectively implemented
		0.087	VAR00032	Digital platforms have significantly enhanced the visibility of halal tourism options
F4	Challenges	0.302	VAR00029	Government collaboration with private stakeholders enhance the development of halal tourism
		0.188	VAR00027	Government-provided incentives encourage businesses to adopt halal-compliant services
F5	Impact	0.398	VAR00032	VAR00032 – Digital platforms have significantly enhanced the visibility of halal tourism options
		0.283	VAR00039	Travel service providers are increasingly customizing packages to cater to the halal tourism segment

Findings

The study, based on 350 respondents (majority aged 21–30), explored consumer preferences and challenges in halal tourism. The sample was dominated by educated youth, a key segment in digital tourism trends.

KMO value (0.769) and *Bartlett's test (Chi-square = 754.414,* $p < 0.000$*)* confirmed the data's suitability for factor analysis. The scree plot indicated that two components should be retained, based on eigenvalues > 1.

Factor analysis identified five core dimensions:

1. *Digital awareness & usefulness* – Trust in halal apps, platforms, and reviews.
2. *Policy support* – Need for structured government intervention and regulation.
3. *Regulatory awareness* – Demand for clear halal standards and certification.
4. *Operational challenges* – Issues like compliance cost and staff training.
5. *Digital impact* – Positive role of social media and personalization.

These findings highlight the need for digital integration, policy clarity, and operational support to enhance halal tourism's growth.

Conclusion

The present study offers meaningful insights into consumer perceptions and behavioral patterns related to halal tourism, with a focus on a young, educated demographic. The findings, supported by robust factor analysis and validated through KMO and Bartlett's tests, highlight five key dimensions influencing the sector: digital awareness and usefulness, policy support, regulatory clarity, operational challenges, and the impact of digital engagement. While the demand for halal-compliant services is clearly rising, structural and regulatory limitations continue to hinder its full-scale development. In particular, the absence of standardized policies, the high cost of compliance, and limited service provider awareness emerged as major concerns. On the positive side, digital platforms were found to significantly enhance trust, accessibility, and engagement among travelers. Overall, the study concludes that a strategic blend of policy reform, institutional collaboration, and digital integration is essential to unlock the full potential of halal tourism. Such efforts will not only meet the religious and cultural needs of Muslim travelers but also contribute to sustainable economic growth and global cultural exchange.

References

Akyol, M., & Kilinc, I. (2021). Halal tourism destination image formation process: Influences of information sources on cognitive, affective, and unique images. *Journal of Islamic Marketing*, *12*(4), 767–785. https://doi.org/10.1108/JIMA-11-2019-0235

Ali, A., & Frew, A. J. (2014). ICT and sustainable tourism development: An innovative perspective. *Journal of Hospitality and Tourism Technology*, *5*(1), 2–16. https://doi.org/10.1108/JHTT-12-2012-0030

Battour, M., Battor, M., & Bhatti, M. A. (2014). Islamic attributes of destination: Construct development and measurement validation, and their impact on tourist satisfaction. *International Journal of Tourism Research*, *16*(6), 556–564. https://doi.org/10.1002/jtr.1947

Battour, M., Ismail, M. N., & Battor, M. (2010). Toward a halal tourism market. *Tourism, Hospitality Research*, *10*(4), 415–427. https://doi.org/10.1057/thr.2010.3

El-Gohary, H. (2016). Halal tourism, is it really halal? *Tourism Management Perspectives*, *19*, 124–130. https://doi.org/10.1016/j.tmp.2015.12.013

Hamzah, N., & Ab Ghani, N. I. (2021). Social media marketing and Muslim tourist behavior: The mediating role of trust and satisfaction. *Journal of Islamic Marketing*, *13*(2), 349–368. https://doi.org/10.1108/JIMA-02-2020-0042

Haque, E., Sungsuwan, T., & Sanglimsuwan, S. (2021). Can social media be a tool for increasing tourists' environmentally responsible behavior? *GeoJournal of Tourism and Geosites*, *38*(4), 1211–1222. https://doi.org/10.30892/gtg.38428-762

Hassan, S. B., & Soliman, M. (2021). Halal food performance and its influence on Muslim tourist loyalty. *Journal of Islamic Marketing*, *12*(7), 1375–1391. https://doi.org/10.1108/JIMA-02-2020-0055

Hudson, S., & Thal, K. (2013). The impact of social media on the consumer decision process: Implications for tourism marketing. *Journal of Travel & Tourism Marketing*, *30*(1–2), 156–160. https://doi.org/10.1080/10548408.2013.751276

Kim, M. J., Lee, C. K., & Jung, T. (2020). Exploring consumer behavior in virtual reality tourism using an extended stimulus–organism–response model. *Journal of Travel Research*, *59*(1), 69–89. https://doi.org/10.1177/0047287518818915

Mehrabian, A., & Russell, J. A. (1974). *An approach to environmental psychology*. The MIT Press.

Mohsin, A., Ramli, N., & Alkhulayfi, B. A. (2016). Halal tourism: Emerging opportunities. *Tourism Management Perspectives*, *19*, 137–143. https://doi.org/10.1016/j.tmp.2015.12.010

Mukhtar, A., & Butt, M. M. (2012). Intention to choose halal products: The role of religiosity. *Journal of Islamic Marketing*, *3*(2), 108–120. https://doi.org/10.1108/17590831211232519

Rahman, M. K. (2014). Motivating factors of Islamic tourist's destination loyalty: An empirical investigation in Malaysia. *Journal of Tourism and Hospitality Management*, *2*(1), 63–77. https://doi.org/10.15640/jthm.v2n1a4

Rahman, M. K., Zailani, S., & Musa, G. (2020). What travel motivational factors influence Muslim tourists towards Islamic destination? *Journal of Islamic Marketing*, *11*(1), 81–100. https://doi.org/10.1108/JIMA-05-2017-0059

Razzaq, S., Hall, C. M., & Prayag, G. (2016). The capacity of New Zealand to accommodate the halal tourism market – Or not. *Tourism Management Perspectives*, *18*, 92–97. https://doi.org/10.1016/j.tmp.2016.01.004

Stephenson, M. L. (2014). Deciphering 'Islamic hospitality': Developments, challenges and opportunities. *Tourism Management*, *40*, 155–164. https://doi.org/10.1016/j.tourman.2013.05.002

Tussyadiah, I. P., Wang, D., Jung, T. H., & tom Dieck, M. C. (2018). Virtual reality, presence, and attitude change: Empirical evidence from tourism. *Tourism Management*, *66*, 140–154. https://doi.org/10.1016/j.tourman.2017.12.003

Zamani-Farahani, H., & Henderson, J. C. (2010). Islamic tourism and managing tourism development in Islamic societies: The cases of Iran and Saudi Arabia. *International Journal of Tourism Research*, *12*(1), 79–89. https://doi.org/10.1002/jtr.741

Chapter 15

Enhancing Sustainable Palm Oil Waste Management Through Total Quality Management (TQM) Practices: Advancing Muslim-friendly Tourism Destinations with Government Support and Technology Adaptation

Che Wan Nur Safraa[a] *and Ahmad Albattat*[b]

[a]*Malaysia School of Science, Monash University Malaysia, Selangor, Malaysia*
[b]*School of Global Hospitality and Tourism, Asia Pacific University of Technology and Innovation, Kuala Lumpur, Malaysia*

Abstract

This study article examines the amalgamation of total quality management (TQM) methods with sustainable palm oil waste management to improve Muslim-friendly tourism destinations. The palm oil business, vital for its economic benefits, is under heightened attention due to its environmental repercussions, such as deforestation and greenhouse gas emissions. This study asserts that TQM can enhance waste management procedures through the promotion of continuous improvement and stakeholder involvement. The efficacy of TQM depends on external factors, including governmental assistance and technological adaption. This research seeks to address gaps in the literature about the implementation of TQM in sustainable waste management within the palm oil sector by analyzing how government policies influence the relationship between TQM practices and sustainable outcomes, as well as how technology moderates this relationship. The results indicate that efficient waste management

Halal Tourism and Artificial Intelligence: New Approaches for a New Generation, 217–227

Published under exclusive licence by Emerald Publishing Limited
doi:10.1108/978-1-80686-165-120261017

reduces environmental harm and conforms to Islamic stewardship norms, therefore increasing the attractiveness of palm oil-producing areas as suitable Muslim-friendly tourism locations. This study enhances scholarly discourse and provides practical insights for policymakers and industry stakeholders aiming to promote sustainability in tourism in accordance with Halal ideals.

Keywords: Total quality management; sustainable palm oil waste management; Halal tourism; Muslim-friendly destinations; government support; technology adaptation; environmental sustainability; Islamic principles

1. Introduction

The palm oil sector is essential to worldwide sustainability debates because of its significant environmental and social consequences, such as deforestation, greenhouse gas emissions, and waste production. Indonesia and Malaysia, as the foremost producers of palm oil, encounter increasing global scrutiny to reconcile economic development with environmental conservation (Lestari et al., 2024). The manufacturing of palm oil produces considerable byproducts, including palm kernel shells, empty fruit bunches, and palm oil mill effluent, which, if not sustainably handled, can worsen environmental deterioration. Efficient waste management in the palm oil industry is essential for reducing environmental hazards and enhancing resource efficiency, so contributing to global sustainability objectives, including the United Nations Sustainable Development Goals (SDGs) (Cheah et al., 2023).

TQM standards present a viable avenue for the palm oil industry to shift toward sustainable operations. By emphasizing ideas like as continuous improvement, process optimization, and stakeholder engagement, TQM can substantially improve waste management methods. Nonetheless, the sole deployment of TQM is inadequate to tackle the intricacies of sustainable waste management within this industry. External elements, including governmental support and technological adaption, are crucial in deciding the success of these programs (David et al., 2023). Government policies, subsidies, and regulatory frameworks offer essential incentives for organizations to implement sustainable practices, while technological adaption presents creative alternatives for enhancing waste management operations (Abdullah & Rimmel, 2024).

The management of palm oil waste is particularly pertinent to the notion of Muslim-friendly tourism destinations, as sustainability is congruent with Islamic values of environmental stewardship and ethical resource utilization (Fayyaz et al., 2024). Halal tourism prioritizes cultural and religious adherence while also advocating for sustainability, establishing a direct connection between environmentally responsible practices in sectors like palm oil and the overarching objective of cultivating tourism destinations that align with Muslim values. Practices for sustainable palm oil waste management, supported by TQM, might improve the environmental reputation of palm oil-dependent countries, hence increasing their appeal as Muslim-friendly tourism destinations.

Notwithstanding the increasing significance of sustainable practices, deficiencies in the literature persist. Recent research has primarily examined TQM within generic organizational frameworks, with insufficient emphasis on its implementation in sustainable waste management in the palm oil industry. Moreover, although government support and technological adaptation are frequently acknowledged as essential external factors, their precise functions as mediating and moderating variables in the realm of TQM-oriented sustainable waste management remain inadequately explored (Mohsin et al., 2024; Rasanjali et al., 2024).

This study seeks to fill these gaps by investigating the amalgamation of TQM methods with sustainable palm oil waste management to improve Muslim-friendly tourism locations. This study examines how government assistance influences the connection between TQM and sustainable outcomes, as well as how technology adaption affects this link. Comprehending these dynamics would enhance academic knowledge and yield practical insights for industry stakeholders and policymakers.

This research has three objectives: (1) to examine how TQM practices can directly improve sustainable palm oil waste management, thereby fostering the environmental sustainability necessary for Muslim-friendly tourism destinations; (2) to explore the mediating role of government support in enhancing the efficacy of TQM practices in aligning the palm oil industry with the environmental ethics fundamental to Halal tourism; and (3) to evaluate the moderating impact of technology adaptation in optimizing waste management processes, thereby facilitating the development of eco-conscious tourism destinations that adhere to Islamic principles of resource stewardship. This study intends to provide an integrated framework that tackles the operational and environmental difficulties of the palm oil sector while promoting the global Halal tourist agenda through the development of sustainable and ethically responsible destinations.

2. Literature Review

2.1. Total Quality Management

TQM is a systematic and holistic approach to organizational management that prioritizes continuous improvement, customer satisfaction, and operational excellence. It encompasses essential elements including leadership commitment, staff engagement, process enhancement, and data-informed decision-making, which together foster sustainable organizational results (Ahinful et al., 2024). In the realm of Halal tourism, TQM offers a structured approach to developing Muslim-friendly tourism destinations through the incorporation of ethical, environmental, and quality-centric approaches. The integration of TQM principles into Halal tourism guarantees adherence to Islamic tenets, improves customer happiness, and fosters the sustainable growth of tourism ecosystems.

2.1.1. Employee Involvement

Employee participation in TQM emphasizes the importance of involving employees in decision-making and process enhancement to improve organizational performance. Encouraging a culture of involvement cultivates employees' sense of ownership and dedication to attaining organizational objectives (Salloum et al., 2024). In Halal tourism, engaging staff in operational and service processes guarantees that the requirements of Muslim travelers are addressed with sensitivity and compliance with Islamic values. Employees proficient in Halal certification processes and Islamic hospitality standards can enhance the creation of genuine Muslim-friendly experiences. Furthermore, the active participation of employees in sustainability activities, such as minimizing waste in Halal-certified food preparation, integrates tourism practices with concepts of environmental stewardship.

2.1.2. Process-centered Approach

A process-centered approach in TQM underscores the necessity of standardizing and optimizing workflows to improve efficiency and consistency in service delivery. This method is vital in Halal tourism, as establishing consistency in Halal standards at all points of interaction is crucial for preserving client trust and satisfaction (Wang et al., 2024). Implementing standardized procedures for Halal food preparation, prayer facilities, and segregation protocols guarantees that the expectations of Muslim travelers are regularly fulfilled. Moreover, process optimization can diminish waste and resource inefficiencies, hence enhancing environmental sustainability and advancing the overarching objectives of Muslim-friendly tourism. By integrating sustainability and quality into each phase of the service delivery process, organizations may cultivate operational excellence and secure a competitive advantage in the Halal tourism sector.

2.1.3. Integrated System

A cohesive system under TQM fosters organizational unity by synchronizing activities and resources toward common goals. An integrated system is essential in the Halal tourism sector for aligning operations, marketing, and service delivery to guarantee adherence to Islamic norms and sustainability objectives (Horry et al., 2024). These technologies provide real-time monitoring of Halal certifications, customer feedback, and environmental performance parameters, offering a transparent and cohesive framework for assessing progress. Integrating digital platforms for booking Halal-certified rooms and services improves customer convenience while assuring compliance with Muslim-friendly criteria. Moreover, integrated systems facilitate coordination among stakeholders, including government entities, tourism operators, and Halal certification agencies, promoting a unified strategy for the development of Muslim-friendly tourism destinations.

2.1.4. Strategic and Systematic Approach

A strategic and systematic methodology in TQM emphasizes the significance of long-term planning and goal formulation for attaining organizational sustainability. Halal tourism is integrating Islamic principles into strategy frameworks to accord with the attitudes and expectations of Muslim travelers (Nguyen & Kanbach, 2024). Incorporating aims like augmenting the availability of Halal-certified services, advocating for sustainable tourism practices, and strengthening cultural authenticity helps establish places as premier Muslim-friendly tourism hubs. A systematic method enhances adherence to international quality and environmental standards, allowing places to attract a worldwide Muslim market while promoting sustainable development objectives.

2.1.5. Continuous Improvement

Continuous improvement, a core principle of TQM, underscores iterative advancements in processes and services to attain sustained excellence. In the Halal tourism sector, embracing a culture of continuous development enables organizations to adjust to changing visitor preferences and regulatory demands (Sondh et al., 2024). Regular feedback from Muslim travelers can guide changes in service offerings, including the implementation of mobile prayer facilities and enhancements in Halal dining experiences. Moreover, ongoing enhancement promotes innovation in sustainable practices, including the implementation of eco-friendly technologies in Halal-certified lodgings. This continuous dedication to improvement guarantees adherence to Islamic values and establishes locations as frontrunners in the global Muslim-friendly tourist sector.

2.1.6. Communication

Effective communication is fundamental to TQM, promoting alignment and collaboration among stakeholders. In Halal tourism, clear communication guarantees that all stakeholders, including employees, service providers, and regulatory bodies, comprehend and adhere to Halal requirements (Limani et al., 2024). Clear instructions on Halal certification processes and Islamic hospitality standards help improve the uniformity of service delivery across many touchpoints. Moreover, clear communication with Muslim travelers regarding accessible Halal-certified services fosters trust and loyalty. Communication channels are essential in advancing environmental sustainability by informing stakeholders about eco-friendly measures that are consistent with Islamic principles.

2.1.7. Decision-making Based on Facts

Fact-based decision-making, a fundamental tenet of TQM, is utilizing data and evidence to inform organizational strategies and actions. In the Halal tourist sector, data-driven decision-making is crucial for evaluating the efficacy of activities designed to attain Muslim-friendly requirements (Adesina et al., 2024).

Performance indicators, including customer satisfaction scores, Halal certification compliance rates, and environmental impact evaluations, can yield significant insights for enhancing service delivery. Organizations can make educated decisions that improve operational efficiency, sustainability, and compliance with Islamic principles by relying on empirical facts. Moreover, data-driven methodologies allow destinations to foresee and react to evolving trends in Muslim travel preferences, so securing sustained competitiveness in the market.

2.2. Sustainable Practices in Halal Tourism and Muslim Friendly Destinations

The expansion of Halal tourism has heightened the emphasis on sustainable tourism practices in places serving Muslim travelers. These sites must comply with Islamic beliefs and guarantee that tourism operations correspond with sustainability objectives. Halal tourism prioritizes the provision of halal cuisine, the accessibility of prayer facilities, and the encouragement of modest attire and conduct. Sustainable tourism in this context transcends religious factors, incorporating environmental, economic, and social sustainability objectives that can beneficially affect local populations and ecosystems (Suyasa et al., 2024).

Studies have shown that Muslim-friendly tourism locations are progressively implementing sustainable measures that exceed mere adherence to Islamic principles, aiming to mitigate adverse environmental effects and foster ethical tourism. The incorporation of energy-efficient technologies, including solar power, water conservation systems, and waste management programs, is an emerging trend among Muslim-friendly tourism locations (Sepawi, 2023). These methods not only appeal to Muslim tourists seeking sites that resonate with their values but also yield enduring advantages for local populations and ecosystems.

Recent research indicates that Muslim-friendly tourism might greatly benefit from circular economy approaches, which minimize and repurpose tourist-related waste products. This methodology has been effectively executed in specific halal tourism locales, where waste management is facilitated by recycling initiatives, and biodegradable materials are emphasized in hospitality services (Sari et al., 2024). These techniques improve environmental sustainability and foster economic opportunities for the local populace, especially in areas where tourism is a primary economic catalyst. Furthermore, the implementation of green certifications and environmentally sustainable hotel practices is increasingly standard in these locations, offering reassurance to Muslim travelers desiring eco-conscious and sustainable holiday experiences.

Notwithstanding the benefits, the implementation of sustainable practices in halal tourism destinations encounters numerous hurdles, such as initial capital expenditures, the incorporation of novel systems, and the necessity for proficient personnel well-versed in both Islamic principles and sustainable tourism methodologies. Recent research indicates that destinations employing comprehensive frameworks, such as TQM, have been more effective in integrating sustainability with tourism operations. The principles of TQM, emphasizing continual development, staff involvement, and customer satisfaction, are crucial for the enduring success of sustainable tourism programs (Ayad et al., 2024). Integrating sustainability into organizational culture enables tourism destinations to tackle these difficulties, leading to increased operational efficiencies and enhanced customer experiences, hence increasing their attractiveness to the expanding demographic of Muslim travelers.

2.3. *Government Support in Promoting Halal Tourism and Muslim-friendly Practices*

Government intervention is essential for promoting the development of halal tourism and ensuring that Muslim-friendly tourism locations adhere to sustainability standards. Governments in prominent Muslim-majority nations, like Malaysia, Indonesia, and Turkey, have established diverse legislative frameworks aimed at advancing Halal tourism while fostering environmental sustainability objectives (Alibašić, 2024). These policies encompass financial incentives, including tax refunds, subsidies for sustainable tourism initiatives, and regulatory frameworks that promote the creation of infrastructure suited to the requirements of Muslim travelers.

Malaysia's initiatives to advance its Halal tourist sector are intricately linked to national sustainability objectives. The government allocates subsidies for the certification of halal restaurants and facilitates the construction of sustainable infrastructure. These programs promote private sector participation in the development of hotels and resorts that are both Muslim-friendly and environmentally sustainable (Alam et al., 2024). The congruence between governmental policies and the tourism sector is essential for guaranteeing that halal tourism is both economically advantageous and conducive to environmental conservation.

Subsequent study indicates that governmental assistance amplifies the efficacy of TQM approaches in Muslim-friendly tourism locales. The collaboration between the public and private sectors facilitates improved resource allocation, knowledge exchange, and the dissemination of best practices, resulting in the formulation of sustainable destination marketing plans (Eruaga, 2024). Furthermore, governmental incentives and laws concerning environmental management, waste reduction, and energy efficiency are pivotal factors in the adoption of sustainable practices within tourism enterprises.

Governments play a vital role in facilitating halal tourism by constructing prayer facilities, halal-certified restaurants, and providing rules for enterprises pursuing halal certification (Teichmann & Wittmann, 2024). By synchronizing governmental policy with the requirements of the tourism sector, Muslim-friendly places can draw visitors while maintaining elevated environmental and ethical standards.

2.4. *Technology Adaptation as a Moderator in TQM for Halal Tourism Destinations*

The adoption of technology has emerged as a crucial element in optimizing management practices within halal tourism destinations, especially in fostering sustainability and optimizing operational efficiencies. The use of technical advancements, such smart tourism systems, automated waste management solutions, and energy-efficient technologies, is crucial for providing a seamless experience for Muslim travelers while achieving sustainability goals (Silvestri et al., 2024).

Technological technologies serve as intermediaries between TQM processes and sustainability outcomes by facilitating real-time monitoring, resource optimization, and enhanced decision-making. Automated waste management systems and smart grids for energy consumption enable tourism companies to monitor and reduce waste output while adhering to sustainability and halal criteria (Segun-Falade et al., 2024). The integration of data analytics and cloud-based platforms for consumer feedback can significantly enhance service quality, enabling tourism organizations to consistently refine their services to accommodate the changing demands of Muslim tourists.

Moreover, developments in digital tools facilitate tourism destinations in effectively managing their halal certification processes and ensuring compliance with environmental sustainability objectives. Research by Gude et al. (2024) emphasizes that technology, including mobile applications, can direct tourists to halal-certified establishments while concurrently supplying real-time information for businesses to enhance their sustainability policies. Moreover, technology-based solutions like online reservation systems can incorporate sustainability metrics into their platforms, offering transparency about a destination's environmental initiatives and halal adherence (Abogunrin-Olafisoye et al., 2024).

Technology adaptation is crucial for improving operational efficiency and attaining sustainability in halal tourism; however, its successful integration depends on tourism organizations' capacity to cultivate a culture of innovation and continuous improvement, as highlighted by TQM principles. Silvestri et al. (2024) contend that organizations excelling in technology integration has robust internal systems for innovation, training, and employee engagement in sustainability projects. Consequently, technology functions not only as a tool but also as a strategic facilitator within the whole structure of TQM, advancing both operational excellence and the sustainable growth of halal tourism destinations.

Evidence indicates that the effective incorporation of technology into TQM frameworks is crucial for sustained development in halal tourism. By implementing new technologies that improve waste management, energy efficiency, and customer satisfaction, destinations may secure their long-term competitiveness while upholding Islamic values. Furthermore, the incorporation of sustainable technology facilitates the attainment of environmental and social sustainability objectives, matching with the overarching goals of Halal tourism to establish responsible and sustainable travel destinations for Muslim tourists.

3. Conclusion

This literature review has comprehensively analyzed the complex relationship between TQM practices and the advancement of Muslim-friendly tourism destinations, highlighting the mediating function of government support and the moderating effect of technology adaption. This evaluation, based on over

50 prominent journal publications, emphasizes that the appropriate incorporation of TQM approaches can substantially improve the sustainability and competitiveness of halal tourism destinations. The results demonstrate that government support serves a crucial mediating function by offering legislative frameworks, financial incentives, and necessary infrastructure. These initiatives not only enable the application of halal tourism standards but also cultivate a culture of ongoing enhancement and sustainability within the tourism sector. Governments can promote the integration of sustainable practices in tourism firms by legislative measures and support mechanisms, aligning with environmental objectives and the ethical standards necessary for Muslim-friendly locations.

The review emphasizes the essential function of technological adaptation as a mediator in improving the correlation between TQM practices and the success of Muslim-friendly tourism locations. Locations that embrace advanced technologies are more adept at executing TQM initiatives, leading to enhanced service quality, operational efficiency, and sustainable practices. The integration of technical advancements, including smart tourism systems, automated sustainability tools, and real-time data analytics, enables tourist enterprises to oversee and enhance their operations. This technological infrastructure not only bolsters sustainability goals but also improves the whole tourist experience, rendering destinations more appealing to the increasing demographic of Muslim travelers pursuing locations that comply with halal standards and sustainability ideals.

This literature study highlights the interrelation of TQM techniques, governmental backing, and technology innovation in realizing the objectives of Muslim-friendly tourism destinations. The results underscore the necessity of using these elements to develop sustainable, high-quality tourism experiences that satisfy the requirements of Muslim travelers while fostering environmental and social accountability. The review promotes ongoing empirical research to further examine these relationships, specifically how the interaction between TQM, government policy, and technology can enhance the development of competitive and sustainable Muslim-friendly tourism destinations in the global tourism market.

References

Abdullah, M., & Rimmel, G. (2024). *Chapter 20: Sustainability reporting model in the Malaysian palm oil industry: Practices, limitations and challenges*. https://www.elgaronline.com/edcollchap/book/9781035316267/book-part-9781035316267-32.xml

Abogunrin-Olafisoye, O. B., Adeyi, O., Adeyi, A. J., & Oke, E. O. (2024). Sustainable utilization of oil palm residues and waste in Nigeria: Practices, prospects, and environmental considerations. *Waste Management Bulletin*, *2*(1), 214–228. https://doi.org/10.1016/j.wmb.2024.01.011

Adesina, A., Iyelolu, T., & Paul, P. (2024). Optimizing business processes with advanced analytics: Techniques for efficiency and productivity improvement. *World Journal of Advanced Research and Reviews*, *22*, 1917–1926. https://doi.org/10.30574/wjarr.2024.22.3.1960

Ahinful, A. A., Opoku Mensah, A., Koomson, S., Cobblah, C., Takyi, G., & Kwarteng, A. H. (2024). Achieving banking industry innovation performance using total quality management: An empirical study. *The TQM Journal*. https://doi.org/10.1108/TQM-10-2023-0327

Alam, A., Nisa, E. L. K., Haque, M. G., & Hamid, A. A. (2024). Halal tourism and the Islamic socio-cultural responsibilities of domestic tourists in Indonesia. *Fikri: Jurnal Kajian Agama, Sosial Dan Budaya*, *9*(2), 221–238. https://doi.org/10.25217/jf.v9i2.4794

Alibašić, H. (2024). Exploring the influence of Islamic governance and religious regimes on sustainability and resilience planning: A study of public administration in Muslim-majority countries. *Public Policy and Administration*, *39*(4), 556–587. https://doi.org/10.1177/09520767231223282

Ayad, T. H., Hafez, N. M., & Hafez, S. M. (2024). Examining interrelationships among tourists guides' professional competencies, service quality, satisfaction, loyalty, destination image and tourism sustainable development. *Przestrzeń Społeczna (Social Space)*, *24*(1), Article 1.

Cheah, W. Y., Siti-Dina, R. P., Leng, S. T. K., Er, A. C., & Show, P. L. (2023). Circular bioeconomy in palm oil industry: Current practices and future perspectives. *Environmental Technology & Innovation*, *30*, 103050. https://doi.org/10.1016/j.eti.2023.103050

David, A., Yigitcanlar, T., Li, R. Y. M., Corchado, J. M., Cheong, P. H., Mossberger, K., & Mehmood, R. (2023). Understanding local government digital technology adoption strategies: A PRISMA review. *Sustainability*, *15*(12), Article 12. https://doi.org/10.3390/su15129645

Eruaga, M. A. (2024). Enhancing global food safety standards through international collaboration and policy harmonization. *International Journal of Scholarly Research in Multidisciplinary Studies*, *4*(1), 020–032. https://doi.org/10.56781/ijsrms.2024.4.1.0027

Fayyaz, A., Liu, C., Xu, Y., & Ramzan, S. (2024). Effects of green human resource management, internal environmental management and developmental culture between lean six sigma and operational performance. *International Journal of Lean Six Sigma*. https://doi.org/10.1108/IJLSS-04-2023-0065

Gude, D. K., Bandari, H., Challa, A. K. R., Tasneem, S., Tasneem, Z., Bhattacharjee, S. B., Lalit, M., Flores, M. A. L., & Goyal, N. (2024). Transforming urban sanitation: Enhancing sustainability through machine learning-driven waste processing. *Sustainability*, *16*(17), Article 17. https://doi.org/10.3390/su16177626

Horry, R., Booth, C. A., & Mahamadu, A.-M. (2024). *Chapter 14: Contributions of environmental management systems (ISO 14001) towards the delivery of sustainable development goal 12*. https://www.elgaronline.com/edcollchap/book/9781035300037/book-part-9781035300037-24.xml

Lestari, S. D., Leon, F. M., Riyadi, S., Qodariah, Q., & Putra, A. H. P. K. (2024). Comparison and implementation of environmental law policies in handling climate change in ASEAN countries: A comparative study of Indonesia, Malaysia, and Thailand. *International Journal of Energy Economics and Policy*, *14*(2), 687–700. https://doi.org/10.32479/ijeep.14998

Limani, E., Hajdari, L., Limani, B., & Krasniqi, J. (2024). Enhancing stakeholder engagement: Using the communication perspective to identify and enhance stakeholder communication in place management. *Cogent Business & Management*, *11*(1), 2383322. https://doi.org/10.1080/23311975.2024.2383322

Mohsin, M., Shamsudin, M. N., Jaffri, N. R., Idrees, M., & Jamil, K. (2024). Unveiling the contextual effects of total quality management to enhance sustainable performance. *The TQM Journal*. https://doi.org/10.1108/TQM-05-2023-0124

Nguyen, H. L., & Kanbach, D. K. (2024). Toward a view of integrating corporate sustainability into strategy: A systematic literature review. *Corporate Social Responsibility and Environmental Management*, *31*(2), 962–976. https://doi.org/10.1002/csr.2611

Rasanjali, W. A., Mendis, A. P. K. D., Perera, B. A. K. S., & Disaratna, V. (2024). Implementing enterprise resource planning for lean waste minimisation: Challenges and proposed strategies. *Smart and Sustainable Built Environment*, *13*(2), 330–353. https://doi.org/10.1108/SASBE-04-2022-0068

Salloum, C., Jarrar, H., Chaanine, N., Al Sayah, M., & Verdie, J.-F. (2024). Winning hearts and minds: The charismatic leader's role in SME productivity. *European Business Review*, *36*(4), 494–509. https://doi.org/10.1108/EBR-04-2023-0126

Sari, R. K., Alfarizi, M., & Talib, M. S. A. (2024). Sustainable strategic planning and management influence on sustainable performance: Findings from halal culinary MSMEs in Southeast Asia. *Journal of Modelling in Management*. https://doi.org/10.1108/JM2-12-2023-0324

Segun-Falade, O., Kedi, O., Ijomah, T., & Abdul-Azeez, P. (2024). *Developing innovative software solutions for effective energy management systems in industry*. 2649–2669.

Sepawi, S. (2023). *Developing talent management hybrid model for business growth and sustainability: The case of Malaysian theme park industry – ProQuest*. https://www.proquest.com/openview/e882839ece1d47f38917728e782223b9/1?pq-origsite=gscholar&cbl=2026366&diss=y

Silvestri, C., Silvestri, L., Piccarozzi, M., & Ruggieri, A. (2024). TQM and sustainability: A study of the methods and CSFs of TQM for achieving sustainability. *Total Quality Management & Business Excellence*, *35*(1–2), 226–272. https://doi.org/10.1080/14783363.2023.2289938

Sondh, S., Upadhyay, D. S., Patel, S., & Patel, R. N. (2024). Strategic approach towards sustainability by promoting circular economy-based municipal solid waste management system – A review. *Sustainable Chemistry and Pharmacy*, *37*, 101337. https://doi.org/10.1016/j.scp.2023.101337

Suyasa, I. G. W., Octafian, R., & Priyanto, S. H. (2024). Vanaprastha tourism: A new foundation for enhancing Bali's cultural tourism resiliency. *Journal of Resilient Economies*, *4*(1), 45–55. https://doi.org/10.3316/informit

Teichmann, F. M. J., & Wittmann, C. (2024). How can sustainability be effectively regulated? *Journal of Financial Crime*, *31*(5), 1156–1165. https://doi.org/10.1108/JFC-07-2022-0174

Wang, P., Wen, Y., Zhou, Y., Li, S., & Zhang, X. (2024). Sustainable design: Circular innovation design method under process reengineering. *Heliyon*, *10*(15). https://doi.org/10.1016/j.heliyon.2024.e35251

Chapter 16

Sustainability and Ethical Considerations in Halal Tourism

C.S. Surti Sharma and Anukrati Sharma

Department of Commerce, University of Kota, Kota, India

Abstract

As the global tourism industry expands, the concept of sustainability has become increasingly vital. This chapter discusses the growing importance of sustainability in the expanding global tourism industry, with a specific focus on halal tourism. With increasing demand for halal tourism, sustainability and ethics have become essential in defining its future.

This chapter examines the convergence of sustainability and ethics in halal tourism, with a focus on the environmental, social, and economic obligations of stakeholders. Sustainable halal tourism encourages environmental friendly practices, for example, minimizing carbon footprints, conservation of natural resources, and proper waste management in line with Islamic principles. Ethical practice includes fair labor practices, responsible business, and inclusiveness while being respectful of cultural and religious values. The contribution of Shariah-compliant accommodations, Halal food certification, and ethical tourism activities is also discussed. It also serves the challenges and opportunities in aligning halal tourism with sustainable tourism principles, such as natural resource conservation, social justice promotion, and generating economic benefits for local communities.

The research points to the necessity of developing industry-wide standards that merge Islamic ethics with universal sustainability models to assure a balanced and responsible approach.

Keywords: Halal tourism; sustainability; ethics; stakeholders; sustainable tourism practices

Halal Tourism and Artificial Intelligence: New Approaches for a New Generation, 229–243

doi:10.1108/978-1-80686-165-120261018

1. Introduction

When compared to other industries, the tourism sector is one of the fastest expanding in the world and the largest in terms of GDP contribution (UNWTO Tourism). According to the World Travel & Tourism Council's (WTTC) research, the tourism industry contributes positively to GDP, economic growth, and the decline in the unemployment rate.

Sustainable tourism, as defined by the United Nation Environment Programme (UNEP) and the United Nation World Tourism Organization (UNWTO) (2005), is

By taking into account current and future demands in terms of social, economic, and environmental impacts on stakeholders (tourists, industry, environment, and community)

For Muslims, halal tourism offers a possible marketplace. The market share of Muslim travelers is predicted to grow rapidly, reaching USD 300 billion by 2026, according to the Global Muslim Travel Index (Masterplan Ekonomi Syariah Indonesia 2019–2024, 2018).

By offering services, events, and goods in accordance with Islamic principles, halal tourism aims to meet the demands of Muslim tourists as the global travel industry grows quickly. The demand for halal travel is rising along with the number of Muslims. Nevertheless, its growth has to be harmonized with international sustainability objectives and ethics in tourism. This chapter analyzes the sustainability and ethical aspects of halal tourism, determining challenges, best practices, and strategic suggestions for promoting a responsible and culturally sensitive tourism industry.

1.1. Understanding Halal Tourism

In accordance with Islamic principles and regulations, "halal" refers to anything that is permissible and legal. This includes not only food and beverages but also banking and financial services, pharmaceuticals, and tourism (Dewi et al., 2023). The idea behind halal tourism is to apply Islamic teachings and practices in all travel-related activities. The term "halal tourism" has no widely recognized definition.

According to study by Battour and Ismail (2016), halal tourism is any travel activity that complies with Islamic principles. The foundation of halal tourism is meeting travelers' needs in accordance with Islamic law. Halal tourism is currently a trend that goes by several names in different countries, such as sharia tourism, Islamic tourism, MFT, etc., thanks to the usage of technology.

Halal tourism is a sub-field of religious tourism. Based on Islamic Sharia law, halal tourism emphasizes the fundamental values of Muslim life from conception to death. In literary work of Feizollah et al. (2021), halal describes everything that covered and permitted by sharia law and also focuses on issues relating to lifestyle, food, tourism, banking, pharmaceuticals, etc.

1.2. Need of Incorporating Sustainability and Ethical Values into Halal Tourism

There are a number of countries that are the biggest importers in the halal industry: Saudi Arabia, the United Arab Emirate, Turkey, Indonesia, and Malaysia (Dinar et al., 2022). Arifin et al. (2023) found in their research that halal industry is not only for Muslims but also covers demand by non-Muslim consumers for halal products and services. The halal sector is also regarded as a viable driver of economic growth and development, especially in nations and regions with large Muslim populations (Dinar et al., 2022). The sector offers prospects for employment, investment, and innovation and can help drive sustainable and inclusive economic growth (Hasan & Pasyah, 2022).

As per research conducted by Fatin Nur et al. (2022), Halal comes under sustainable development since it's not just a matter of religion and food but also includes industries engaging in business and economy. The development of the halal industry has to be made in a sustainable manner, and it is in direct connection to the halal industry players namely the stakeholder, supplier, manufacturer, seller, and consumer. Based on the information around us, the fact that it is information of environmental and society degradation will never be enough for people to move into action. Action can be brought about only when people and society possess a belief system which recognizes the significance of the natural world to human evolution, and then they will become able to take action for sustainable development.

There is possibility for halal tourism to contribute more broadly and sustainably to Islamic principles, the environment, and society. Halal infrastructure development, including provision of places of worship, men's and women's toilets, and halal marking of tourism products, are examples of socio-cultural commitments in favor of halal tourism. This research not only fulfils the demand of Muslim tourists but also enhances comfort and safety for everyone (Arintyas & Budiman, 2023; Haryanti, 2020).

Ethics play a vital role for focusing on actions toward sustainability in Muslim-friendly tourism as well. The importance of sustainable tourism, including ecological and societal aspects, is most important in the field of travel ethics. The above assertion is reflective of the Islamic teachings that advocate for the preservation of the environment and the development of positive social relationships, which include acts of charity toward host communities (Khairuldin, 2020).

One key to achieving sustainability in the tourism sector is generating tourist satisfaction, which has been studied extensively by many studies (Zulvianti et al., 2022; Zhang et al., 2019). The majority of studies have argued that tourism managers must develop competence to deliver an attractive tourist experience.

Furthermore, Islamic ethics in tourism that prioritizes justice, honesty, and social responsibility are also a crucial pillar in the management of halal tourist destinations (Ilmi & Ambariyanto, 2024; Samiul & Chatterjee, 2023).

Halal tourist destinations encourage positive interactions and mutual respect between guests, which is consistent with Islamic principles of fraternity and humility to others. Such brotherhood fosters harmony and inclusiveness in the environment among all visitors, irrespective of their origin (Ramadhan et al., 2024).

2. Literature Review

2.1. Halal Tourism

Research on the growth of halal tourism has been outlined by Sunarya and Qital (2022). They found that 191 publications (journal articles, conferences, editorials, and others) have been published by media outlets that were indexed by Scopus as of May 11, 2022. These research clarified that the development of halal tourism was driven by demand. This would grow the tourism business based on the needs of travelers and the halal tourism sector.

Since both experience and satisfaction are key factors in motivating tourists to return and recommend a tourism destination, research done by Amalia et al. (2024) indicates that delivering great experiences in the destination (both the attraction and halal products and services) and satisfying Muslim tourists are crucial for building the business sustainability of a tourism destination and its business actors.

This study identifies two essential components of delivering an outstanding tourism experience: innovation and environmental sensitivity. This study emphasizes how crucial environmental concerns are to improving visitors' experiences with local attractions and halal goods and services.

In his book, Ali (2020) discusses the possibility of encounters between Muslim and non-Muslim tourists, allowing them to recognize religious distinctions and potentially work toward unity. This allows for the promotion of positive interfaith communication.

As per Perano (2018), halal tourism is synonymous with Islamic tourism, MFT, Shariah tourism, halal lifestyle, and many more.

By incorporating economic importance of halal tourism in Muslim populated area, it may improve quality and sustainability in tourism sector (Ejigu & Hamid, 2023).

2.2. Sustainability in Halal Tourism

Al Mustaqim (2023) discovered in his research work that halal tourism is able to contribute toward sustainable development in positive manner. Furthermore, Suharto (2017), in their research, clarified that social and cultural responsibility encompasses economic empowerment, which is a basic pillar that assists in enhancing the quality of life in society and lowering the level of social inequality. Social and cultural responsibility also encompasses empowering individuals and communities to help them contribute to setting their priorities and what is appropriate for them effectively. Here, it is evident that economic empowerment should be accompanied by the proper contribution of people to social work and deciding all aspects of their life matters.

Sugito et al. (2022) described that participatory communication in corporate social responsibility initiatives also has a crucial role in empowering people. They stressed that cooperation among the government, private sector, and community is needed to establish conditions favorable to local economic development and enhance the quality of life of the community. In general, economic empowerment as a part of socio-cultural obligations can enhance the partnership among people, communities, and institutions in attaining sustainable development objectives.

2.3. Halal Tourism Ethics

Itang and Hadi Peristiwo (2023) did work on ethics in halal. On the basis of which it is possible to assume that halal tourism from an Islamic business ethic point of view means that by analogy with the idea of monotheism, the elements of halal tourism in human existence serve as a cohesive unity, one and the same from inside, and harmonized with nature overall.

This is the vertical aspect of Islam. Aforementioned with the idea of oneness is harmony between different human activities such as halal tourism to develop the optimum social norms. Such a feeling of harmony is achieved through purposeful aims, and it belongs to the horizontal aspect of Islam. Associated with free will is human power to act voluntarily without outside compulsion in relation to Allah SWT's creation as Allah SWT's caliph on earth.

The relationship between ethics and philosophy in the framework of Muslim-friendly tourism was thoroughly examined in this research. A re-examination of this idea shows that Muslim-friendly tourism entails adherence to Sharia law, respect for an indigenous way of life and a thorough comprehension of Islam.

Tourism ethics plays a crucial role in ensuring positive traveler behavior and promoting interfaith dialog. The implications of Muslim-friendly tourism are both at the regional and global levels with positive effects on the local economy, strengthening the image of the destination, and generating mutually beneficial cultural interactions. The work makes a contribution to a broader understanding of the concepts that underlie the tourist sector, in this case, concerning the provision of the demands of Muslim tourists. It provides valuable insights and suggestions to improve the quality of services offered by the tourism industry to this specific group (Khairuldin et al., 2024).

Hasanah et al. (2024) have conducted a study that indicates Islamic morality can facilitate greater awareness of tourists regarding the significance of halal and ethics in tourism. High-aware tourists are more likely to select halal destinations. Asyifa et al. (2023) detailed in their study that Islamic morality is necessary for fostering socio-cultural responsibility in halal tourist destinations. Islamic ethics can be utilized to raise tourist consciousness regarding the significance of halal and ethics in tourism.

Going back to Tayob's (2021) study, the literature review emphasizes the scrutiny of the ethical transformation introduced by Halal certification. This investigation touches on the intersectionality of sustainable capitalism with the state of labor and the environment.

Golnaz Rezai and Shamsudin (2015) conduct a study that revealed non-Muslim consumers still perceive the halal process from the religious rather than the sustainability side. Consumer ethics contribute notably to advancing Muslim-friendly tourism by fostering respect, understanding, and accommodation of Islamic cultural and religious practices. Convergence of MFT with various SDGs shows that MFT has the capability to aid in sustainable global development. While MFT keeps increasing, it is critical that stakeholders ensure ethical approaches and sustainability for long-term viability and benefit for host communities and environments (Shabudin, 2023).

3. Research Methodology

3.1. Research Design

Qualitative, exploratory research design was adopted in this research to explore the sustainability and ethical aspects of halal tourism. The method is appropriate given the developmental stage of halal tourism as a discipline and the necessity to achieve deep insights into values, perceptions, and practices in multicultural and multifaith settings.

The study incorporates documentary analysis and case studies in order to investigate existing halal tourism practices, challenges, and prospects for sustainable and ethical halal tourism.

3.2. Study Aims

- In order to investigate the ways in which sustainability is incorporated into halal tourism practice in various regions.
- In order to establish halal tourism-specific ethical considerations and assess their application.
- To offer strategic advice to policymakers and tourism stakeholders.

3.3. Data Collection Methods

3.3.1. Secondary Data

Literature review was carried out through academic journals, books, government reports, industry white papers, and publications by international organizations (e.g., UNWTO, OIC, Islamic Tourism Centre). These sources gave basic knowledge and pointed out important issues in halal tourism, sustainability, and ethics.

3.3.2. Case Studies

Three case studies – United Arab Emirates, Indonesia, and Malaysia – were chosen for their position at the fore of halal tourism and differing models of sustainability development. Data were collected via:

- Government tourism plans
- Halal certification body reports
- Sustainability audits
- Media reports

These examples served to demonstrate practical applications and differing strategies for sustainable halal tourism.

4. Convergence of Sustainability in Halal Tourism

The term "tourism sustainability" describes the long-term viability of the sector with few adverse repercussions on the environment, society, or economy. Concerns about sustainable development have been discussed among professionals since the 1990s. Sustainable development is the process of using human and environmental resources as efficiently as possible. Sustainability is not just about the physical; social factors also need to be taken into account (Sulistyadi et al., 2019).

For halal tourism, sustainability includes the following sections.

4.1. Environmental Sustainability

According to Sulistyadi et al. (2019), their research revealed that tourism in some places can have a favorable impact on the local population's economic well-being and even grow their incomes.

Therefore, appropriate rules must be implemented in order to preserve the sustainability of the natural environment that is a sightseeing spot. These are detailed here below:

- *Eco-friendly infrastructure*: Developing accommodations as well as attractions that reduce carbon footprints and maximize energy efficiency.
- *Waste management*: Ensuring sustainable mechanisms in food waste, particularly in Halal food preparation.
- *Nature-based tourism*: Ensuring eco-tourism practices that are compatible with Islamic values such as respect for the natural world, protecting animals, and environmental management

4.2. Economic Sustainability

Halal tourism provides local economies with a wide range of opportunities. One of them is the creation of economic resources and a decrease in the level of economic inequality between an area and another. Tourism is now regarded as one sector that can grow local communities and the country by boosting the economy (Haikal, 2022).

Advantages of halal tourism to economy can be realized by below points:

- *Local economic empowerment*: Involvement of local communities, especially Muslim communities, in tourism activities ensures equitable economic benefits and support for local Halal producers.

- *SMEs support*: Promoting small- and medium-sized enterprises in the Halal value chain ensures diversified and sustainable economic growth.

4.3. Socio-cultural Sustainability

Socio-cultural responsibilities, in this regard, entail economic, environmental, artistic, and spiritual dimensions. For instance, for halal tourism development, socio-cultural responsibilities are to offer halal food and drinks, Muslim-friendly accommodations, and interaction in accordance with religious practice, which generates an environment based on Maqashid Sharia (Suhandi, 2023).

Halal tourism also encompasses elements like halal food and drinks but additionally consists of places for worship, a social setting in accordance with Islamic guidelines, and services that are privacy- and comfort-conscious to Muslim tourists (Abdullah et al., 2020; Vargas-sánchez & Moral-Moral, 2020). These guidelines are imperative to Muslim tourists and have wider implications for the social and cultural responsibility of the tourist destination (Akbar, 2021; Rachmiatie et al., 2023).

Halal tourism would take into consideration the following points as social responsibility:

- *Cultural conservation*: Halal tourism has to preserve and protect local customs and traditions, that is, Islamic history and heritage.
- *People-to-people contact*: Contact with the local populace so that the expansion of tourism does not lead to social unrest or is against local values.

5. Ethical Implication in Halal Tourism

The ethics concept within Muslim-friendly tourism refers to the behavior of tourists who act with respect toward local culture and values, alongside observing proper conduct in an Islamic-friendly environment that is supportive of Islamic principles (Khan & Duman, 2017).

Ethics provides fundamental values to people for operating along with the halal supply chain that are connected with the halal industry. Ethical practices in halal can be understood through following points.

5.1. Religious Authenticity and Integrity

Tourism services offered as Halal must actually be Sharia-compliant. Misleading or artificial promotion of Halal offerings, also known as "Halal-washing," undermines consumer trust and violates ethical marketing standards.

5.2. Gender Sensitivity

Islamic teachings about gender encounters call for careful planning of facilities and services. Gender-separated facilities, women-only facilities, and women staff for women visitors enhance ethical service provision without stereotyping or exclusion.

5.3. Animal Welfare in Halal Food

Halal food supply chains are concerned with humane animal handling. Ethical halal tourism calls for transparency in sourcing, slaughter conditions, and food handling according to religious and global ethical expectations.

5.4. Fair Labor Practices

Tourism should ensure fair remuneration, decent working conditions, and respect for workers' rights, particularly in Halal-certified outlets that may include migrant or low-wage labor.

5.5. Cultural Sensitivity

Halal tourism needs to avoid commodifying Islamic culture or religious practice in a way that is disrespectful to or exploitative of religious aspects. Sensible cultural representation needs to be balanced with educational components for non-Muslim tourists.

6. Best Practices and Case Studies

Indonesia: Halal Tourism, Innovation, and Environmental Issue

1. Lombok, Indonesia: Tackling Ethical Issues in halal tourism
   Lombok is marketed as one of the leading halal tourist destinations. With the island becoming increasingly involved with halal tourism, there has been a need to address concerns regarding the rapid development of tourism, such as possible cultural commodification and environmental degradation (Puput Yanita Senja et al., 2024).
2. Benteng Ciampea, Indonesia: while working on Sustainable halal tourism in this village, major improvements in environmental, social, cultural, and economic circumstances have been noted post development. This illustration demonstrates the significance of community participation and cultural conservation in sustainable halal tourism (Harini et al., 2025).

Malaysia: Propelling sustainable and moral halal tourism

Conducting tourism practices in a way that follows Islamic values will increase the sustainability of tourist destinations as well as the experience of Muslim tourists. Malaysia, leading the way in bringing together sustainability and halal tourism, has robust certification systems in place and green-friendly Halal resorts (Saffinee et al., 2024).

United Arab Emirates: Ethical and sustainable Halal tourism development

Important determinants like safety, family leisure, halal food variety, and global restaurant chains offering halal cuisine strongly impact tourists' decisions and satisfaction, highlighting the UAE's adherence to ethical and sustainable halal tourism experiences. Offers luxury Halal experiences with a focus on sustainability through green buildings, solarization of mosques, and socially conscious tourism charters (Echchabi et al., 2022).

These case studies depict the complex dimensions of applying sustainability and ethics to halal tourism. They reflect the significance of community engagement, cultural conservation, religious values, innovation, and environmental stewardship in creating sustainable halal tourism practices.

They underscore the significance of ethical standards, environmentally friendly hospitality, and technological innovation in promoting sustainable halal tourism practices.

7. Challenges and Opportunities

7.1. Challenges in Aligning Halal Tourism with Sustainable Tourism Practices

- *Lack of global standards*: Differences in Halal certification and sustainability standards between nations can confuse tourists and providers.
- *Over-tourism and environmental degradation*: Islamic heritage places of interest risk overcrowding, pollution, and loss of cultural essence.
- *Balancing commercial and religious objectives*: Tourism players might offer profit over ethical or religious truth, endangering the loss of essential values.

7.2. Stakeholder Opportunities as a Result of Sustainability and Ethical Factors in Halal Tourism

1. Creation of green halal resorts and hotels
    - Stakeholders can make investments in the accommodations that mix halal friendliness (such as halal food, prohibition of alcohol, prayer rooms) with green efforts (solar power, conservation of water, zero-waste policies).
    - *Opportunity*: Grab a rising niche of environmentally aware Muslim tourists.
2. Promoting ethical and local experiences
    - Providing genuine, ethical tourism experiences – such as community-based tourism in which Muslim communities are directly benefited – can be a point of differentiation.
    - *Opportunity*: Encourage trust and loyalty from ethically conscious tourists.
3. Certification and branding opportunities
    - Creating and selling certifications such as "Eco-Halal Certified" or "Sustainable Halal Destination" can generate a competitive advantage.
    - *Opportunity*: Be a trusted standard-bearer of quality and ethics in halal tourism.

4. Agro-tourism and organic halal food experiences
   - Farm tours, halal organic food excursions, and sustainable culinary tours can be established in rural Muslim communities.
   - *Opportunity*: Capitalize on both food- and sustainability-oriented tourism streams.
5. Investment in green transportation services
   - Electric car rentals, green shuttle buses between halal hotels and sightseeing places, or bike tours.
   - *Opportunity*: Capture low-carbon halal travel demand.
6. Support for social enterprises and charity-linked tourism
   - Designing travel packages in which a percentage of earnings is directed towards local zakat (philanthropic) programs or sustainable community development projects.
   - *Opportunity*: Engage socially driven travelers and Islamic ethical giving principles.
7. Technology integration for ethical tourism transparency
   - Apps or platforms authenticating halal compliance and sustainability indicators of tourism products.
   - *Opportunity*: Tech-literate Muslim travelers increasingly demand transparency and certainty.
8. Workforce development and training
   - Providing training courses to educate tourism staff on halal ethics, sustainability, and customer service.
   - *Opportunity*: Create a highly skilled, culturally competent personnel.

8. Final Results and Strategic Recommendations

The industry of travel has recently been shifting toward Islamic and sustainable travel has also started gaining popularity among the tourists, either from Islamic or non-Islamic countries. The idea of Sustainable Tourism Destinations has pointed out that the destinations should pay extra attention to the development of tourism, which can be divided into three key criteria: economy, social, and environment. The integration of Islamic tourism with sustainable tourism features can lead to innovation in the tourism industry that is likely to enhance and contribute to the competitiveness of destinations.

In the study of Cyntia Keliat et al. (2022), since there are Islamic values in halal tourism, it is not just good for the tourism sector but also for the community in rising faith, to be a good human being and to avoid activities that may threaten the neighborhood, and the locals who live close to tourist destinations gain even more from an expanding economy.

The significance of the halal tourism industry and its growth is owed to a number of reasons. The rise in financial resources and available time within Muslim communities' middle class (Yousaf, 2023) has promoted increased involvement of Muslims in worldwide travel activities.

The notion of halal tourism is more than just adhering to dietary requirements; it's a comprehensive approach to travel that is in accordance with the moral and religious codes of Muslim travelers. Consequently, places that can provide an environment conducive to being Halal-friendly are in demand by this segment of tourists. The economic potential of tapping the Muslim travel market is also huge, with the estimate that spending by Muslim tourists will reach over USD 200 billion by 2026 (Mastercard & Crescent Rating, 2019).

Strategic Recommendations

- *Develop harmonized standards*: International collaboration to develop recognized standards for sustainable and ethical halal tourism.
- *Capacity building*: Train tourism industry players, chefs, and service providers in sustainability and Sharia compliance.
- *Policy integration*: National Halal tourism policy shall incorporate sustainability as a means to offer long-term vision and cohesion with the UN Sustainable Development Goals (SDGs).
- *Monitoring and evaluation*: Employ independent institutions in order to audit and certify the sustainability and ethics compliance in destinations of halal tourism.

The convergence of Islamic ethics and sustainable principles offers a strong platform for ethical tourism growth. Halal tourism, if executed in sincerity and forward vision, can become a model of ethical travel that serves tourists, locals, and the environment with equal efficacy. Its nourishment and ethical integrity are not simply a religious requirement but an international necessity to realize equitable, inclusive, and environmentally compliant tourism practices.

References

Abd Hamid, M., Ismail, N., Mohd Fuza, Z. I., Othman, N., & Mohamed Rani, Z. (2022). Review of Islamic tourism and sustainability. *International Journal of Social Science Research*, *4*(1), 447–456.

Abdullah, A. A., Awang, M. D., Abdullah, N., Amir Abdullah, A., Daud Awang, M., & Abdullah, N. (2020). *Islamic tourism: The characteristics, concept and principles*. International conference on Islam, Economy, and Halal Industry 2020, 196–215.

Akbar, M. F. (2021). Halal tourism opportunities to increase tourist visits in Indonesia. *Journal of Indonesia Tourism and Policy Studies*, *6*(2), 1–8.

Al Mustaqim, D. (2023). Strategi Pengembangan Pariwisata Halal Sebagai Pendorong Ekonomi Berkelanjutan Berbasis Maqashid Syariah. *AB-JOIEC: AlBahjah Journal of Islamic Economics*, *1*(1), 26–43.

Amalia, F. A., Muhamad Nova, M., Koh, C., & Suhartanto, D. (2024). *Sustainable development in halal tourism industry: The role of innovation and environmental concern E3S Web of Conferences*, 479, 07038. https://doi.org/10.1051/e3sconf/202447907038

Arifin, M. R., Raharja, B. S., & Nugroho, A. (2023). Do young Muslim choose differently? Identifying consumer behavior in industry. *Journal of Islamic Marketing*, *14*(4), 1032–1057.

Arintyas, A. P. R. D. A., & Budiman, R. C. P. (2023). Halal tourism towards equity representation of multicultural identity and human development. *Jurnal Kepariwisataan: Destinasi, Hospitalitas Dan Perjalanan*, *7*(2), 154–166.

Asyifa, N., Pratama, R. K., Andjanie, I. F., & Furqan, A. (2023). Pendekatan Pariwisata Berbasis Masyarakat/Community Based Tourism (CBT) Di Desa Wisata Lumajang, Kabupaten Bandung. *Jurnal Master Pariwisata (JUMPA)*, *10*(1), 220–253. https://doi.org/10.24843/jumpa.2023.v10.i01.p09

Battour, M., & Ismail, M. N. (2016). Halal tourism: Concepts, practises, challenges and future. *Tourist Management Perspectives*, *19*, 150–154. https://doi.org/10.1016/j.tmp.2015.12.008

Crescent Rating. (2022). *Global Muslim Travel Index 2022*. Retrieved February 5, 2023, from https://www.crescentrating.com/

Cyntia Keliat & I Gede Eko Putra Sri Sentan. (2022). Sustainable Halal Tourism in the post pandemic era: Opportunity and challenges. *Journal of Research on Business and Tourism*, *2*(1), 69–77.

Dewi, K. R., Ismayati, M., Solihat, N. N., Yuliana, N. D., Kusnandar, F., Riantana, H., Heryani, H., Halim, A., Acter, T., Uddin, N., Uddin, N., & Kim, S. (2023). Advances and key considerations of liquid chromatography–mass spectrometry for porcine authentication in halal analysis. *Journal of Analytical Science and Technology*, *14*(1).

Dinar Standard & Salam Gateway. (2022). State of the global Islamic economy report: Unlocking opportunity. *State of the Global Islamic Economy Report*, *21*, 4–202.

Echchabi, A., Bocanet, A., & Grassa, R. (2022). Determinants of selection of Halal Tourism destination: A case study of the UAE. *Global Journal Al Thaqafah*, *12*. 186–203. 10.7187/GJAT072022-12

Embong, A. H. (2022). Ethical issues in academic authorship: A study on group writing. *Academic Journal of Interdisciplinary Studies*, *11*(1), 226–231. https://doi.org/10.36941/ajis-2022-0020

Feizollah, A., Mostafa, M. M., Sulaiman, A., Zakaria, Z., & Firdaus, A. (2021). Exploring halal tourism tweets on social media. *Journal of Big Data*, *8*(1). https://doi.org/10.1186/s40537-021-00463-5

Golnaz Rezai, Z. M., & Shamsudin, M. N. (2015). Can Halal be sustainable? Study on Malaysian consumers' perspective. *Journal of Food Products Marketing*. https://doi.org/10.1080/10454446.2014.883583

Haikal, A. (2022). Analisis Dampak Pariwisata Halal Dalam Menunjang Keberlanjutan Ekonomi, Sosial, Dan Budaya Masyarakat Di Kecamatan Lhoknga Kabupaten Aceh Besar. *Journal of Economic Perspectives*, *2*(1), 1–4. https://doi.org/10.37598/jeips.v2i1

Harini, S., Rahmawati, R., Silaningsih, E., Nurhayati, I., Mutmainah, I., Rainanto, B. H., & Endri, E. (2025). Development of Halal tourism villages based on local culture and sustainability. *Tourism and Hospitality*, *6*(2), 55. https://doi.org/10.3390/tourhosp6020055

Haryanti, T. (2020). Pengembangan Halal Tourism Dalam Menjamin Perlindungan Hukum Bagi Wisatawan Muslim. *Tahkim*, *15*(2), 276–288. https://doi.org/10.33477/thk.v16i2.1500

Hasan, K. N. S., & Pasyah, T. (2022). Challenges of Indonesian Halal industry in the digital economic era. *Sriwijaya Law Review*, *6*(2), 319–335. https://doi.org/10.28946/slrev

Hasanah, A., Yahya, A., Winata, S., Setyawan, A., & Mustikowati, R. I. (2024). Measuring marketing agility, Halal tourism attributes and interest in revisiting tourist destinations in Bangkalan. *COSTING: Journal of Economic, Business and Accounting*, *7*(2), 3682–3690. https://doi.org/10.31539/costing.v7i2.8676

Hashim, P., & Mat Hashim, D. (2013). A review of cosmetic and personal care products: Halal perspective and detection of ingredient. *Pertanika Journal of Science and Technology*, *21*(2), 281–292.

Ilmi, H., & Ambariyanto, A. (2024). Does Halal tourism development support achievement of SDGs goals? A systematic literature review. *Jurnal Ilmiah Ekonomi Islam*, *10*(1), 1–11. https://doi.org/10.29040/jiei.v1i1.12376

Itang & Hadi Peristiwo. (2023). Halal tourism in Islamic business ethics perspective. *Journal of Namibian Studies*, *34*(2023), 483–502.

Khan, A. N., & Duman, T. (2017). The impact of halal tourism on economic growth and environment. In S. A. Shibli (Ed.), *Economic and environmental dimensions of sustainability and governance in tourism* (pp. 239–249). IGI Global.

Khairuldin, W. M. K. F. W., Anas, W. N. I. W. N. , Imas, M., Hassan, A., Embong, A. H., Lukman, N. H. Z., & Yusuf, M. A. I. M. (2024). Philosophy and ethics in halal tourism: A conceptual analysis. *International Journal of Religion*, *5*(11), 486–493. https://doi.org/10.61707/gsrdnf74

Master card & Crescent Rating. (2019). *Global Muslim Travel Index (GMTI) 2019*. https://www.crescentrating.com

Masterplan Ekonomi Syariah Indonesia 2019–2024. (2018). *Masterplan Ekonomi Syariah Indonesia 2019-2024*. Kementerian Perencanaan Pembangunan Nasional/Badan Perencanaan Pembangunan Nasional, 1–443.

Mohd Salleh, N. Z., et al. (2014). Halal tourism: Conceptualizations, practices, and challenges. *Journal of Emerging Economies and Islamic Research*, *2*(1), 1–17.

Nafis, A. A., Slamet Sukardi, A., & Muhammedi, S. (2024). An analysis of the Halal certification movement for MSME (micro, small, and medium enterprises) actors: A case study on Halal tourism in Kudus regency. *Journal of Islamic Economic Laws*, *7*(1), 1–17.

Perano, A. V.-S. M. (2018). Halal tourism through the lens of Generation Z in a Muslim majority country: Implications on tourist services. *International Journal of Business and Management*, *13*(9).

Rachmiatie, A., Zakiah, K., Yusdiansyah, E., Setiawan, E., & Martian, F. (2023). *Model of stakeholder engagement in Halal tourism ecosystems in rural areas*. 5th Sores social and Humaniora Research Symposium (SoRes) Volume 2023 Research, 707–716.

Saffinee, S., Jamaludin, M., Rosli, N., & Hashim, K. (2024). Sustainable and ethical Vicegerency in Halal tourism practices. *Journal of Event, Tourism and Hospitality Studies*, *4*, 111–126. https://doi.org/10.32890/jeth2024.4.8

Samiul, & Chatterjee, K. (2023). Social values and morality of few Islamic rituals. *International Journal of Creative Research Thoughts (IJCRT)*, *11*(5), 922–929. https://doi.org/10.6084/m9.doi.one.IJCRT23A5087

Senja, P. Y., Silviani, W. D., & Shah, S. M. A. R. (2024). Can Halal tourism in Lombok be sustainable? A case study of stakeholder perspective. *Journal of Islamic Economic and Business Research*, *4*(2), 190–212. https://doi.org/10.18196/jiebr.v4i2.309

Shabudin, J. (2023). Consumer ethics and sustainability in Muslim-friendly tourism: Aligning religious principles with global development goals. *AL-MAQASID: The International Journal of Maqāṣid Studies and Advanced Islamic Research*, *4*(2), 39–41.

Sugito, T., Windiasih, R., Prastiyanti, S., & Sulaiman, A. I. (2022). Empowerment communication in the corporate social responsibility program in rural areas. *Technium Sustainability*, *2*(4), 1–16. https://doi.org/10.47577/sustainability.v2i4.7299

Suhandi, A. (2023). Strategi Pengembangan Pariwisata Halal Sebagai Pendorong Ekonomi Berkelanjutan Berbasis Maqasid Syariah. *AB-JOIEC: Al-Bahjah Journal of Islamic Economics*, *1*(1), 44–55. https://doi.org/10.61553/abjoiec.v1i1.22

Suharto, I. K. S. (2017). The role of community economic empowerment to social capital and the implication of community welfare in Karawang Regency West Java

Indonesia. *European Journal of Business and Management*, *9*(32), 65–72. https://doi.org/10.7176/EJBM

Sulistyadi, Y., Eddyono, F., & Entas, D. (2019). *Indikator Perencanaan Pengembangan Pariwisata Berkelanjutan*. Aura.

Sunarya, S. L., & Qital, S. A. (2022). A mapping halal tourism management research: Text mining using NVivo. *Juwita*, *1*, 98–107. https://doi.org/10.20414/juwita.v1i2.5525

Susilawati, C. (2023). Identification and effectiveness of halal tourism laws in Indonesia. *Journal of Islamic Economic Laws*, *6*(2), 110–132. https://doi.org/10.23917/jisel.v6i2.22597

Tayob, S. (2021). Sustainability and halal: Procedure, profit, and ethical practice. *Journal of Digital Marketing and Halal Industry*, *3*(2), 95–110.

UNWTO. (2019). *Tourism and Sustainable Development Goals – Journey to 2030 [especially chapters relating to responsible tourism]*.

Vargas-sánchez, A., & Moral-Moral, M. (2020). Halal tourism: Literature review and experts' view. *Journal of Islamic Marketing*, *11*(3), 549–569. https://doi.org/10.1108/JIMA-04-2017-0039

Yousaf, S. (2023). Understanding Halal leisure: A preliminary view. *Leisure Studies*, *42*(2), 314–323.

Zhang, T., Chen, J., & Hu, B. (2019). Authenticity, quality, and loyalty: Local food and sustainable tourism experience. *Sustainability*, *11*, 3437.

Zulvianti, N., Aimon, H., & Abror, A. (2022). The influence of environmental and non-environmental factors on tourist satisfaction in halal tourism destinations in West Sumatra, Indonesia. *Sustainability*, *14*, 9185.

Chapter 17

Ethical and Religious Considerations in AI-driven Halal Tourism: Focusing on Future with the Use of Technology

Vivek Sharma

Department of Commerce, Government Mahendra Karma Girls College, Dantewada, Chhattisgarh, India

Abstract

Halal tourism is a fast-emerging segment of the international travel market, fueled by the growing need for services that are compliant with Islamic values. The application of artificial intelligence (AI) is transforming this industry by improving the experiences of travelers, streamlining service delivery, and maintaining halal compliance. AI-based technologies like chat bots, recommendation engines, and customized travel assistants are revolutionizing the manner in which halal-aware travelers plan and experience their trips. Moreover, machine learning and big data analytics allow companies to learn about consumer preferences and enhance customized offerings.

This chapter discusses the role of AI in defining the future of Halal tourism, with a focus on how technologies like natural language processing, computer vision, and block chain help in authentication, frictionless travel, and increased customer satisfaction. It also touches on the challenges of AI adoption, such as ethical issues, data privacy, and standardization in halal certification procedures. In addition, practical case studies show effective applications of AI in the Halal tourism sector. Through these key areas, this chapter offers insights into how AI-powered innovations can transform Halal tourism for future generations of Muslim tourists.

Keywords: Halal tourism; artificial intelligence; machine learning; travel technology; personalization; halal compliance; smart tourism

Halal Tourism and Artificial Intelligence: New Approaches for a New Generation, 245–259

doi:10.1108/978-1-80686-165-120261019

1. Introduction

Tourism is a keystone of global economic activity, promoting cultural understanding, economic development, and the creation of jobs worldwide. For the last decades, technological advancement has transformed travel planning, bookings, and the experience of the trip. Technology has become intimately involved in each and every corner of the tourism value chain from the early steps of trip planning to post-visit feedback and suggestions.

The convergence of technology and tourism has revolutionized the travel sector, with AI spearheading innovation and efficiency. Halal tourism, a specialist sector catering to the religious and lifestyle needs of Muslim visitors, has experienced immense growth over the last few years. With the sector evolving, AI presents new opportunities for the enhancement of traveler experience, operations optimization, and compliance with Islamic principles.

The advent of web-based travel booking platforms and aggregators, which have enabled the democratic access to information and travel services, is likely the most obvious trend of recent years. Nowadays, consumers may easily and conveniently utilize computers or portable devices in their domiciles to compare prices, read user reviews, and make reservations for travel, accommodations, and activities.

This movement toward online channels has not only equipped consumers with increased choice and transparency but has also brought new challenges and opportunities for businesses in the tourism industry. Furthermore, the rise of social networking sites and content created by users has completely changed how tourists ask for advice, share their experiences, and seek inspiration.

Technologies like augmented reality (AR) and virtual reality (VR) are also starting to be used to improve the pre-trip planning process and make on-site experiences much richer so that travelers are able to experience destinations, attractions, and accommodations in advance in immersive and interactive formats. In a nutshell, the tourism sector is undergoing a technological revolution, with digitalization, personalization, and connectivity at the forefront of defining the future of travel. As tourists increasingly use technology as a part of their experience, tourism enterprises must transform and become innovative to address changing consumer behaviors and expectations by utilizing technology to provide unique, seamless, and memorable travel experiences. This chapter explains the revolutionary role of AI in Halal tourism and examines how smart systems are guiding its future in accordance with Shariah compliance, ethical values, and global digital trends.

1.1. Overview of Technological Trends Within the Tourism Sector

New technological innovations fueled by AI like virtual hosts and virtual tour guides, Chatbots, smart rooms, and digital personal assistants have revolutionized the experience in the tourism sector (Battour et al., 2023).

The use of AI in the tourism sector presents great opportunities since it can facilitate growth between 7% and 11.6% of the sector's total revenue (Kirtil & Askun, 2021).

AI is extensively used across different sectors such as tourism in order to assist with decision-making and problem-solving in addition to maximizing revenues.

However, few studies have been done on AI usage in Islamic tourism (Abas et al., 2022; Battour et al., 2023; Mastercard-Crescent Rating, 2023; MOTAC, 2020; OIC, 2020). Since the demand for the halal sector is thriving because of global acceptance of Islam as the fastest-growing religion, it is essential for the halal sector to embrace AI. In the travel sector, AI is extensively employed in the Global Distribution System (GDS) through cloud computing.

This system allows tourism stakeholders to share resources and receive updated product lists from the partners 24/7, broader market reach, improved service quality, efficient business model, energy efficiency, bulk data acquisition, narrower information and services, less business downtime, higher security and privacy, thus leading to increased performance to all stakeholders and acquire competitive edge over their competitors (Abas et al., 2022; Agrawal, 2021; Kansakar et al., 2019).

1.2. Need of Innovation in Halal Tourism

Halal tourism comprises tourist services under Islamic law, including Halal food, prayer rooms, gender-segregated facilities, and conservative entertainment.

AI technologies have the potential to offer personalization opportunities, automate screening for compliance, monitor traveler behavior, and provide real-time recommendations that take into account Islamic values. This transformation is imperative not only to enhance the user experience but also to expand market reach as well as build consumer confidence.

AI and the Halal sector collaborate to increase both the quantity and effectiveness of manufactured items while ensuring their halal ness.

The impact of AI has been considered in many sectors like- the South Korean Halal tourism sector (Marlinda et al., 2021), the food sector (Kakani et al., 2020; Mavani et al., 2022), the manufacturing sector (Lee et al., 2018), the healthcare sector (Gautam et al., 2022), the construction sector (Abioye et al., 2021), the accounting sector (Luo et al., 2018), and the oil and gas sector (Sircar et al., 2021).

In addition, with gen Y (1981–1996), gen Z (1997–2012), and women travelers as three major key segments holding global Islamic tourism market and gen alpha (2010–2024) as a precursor, Islamic tourism stakeholders need to be aware of these segments' own characteristics, travel habits, motivation, decision-making and uses the latest technology as AI to provide quality product and services based on the customers' characteristics (Mastercard-Crescent Rating, 2022, 2023).

By having these tech-enabled segments, the Islamic tourism industry is expected to register USD 225 billion receipts via 230 million arrivals by 2028 (Mastercard-Crescent Rating, 2023). In tandem, it is aimed that, by the year 2030, 60% of Muslim travel expenditures will be booked online and the AI market will register USD $15.7 trillion Mastercard-Crescent Rating (2022).

With such immense potential, studies in this field are thus urgently needed to guide Islamic tourism stakeholders in understanding the potential threats and advantages of technology adoption and boost their preparedness to meet the market demand.

2. Literature Review

In order to create expert systems that can simulate, make forecasting, or classify data to help with solving issues and making decisions, AI combines computer science with large datasets of algorithms (IBM, 2023).

The example is in the captcha or as we watch YouTube videos where the subsequent video suggestion or the advertisement displayed are based on the algorithms.

In a relevant study, it was found that tourists' adoption of AI devices for both airlines services and hospitality industry are strongly influenced by social influence, entertainment motivation, humanoid, performance, and effort expectancy and emotions toward the AI devices (Chi et al., 2022). Besides, as technologies are improved by highly interactive systems, increased capability and have more user-friendly interfaces, it is vital to explore the perceived interactivity (Go et al., 2020). In addition, leveraging AI in Islamic tourism provision results to enhanced customer service, personalized recommendation, optimized offerings, streamlined trip planning, and targeted marketing (Mastercard-CrescentRating, 2023).

As per IBM Global AI Adoption Index, 2022, 44% AI applications are recorded and processed by organizations involving 7,502 businesses worldwide while (66%) of companies are either presently employing or planning to use AI in their sustainability goals (IBM, 2023). Furthermore, the worldwide AI market value is estimated at 100 billion USD and is expected to grow to reach two trillion by the year 2030 (Thormundsson, 2023).

The Asian Banker (2023) report indicated that AI adoption in Singapore has surged to 51% for weak AI and 57% for generative (strong AI), respectively. The same source also indicated that the figure is expected to grow continuously with 92% of the firms studied are planning to adopt the technology in the next 12 months from the current 67%. Data from https://www.statista.com also indicated that in 2022, the online travel market in Southeast Asia is worth nearly 17 billion USD and is projected to rise to 44 billion USD by 2025 (Gambold, 2023).

By providing a thorough overview of the present research instance, Li et al. (2021) offer insights into the trends, subjects, and key authors in the area through their bibliometric study.

It requires the stakeholders to invest in the strong AI to avoid customers' frustration while enjoying stronger competitive advantage. Besides, a larger volume of Muslim AI experts helps to eliminate biases in information dissemination which according to (Abas et al., 2022) helps to maintain Islamic tourism sanctity and uphold the objective of Syariah (Maqasid Syariah).

African American entrepreneurs with the use of Generative AI become able to mitigate digital divide and also addresses resource constraints. Generative AI provides cost effective tools for several works like marketing, customer interactions, and creation of content. It is beneficial for entrepreneurs to use AI as it generate multilingual content and perform operational tasks automatically that will enable them to compete in tourism industry (George & Mattathil, 2025).

According to Tussyadiah (2020) and Rahmadian et al. (2022), the integration of big data, IoT, and AI tools in the chain of tourism services enables the smart tourism environment. However, Kirtil and Askun (2021) clarified that chatbots and virtual assistants driven by AI can encourage visitors to make well-informed travel decisions, hence promoting sustainable tourism practices.

Research done by Euromonitor International (2023) indicates about the shifting toward value-based tourism practices that are expected to perform as per standard over the 2023–2027 period, along with average growth of 12% or more per annum. Also sustainability has become key area within the tourism industry.

With the use of Generative AI, it has been anticipated a transformative effect on hotel and tourism sector that offers personalized and efficient services to meet travelers need. AI also helpful in management of hotels and tourism business as it enhance operational efficiency, security measures, reduce the cost, and boost up competitiveness in market. It has been observed that by the use of AI tools in creation of high-quality content, a significant implication on future of market in hospitality and tourism industry arises (Yang & Chew, 2021).

Halal is becoming more and more essential to Muslims every day. It will be easier for businesspeople to handle their work with greater tact if people are conscious of halal items.

It has been seen that halal not only is focusing on production of halal goods and services but also provides strong business strategy (Utomo et al., 2020).

Islamic tourism refers to tourism-related activities that comply with Islamic jurisprudence. In terms of market and dynamic, the worldwide Muslim market is accounted for 1.46 billion. Of this figure, the market composition is made up of 22.9% millennial, 27.2% gen Z, and 21.5% gen alpha. Based on the market profiling, it technically indicates that the industry is currently dominated by the gen Y or known as the millennial (Debra Kamin, 2019; Mastercard-Crescent Rating, 2023; MOTAC, 2020).

By using AI halal certification process becomes easy as it provides automatic verification and validation facilities in speedy manner. The Indonesian Ministry of Religion's Halal Product Guarantee Administering Agency (BPJPH) is concentrating on employing AI to provide halal activities. AI will benefit the Halal tourism sector by lowering costs, improving product quality and safety, and assessing patterns for halal credentials (KEMENKOPUKM, 2023).

3. Research Methodology

1. Research design
   The research employs a descriptive and exploratory research design.
   It seeks to examine, interpret, and synthesize secondary data in order to comprehend how AI is impacting the future of Halal tourism in the world and in the region.

2. Data collection method
   The research relies solely on secondary data.

Sources include:

- Peer-reviewed journal articles
- Conference papers
- Books and book chapters
- Reports from international organizations (e.g., UNWTO, Crescent Rating, Dinar Standard)
- Industry white papers and market research reports
- Case studies of Halal tourism destinations and AI uptake
- Relevant government reports
- Quality news reports on AI and tourism

The literature collection is specifically geared toward 2015–2025 to guarantee relevance and current information.

3. Data sources

- *Academic databases*: Scopus, Web of Science, Google Scholar
- *Tourism industry reports*: Global Muslim Travel Index (GMTI), State of the Global Islamic Economy Report
- *AI reports*: PwC, McKinsey, and World Economic Forum reports
- *Halal industry reports*: Crescent Rating, Salaam Gateway
- *Official websites*: Ministry of Tourism websites of major Muslim-majority nations (e.g., Malaysia, Indonesia, UAE)
- *Technology blogs and research portals*: AI-related perspectives with regard to the tourism industry

4. Research objectives

- To outline current and emerging AI technologies utilized in Halal tourism.
- To comprehend the advantages and disadvantages of AI to the Halal tourism sector.
- To predict future directions in Halal tourism influenced by AI developments.
- To offer advice to policymakers, Halal tourism operators, and technology creators.

5. Limitations

- Because the research is based only on secondary data, primary data findings (e.g., customer questionnaires or interviews) are not provided.
- Some of the secondary sources may vary in credibility; efforts are made to select peer-reviewed or verified information.

4. Application of AI in Halal Tourism

It has been observed by Fitriani Tobing et al. (2024) in their research work that use of AI in halal sector plays a very important role. AI might be used to track the flow of halal items, ensuring their long-term reliability and validity by monitoring the whole process from manufacturers to consumers.

A chat bot is a software application that may be termed a robot or a bot, but it works to conduct conversations with customers through the use of natural language (Melián-González et al., 2021). This is accomplished by voice or text using specific gadgets like as PCs, cellphones, Google, Siri, and Amazon Alexa (Pillai & Sivathanu, 2020).

4.1. Personalized Halal Travel Experiences

AI-powered recommendation tools can analyze user data – such as travel history, eating patterns, prayer times, and language needs – to offer customized itineraries and service options. For instance:

- Smart itinerary advisors suggest destinations with Halal-approved facilities.
- AI-powered chatbots converse in local dialects and answer Shariah-associated queries regarding travel.
- Machine-learning trends track users' preferences to enhance future recommendations.

4.2. Halal Compliance Verification

One of the biggest issues in Halal tourism is maintaining religious compliance among service providers. AI can assist with:

- Automated checks for Halal certification through international database integration.
- Image and text recognition programs to interpret restaurant menus, product packaging, and facility information for Halal checking.
- Blockchain–AI hybrids to ensure end-to-end transparency in Halal food provenance and ethical supply chains.

4.3. Sentiment and Behavior Analysis

- NLP software reviews, social media, and feedback to measure consumer satisfaction and issues of non-compliance.
- Real-time monitoring of online content can identify ethical concerns or non-compliance by Halal-certified plants.
- AI sentiment analysis helps tourism boards and operators know what Muslim travelers expect and experience.

4.4. Virtual Assistants and Multilingual Support

AI-powered assistants (e.g., kiosks and mobile apps) provide:

- Real-time Qibla direction
- Prayer time reminders
- Halal restaurant finders
- Cultural etiquette advice

These technologies enhance convenience and spiritual comfort, vital for faith-aware travelers.

4.5. Intelligent Infrastructure and Predictive Analytics

AI facilitates the planning and management of intelligent tourism infrastructure:

- Crowd management systems to preserve modesty and mitigate over-tourism at holy Islamic sites.
- Predictive analytics for demand forecasting, enabling tour operators to coordinate their services with Muslim holiday calendars (e.g., Ramadan, Hajj).
- Sustainability modelling ensures green practices consistent with Islamic environmental ethics.

➢ Advantages of AI in tourism:

1. Improvement of customer satisfaction and service
    - Chatbots and virtual assistants powered by AI offer real-time assistance and customized support.
    - They respond and offer suggestions in a fast manner.
    - This promotes customer satisfaction and a positive experience throughout the journey.
2. More personalization and customization of travel experiences
    - AI analyzes large amounts of data about preferences, behavior, and history.
    - It customizes recommendations and services to suit unique traveler requirements.
    - Personalized experiences promote greater customer attachment, loyalty, and repeat business.
3. Effective operations and resource utilization
    - AI makes it easier to automate client inquiries, route scheduling, and booking operations.
    - This enhances operational efficiency, eliminates manual labor, and optimizes productivity.
    - Predictive analytics provide precise demand forecasts, price optimization, and inventory control, thereby optimizing revenue opportunities.
4. Data-based decision-making in marketing and business strategies
    - AI processes data from varied sources such as customer preferences, market trends, and competitors.
    - Companies utilize these insights to enhance marketing campaigns, products, and growth strategies.
    - Data-driven decision-making enhances marketing effectiveness, customer targeting, and business growth amid competition.

5. Ethical and Religious Considerations in AI-driven Halal Tourism

Implementation of AI adoption carries substantial risk and ethical concerns that need to be managed for safe and accountable use. Of utmost concern among ethical issues are algorithmic bias, transparency, and accountability that have the potential to produce unequal and unjust results and amplify prevalent disparities in other fields, including healthcare. Ensuring ethical inputs in AI systems is necessary with paradigms proposing beneficence, justice, and explainability to manage AI technology development and deployment (Carson et al., 2021).

5.1. Ensuring Shariah Compliance in Algorithms

AI algorithms must be trained with culture-conscious datasets to Islamic principles. Biases in algorithms can lead to inappropriate suggestions or exclusion of religious requirements.

5.2. Data Privacy and Protection

Handling religious and personal data requires high ethical standards:

- Use of personal data by consent
- Encryption of data and secure transfer of sensitive data
- Compliance with global data law (e.g., GDPR) and Islamic ethics regarding privacy

5.3. Cultural Sensitivity in AI Interactions

AI interfaces should not stereotype, misrepresent Islamic culture, or misinterpret religious norms. Scholars of Islam and culture experts should work together with developers to define AI development.

6. Case Studies and Industry Adoption

➢ Crescent rating's AI-powered halal travel intelligence
  Leading Halal tourism authority Crescent Rating launched AI-driven travel intelligence solutions to help destinations better serve Muslim travelers.
  Their AI platform predicts travel trends, Muslim consumer behavior, and offers intelligence on popular Halal-friendly amenities. Destinations like Malaysia, Singapore, and Japan used Crescent Rating's AI solutions to optimize their marketing efforts for Muslim tourists.
  AI contribution:

  - Predictive analytics on Muslim traveler behavior
  - Market profiling and segmentation
  - Enhancing destination readiness for Halal compliance (Mastercard-CrescentRating, 2022)

➢ Halal trip's AI chatbot for Muslim travelers
Halal trip, a Muslim travel services platform, introduced an AI chatbot providing real-time Halal restaurant recommendations, prayer notifications, and Muslim traveler destination insights.
AI contribution:

- 24/7 personalized travel assistance
- Real-time location-based Halal service recommendations
- Building customer trust through religious compliance while traveling (HalalTrip, 2021)

➢ Japan's smart tourism cities with Halal integration
Japan's government promoted "Smart Tourism Cities" which integrated AI technologies like facial recognition, automated translation, and information centers based on AI.
In areas like Osaka and Kyoto, AI apps provide Muslim tourists Halal food finder services, locators for prayer facilities, and cultural etiquette guidance.
AI contribution:

- AI translation and communication for non-Japanese Muslim tourists
- Mobile apps that recommend Halal-certified outlets
- Immersive, personalized tourist experiences with cultural sensitivity (MLIT, 2022)

➢ Malaysia's AI-driven Halal certification system
Malaysia's Halal development corporation (HDC) is constructing AI-driven systems for quicker, more efficient Halal certification processing.
AI streamlines document verification, compliance verification, and inspection schedules, reducing human error and time.
AI contribution:

- Enhanced streamlined Halal certification for business-to-tourism industry ventures (hotels, restaurants, spas)
- Increased trust and integrity in Halal compliance
- Sustaining Malaysia's vision of remaining a world leader in Halal tourism (HDC, 2023)

➢ OIC nations utilizing AI for Halal tourism growth
OIC countries, including UAE and Turkey, are integrating AI into tourism apps to recommend Muslim-compliant hotels, Halal restaurants, and prayer rooms according to travelers' live profiles and needs.
AI contribution:

- AI-based recommendation systems
- Customized Halal travel packages
- Enhancing Muslim tourist satisfaction and loyalty (Salaam Gateway, 2023)

7. Challenges and Opportunities

AI has wide and far-reaching social consequences that can be either a "curse or a blessing" due to the potential for beneficial as well as adverse impacts (Aly, 2020). A range of emotions, from excitement to fear, are caused by the possible role of AI in the near future (D'Cruz et al., 2022). Positively, by boosting productivity and efficiency, AI technology has the potential to revolutionize a number of industries (Yang, 2022). Nevertheless, the arrival of AI is not without problems, including data and privacy security and the ethical issues related to AI use (Gerke et al., 2020).

Additionally, Li et al. (2021) highlight certain restrictions and difficulties when integrating internet data for tourism projections. For example, the effectiveness of tourism forecasting may be impacted by the quality of online search engine data, such as keyword accuracy and frequency. On the other hand, social media data may contain noise or unrelated information, which could affect the accuracy of predicting models.

Issues like data complexity, bias in algorithms, financial issues, and socio-ethical issues have to be addressed to harness all the possibilities of these advances in tourism (Samara et al., 2020).

7.1. Issues in the Application of AI in Tourism

1. Privacy and security issues:
   - The possibility of data breaches, violation of privacy, and unauthorized use of sensitive customer data.
   - Requirement for strong security practices, data protection, and compliance with regulations.
2. Integration with existing infrastructure:
   - Challenge in integrating AI with legacy or siloed systems.
   - Requires investment in compatible infrastructure and diligent planning.
3. Workforce training and the skill gap:
   - Insufficient internal resources and expertise to develop, implement, and maintain AI solutions.
   - Need for employee upskilling, workforce training programs, and an innovation culture.
   - Shortage of AI literacy among providers of tourism
4. High implementation cost of SMEs
5. Ethical issues in autonomous decision-making
6. Insufficient Muslim-applicable data in AI training sets

7.2. Opportunities in Applying AI in Tourism

1. Increased personalization and automation:
   - The capability to personalize the customer experience and automate processes.
2. Data-driven decision-making:
   - Increased efficiency and productivity through data analytics insights.
3. Operational streamlining and resource optimization:
   - Improved resource allocation, resulting in greater profitability.
4. Innovative products and services:
   - Creation of AI-based solutions such as chatbots for individualized customer support and predictive analytics for demand planning.
5. Competitive advantage:
   - Standing out from the competition by providing superior, tech-savvy experiences.
   - New customer acquisition and retention in a competitive marketplace.
   - AI provides global platform to Halal tourism with no compromise in quality.

8. Conclusions and Future Outlook

AI by improvement in productivity and economic performance enhanced competitiveness among tourism companies along with transforming customer experiences. This will result increased operational efficiency and provide competitive advantage in market (Adam et al., 2020). Application of AI explored at different levels of tourism sector including Halal tourism that is mostly depends on customer services (Aldoseri, 2024). AI adoption is essential to realize higher tourist satisfaction, increased efficiency, enhanced productivity, and delivering positive experiences that ensure repeated visits and customer loyalty.

Analysis of successful AI deployments identifies a number of key strategies and results:

- *Personalization*: Recommendation systems powered by AI allow tourism companies to provide personalized travel recommendations based on individual tastes, resulting in higher customer interaction and conversion rates.
- *Efficiency*: AI-powered automation simplifies processes and minimizes manual labor, enhancing efficiency and productivity in tourism companies.
- *Customer satisfaction*: Virtual assistants and AI-driven chatbots improve customer service through immediate support and tailored assistance, which results in greater satisfaction to customer.
- *Optimization of revenue*: Through the use of AI demand forecasting and estimation of pricing is possible which will enable companies to increase revenue by adopting dynamic price as per market conditions.

Together, these effective AI applications show how AI is revolutionizing the travel and tourism industry by opening up new opportunities for creativity, efficiency, and better customer service. As tourism businesses keep using AI technology, deliberate adoption and evaluation of key results will be critical to sustaining achievement and competitiveness in the digital age.

AI is revolutionizing the way Halal tourism is being offered and consumed. By personalization, operational efficiency, and higher compliance, AI can make Halal tourism a highly responsive and inclusive travel market. Its success, however, depends on ethical deployment, cultural sensitivity, and strategic management. As Muslim visitors place a greater emphasis on efficient and Shariah-based experiences, the incorporation of AI – driven by Islamic values – will play an important part in determining the future of this vibrant sector.

In general, AI has a wide range of possible uses in the travel industry, from customer service and customization to data analysis and revenue management. With the power of AI technologies, tourism companies can tap into new areas of innovation, efficiency, and competitiveness and, ultimately, improve the overall travel experience for consumers and fuel sustainable growth in the tourism sector.

Strategic Recommendations

- *Develop AI Halal tourism guidelines*: Collaborate with Shariah boards, AI programmers, and tourism experts to formulate moral guidelines.
- *Invest in Muslim-specific tech startups*: Foster innovation in apps, platforms, and tools aimed at faith tourism.
- *Capacity building*: Train Halal tourist operators in digital skills and AI application.
- *Government incentives*: Grant tax relief and subsidies for embracing technology in Halal tourism.
- *Public–private partnerships*: Encourage partnerships between technology firms, tourist boards, and Islamic institutions.

References

Abas, R., Mohd Zahari, M. S., & Mohd Radzi, S. (2022). The influence of technology in tapping the full potential of Islamic tourism. *International Journal of Social Science Research (IJSSR)*, *4*(1), 2710–62761. https://myjms.mohe.gov.my/index.php/ijssr/article/view/17006

Abioye, S. O., Oyedele, L. O., Akanbi, L., Ajayi, A., Davila Delgado, J. M., Bilal, M., Akinade, O. O., & Ahmed, A. (2021). Artificial intelligence in the construction industry: A review of present status, opportunities, and future challenges. *Journal of Building Engineering, 44,* 103299. https://doi.org/10.1016/j.jobe.2021.103299

Adam, M., Wessel, M., & Benlian, A. (2020). AI-based Chatbots in customer service and their effects on user compliance. *Electron Mark*, *31*, 427–445.

Agrawal, R. (2021). Internet of things in tourism: Challenges and opportunities in "The New Normal." *International Journal of Science and Research*, *10*(7), 513–516.

Aldoseri, A. (2024). methodological approach to assessing the current state of organizations for AI-based digital transformation. *Applied System Innovation*, *7*, 14.

Aly, H. (2020). Digital transformation, development and productivity in developing countries: Is artificial intelligence a curse or a blessing? *Review of Economics and Political Science*, *7*, 238–256.

Battour, M., Mady, K., Salaheldeen, M., Elsotouhy, M., Elbendary, I., & Boğan, E. (2023). AI-enabled technologies to assist Muslim tourists in Halal-friendly tourism. *Journal of Islamic Marketing*, *14*(5), 1291–1309. https://doi.org/10.1108/JIMA-01-2022-0001

Carson, S., Casillas, A., Castellon-Lopez, Y., Mansfield, L., Morris, D., Barron, J., & Brown, A. (2021). COVID-19 vaccine decision-making factors in racial and ethnic minority communities in Los Angeles, California. *JAMA Network Open*, *4*, e2127582.

Chen, M., Jiang, Z., Xu, Z., Shi, A., Gu, M., & Li, Y. (2022). Overviews of Internet of Things applications in China's hospitality industry. *Processes*, *10*, 1256.

CrescentRating. (2022). *AI to revolutionize Muslim travel market*.

D'Cruz, P., Du, S., Noronha, E., Parboteeah, K. P., Trittin-Ulbrich, H., & Whelan, G. (2022). Technology, megatrends and work: Thoughts on the future of business ethics. *Journal of Business Ethics*, *180*, 879–902.

Debra Kamin. (2019). The rise of Halal tourism. *The New York Times*, 1–4.

Euromonitor International. (2023, May 23). *Top three travel trends for 2023*. Euromonitor International. https://www.euromonitor.com/article/top-three-travel-trends-for-2023

Gautam, A., Chirputkar, A., & Pathak, P. (2022). Opportunities and challenges in the application of artificial intelligence-based technologies in the healthcare Industry. *International Interdisciplinary Humanitarian Conference for Sustainability, IIHC 2022 – Proceedings,* 1521–1524. https://doi.org/10.1109/IIHC55949.2022.10059767

George, B., & Mattathil, A. P. (2025). Empowering African American tourism entrepreneurs with generative AI: Bridging innovation and cultural heritage. *Societies*, *15*, 34. https://doi.org/10.3390/soc15020034

Gerke, S., Minssen, T., & Cohen, G. (2020). Ethical and legal challenges of artificial intelligence-driven healthcare. In *Artificial intelligence in healthcare* (pp. 295–336). Elsevier.

Go, H., Kang, M., & Suh, S. B. C. (2020). Machine learning of robots in tourism and hospitality: Interactive technology acceptance model (iTAM) – Cutting edge. *Tourism Review*, *75*(4), 625–636.

Halal Development Corporation (HDC), Malaysia. (2023). *Harnessing AI in Halal certification*.

HalalTrip. (2021). *Innovations in Muslim travel services*. https://www.halaltrip.com/

https://hdcglobal.com/

https://www.mlit.go.jp/en/

IBM. (2023). *AI vs. machine learning vs. deep learning vs. neural networks: What's the difference?* https://www.ibm.com/blog/ai-vs-machine-learning-vsdeep-learning-vs-neural-networks/

Kakani, V., Nguyen, V. H., Kumar, B. P., Kim, H., & Pasupuleti, V. R. (2020). A critical review on computer vision and artificial intelligence in food industry. *Journal of Agriculture and Food Research, 2*(February), 100033. https://doi.org/10.1016/j.jafr.2020.100033

Kansakar, P., Munir, A., & Shabani, N. (2019). Technology in the hospitality industry: Prospects and challenges. *IEEE Consumer Electronics Magazine*, *8*(3), 60–65. https://doi.org/10.1109/MCE.2019.2892245

KEMENKOPUKM. (2023). *Artificial intelligence in Halal certification process automation*. SMESTA.

Kirtil, I. G., & Askun, V. (2021). Artificial intelligence in tourism: A review and bibliometrics research. *Advances in Hospitality and Tourism Research-AHTR*, *9*, 205–233.

Lee, J., Davari, H., Singh, J., & Pandhare, V. (2018). Industrial artificial intelligence for industry 4.0-based manufacturing systems. *Manufacturing Letters*, *18*(September), 20–23. https://doi.org/10.1016/j.mfglet.2018.09.002

Li, X., Law, R., Xie, G., & Wang, S. (2021). Review of tourism forecasting research with internet data. *Tourism Management*, *83*, 104245.

Luo, J., Meng, Q., & Cai, Y. (2018). Analysis of the impact of artificial intelligence application on the development of accounting industry. *Open Journal of Business and Management*, *06*(04), 850–856. https://doi.org/10.4236/ojbm.2018.64063.

Marlinda, A. P., Cipto, B., Al-Fadhat, F., & Jubba, H. (2021). The influence of artificial intelligence to support halal tourism policy in South Korea. *IOP Conference Series: Earth and Environmental Science*, *717*(1). https://doi.org/10.1088/1755-1315/717/1/012027

Mastercard-Crescent Rating. (2022, 2023). *Global Muslim Travel Index (GMTI) 2022, 2023*. https://www.crescentrating.com/halal-muslim-travel-market-reports.html

Mastercard-Crescent Rating. (2023). *Global Muslim Travel Index (GMTI) 2023*. https://www.crescentrating.com/reports/global-muslim-travel-index-2023.html

Mavani, N. R., Ali, J. M., Othman, S., Hussain, M. A., Hashim, H., & Rahman, N. A. (2022). Application of artificial intelligence in food industry – A guideline. *Food Engineering Reviews*, *14*(1), 134–175. https://doi.org/10.1007/s12393-021-09290-z

Melián-González, S., Gutiérrez-Taño, D., & Bulchand-Gidumal, J. (2021). Predicting the intentions to use chatbots for travel and tourism. *Current Issues in Tourism*, *24*(2), 192–210. https://doi.org/10.1080/13683500.2019.1706457

Ministry of Land, Infrastructure, Transport and Tourism Japan (MLIT). (2022). *Smart tourism initiatives*.

MOTAC. (2020). *National Tourism Policy (2020–2030)*. https://www.tourism.gov.my/files/uploads/Executive_Summary.pdf

OIC. (2020). *International tourism in the OIC countries: Prospects and challenges 2020*.

Pillai, R., & Sivathanu, B. (2020). Adoption of AI-based chatbots for hospitality and tourism. *International Journal of Contemporary Hospitality Management*, *32*(10), 3199–3226. https://doi.org/10.1108/IJCHM-04-2020-0259

Rahmadian, E., Feitosa, D., & Zwitter, A. (2022). A systematic literature review on the use of big data for sustainable tourism. *Current Issues in Tourism*, *25*, 1711–1730.

Salaam Gateway. (2023). *AI's emerging role in Muslim travel and halal tourism*.

Sircar, A., Yadav, K., Rayavarapu, K., Bist, N., & Oza, H. (2021). Application of machine learning and artificial intelligence in the oil and gas industry. *Petroleum Research*, *6*(4), 379–391. https://doi.org/10.1016/j.ptlrs.2021.05.009

Tobing, F. et al. (2024). The role of artificial intelligence in the halal industry. *Information Management and Business Review*, *16*(3), 159–166.

Tussyadiah, I. (2020). A review of research into automation in tourism: Launching the annals of tourism research curated collection on artificial intelligence and robotics in tourism. *Annals of Tourism Research*, *81*, 102883.

Utomo, S. B., Sekaryuni, R., Widarjono, A., Tohirin, A., & Sudarsono, H. (2020). Promoting Islamic financial ecosystem to improve halal industry performance in Indonesia: A demand and supply analysis. *Journal of Islamic Marketing*. https://doi.org/10.1108/JIMA-12-2019-0259

Yang, C.-H. (2022). How artificial intelligence technology affects productivity and employment: Firm-level evidence from Taiwan. *Research Policy*, *51*, 104536.

Yang, J., & Chew, E. (2021). A systematic review for service humanoid robotics model in hospitality. *International Journal of Social Robotics*, *13*, 1397–410.

Chapter 18

Promoting Halal Tourism via University Curriculum

Mohamed Jaafari[a] *and Mohamed Louza*[b]

[a] *University Sultan Moulay Slimane, Morocco*
[b] *University Cadi Ayyad, Morocco*

Abstract

The current study investigates how universities can mainstream halal tourism into study programs in order to prepare future industry experts with the skills needed for this burgeoning industry all over the world. The research that is conducted with 146 participants from universities, academics, and industry experts examines their views on halal tourism, its key characteristics, advantages of incorporating it into study programs, and optimal teaching methods. The survey respondents perceive halal tourism as being family-oriented and embracing, with its key characteristics being cultural experiences and halal food. The respondents believe incorporating halal tourism into academic programs would be more effective in preparing graduates for the profession of tourism and hospitality, stimulate industry growth, and promote cultural exchange. The survey highlighted the first-hand experience, with internships considered the best way of educating on halal tourism. The respondents also had a preference for interactive methods, such as oral and written presentations and audio–visual devices, for communication and interaction. The interest in research on halal tourism was highest among young respondents, with a substantial response from female respondents, under 25, highlighting its broad attraction across age and gender categories. The study underscores the importance of a holistic approach toward research on halal tourism, with experience and knowledge blended. To this end, universities must foster industry mutual partnerships and apply up-to-date teaching technologies and cultural understanding in

Halal Tourism and Artificial Intelligence: New Approaches for a New Generation, 261–277

Published under exclusive licence by Emerald Publishing Limited
doi:10.1108/978-1-80686-165-120261020

order to ready and empower their forthcoming graduates and stakeholders for career growth in this rapidly developing and spreading industry.

Keywords: Halal tourism education; halal tourism; university curriculum; cultural sensitivity; tourism education

1. Introduction

The global tourism industry is undergoing a significant transformation, increasingly embracing inclusivity and cultural sensitivity. Halal tourism, which provides for the specific requirements of Muslim travelers by providing services and facilities that comply with Islamic principles, is one of the fastest-growing segments in this field. Key components of halal tourism include halal-certified food and beverages, prayer facilities, gender-segregated recreational areas, modest clothing options, and Islamic financing options for travel and accommodation. These components ensure that Muslim travelers can maintain their religious practices while enjoying their travel experiences. Accordingly, Battour and Ismail (2016) report that halal tourism is "any tourism object or action which is permissible according to Islamic teachings to use or engage by Muslims in tourism industry" (p. 151). The promotion of halal tourism is essential in tapping into the lucrative Muslim travel market, which is projected to continue growing in the coming years.

Indeed, in the recent past, the concept of "halal tourism" has emerged as a growing trend in the travel industry. The global Muslim population is significant, and with increasing disposable incomes and a growing desire to explore the world, the demand for halal-compliant tourism services has surged. Hence, on the basis of the growing Muslim population worldwide, the travel industry is witnessing a rising demand for experiences that adhere to Islamic ethics and values. According to the Global Muslim Travel Index (GMTI) 2020, the number of Muslim international travelers is projected to reach 230 million by 2026, representing more than 10% of the global travel market (CrescentRating, 2020). This evolution is driven by factors such as rising disposable incomes, a youthful demographic, and a growing awareness of halal-friendly travel options. As the report CrescentRating (2020) highlights, "Muslim travelers spent an estimated $194 billion in 2019, and this figure is expected to grow significantly in the coming years" (p. 4). More recent and ampler news report is published by Aamer Yaqub as follows:

> The Global Muslim Travel Index has highlighted a significant increase in Muslim travelers worldwide. In 2013, 108 million Muslims traveled internationally, and by 2019, this number had surged to 160 million. Post-pandemic recovery is evident, with 140 million Muslims expected to travel in 2023. Experts predict that by 2028, 230 million Muslim travelers will be spending an estimated $225 billion annually. (*Halal Times,* 2024)

In fact, the integration of halal tourism into the broader tourism strategy can lead to significant economic benefits, including job creation, increased investment, and cultural exchange (Henderson, 2016). Several countries and companies have emerged as leaders in the halal tourism market. For example, destinations like Turkey, Malaysia, and the United Arab Emirates have become leaders in halal tourism, attracting millions of Muslim tourists annually. Malaysia, more particularly, has consistently ranked as the top halal-friendly destination due to its comprehensive halal certification system and Muslim-friendly facilities. Mohsin et al. (2016) note that "Malaysia's commitment to halal tourism is evident in its extensive network of halal-certified restaurants, prayer facilities, and family-friendly attractions" (p. 138). Similarly, Turkey and Indonesia have invested heavily in promoting their halal tourism offerings, attracting millions of Muslim tourists each year.

Recognizing the growing potential of the halal tourism market, "with or without a majority Muslim population, many countries boast businesses focusing on this segment" (Pamukcu & Sariisik, 2021, p. 391). Indeed, regions around the world, including Europe, North America, and Southeast Asia, are actively developing initiatives to cater to Muslim travelers. These efforts involve creating Muslim-friendly amenities, certification programs, standards of Muslims expectations (Pamukcu & Sariisik, 2021), and culturally inclusive marketing strategies to tap into this lucrative market.

As halal tourism continues to expand globally, it is essential to address the educational needs that arise from this growth. Accordingly, partnerships between universities and industry are essential for translating academic theory into practical halal tourism education. Such collaborations can significantly improve the quality and relevance of halal tourism curricula.

The increasing demand for culturally inclusive services highlights the importance of equipping future tourism professionals with the necessary knowledge and skills. Integrating halal tourism into university curricula becomes vital for meeting these industry standards of quality profile of workforce. This assumption synchronizes with Pamukcu and Sariisik's (2021, p. 338) emphasis on standardization "to gain customers' trust in the products and services offered," underscoring the need for specialized education to uphold these standards and foster a culturally competent workforce. Therefore, Hsu (2018) published a paper advocating for the integration of academic understanding and practical implementation. She says:

> In the context of the changing economic, social, and technological environments, this paper projects the need for radical transformations of tourism education, including curriculum, program offering, pedagogy, and learning environment. Entrepreneurship, innovation, crisis management, data analytics, humanities, and communication are essential elements of broad-based tourism curricula … Graduates equipped with conventional management competencies, such as marketing, finance, and human capital, are no longer sufficiently prepared for their future. Entrepreneurship

> and innovation should also be embedded in their learning. The curriculum and extracurricular activities should be designed to nurture the students' entrepreneurial and innovative spirit and level of excitement. (p. 1)

Accordingly, promoting halal tourism is crucial, both within the industry and through educational institutions. In this context, this article explores integrating halal tourism into university academic curricula and its potential impact on the industry. Incorporating halal tourism into university programs is essential to equip the next generation of tourism professionals with standardized certifications to accommodate this thriving market. This investigation explores the current state of halal tourism education in Morocco, including the preferred teaching methods and key objectives identified by industry stakeholders.

Research questions:

- What are the primary characteristics and teaching methods preferred for halal tourism education?
- How do demographic factors (gender, age, educational status) influence the interest in halal tourism education?
- What are the key objectives for integrating halal tourism into university curricula?

2. Literature Review

This literature review explores existing research on this subject, underscoring significant results and detecting gaps in the current academic landscape. The integration of halal tourism into academic curricula is crucial for the development of halal tourism industry. This sentiment is echoed by Liburd et al. (2018), who argue that "The continued growth, complexity, and socio-economic significance of tourism have played a part in prompting universities to meet the demands and opportunities created by the tourism industry" (p. 100). Indeed, tourism higher education is crucial for addressing misconceptions and stereotypes, as it provides a platform for accurate information and open dialog. Thus, it is evident that the incorporation of halal tourism studies into university programs not only enhances the educational framework but also heavily influences the wider development of the tourism industry as a whole.

2.1. Identifying Relevant Academic Disciplines

Integrating halal tourism into the academic curriculum requires a multidisciplinary approach, involving various fields such as tourism management, hospitality, religious studies, and business. Universities can create specialized modules within these disciplines to address the unique aspects of halal tourism, ensuring that students gain a holistic understanding of the industry. Hsu (2018) suggests that a multidisciplinary approach is essential for effectively integrating halal tourism into the academic curriculum, as "tourism degree graduates will need higher-level soft skills, such as critical thinking, problem solving, and lifelong learning" (p. 181). This comprehensive, multidisciplinary approach ensures that graduates are well-equipped with the necessary skills to navigate and innovate within the complex landscape of the Halal tourism industry.

2.2. Case Studies and Success Stories

Leading universities have pioneered the integration of halal tourism studies into their curricula, setting benchmarks for others to emulate. In a similar vein, institutions in Turkey witness a "rapid increase in tourism programs in many forms as a department in faculties, and as a main branch of science within the body of academic institutes" (Pirnar, 2014, p. 5070). Afyon Kocatepe University and Akdeniz Üniversitesi are prominent examples, which have cooperated with Turkish and international universities, tourism institutions and governmental bodies to organize the 3rd International Halal (Muslim-Friendly) Tourism Congress in May 2024 in Izmir Royal Teos Thermal Resort. This reflects an interest in halal tourism development on the part of Turkish universities that are actively incorporating halal tourism development into their strategic plans to capitalize on the growing demand in this market.

In the same vein, Indonesia also has established specialized programs focused on halal tourism, underscoring the significance of cultural awareness and religious adherence within this industry. These programs encompass a diverse range of subjects, such as halal hospitality, Islamic finance, and cultural tourism. The global appeal of these initiatives has drawn students from across the globe, further promoting the growth of halal tourism worldwide. Below are summaries of two notable references that review successful integrations between tourism industry and higher education.

The article by Liburd et al. (2018) discusses the integration of values in tourism higher education, with a particular focus on the European Master in Tourism Management program (EMTM), "a joint international MSc programme in tourism management jointly delivered by three European Universities" (p. 100). This program exemplifies the growing emphasis on ethical and responsible tourism in academic settings, reflecting broader industry trends such as the emergence of tourism studies on a global level. The authors argue for a curriculum that not only imparts technical knowledge and skills but also cultivates moral and ethical sensibilities among students. They highlight the importance of such educational initiatives in preparing graduates to navigate and lead in the increasingly diverse and globalized tourism sector. As they note,

> In this context of trans-institutional, trans-disciplinary and trans-cultural experience, the EMTM aims to educate graduates who can manage the complex challenges and opportunities in international tourism. This calls for a holistic approach to tourism education where broader aims of the industry and society are explicitly addressed in the curricula. In order to do so the EMTM programme is committed to the values of the Tourism Education

> Futures Institute (TEFI) where notably ethics, responsibility and sustainability are centre stage. (Liburd et al., 2018, p. 101)

This perspective underscores the significance of tourism education as part of broader efforts to adapt tourism curricula to meet the changing demands and values of the world market.

The second example is a systematic literature review that examines the contribution of the Indonesian universities in advancing halal product innovation and education in the global halal market. The review synthesizes findings from various scholarly articles published between 2015 and 2023, focusing on curriculum development, research initiatives, and industry-academia collaboration. This review covers three key topics: the integration of halal standards into academic programs, university involvement in halal certification, and the nurturing of halal product entrepreneurs on campus.

To sum up the reviewed literature, the addition of halal tourism study into universities has played a significant contribution toward the universities, the tourism sector, and the students. Students gain valuable knowledge and skills, and their job marketability and careers thus improve. Universities gain increased admission and international recognition, while the tourism sector gains the skilled workforce needed to provide for the Muslim tourists. These successes demonstrate the potential of tourism education, particularly the study of halal tourism, toward causing improvement and transformation in the tourism sector.

3. Theoretical Framework

The integration of halal tourism into university curricula can be analyzed through several theoretical lenses, including educational theory, cultural competency theory, and experiential learning theory. These frameworks help to understand the importance of incorporating halal tourism education and the preferred teaching methods identified by the respondents.

3.1. Educational Theory

Educational theory provides a foundation for understanding how best to develop and apply curricula that cater to the needs of students and the industry. Constructivist learning theories, such as those proposed by Piaget et al. (1969) and Vygotsky (1978), emphasize the importance of active learning and the construction of knowledge through experience. Piaget et al. (1969) asserts that learning and knowledge is gained through active engagement with one's surroundings, underscoring the need for hands-on learning. Vygotsky (1978) further elaborates that learning is a social process, where interaction with peers and mentors plays a crucial role. This theoretical perspective supports the finding that practical, experiential learning methods, such as internships and field experiences, are highly valued by respondents. By engaging in real-world halal tourism activities, students can construct meaningful knowledge that is directly applicable to their future careers.

3.2. Cultural Competency Theory

Cultural competency theory is crucial for understanding the significance of halal tourism and its integration into educational programs. This theory, as outlined by Cross et al. (1989), posits that effective services must be culturally relevant and responsive to the needs of diverse populations. Cross et al. (1989) state that "cultural competence is a set of congruent behaviors, attitudes, and policies that come together in a system, agency, or among professionals and enables effective work in cross-cultural situations" (p. 28). In the context of halal tourism, this means providing services that align with Islamic principles and values. The survey findings, which highlight the importance of cultural inclusivity and family-friendly services, align with the principles of cultural competency. Educational programs that incorporate halal tourism must, therefore, aim to develop students' cultural competency, ensuring they can meet the needs of Muslim travelers.

3.3. Experiential Learning Theory

Experiential learning theory, proposed by Kolb (1984), emphasizes the impact of experience on learning outcomes. Kolb (1984) describes learning as "the process whereby knowledge is created through the transformation of experience" (p. 26). This theory supports the survey finding that field experience and internships are considered the most important teaching methods for halal tourism education. By engaging in hands-on activities and real-world experiences, students can apply theoretical knowledge in practical settings, leading to deeper learning and skill development. Hence, students learn most effectively when they actively engage in a process of meaning-making and self-reflection.

3.4. Integration of Theories

The integration of educational theory, cultural competency theory, and experiential learning theory provides a comprehensive framework for understanding the effective incorporation of halal tourism into university curricula. Constructivist learning theories emphasize the need for active, student-centered learning experiences, while cultural competency theory highlights the importance of cultural relevance and responsiveness. Experiential learning theory underscores the value of practical, hands-on experiences in the learning process.

This theoretical framework suggests that effective halal tourism education should combine practical experiences, such as internships and field trips, with culturally relevant content that enhances students' understanding of Islamic principles and practices. Additionally, it should foster intercultural exchange and sensitivity, preparing students to work in a diverse and inclusive tourism industry.

4. Integrating Halal Tourism in Moroccan University

This section presents a case study from Morocco on integrating halal tourism into university curricula. Using a systematic methodology, the study defines the objectives, topics, teaching methods, and activities involved in this integration. The research reports empirical findings from surveys of students and tourism industry practitioners, exploring the characteristics of Morocco's halal tourism experience. Finally, the study assesses the success of the halal tourism integration experiment at Cadi Ayyad University, focusing on its teaching methods, activities, and partnerships.

4.1. Rationale for the Implementation

Incorporating Muslim-friendly tourism into university curricula is crucial for preparing the next generation of tourism professionals to cater to the diverse global market. This approach can enhance cultural understanding and promote inclusive practices in the industry. There are three main reasons behind the effort to integrate halal tourism into university programs:

- The rapidly expanding tourism market in Morocco offers substantial economic potential for destinations that cater to the specific requirements and preferences of halal tourists, including families, local and international organizations, and sports clubs.
- Promoting Muslim-friendly tourism can foster greater intercultural understanding, enabling visitors to immerse themselves in diverse Islamic traditions and customs. This commitment to diversity can attract a wider range of international visitors across age, gender, race, and religion.
- Muslim-friendly tourism can make a substantial contribution to enhancing sustainable development in destinations, as it frequently upholds environmentally and socially responsible principles.

Incorporating these key incentives can help universities better endow future tourism specialists to serve the requirements of a varied global market and promote inclusive, culturally sensitive tourism practices.

5. Methodology

To gather comprehensive opinions and insights regarding the integration of halal tourism into university programs, we employed an online survey using Google Forms. This tool was chosen for its accessibility and ease of use, allowing us to reach a wide audience efficiently. The survey was designed to capture both quantitative and qualitative data through a variety of question types.

5.1. Survey Design

The Google Form included several sections aimed at gathering detailed information from respondents. The first section collected demographic information, including age, gender, and occupation. These data helped to contextualize the responses and analyze trends across different demographic groups.

The next section comprised multiple-choice questions designed to gauge respondents' understanding and opinions about halal tourism. These questions focused on the perceived benefits and challenges of integrating halal tourism into university curricula. Additionally, ranking questions were included to allow respondents to prioritize various factors related to halal tourism and its academic integration.

To gain deeper insights, the survey also featured open-ended commentary slots. These sections provided respondents with the opportunity to offer detailed feedback, suggestions, and personal insights regarding halal tourism education. These qualitative data were crucial for understanding the nuances of respondents' opinions and capturing a broad range of perspectives.

5.2. Targeted Population

The survey targeted three specific groups within the Moroccan context: university students, university professors, and tourism sector practitioners. University students, particularly those enrolled in tourism and hospitality programs, provided insights from the perspective of future professionals in the field. Professors specializing in tourism and hospitality subjects contributed their academic and practical expertise. Tourism sector practitioners, including those involved in halal tourism, offered a professional viewpoint on the industry's needs and trends.

5.3. Delivery Method

To ensure a wide and relevant reach, the survey was distributed through professional and class WhatsApp groups. Professional WhatsApp groups included networks of tourism industry professionals and academic faculty, facilitating the involvement of knowledgeable and experienced individuals. Class WhatsApp groups, formed by university students for communication and collaboration, helped to reach a substantial number of students.

5.4. Purpose of Inquiry

The primary objective of this inquiry was to gather comprehensive opinions and insights regarding the integration of halal tourism into university programs. Specifically, the survey aimed to assess the level of awareness and understanding of halal tourism among the targeted population, identify the perceived benefits and challenges of incorporating halal tourism into academic curricula, and collect suggestions and feedback on how best to implement halal tourism education in Moroccan universities.

By utilizing this methodology, the study aimed to provide valuable data that can inform the development and enhancement of university programs. This, in turn, would help prepare future tourism professionals to meet the needs of a diverse and inclusive global market, promoting culturally aware and sustainable tourism practices.

6. Findings

This section presents findings from a survey of Moroccan university students, professors, and tourism professionals. The survey explored attitudes toward integrating halal tourism into university curricula. The results provide a comprehensive overview of respondents' awareness, perceptions, and attitudes regarding halal tourism education. Key benefits, challenges, and recommendations for effective implementation are highlighted. Both quantitative and qualitative data offer valuable insights to inform the development of inclusive, culturally sensitive tourism programs at universities.

6.1. Demographic Profile of Survey Respondents

The survey results underscore the importance of Muslim-friendly tourism through the lens of gender, age, and educational status among Moroccan university students, professors, and tourism sector practitioners.

The image presents three graphs illustrating the demographics of 146 respondents (see Fig. 18.1), who participated in a questionnaire aimed at understanding perspectives on integrating Muslim friendly tourism in the Moroccan university curriculum.

1. *Gender distribution*: A pie chart (Fig. 18.1, top left) showing that 83 respondents (56.8%) are female and 63 respondents (43.2%) are male.
2. *Age distribution*: As depicted in the pie chart (Fig. 18.1, top right), the age breakdown includes:
   - Under 25 years old: 90 respondents (61.6%)
   - Ages 25–35: 18 respondents (12.3%)
   - Ages 35–45: 17 respondents (11.6%)
   - Over 45 years old: 21 respondents (14.4%)
3. *Occupation distribution*: A bar chart (Fig. 18.1, bottom) outlines respondents' occupations, with bachelor students (54.8%), university professors (17.1%), master students (13%), educators (7.5%), tourism promoters (5.5%), tourism trainers (4.1%), tourism trainees (4.8%), and a small number of doctoral students (0.7%).

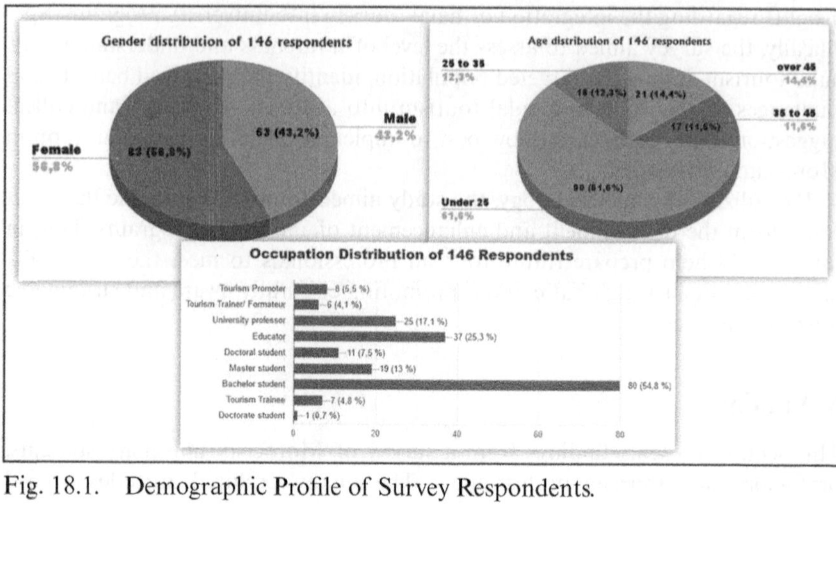

Fig. 18.1. Demographic Profile of Survey Respondents.

The analysis reveals key demographic trends that highlight the growing interest and demand for halal tourism services and education. Given the context of the survey, the demographic data suggest that young, university-level students, particularly those at the bachelor's degree level, are the primary participants in the study. This could imply an interest or relevance of the topic among young academics and future professionals in the tourism sector.

6.2. Respondents' Views on Halal Tourism Characteristics

The survey data reveal several key characteristics of the halal tourism industry as perceived by the respondents. The findings are visually summarized in Fig. 18.2, which displays the frequency and percentage of endorsements for each characteristic of halal tourism.

1. *Suitability for people from different cultural backgrounds*: This characteristic receives the highest endorsement, with 130 respondents (89%) agreeing that halal tourism is suitable for people from various cultural backgrounds (Fig. 18.2). This suggests a broad acceptance and potential appeal of halal tourism to a diverse audience.
2. *Suitability for any family (local and international)*: 79 respondents (54.1%) believe that halal tourism is suitable for any family, whether local or international (Fig. 18.2). This indicates that halal tourism is seen as family-friendly and capable of accommodating the needs of diverse family groups
3. *Offers halal food and drinks*: 67 respondents (45.9%) identified the availability of halal food and drinks as a significant characteristic (Fig. 18.2). This underscores the importance of halal-certified consumables in attracting Muslim tourists.
4. *Organizes cultural activities*: 86 respondents (58.9%) highlighted the organization of cultural activities as a key feature of halal tourism (Fig. 18.2). This reflects the value placed on cultural enrichment and activities that align with Islamic values.

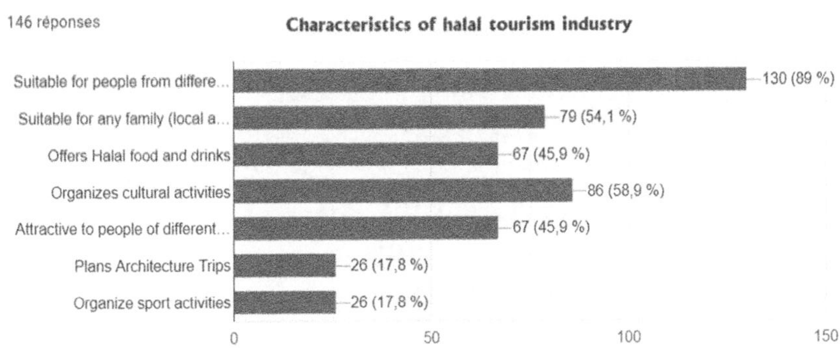

Fig. 18.2. Characteristics of Halal Tourism Industry.

5. *Attractiveness to people of different ages*: 67 respondents (45.9%) noted that halal tourism is attractive to people of different ages (Fig. 18.2). This indicates its potential to cater to a wide age demographic, making it an inclusive travel option.
6. *Plans architecture trips*: This characteristic was less prominent, with only 26 respondents (17.8%) acknowledging it (Fig. 18.2). This suggests that architectural trips are not a primary focus for most respondents when considering halal tourism.
7. *Organizes sports activities*: Similarly, organizing sports activities was noted by 26 respondents (17.8%), indicating that sports are not seen as a major feature of halal tourism by the majority (Fig. 18.2).

Overall, the data suggest that the most valued characteristics of halal tourism are its cultural inclusivity, family-friendliness, and provision of halal food and cultural activities. These features highlight the industry's potential to appeal to a broad and diverse audience, while aspects like architectural and sports trips are considered less central by the respondents.

6.3. Key Topics for Halal Tourism Curriculum

The survey data outline the key topics that respondents believe should be included in a halal tourism curriculum. The responses highlight a diverse range of skills and knowledge areas deemed essential for a comprehensive education in halal tourism.

1. *Intercultural tolerance and communication skills*: This topic received the highest endorsement, with 116 respondents (79.5%) indicating its importance (Fig. 18.3). This emphasizes the necessity for students to understand and effectively communicate across diverse cultures, which is crucial for the success of halal tourism.
2. *International relations*: 107 respondents (73.3%) highlighted the significance of international relations (Fig. 18.3). This suggests a strong need for future

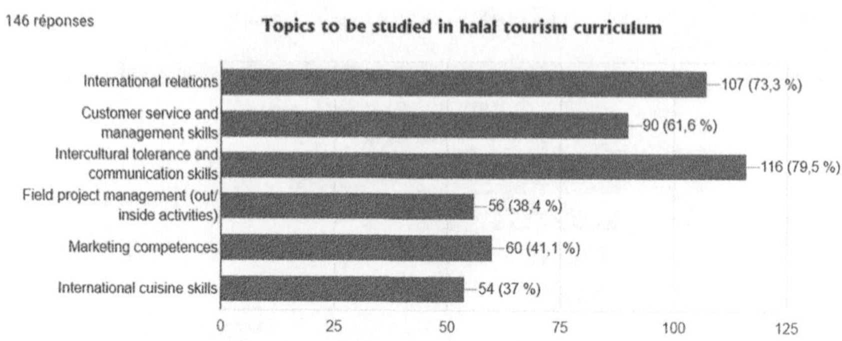

Fig. 18.3. Topics for Study in Halal Tourism Curriculum.

professionals to be well-versed in global dynamics and how they impact the tourism industry, particularly in the context of halal tourism.

3. *Customer service and management skills*: 90 respondents (61.6%) identified customer service and management skills as crucial (Fig. 18.3). This reflects the importance of delivering high-quality service and effective management in halal tourism operations.
4. *Marketing competences*: 60 respondents (41.1%) recognized the importance of marketing skills (Fig. 18.3). This indicates that promoting halal tourism services effectively is seen as vital for attracting and retaining Muslim tourists.
5. *Field project management (outdoor/indoor activities)*: 56 respondents (38.4%) considered field project management essential (Fig. 18.3). This highlights the need for practical skills in planning and executing tourism-related projects, both indoors and outdoors.
6. *International cuisine skills*: 54 respondents (37%) pointed out the significance of international cuisine skills (Fig. 18.3). This underscores the role of culinary knowledge in providing halal-compliant food options and enhancing the overall travel experience.

Overall, the data suggest that the most valued topics for a halal tourism curriculum include intercultural communication, international relations, and customer service. These areas are seen as critical for equipping students with the necessary skills to succeed in the halal tourism industry. Marketing, project management, and culinary skills are also important, though slightly less prioritized.

6.4. Respondents' Evaluation of Halal Tourism Teaching Objectives

The survey results provide insights into the respondents' views on the primary objectives for teaching halal tourism at universities. The following data (see Fig. 18.4) indicate varying degrees of importance attributed to different educational goals.

The survey results indicate a strong consensus on the importance of teaching halal tourism at universities. The primary objectives identified include preparing students for jobs in cultural hospitality and tourism (87.6% rating it very important or important) (Fig. 18.4, top left), developing the halal tourism industry (87.7%) (Fig. 18.4, top right), and encouraging intercultural exchange (87.6%) (Fig. 18.4, bottom left). Promoting research in halal tourism is also considered important, though to a slightly lesser extent, with 78.1% of respondents rating it as very important or important (Fig. 18.4, bottom right). These findings underscore the need for university curricula to focus on practical skills, industry development, and cultural understanding while also supporting academic research in halal tourism.

6.5. Respondents' Assessment of Halal Tourism Teaching Methods

The survey data highlight respondents' views on the importance of various teaching methods for halal tourism education. The responses displayed in Table 18.1

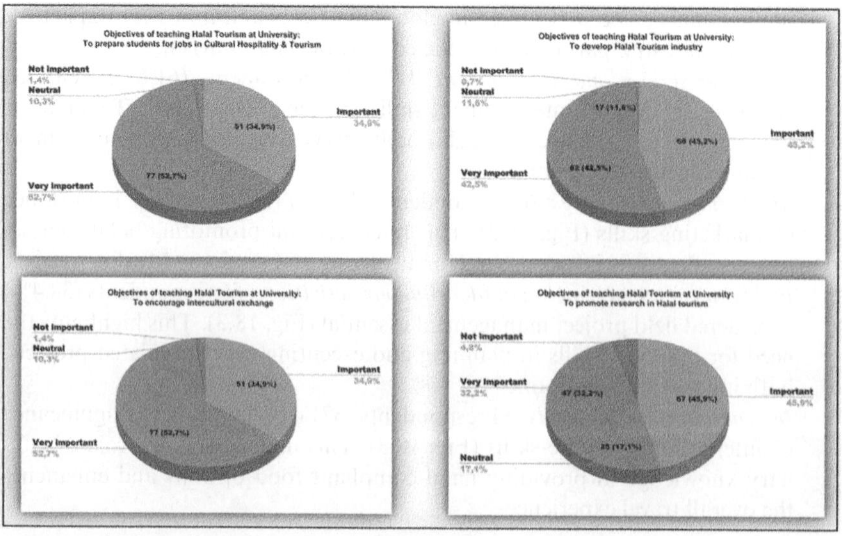

Fig. 18.4. Halal Tourism Teaching Objectives.

Table 18.1. Halal Tourism Teaching Methods.

Teaching Method	Not Important 1/5	Slightly Important 2/5	Important 3/5	Fairly Important 4/5	Very Important 5/5
Theoretical lectures	3 (2.1%)	26 (17.8%)	36 (24.7%)	48 (32.9%)	33 (22.6%)
Audio–visual tools	–	8 (5.5%)	31 (21.2%)	35 (24.0%)	72 (49.3%)
Field experience (internship)	1 (0.7%)	–	17 (11.6%)	27 (18.5%)	100 (68.5%)
Oral & written presentations	4 (2.7%)	12 (8.2%)	25 (17.1%)	45 (30.8%)	63 (43.2%)
Field research	4 (2.7%)	8 (5.5%)	35 (24.0%)	38 (26.0%)	61 (41.8%)

(p. 13) reflect diverse preferences for instructional strategies to effectively teach halal tourism.

The survey results indicate that respondents highly value practical and interactive teaching methods for halal tourism education. Field experience (internships) is rated as the most important method, with 98.6% (Table 18.1) of respondents considering it from fairly important to very important. Audio–visual tools and oral and written presentations are also highly regarded, with 93.3% and 91.1%, respectively, viewing them as important (Table 18.1). While theoretical lectures and field research are slightly less emphasized, they are still considered significant by 80.2% and 91.8% of respondents, respectively (Table 18.1). Overall, the data underscore the necessity of a balanced approach that combines practical, hands-on learning with theoretical and research-based instruction in halal tourism curricula.

7. Discussion and Conclusion

The survey data reveal significant insights into the preferences and priorities of respondents regarding the characteristics, topics, objectives, and teaching methods of halal tourism education. There is a clear emphasis on practical, experiential learning, with field experience (internships) being considered the most crucial method by 98.6% of respondents (see Table 18.1). This preference aligns with the literature and theoretical background, which underscores the importance of hands-on training in preparing students for real-world challenges in the halal tourism industry.

Audio–visual tools and oral and written presentations are also highly valued, with 93.3% and 91.1% of respondents, respectively, viewing them as important (Table 18.1). These methods enhance engagement and communication skills, aligning with scholars' assertion that innovative teaching and learning methods, such as online platforms and experiential learning, are crucial for delivering effective halal tourism education. Theoretical lectures and field research, while slightly less emphasized, remain significant, with 80.2% and 91.8% of respondents, respectively, recognizing their importance (Table 18.1). This suggests a balanced curriculum that combines both practical and theoretical components is essential for effective halal tourism education.

In terms of educational objectives, the data (Fig. 18.4) reveal a strong consensus on the importance of preparing students for careers in cultural hospitality and tourism, developing the halal tourism industry, and encouraging intercultural exchange. These objectives align with Henderson's (2016) view that education is key to promoting cultural awareness and sensitivity, which are essential for the success of tourism industry. Promoting research in halal tourism is also valued, though to a slightly lesser extent, indicating a recognition of the need for academic contributions to advance the field. Hsu (2018) highlights the value of integrative, multidisciplinary tourism curriculum as follows:

> A Tourism Design program will enable students to develop scientific, culturally sensitive, and holistic approaches along with ethical frameworks and legal policies to address challenges faced by various stages of economic development and shape and support sustainable tourism development. (p. 182)

Universities can effectively contribute to the growth and development of the halal tourism industry by adopting a well-rounded curriculum that integrates practical experience, theoretical knowledge, and research. Incorporating these objectives into university programs will not only supply students with vital skills and expertise but also promote a more inclusive and culturally aware tourism sector.

The findings have several implications for the design and implementation of halal tourism curricula in universities. First, the strong preference for practical learning methods highlights the need for universities to establish partnerships with the tourism industry to provide internships and field experiences. Second, the importance placed on audio–visual tools and presentations suggests that universities should invest in modern teaching technologies and interactive platforms to engage students effectively. Lastly, the focus on intercultural exchange and developing the halal tourism industry underscores the need for a curriculum that not only covers the operational aspects of tourism but also cultivates cultural awareness and global understanding.

References

Battour, M., & Ismail, M. N. (2016). Halal tourism: Concepts, practises, challenges and future. *Tourism Management Perspectives*, *19*, 150–154. https://doi.org/10.1016/j.tmp.2015.12.008

CrescentRating. (2020). *Global Muslim Travel Index (GMTI) 2020*. CrescentRating and Mastercard.

Cross, T. L., Bazron, J., Dennis, W., & Isaacs, R. (1989). *Towards a culturally competent system of care: A monograph on effective services for minority children who are severely emotionally disturbed* [Monograph, Georgetown University Child Development Center]. http://files.eric.ed.gov/fulltext/ED330171.pdf

Dinar Standard. (2021). *State of the global islamic economy report 2020/21*. https://salaamgateway.s3.us-east-2.amazonaws.com/special-coverage/sgie22/pdf/

Duman, T. (2011). Value of Islamic tourism offering: Perspectives from the Turkish experience. *Islamic Marketing*, *2*(4), 356–365. https://doi.org/10.1108/17590831111182051

Henderson, J. C. (2016). Halal food, certification and halal tourism: Insights from Malaysia and Singapore. *Tourism Management Perspectives*, *19*, 160–164. https://doi.org/10.1016/j.tmp.2015.12.006

Hsu, C. H. C. (2018). Tourism education on and beyond the horizon. *Tourism Management Perspectives*, *25*, 181–183. https://doi.org/10.1016/j.tmp.2017.11.022

IIUM (International Islamic University Malaysia). (2021). *Bachelor of tourism planning and hospitality management*. Retrieved from IIUM website.

Kolb, D. A. (1984). *Experiential learning: Experience as the source of learning and development*. Prentice-Hall.

Liburd, J. J., Mihalič, T., & Guia, J. (2018). Values in tourism higher education: The European master in tourism management. *Journal of Hospitality, Leisure, Sport and Tourism Education*, *22*, 100–104. https://doi.org/10.1016/j.jhlste.2017.09.003

Mohsin, A., Ramli, N., & Alkhulayfi, B. A. (2016). Halal tourism: Emerging opportunities. *Tourism Management Perspectives*, *19*, 137–143. https://doi.org/10.1016/j.tmp.2015.12.010

Pamukcu, H., & Sariisik, M. (2021). Suggestions for standardization of halal tourism in hospitality industry. *Journal of Islamic Marketing*, *12*(2), 389–407. https://doi.org/10.1108/JIMA-04-2019-0078

Piaget, J., Inhelder, B., & Weaver, H. (1969). *The psychology of the child*. http://ci.nii.ac.jp/ncid/BA21022515

Pirnar, I. (2014). Tourism education universities in Turkey: Comparison of different structures and related effects on education quality. *Procedia: Social & Behavioral Sciences*, *116*, 5070–5074. https://doi.org/10.1016/j.sbspro.2014.01.1075

Risza, H. (2024). The role of universities in pioneering halal product innovation and education in Indonesia. *AL-ISHLAH: Jurnal Pendidikan*, *16*(2), 821–829. https://doi.org/10.35445/alishlah.v16i2.5218

Vygotsky, L. S. (1978). *Mind in society: The development of higher psychological processes*. Harvard University Press.

Yaqub, A. (2024, June 15). Vietnam aims to attract affluent Muslim travelers. *The Halal Times*. https://www.halaltimes.com/vietnam-aims-to-attract-affluent-muslim-travelers/

Webpage

Third International Halal (Muslim-Friendly) Tourism Congress – Muslim-friendly Events. (s.d.). https://www.halaltourismcongress.com/

Chapter 19

Halal Tourism in the Age of Artificial Intelligence: Innovations, Challenges, and Future Prospects

Manabhanjan Sahu

SVKM's Narsee Monjee Institute of Management Studies (Deemed to be University), Hyderabad, India

Abstract

Technology has remodeled every aspect of contemporary life, and Halal tourism is no exception. Artificial intelligence (AI), blockchain, augmented reality (AR), and virtual reality (VR) are transforming travel by reinventing the experiences of Muslim travelers. This chapter examines how these technologies can adjust to Islamic values, providing faith-based customization, transparent communications, and ethically conscious content delivery in a fast-changing digital world. The study adopts a qualitative approach, drawing on real-life case scenarios and field observations to reflect the impact of AI and the digital ecosystem across Halal tourism. The results indicate that immersive tools can enhance destination marketing, facilitate pilgrimage, and enable personalized, culturally considerate travel. Blockchain, in particular, introduces trust and transparency in Halal compliance by simplifying verification processes through smart contracts. Together, these technologies offer a future-ready model of travel that integrates religious sensitivities with convenience and inclusivity. The chapter provides practical guidelines for tourism boards, Halal certification agencies, and developers, emphasizing collaboration to create ethically oriented, digitally inclusive travel systems. It also highlights potential challenges, such as digital divides and algorithmic biases, which may hinder technological advancement. Overall, the chapter underscores

Halal Tourism and Artificial Intelligence: New Approaches for a New Generation, 279–294

Published under exclusive licence by Emerald Publishing Limited
doi:10.1108/978-1-80686-165-120261021

the importance of applying technology in the international Halal tourism sector in a purposeful, non-biased, and value-centered manner.

Keywords: Halal tourism; artificial intelligence; metaverse; blockchain; augmented reality; virtual reality

1. Introduction

A digital revolution is reshaping the global tourism sector, driven by the integration of advanced technologies such as AI, AR, VR, and blockchain. This technological evolution is especially transformative for Halal tourism, a sector that caters to the religious, ethical, and cultural needs of Muslim travelers. As more tourists place more and more demand for experiences based on their values, the meeting of immersive technologies and AI is transforming how destinations are configured, marketed, and experienced.

The proliferation of AI-powered platforms, smart devices, and immersive metaverse environments allows for real-time customization of travel services from itinerary planning and virtual prayer room access to halal dining navigation and culturally sensitive hospitality training ("Blockchain, Internet of Things, and Artificial Intelligence," 2021). These AI-driven solutions enhance both the convenience and trust required in Halal tourism, especially among younger, tech-savvy Muslim travelers.

However, this shift from the conventional paradigm brings a new wave of ethical, cultural, and security challenges. Just as the reliance on IoT and intelligent systems in other sectors raises issues of data integrity, bias, and access inequality, the Halal tourism ecosystem must also contend with data privacy concerns, cultural misrepresentation in virtual environments, and the digital divide affecting travelers from less technologically developed regions (Tiainen, 2024).

To address these challenges, AI and blockchain integration emerges as a promising solution. Blockchain, with its immutable and transparent data infrastructure, can ensure Halal compliance in supply chains, booking systems, and reviews. At the same time, AI systems can deliver personalized, adaptive travel experience, but be able to identify and prevent possible risks, such as cultural insensitivity or misinformation.

Despite the potential of these innovations, the adoption of AI and blockchain in Halal tourism remains limited, hindered by regulatory uncertainty, resource-intensive implementations, and a lack of empirical evidence showcasing successful field applications. There are not many real-world current examples that fuse these technologies within culturally specific tourism contexts.

This chapter aims to bridge that gap by conducting a qualitative, exploratory study of AI and metaverse applications in Halal tourism. It assesses research publications, combines the theoretical frameworks, and presents a conceptual model to promote culturally respectful, technologically enabled tourism ecosystems. By so doing, it offers practical lessons to developers, stewards of tourism and policymakers on how to create inclusive, secure and value aligned experiences for the world's Muslim traveler.

2. Literature Review and Theoretical Framework

The digital revolution has revolutionized the global tourism sector, and Halal tourism is not an exception. The convergence of AI, blockchain, and immersive technologies like AR and VR is redefining the way Muslim travelers interact with travel services (Zambrano et al., 2024). With religious values, moral expectations, and cultural sensitivities having to be respected in such an environment, the overlap of technology and Islamic tourism concepts is building a more tailored, safe, and accessible experience. This section discusses how these digital technologies are transforming Halal tourism, ranging from fully engaged virtual experiences to AI-powered personalization and blockchain-locked trust mechanisms.

2.1. Digital Transformation in Halal Tourism

Halal tourism, based on Islamic values, demands meticulous selection of services like Halal food, prayer rooms, gender-segregated facilities, and culturally sensitive entertainment. With the changing travel requirements of Muslim tourists, so does the need for innovative digital solutions that provide compliance and convenience. New digital technologies such as AR/VR interfaces, AI travel planners, and mobile Halal service finders now provide Muslim travelers with increased control over their trip. For instance, AR can superimpose prayer times and directions to Qibla onto real-life landscapes, whereas VR allows previews of accommodations, dining, and places of worship in immersive detail before actual travel arrangements are finalized. AI personal assistants assist in tailoring itineraries according to Halal requirements, previous travel habits, and instant feedback from other Muslim travelers.

2.2. AI in Personalization and Predictive Services in Halal Tourism

Whereas blockchain safeguards trust, AI brings intelligence to the travel journey. AI engines can process travel history, behavioral patterns, religious inclinations, and contextual information to suggest personalized travel itineraries, eating places, and local activities all Halal-compliant. Principal AI applications in Halal tourism are: Real-time personalization is recommending Halal restaurants, mosques, and gender-segregated recreational activities; anomaly detection is alerting content or places that might contravene Islamic rules; predictive modeling is recommending travel destinations based on prayer calendar dates, regional festivities (e.g., Ramadan-friendly packages), or seasonal variations in Halal tourism offerings. AI's predictive power is further enhanced when combined with verified blockchain data ensuring that recommendations are not only customized but also ethically and religiously verified. These smart systems reduce user burden and build loyalty by offering safe, respectful, and enjoyable travel experiences.

2.3. Blockchain for Transparency and Trust in Halal Tourism

Trust is everything in Halal tourism whether in the Halal certifications, safety of travel plans, or authenticity of user ratings. Blockchain technology can offer a tamper-proof, decentralized ledger that can significantly enhance transparency across the Halal tourism value chain. Blockchain makes it possible to manage immutable records of Halal certification verifications (e.g., restaurants, hotels, packages tours), smart contracts to guarantee service terms are automatically applied, such as promised prayer times or Halal food, and decentralized authentication eliminating reliance on central authorities and reducing fraud (Forensics, 2024). This technology is particularly precious for Muslim travelers moving around areas with uncertain Halal governance or limited local regulation. By using blockchain, tourists can get access to validated information regarding products and services while ensuring their values are respected.

2.4. Ethical and Privacy Considerations in AI-enabled Halal Tourism

The greater application of AI and analytics to data within Halal tourism presents new risks in terms of data privacy, cultural sensitivity, and ethical suitability. The computer infrastructure that facilitates tailored services hinges on gathering and processing sensitive customer information, for example, eating habits, spiritual behaviors, sex, and locations. Poor encryption of data or user information misuse can result in breaches of religious or ethical trust, for example, suggesting non-Halal venues or revealing user data to third parties. Additionally, if algorithms are not trained on culturally relevant data, they might perpetuate bias or suggest irrelevant content, defeating the aim of Halal tourism. The threat of surveillance, algorithmic profiling, or manipulation is especially concerning in areas with less robust data protection legislation or where Muslim travelers are minorities. There is a pressing need for regulatory frameworks, digital ethics charters, and culturally informed AI design to protect user dignity and faith-based preferences.

3. Research Methodology

3.1. Research Design and PRISMA Strategy

This research employs a systematic literature review method to investigate the ways in which AI, blockchain, and immersive technologies such as AR and VR are transforming Halal tourism, especially in the context of the metaverse as mentioned in Table 19.1. Based on the PRISMA 2020 guidelines and Kitchenham's guidance, this research methodology promotes transparency, reproducibility, and analytical strength in the understanding of technological innovation based on the requirements of Muslim travelers. A total of 92 peer-reviewed and gray literature papers published between 2015 and 2024 were examined. The research utilized thematic coding for the extraction and synthesis of insights on digital technology, smart ecosystems, and Sharia-compliant travel experiences.

Table 19.1. Mapping of Research Questions to Methods and Analytical Dimensions.

Research Question (RQ)	Methodological Activity	Analytical Dimension
RQ1: How does blockchain technology ensure trust and transparency in Halal tourism experiences?	Literature search and content coding	Blockchain use cases (traceability, smart contracts, trust verification)
RQ2: What are the roles of AI, AR, and VR in enhancing culturally aligned digital tourism experiences?	Thematic extraction from literature	AI/AR/VR techniques (personalization, immersion, experience simulation)
RQ3: What barriers hinder the adoption of AI and immersive tech in Halal tourism ecosystems?	Comparative analysis	Implementation challenges (digital divide, religious alignment, interoperability)
RQ4: What frameworks exist or are proposed for integrating AI and metaverse tools in Halal tourism?	Synthesis of frameworks and models	Tourism-tech integration models, ethical validation, socio-cultural compliance

3.2. Search, Inclusion/Exclusion Criteria

Literature searching covered academic and grey literature publications from January 2015 to March 2024, encapsulating the accelerated post-COVID technology-driven digitization of tourism. The keywords were chosen cautiously to cover the main themes in Halal tourism and technology adoption. Scopus, IEEE Xplore, Web of Science, ScienceDirect, SpringerLink, and ACM Digital Library were the databases covered. White papers, industry reports, and policy briefs by tourism regulators and technology companies were also perused.

3.2.1. Boolean Search Strategy

("Halal Tourism" OR "Muslim Traveler" OR "Sharia Tourism") AND ("Artificial Intelligence" OR "AI" OR "Machine Learning") AND ("Blockchain" OR "Smart Contracts") AND ("Augmented Reality" OR "Virtual Reality" OR "Metaverse") AND ("Digital Experience" OR "Cultural Tourism" OR "Islamic Travel").

3.3. Inclusion and Exclusion Criteria

Inclusion criteria include the following: Peer-reviewed articles and reliable grey literature between 2015 and 2024; focus on AI, blockchain, or immersive technologies in the tourism sector; specific mention of Halal travel, Muslim tourists, or Sharia-compliant services; understanding of ethical, technological, or implementation paradigms.

Exclusion criteria exclude the following: Non-tourism or non-cultural/religious context articles; research not on Muslim travelers or Halal-directed services; publications in non-English languages; duplicate entries or papers without empirical/technical substance.

3.4. Analytical Framework

The analysis process was a three-stage thematic approach. First, studies were classified based on technological domain (AI, blockchain, AR/VR), followed by grouping them by tourism function (marketing, service delivery, compliance). Elaborate coding allowed for grouping into themes like religious personalization, data ethics, system interoperability, and consumer trust.

4. Findings and Analysis

This chapter offers synthesized findings from qualitative analysis of gray and peer-reviewed literature on Halal tourism, AI, and VR immersive technologies. The results coalesce on three key axes: the contribution of AI and immersive technologies to creating enriched Halal travel experiences, the cultural and ethical considerations surrounding their adoption, and the governance and infrastructure structures required to enable inclusive Halal tourism economies.

4.1. Keyword and Trend Analysis

Keyword frequency analysis was carried out to determine the most prevalent themes in the literature on Halal tourism within the context of AI and digital transformation. Table 19.2 illustrates the frequency distribution of key terms and their co-occurrence and centrality-based relevance scores in academic discourse.

This keyword density reflects an emerging intersection of tourism, AI, and religious compliance that is changing very rapidly. It suggests a transition from straightforward conceptualization of Halal services to sophisticated implementations like AI-based personalization, VR environments, and blockchain-based assurance tools. Notably, the visibility of "Covid" suggests that the pandemic stimulated demand for contactless, virtual, and AI-enhanced tourism paradigms that are compatible with Halal principles.

4.1.1. Network Visualization of Keywords

Fig. 19.1 illustrates a network visualization placing thematic groups like AI, immersive technologies (VR/AR), blockchain, and Muslim-themed concepts of tourism. The visualization indicates how words such as AI and blockchain closely relate with trust, transparency, personalization, and compliance. It

Table 19.2. Summary of Keyword Occurrences in Literature.

Term	Occurrences	Relevance Score
Halal tourism	48	0.1639
Artificial intelligence	20	0.203
Muslim tourist	9	1.922
Muslim traveler	6	1.1431
Sharia tourism	6	3.259
Smart city	28	0.8214
Smart economy	6	0.1319
Digital technology	9	2.7588
Covid	36	0.8366
Publication	10	0.6487
Sector	16	0.194
Review	13	0.014

Fig. 19.1. Network Visualization of Keyword Cloud.

reaffirms that AI is not considered just a means of automation but as a facilitator of religious authenticity and customer-oriented innovation within the Halal tourism sector.

4.2. The Role of Blockchain in Halal Tourism Security and Trust

Blockchain became an innovative technology in Halal tourism by promoting trust, transparency, and compliance guarantee in service provision. Similar to smart agriculture, where data integrity is secured and processes are automated by smart contracts, its application potential in Halal tourism is that it can certify Halal compliance, validate service standards, and handle decentralized transactions. Blockchain contributes the Halal tourism industry in three major featured areas as mentioned in Table 19.3.

Table 19.3. Blockchain Contributions to Halal Tourism.

Blockchain Feature	Halal Tourism Benefit
Immutability	Protects the integrity of certification, booking, and feedback records
Smart contracts	Automates Halal-specific services and enforces contractually-bound faith-compliant conditions
Traceability	Enables full-service authentication – from Halal food sourcing to ethical tour operations

Table 19.4. AI Contributions to Halal Tourism Experience and Security.

AI Technique	Application in Halal Tourism
Anomaly detection	Monitors changes in service compliance or customer feedback for irregularities
Predictive analytics	Anticipates seasonal and user-specific needs to offer personalized, Shariah-compliant experiences
Machine learning	Adapts recommendations and service filters based on evolving travel behavior

4.3. AI Contributions to Experience Personalization and Ethical Compliance in Halal Tourism

Where blockchain offers structural integrity and trust, AI adds dynamic responsiveness and cultural intelligence to Halal tourism services. AI technologies such as machine learning, predictive analytics, and real-time recommendation engines are used to predict traveler requirements, optimize journeys, and offer personalized faith-based experiences. Blockchain contributes the Halal tourism industry in the areas of platform mediated experience and security in three major featured areas as mentioned in Table 19.4.

4.4. Comparative Analysis of Blockchain and AI Integration in Halal Tourism

While AI and blockchain integration is extensively researched in agriculture, its application in Halal tourism is yet to emerge. Table 19.5 recontextualizes this analysis for the tourism sector, determining how these technologies might be used and what are the remaining barriers.

These illustrations suggest that although conceptual blueprints and prototypes are available, scalable, inclusive, and validated models are scarce. The industry needs more empirical proof, wider stakeholder uptake, and user-friendly interfaces to unlock the full potential of blockchain and AI integration.

Table 19.5. Comparative Analysis of Blockchain and AI Integration in Halal Tourism Context.

Study	Technology Focus	Key Contributions	Limitations	Application Context
Nilashi et al. (2019)	Blockchain + AI	Proposed blockchain-backed Halal certification system with AI monitoring user feedback	Not field-deployed; lacked consumer interface	Halal food tourism (Malaysia)
Battour et al. (2023)	AI (Chatbots)	Developed culturally aware AI travel assistant for Muslim travelers	Low context adaptability for regional practices	Urban Islamic tourism (UAE)
Trad et al. (n.d.)	Blockchain	Piloted blockchain ledger for Umrah package verification	Limited to transportation data	Religious pilgrimage travel (Saudi Arabia)
Putra et al. (n.d.)	AI + AR	Combined AI with AR to offer virtual mosque tours with real-time prayer timings	Expensive deployment and VR hardware dependency	Spiritual tourism (Indonesia)
Basarud-din et al. (2024)	AI (Predictive)	Predicted Halal travel trends based on search engine data and seasonal behaviors	Limited geographical scope	Muslim millennial travel patterns

5. Proposed Integrated Architecture: Conceptual Framework for Smart Halal Tourism

The swift digital evolution of tourism, fueled by AI, blockchain, and immersive interfaces, is transforming the way Muslim travelers plan, experience, and assess trips. This part suggests a four-layered conceptual framework for smart Halal tourism systems that combine these technologies to enable personalization, compliance, and digital trust.

As opposed to previous siloed methodologies, this combined structure infuses adaptive intelligence and auditable trust within an uninterrupted system, allowing for Halal-aware travel experiences that not only are immersive and bespoke but also are aligned ethically and transparent.

5.1. Overview of the Layered Framework

Depicted in Table 19.6, the overview of layered architecture includes four functional tiers: data interaction, processing, integrity, and acquisition – connected by secure communication schemes. The system will be able to work through mobile apps, tourism websites, and smart city interfaces to address the specific requirements of Muslim travelers in real-time.

This architectural framework serves as a model for future AI-powered Halal tourism systems with personalization, trust, inclusivity, and transparency. It guarantees that Muslim tourists can approach tourism platforms without fear, confident that their religious and ethical requirements are upheld and supported by advanced technologies.

5.2. Proposed Proof-of-concept Architecture for AI-driven Halal Tourism in the Metaverse

This conceptual architecture (Fig. 19.2) offers a future-proof architectural framework for an AI, blockchain, and immersive technology-driven secure, immersive,

Table 19.6. Overview of the Layered Framework.

Layer	Components	Contribution to Halal Tourism
1. Data acquisition layer	Mobile sensors, geolocation APIs, user preferences	Enables real-time responsiveness to user needs and environment
2. Integrity layer (blockchain ledger)	Smart contracts, certification hashes, compliance logs	Guarantees trust in Halal-compliant services and provider claims
3. Processing layer (AI analytics engine)	Recommendation systems, sentiment analysis tools, edge AI modules	Provides context-aware, ethical, and user-aligned travel experiences
4. Interaction layer (stakeholder interfaces)	Mobile apps, VR/AR interfaces, booking dashboards	Fosters user engagement while maintaining cultural and religious integrity
Cross-layer flow	APIs, secure encryption protocols, identity verification tools	Protects user privacy and secures transactions

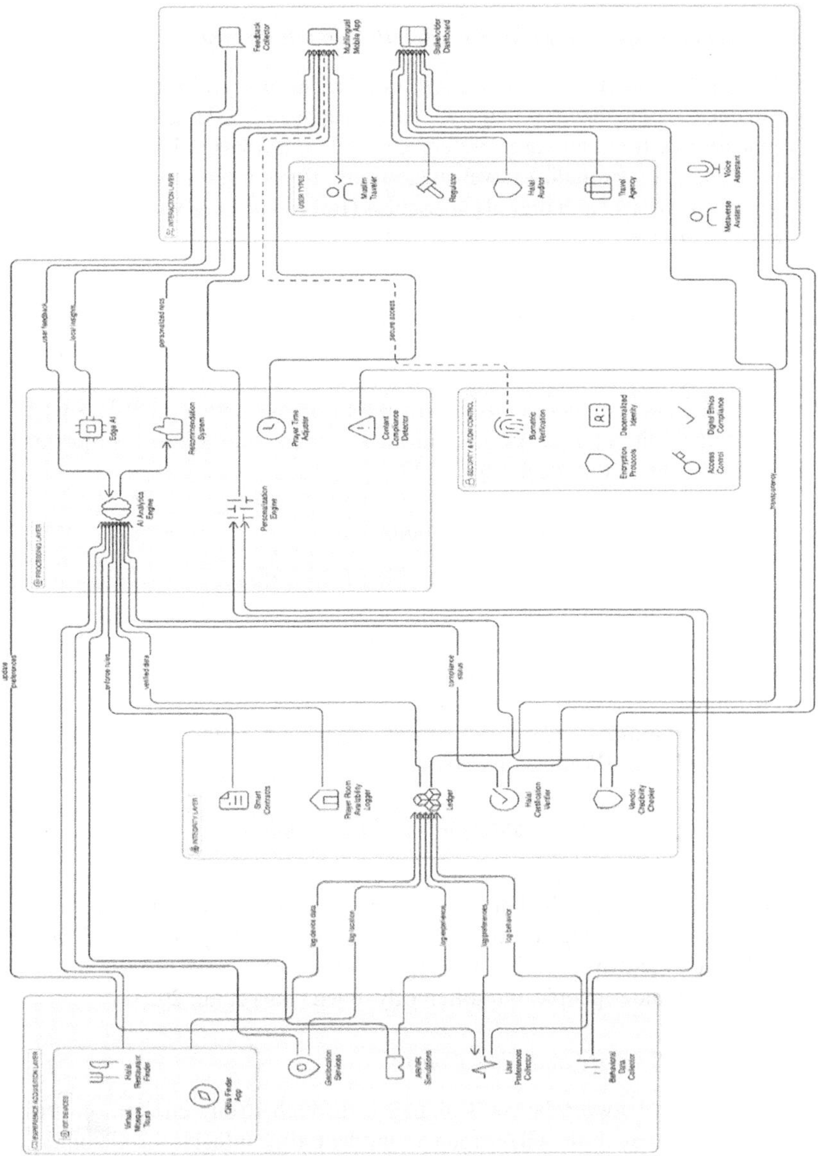

Fig. 19.2. Conceptual Architecture for AI-enabled Halal Tourism Ecosystem in the Metaverse.

and personalized Halal tourism ecosystem. It sees a five-layer modular architecture that fosters religious compliance, maximizes user trust, and scales across various Islamic tourism use cases ranging from pilgrimage planning and travel guides compliant with Halal principles to ethical hospitality experiences in the metaverse.

5.2.1. Experience Acquisition Layer (AR/VR & IoT Interfaces)

This layer gathers contextual inputs via AR/VR simulations, geolocation services, and intelligent tourism devices (e.g., virtual mosque tours, Halal restaurants, Qibla applications). It gathers user preferences and behavioral information from immersive spaces to personalize travel suggestions. These interfaces serve as the sensory portal to physical and digital experiences (Bobrownicki & Valentin, 2022).

5.2.2. Integrity Layer (Blockchain Ledger)

To provide authenticity, transparency, and religious trust, all transactional and experiential data are recorded onto a decentralized blockchain. Whether confirming Halal food certification, prayer room availability, or vendor credibility, this layer ensures Muslim travelers can trust immutable, time-stamped records. Smart contracts enforce adherence to Islamic norms for accommodation, transportation, and entertainment (Shakeel et al., 2023).

5.2.3. Processing Layer (AI Analytics Engine)

This is the central layer of intelligence in which AI algorithms do real-time analysis, predictive modeling, and context-aware personalization. These include suggesting Halal-compliant holiday packages based on historic behavior; adjusting digital itineraries during prayer times; identifying inconsistencies in religious content in tourism offerings; adding edge AI improves responsiveness in low-connectivity environments (e.g., out-of-way pilgrimage sites), allowing for near-source intelligence (Wang et al., 2024).

5.2.4. Interaction Layer (User and Stakeholder Interfaces)

This layer supports multilingual mobile applications, metaverse avatars, voice assistants, and dashboards. Muslim travelers, Halal auditors, travel agencies, and government regulators engage on this layer to utilize insights, provide feedback, and make knowledge-driven decisions. It focuses on accessibility across all generations, including older people and differently-abled (Barj et al., 2023).

5.2.5. Cross-layer Security and Flow Control

Secure transmission between layers is managed through strong encryption protocols that are in line with the CIA model (confidentiality, integrity, availability). Privacy of data, particularly regarding religious choice and biometric authentication (e.g., Hajj e-visas), is safeguarded through decentralized identity systems. This layer also manages data access among various stakeholders while maintaining digital ethics compliance (Tan et al., 2014).

5.2.6. Implications of the Architecture

This modular design shows how AI, blockchain, and immersive technology can converge to enable an active Halal tourism ecosystem. Some of the main outcomes are real-time personalization with Islamic principles; transparent, verifiable Halal compliance; culturally responsive digital interaction in real-world and virtual spaces; and secure, user-managed data flows. Through meeting the demands of faith-based tourists while guaranteeing inclusivity, transparency, and technological strength, this design offers a plausible blueprint for future ethical, AI-powered global tourism.

6. Discussion

The convergence of AI and blockchain technologies into Halal tourism represents a profound shift not only of digital technology in travel, but also of the underlying assumptions regarding trust, personalization, inclusivity, and religious compliance in Muslim-friendly travel. This conversation goes beyond superficial descriptions to explore the theoretical, technological, and practical implications of AI-powered Halal tourism in a digitally immersive, metaverse-enabled future.

6.1. Theoretical Implications

The intersection of AI, blockchain, and Halal tourism forces a reexamination of traditional models of travel behavior and service design. Traditionally, Halal tourism has been characterized as a niche market that demands faith-compliant logistics Halal food, prayer rooms, and modest accommodations. But with the addition of intelligent systems, this terrain shifts from a compliance model to a cyber-ethical tourism model in which digital infrastructure enforces, personalizes, and even anticipates Islamic values (Fisher et al., n.d.).

Blockchain decentralizes trust in service providers. Halal certification historically depended on accepted authorities. With a blockchain-based system, digital records that are immutable, smart contracts, and peer-verifiable certifications transfer trust from centralized organizations to open, decentralized systems. For Muslim travelers, this change guarantees that statements regarding Halal compliance can be objectively verified among service providers worldwide (Chen, 2023).

AI introduces a level of cognitive personalization. With machine-learning algorithms trained on cultural tastes and Shariah principles, systems can personalize recommendations, identify potentially non-compliant offerings, and dynamically adjust to individual travel tastes. This real-time, culturally aware interaction repositions the Muslim traveler from a passive recipient of faith-compliant services to an active participant in co-creating their own ethical travel experience (Pham, 2024).

Jointly, AI and blockchain form a double epistemic structure one providing compliance through verifiable truth (blockchain), while the other supports adaptation through perpetual learning (AI). This recasting defies conventional roles for tour operators, regulatory agencies, and even the travelers themselves, bringing a fresh digital ethos in Halal tourism (Mohi-ud-Din Qadri, 2024).

6.2. Practical Implications

Whereas technological potential is enormous, fulfilling the dream of AI-based Halal tourism relies on filling the gap between theory systems and on-ground execution.

Initial pilot projects need to be initiated in culturally important Muslim travel destinations Makkah, Istanbul, Jakarta, and new Halal hotspots such as Bosnia and Uzbekistan. These pilots can showcase combined AR/VR-led tours, blockchain-secured Halal certifications, and AI-driven trip planning. Field testing is necessary to evaluate user trust, usability, and cultural sensitivity (Ioannidis & Tourism, 2023).

Second, the tourism sector has to develop Shariah-compliant digital compliance guidelines. These guidelines must tackle the challenges of data privacy, algorithmic bias, and content moderation in immersive tourism spaces such as the metaverse. Lacking these controls, AI can inadvertently suggest content or experiences that run contrary to Islamic values, compromising user trust (Casare et al., 2024).

Third, digital literacy initiatives specific to Muslim societies must ride alongside tech rollout. Just as food ethics is taught by Halal certification organizations, emerging institutions or partnerships can instruct visitors on blockchain-protected travel history, AI-powered privacy settings, and metaverse wayfinding. Trust is a product of comprehension, not merely infrastructure (Polcumpally et al., 2024).

Lastly, stakeholders need to understand AI in Halal tourism as a socio-technical revolution. This revolution recasts access, authority, and influence within Muslim travel across the world. Faith-based tour operators, Islamic academics, developers, and travelers need to co-design governance models that are inclusive, accountable, and ethically innovative.

7. Conclusion

This chapter has illustrated how AI technologies can improve the Halal tourism value chain dramatically – right from itinerary planning to in-trip support and post-trip feedback. Smart recommendation systems, language translation engines, and facial recognition-based security features deliver tailored and seamless experiences, particularly for younger Muslim tourists who are digital natives. When combined with AR and VR, these technologies allow virtual discovery of Halal-friendly destinations, mosques, and cultural sites, enabling tourists to make informed decisions prior to committing to physical travel. Also important is how blockchain technology plays a part in ensuring and validating Halal compliance in an industry frequently marred by inconsistency and transparency issues. Smart contracts can enforce ethical business practices and validate that service providers adhere to defined Halal standards. Blockchain-supported transaction records and decentralized identity validation provide travelers with trust and control, both important values in Islamic ethical systems. But the deployment of these technologies poses challenges. Data privacy, bias in AI, digital inequality, and the lack of strong Shariah-compliant technological standards all constitute strong barriers to overcome. These can only be addressed through multi-stakeholder engagement between policymakers, Halal certification organizations, Islamic scholars, tech developers, and the tourism sector. As significant is the imperative to educate and raise awareness among Muslim travelers to enable them to navigate and have faith in these digital environments. This chapter concludes that the intersection of AI and metaverse technologies with Halal tourism presents a massive opportunity to reimagine the global tourism sector through ethical, inclusive, and sustainable innovation. Intelligent and immersive technologies do not weaken the spiritual essence of Halal tourism; on the contrary, they increase its accessibility, engagement, and integrity in a globalized and digitized world. In order to fully achieve this potential, future deployments need to be informed by Islamic ethical values, socio-cultural awareness, and responsible technological stewardship.

References

Barj, S., Ouaddah, A., & Mezrioui, A. (2023). Cryptography in distributed ledger technologies from a layered perspective: A state of the art. *Lecture Notes in Networks and Systems*, *669*, 210–220. https://doi.org/10.1007/978-3-031-29860-8_22

Basarud-din, S. K., Nik Abdullah, N. S., & Mohd Najib, N. W. (2024). The role of culinary digital tools in enhancing the gastronomic experience for Muslim travelers. *International Journal of Research and Innovation in Social Science*, *VIII*(XI), 3113–3122. https://doi.org/10.47772/IJRISS.2024.8110242

Battour, M., Mady, K., Salaheldeen, M., Elsotouhy, M., Elbendary, I., & Boğan, E. (2023). AI-enabled technologies to assist Muslim tourists in Halal-friendly tourism. *Journal of Islamic Marketing*, *14*(5), 1291–1309. https://doi.org/10.1108/JIMA-01-2022-0001

Blockchain, Internet of Things, and Artificial Intelligence. (2021). *Blockchain, internet of things, and artificial intelligence*. https://doi.org/10.1201/9780429352898

Bobrownicki, R., & Valentin, S. (2022). Adding experiential layers to the transnational-athlete concept: A narrative review of real-world heterogeneous mobility experiences. *Psychology of Sport and Exercise*, *58*. https://doi.org/10.1016/J.PSYCHSPORT.2021.102075

Casare, A. R., da Silva, C. G., & Moraes, R. (2024). User perception as a factor for improving trustworthiness in e-commerce systems. *Sol.Sbc.Org.Br*, *15*, 1. https://doi.org/10.5753/jis.2024.3748

Chen, M. T. (2023). *A study of the influence of introduction of block chain into traceability certification on consumer's acceptance of smart agriculture*. 2023 International conference on consumer electronics – Taiwan, ICCE-Taiwan 2023 – Proceedings, 367–368. https://doi.org/10.1109/ICCE-TAIWAN58799.2023.10226712

Fisher, J. A., & Bolter, J. D., (2018). *Ethical considerations for AR experiences at dark tourism sites*. Ieeexplore.Ieee.Org. Retrieved January 29, 2025, from https://ieeexplore.ieee.org/abstract/document/8699186/

Forensics, R. R. C. I. & D. (2024, July 4). *Data breach fraudulence and preventive measures in e-commerce platforms*. Taylorfrancis.Com. https://www.taylorfrancis.com/chapters/edit/10.1201/9781003369479-8/data-breach-fraudulence-preventive-measures-commerce-platforms-raja-rajendran

Ioannidis, S., & Tourism, A. K.-I. T. (2023). *Metaverse for tourists and tourism destinations*. Springer. Retrieved January 16, 2025, from https://link.springer.com/article/10.1007/s40558-023-00271-y

Mohi-ud-Din Qadri, H. (2024). *The global halal industry: A research companion*. 1–196. https://doi.org/10.4324/9781003441540

Nilashi, M., Samad, S., Manaf, A. A., Ahmadi, H., Rashid, T. A., Munshi, A., Almukadi, W., Ibrahim, O., & Hassan Ahmed, O. (2019). Factors influencing medical tourism adoption in Malaysia: A DEMATEL-Fuzzy TOPSIS approach. *Computers and Industrial Engineering*, *137*. https://doi.org/10.1016/J.CIE.2019.106005

Pham, M. (2024). *Exploring privacy concerns and consumer behaviors towards personalization tools*. https://aaltodoc.aalto.fi/items/ac0041d5-3ba8-4524-b659-257880cb5b80

Polcumpally, A. T., Pandey, K. K., Kumar, A., & Samadhiya, A. (2024). Blockchain governance and trust: A multi-sector thematic systematic review and exploration of future research directions. *Heliyon*, *10*(12). https://doi.org/10.1016/J.HELIYON.2024.E32975

Putra, D. T., Mahmudin, T., Gede, N., Wiartha, M., Made, I., Adnyana, S., Istri, A. A., Septiviari, M., Tinggi, S., Pariwisata, I. E., & Semarang, I. (n.d.). *The existence of the metaverse tourism in Indonesia: Between opportunities and threats*. Journal. Laaroiba.Com. https://doi.org/10.47476/reslaj.v6i3.6162

Shakeel, M., Krishnammal, P. M., Vekariya, V., Akram, S. V., Kumar, P. P., & Kapila, D. (2023). *The design and implementation of a double layered security network with an authentication system through block chain technology*. 2023 3rd International conference on advance computing and innovative technologies in engineering, ICACITE 2023, 1469–1474. https://doi.org/10.1109/ICACITE57410.2023.10182566

Tan, Z., Zhang, P., Tan, J., & Guo, L. (2014). A multi-layer event detection algorithm for detecting global and local hot events in social networks. *Procedia Computer Science*, *29*, 2080–2089. https://doi.org/10.1016/J.PROCS.2014.05.192

Tiainen, M. (2024). *Ethical issues in the industrial metaverse*. https://aaltodoc.aalto.fi/items/321f5752-64fe-4be0-8861-ced703bdf9b2

Trad, N., & Al Dabbagh, M. A. (2020). *Use of social media as an effective marketing tool for fashion startups in Saudi Arabia*. Scirp.Org. Retrieved August 12, 2023, from https://www.scirp.org/journal/paperinformation.aspx?paperid=104448

Wang, W., Ikegaya, N., Hirose, C., & Mohamad, M. F. (2024). Indoor flow datasets of two-layered cross-ventilation models by particle image velocimetry and hot wire anemometry. *Data in Brief*, *52*. https://doi.org/10.1016/J.DIB.2023.109856

Zambrano, J. L. V., Cedeño, A. K. A., Escobar, J. C. P., & Mera, A. F. S. (2024). Immersive virtual reality for the preservation of cultural heritage. Ieeexplore.Ieee.Org. Retrieved January 29, 2025, from https://ieeexplore.ieee.org/abstract/document/10702094/

Chapter 20

Sustainable Halal Tourism: A Pathway Toward Ethical and Inclusive Travel

Gobinathan Manickam[a], *Ihtisham Ullah*[b], *Nohman Khan*[b] *and Ravindra Kumar Perumal*[c]

[a]*School of Marketing and Management, Asia Pacific University of Technology and Innovation (APU), Technology Park Malaysia, Kuala Lumpur, Malaysia*
[b]*Strategic Research Institute (SRI), Asia Pacific University of Technology and Innovation (APU), Technology Park Malaysia, Kuala Lumpur, Malaysia*
[c]*School of Global Hospitality and Tourism, Asia Pacific University of Technology and Innovation (APU), Technology Park Malaysia, Kuala Lumpur, Malaysia*

Abstract

Sustainable Halal Tourism integrates Islamic values with global sustainable development goals. As the Muslim population grows and travel increases, demand for experiences respecting Islamic principles while championing environmental stewardship, socio-cultural preservation, and economic viability surges. This chapter explores the foundational concepts of Halal tourism and sustainability, synthesizing their convergence theoretically. It proposes a framework for Sustainable Halal Tourism, drawing lessons from case studies in Muslim-majority and non-Muslim-majority nations (Malaysia, Turkey, Japan). The chapter examines challenges, opportunities, and essential policy interventions to cultivate an inclusive, ethically grounded, and environmentally conscious tourism sector serving Muslim travelers without compromising global sustainability standards. Analysis is supported by market data and academic frameworks, incorporating peer-reviewed literature.

Keywords: Sustainable Halal Tourism; Islamic values; Sustainable Development Goals; Muslim travelers; environmental sustainability; socio-cultural sustainability; economic sustainability; Islamic ethics; tourism development theory

---

Halal Tourism and Artificial Intelligence: New Approaches for a New Generation, 295–307

doi:10.1108/978-1-80686-165-120261022

1. Introduction

The tourism sector, a significant force in the global economy, holds immense potential for sustainable development. Its intersection with socio-economic and environmental systems makes its sustainable transformation crucial. Concurrently, demographic shifts and evolving consumer values increasingly drive a preference for responsible, ethical, and inclusive tourism models. Within this landscape, "Halal Tourism" – defined by adherence to Islamic law (Shariah) in services and facilities – has gained considerable attention. This encompasses provisions meeting faith-based needs, including Halal-certified food, prayer facilities, alcohol/gambling-free environments, and modesty-aligned recreational options.

Despite growing recognition and economic significance, the sustainability of Halal tourism is often overlooked. Sustainable Halal Tourism integrates meeting Muslim travelers' religious needs with broader sustainability imperatives, consciously incorporating the "triple bottom line" – environmental protection, socio-cultural sensitivity, and equitable economic benefits – into every facet of Halal travel. This chapter investigates how sustainability principles and Halal tourism can coexist to build a more inclusive, ethical, and resilient global tourism sector. The economic impetus is substantial: the global Halal tourism market, estimated at USD 256.5 billion in 2023, is projected to reach USD 410.9 billion by 2032 (Credence Research, 2025; Tehran Times, 2025). Other estimates place the 2024 market at USD 450 billion, with a projected CAGR of 10.5% (Future Data Stats, n.d.). Increasing Muslim mobility is a key driver, with international Muslim tourist arrivals at 80 million in H1 2024, forecasted to climb to 230 million by 2028 (Ghani, 2025). Academic interest has also surged, highlighting its emergence as a prominent study area (Nor, 2023).

2. Conceptual Foundations

Understanding the convergence of Halal tourism and sustainability requires defining each concept and exploring their theoretical intersection.

2.1. What Is Halal Tourism?

Halal tourism, a specialized segment, adheres to Islamic principles (Shariah) in providing tourism services. This is rooted in Muslim travelers' religious obligations and lifestyle choices. Key differentiating components include:

- *Halal-certified food and beverages*: Meticulous sourcing, preparation, and serving to comply with Islamic dietary laws (Ghani, 2025). Certification recognized by Halal bodies is crucial for trust (Halal Food Council USA, 2025).
- *Prayer and ablution facilities*: Easily accessible and equipped (musallas and wudu areas) in hotels, airports, and tourist sites, clean and clearly marked (Ghani, 2025; Islamic Tourism Centre (ITC), n.d.-b). Availability significantly influences satisfaction (Zainol & Mustafa, 2021).

- *Alcohol and gambling-free environments*: Strictly prohibited in Islam (Ghani, 2025), often translating to alcohol-free hotel premises, fostering a family-friendly atmosphere.
- *Accommodation respecting modesty and privacy*: Rooms with Qibla indicators, private pools/beaches, or gender-segregated facilities (Islamic Tourism Centre (ITC), n.d.-b). Such facilities are key for Muslim travelers (Rahmawati et al., 2025).

While primarily for Muslims, ethical considerations, cleanliness, and family-friendly nature appeal to broader audiences. The rapid market growth (Credence Research, 2025; Future Data Stats, n.d.; Ghani, 2025; Tehran Times, 2025) underscores increasing demand, evolving from a niche to a mainstream component.

2.2. What Is Sustainable Tourism?

Sustainable tourism balances the needs of visitors, industry, environment, and host communities, ensuring long-term viability and positive contributions to destination well-being. It is structured around the "triple bottom line":

- *Environmental sustainability*: Minimizing negative impacts and maximizing conservation. Focus areas include efficient resource use, biodiversity preservation, pollution reduction, and responsible waste management. The aim is to prevent degradation of environmental assets.
- *Socio-cultural sustainability*: Respecting host communities' social and cultural authenticity. This involves preserving heritage, protecting traditional values, fostering inter-cultural understanding, and preventing social disruption or exploitation. Community involvement is central.
- *Economic sustainability*: Ensuring long-term economic viability and prosperity. This involves generating equitable benefits for all stakeholders, creating stable employment, fostering local entrepreneurship, and reducing poverty. Minimizing economic leakage is key.

Sustainable tourism requires careful planning, effective management, and active stakeholder participation to maximize benefits and minimize negative impacts across these dimensions.

2.3. The Convergence of Halal and Sustainable Tourism

The convergence of Halal and sustainable tourism is deeply rooted in Islam's ethical framework. Islamic teachings emphasize concepts resonant with sustainability. "Khilafah" (stewardship) posits humanity's responsibility to care for Earth as a trust (amanah) from God, instilling guardianship. "Mizan" (balance) highlights maintaining equilibrium in all life aspects, including human activities and the environment, encouraging balanced development. "Israf" (extravagance, waste) is strongly discouraged, promoting mindful consumption and efficient resource management. These values provide a powerful ethical foundation for sustainable practices, including in tourism.

Sustainable Halal Tourism thus emerges as a natural and consistent convergence point, seamlessly integrating Islamic ethics with responsible, environmentally conscious, and socially equitable travel. Academic research confirms this alignment, showing that sustainable practices informed by Islamic values effectively meet faith-based needs and mitigate environmental impacts of mass tourism (Chantarungsri & Alam, 2024). This integrated approach also fosters cultural sensitivity, promotes social cohesion, and enhances economic viability for host communities (Chantarungsri & Alam, 2024). This inherent compatibility provides a strong foundation for developing tourism models that are both faith-compliant and globally responsible. The convergence can be understood through Stakeholder Theory, recognizing diverse interests. Research also highlights Muslim travelers' increasing motivation by global sustainable development goals, reinforcing the link (Battour et al., 2021).

3. Dimensions of Sustainable Halal Tourism

Sustainable Halal Tourism manifests across the three core dimensions of sustainability, each with unique opportunities, challenges, and practical considerations.

3.1. Environmental Sustainability

Integrating environmental sustainability into Halal tourism aligns with Islamic teachings on stewardship and is crucial for long-term viability. Halal tourism operators can contribute to preservation and resource efficiency through green practices:

- *Prioritizing eco-friendly accommodations*: Designed for minimal environmental impact, utilizing renewables, rigorous water conservation, and locally sourced, non-toxic materials (Pongsakornrungsilp et al., 2024). Some Halal-friendly resorts use solar panels and rainwater harvesting, aligning with "israf" avoidance. Green hotel practices contribute to SDGs 6, 7, 12, and 13 (Khan et al., 2024). Research in Malaysia found positive links between environmental advertising and green attitudes among guests (Khan et al., 2024).
- *Implementing comprehensive waste management and recycling*: Minimizing landfill waste and pollution through reducing single-use plastics, composting organic waste, and clear segregation guidelines. Islamic principles emphasize resource value, motivating such initiatives (Khan et al., 2024).
- *Promoting sustainable transportation options*: Encouraging electric vehicles, efficient public transport, or non-motorized options. Reducing carbon emissions is vital for eco-tourism. Research on COVID-19's impact on Halal tourism transportation in Indonesia highlighted health and sustainability priorities (Peristiwo, 2021).
- *Developing nature-based halal tourism experiences*: Marketing experiences emphasizing conservation and natural appreciation, such as Halal-compliant eco-lodges offering hiking or bird watching in protected areas. This aligns with preserving God's creation and can boost rural economies.

- *Adopting sustainable design principles*: In construction and renovation, focusing on low-impact strategies and adaptive reuse (Chantarungsri & Alam, 2024). This includes maximizing natural light/ventilation, incorporating green spaces, or restoring historical buildings. Halal certification bodies increasingly integrate environmental consciousness into standards (Halal Food Council USA, 2025). An example is a Halal-certified hotel with a plastic reduction program, using biodegradable alternatives and educating guests on marine conservation, resonating with Muslim travelers' stewardship values.

3.2. Socio-cultural Sustainability

Respect for local traditions and heritage is a cornerstone shared by sustainable tourism and Islamic values. Halal tourism fosters socio-cultural sustainability by promoting understanding, preserving authenticity, and empowering communities:

- *Promoting and preserving local heritage*: Actively supporting visits to Islamic historical sites, mosques, and cultural centers (Harini et al., 2025). In Turkey, sites like Hagia Sophia and Mevlâna Museum attract millions, offering spiritual and cultural experiences (Bozkurt & Tümbek Tekeoğlu, 2024). Responsible visitation and contributing to preservation are key. Research highlights how Halal principles enhance socio-cultural responsibility (UN Tourism, 2024).
- *Facilitating cross-cultural understanding and interaction*: Through organized cultural exchange, guided tours by locals, and authentic interactions (Harini et al., 2025). Community-based tourism (CBT) in Muslim-majority regions (e.g., Bangladesh, Indonesia) offers immersive experiences like homestays and traditional activities (Harini et al., 2025; Islamic Tourism Centre (ITC), n.d.-b; Solimar International, n.d.). These foster mutual respect and break stereotypes.
- *Empowering local Muslim communities*: Directly involving them equitably in the tourism value chain, especially through CBT (Chantarungsri & Alam, 2024). In Aceh, Indonesia, local involvement is key for Muslim-friendly tourism success (Adinugraha et al., n.d.). Projects like Sundarbans EcoVillage Network combine homestays with local artisan products, boosting local economy and cultural exchange (Solimar International, n.d.). Engaging residents ensures equitable benefits and mitigates negative impacts (Chantarungsri & Alam, 2024). Research emphasizes social capital for economic empowerment (UN Tourism, 2024).
- *Respecting local social norms and values*: Providing facilities catering to Islamic modesty and privacy, such as separate recreational facilities. This includes promoting respectful dress codes and behavior, creating a harmonious environment. An example is community homestay programs for Muslim families, offering private accommodation with Halal amenities and authentic cultural experiences, generating income and fostering understanding.

By prioritizing socio-cultural sustainability, Halal tourism contributes to stronger, more resilient communities, preserving unique cultural heritage and ensuring tourism benefits locals.

3.3. Economic Sustainability

Sustainable Halal Tourism can generate equitable and lasting economic benefits for destinations. This dimension focuses on maximizing local economic gains, distributing them fairly, and building long-term resilience:

- *Creating entrepreneurship and business opportunities*: Significant opportunities arise in Halal food production, modest fashion, Islamic art/crafts, and faith-based wellness services (Hidayat et al., 2024). The industry's growth necessitates a workforce, creating jobs and income for regions developing this sector (Rachmat et al., 2019). Studies show Halal tourism creates jobs, increases income, and stimulates local economic development (Rachmat et al., 2019).
- *Developing tailored halal travel packages*: Catering to the growing global Muslim middle class, offering luxury resorts, community-based tourism, and budget-friendly options to ensure broad economic distribution.
- *Ensuring local business involvement and supply chains*: Maximizing revenue retention by prioritizing local procurement for goods and services (e.g., local Halal food, artisans, transportation). This mitigates "leakage" and directly benefits local well-being.
- *Contributing to overall economic boost*: Attracting Muslim tourists, often a valuable market segment with higher disposable incomes and longer stays, increases revenue for hotels, restaurants, and retail (Rachmat et al., 2019).
- *Generating additional employment opportunities*: Across hospitality, food services, guiding, transportation, and retail (Rachmat et al., 2019). In Indonesia, Halal tourism growth is expected to boost regional economic growth, welfare, and reduce unemployment/poverty (Rachmat et al., 2019). Community-based projects, like in Bangladesh, provide income and training in valuable skills (Solimar International, n.d.). The social impact can extend beyond economic, fostering community development (Marlinda et al., 2024).

By focusing on equitable economic participation and local benefit retention, Sustainable Halal Tourism serves as a powerful tool for local economic development, poverty alleviation, and a more equitable distribution of tourism benefits.

4. Challenges to Sustainable Halal Tourism

Realizing Sustainable Halal Tourism faces significant obstacles, requiring strategic addressing for long-term growth.

4.1. Lack of Standardization

A major hurdle is the absence of a universally accepted framework for Halal tourism certification (Credence Research, 2025; UN Tourism, 2024). This leads to variations in quality and reliability, confusing Muslim travelers seeking assurance (Chantarungsri & Alam, 2024; Credence Research, 2025). This challenge, framed within Institutional Theory, highlights the need for unified regulatory pillars. Developing clear, internationally recognized guidelines, aligned with

SDGs, is crucial for credibility and market growth (UN Tourism, 2024). UN Tourism is actively exploring a unified certification framework (UN Tourism, 2024).

4.2. Limited Infrastructure

Many non-Muslim majority countries, despite attracting Muslim travelers, lack Halal-friendly infrastructure (Khan et al., 2024). This includes insufficient prayer spaces, limited Halal-certified restaurants, and scarcity of accommodations catering to specific needs like bidets or gender-segregated facilities (Khan et al., 2024; Islamic Tourism Centre (ITC), n.d.-b). This significantly impacts Muslim travel comfort and choices. Upgrading facilities requires substantial investment, often through public–private partnerships, to enhance quality and appeal (Islamic Tourism Centre (ITC), n.d.-b).

4.3. Misconceptions and Stereotypes

Sustainable Halal Tourism can face misconceptions and negative stereotypes, perceived as restrictive or exclusive. Such perceptions, fueled by lack of understanding, limit its acceptance (Rachmat et al., 2019). This is a communication challenge. From a socio-cultural perspective, misconceptions create barriers to cross-cultural understanding. Promoting Halal tourism through accurate information, transparency, and highlighting its inclusive, ethical, and environmentally conscious aspects is essential (Wahizan Saidin et al., 2025). Concerns about cultural impact in diverse destinations require open dialog and community engagement (Rachmat et al., 2019).

4.4. Environmental Concerns

Tourism growth, even Halal tourism, can cause environmental degradation if not managed responsibly. Without planning and regulations, expansion could exacerbate issues like increased carbon emissions, over-tourism, and localized pollution. Integrating robust environmental management systems, promoting eco-friendly options, and prioritizing sustainable design are crucial to mitigate these impacts (Chantarungsri & Alam, 2024). Ensuring Halal compliance integrates with environmental responsibility is key to long-term sustainability.

5. Opportunities for Growth

Despite challenges, Sustainable Halal Tourism offers significant opportunities for innovation, expansion, and positive impact, driving economic growth and broader sustainability goals.

5.1. Technology Integration

Technology can enhance the Muslim traveler experience, improve accessibility, and facilitate sustainable practices. Mobile apps offer prayer times, Halal restaurant/mosque locators, and destination guides (UnivDatos, 2024). Technology also enables tailored online booking platforms, virtual tours, and gamified experiences educating travelers on local culture and sustainability. This appeals to tech-savvy Muslim millennials and Gen Z (UnivDatos, 2024). Technology can also aid environmental monitoring and resource management. AI-enabled technologies can assist in finding Halal-friendly options (Battour et al., 2022).

5.2. Faith-based Wellness Tourism

The convergence of Halal principles with wellness tourism offers a promising niche. Developing faith-based wellness experiences – Halal spas with privacy/segregation, retreats with organic Halal food and Islamic mindfulness, and activities incorporating prayer/meditation – attracts those seeking ethical, holistic, and health-conscious travel (Ghani, 2025). This appeals to both Muslims and non-Muslims interested in enriching wellness experiences, aligning with broader sustainability principles.

5.3. Women-led Halal Tourism

Growing demand for travel tailored to Muslim women presents a substantial opportunity for safe, comfortable, and empowering options respecting modesty and privacy (Islamic Tourism Centre (ITC), n.d.-b; Pongsakornrungsilp et al., 2024). Services like women-only tours, accommodations with private/segregated facilities, and activities designed for Muslim women tap into this underserved market. Empowering local Muslim women as guides and entrepreneurs also contributes to socio-economic sustainability and gender equality.

5.4. Cross-cultural Collaboration

Non-Muslim majority countries increasingly recognize the economic potential and cultural enrichment of the Muslim travel market, investing in Halal-friendly infrastructure (Halal Food Council USA, 2025; Islamic Tourism Centre (ITC), n.d.-b; Pongsakornrungsilp et al., 2024). This includes Halal certification bodies, increased Halal food options, and accessible prayer facilities. Japan, South Korea, and Thailand demonstrate strategic commitment to inclusivity (Halal Food Council USA, 2025; Islamic Tourism Centre (ITC), n.d.-b; Pongsakornrungsilp et al., 2024). This collaboration fosters understanding, breaks stereotypes, and drives global growth, aligning with SDGs.

6. Case Studies

Examining experiences from different countries provides practical insights into Sustainable Halal Tourism implementation and impact.

6.1. Malaysia: A Global Halal Tourism Hub

Malaysia is a global leader in comprehensive Halal tourism, with strong government support from agencies like the Islamic Tourism Centre (ITC). The ITC develops standards, provides training, and promotes Malaysia as a premier Muslim-friendly destination (Islamic Tourism Centre (ITC), n.d.-a, n.d.-b). Malaysia's success extends beyond basic provisions to an integrated ecosystem including Islamic finance, robust Halal certification, and a focus on Halal Total Quality Management (TQM) (Wahizan Saidin et al., 2025). Its consistent top ranking in the Mastercard-CrescentRating Global Muslim Travel Index (GMTI) since 2015 reflects its effective long-term strategy and comprehensive approach (Islamic Tourism Centre (ITC), n.d.-b). Malaysia offers diverse Halal-friendly options, from certified hotels to Muslim-friendly tours and wellness centers. This integrated approach, supported by clear policies and dedicated institutions, solidifies Malaysia's benchmark position.

6.2. Turkey: Blending Culture and Faith

Turkey leverages its rich historical and cultural heritage, intertwined with Islamic civilization, to attract Muslim travelers while integrating sustainability. As a transcontinental nation, it boasts significant Islamic historical sites and mosques. Iconic sites like Hagia Sophia and Mevlâna Museum attract millions, offering spiritual and cultural experiences (Bozkurt & Tümbek Tekeoğlu, 2024). Promoting responsible visitation and contributing to preservation are key for socio-cultural sustainability. Turkey blends these offerings with modern infrastructure. While already popular, Turkey actively works to capitalize on its faith tourism potential (Bozkurt & Tümbek Tekeoğlu, 2024). The Ministry of Culture and Tourism is involved in sustainable tourism and cultural heritage preservation (Raj, 2020). The growing focus on cultural preservation and eco-tourism resonates with Muslim travelers. Turkey's experience highlights the opportunity for countries with rich Islamic heritage to develop faith-based tourism that is culturally immersive and increasingly sustainable.

6.3. Japan: Embracing Halal for Muslim Travelers

Japan, a non-Muslim majority country, has proactively positioned itself as a welcoming Muslim-friendly destination, recognizing the economic potential from Southeast Asia (Ahmed, 2025; Islamic Tourism Centre (ITC), n.d.-b; Pongsakornrungsilp et al., 2024). The Japan National Tourism Organization (JNTO) leads initiatives, collaborating with local businesses to raise awareness and encourage Halal-friendly services (Ahmed, 2025). Key initiatives include facilitating Halal certification and increasing prayer facilities in airports, railway stations, shopping centers, and tourist sites (Halal Food Council USA, 2025; Islamic Tourism Centre (ITC), n.d.-b; Pongsakornrungsilp et al., 2024). The availability of Halal food options is a positive aspect for Muslim travelers (Ahmed, 2025). Japan's success in attracting Muslim tourists, reflected in its high GMTI ranking among non-OIC countries, demonstrates that strategic planning and investment in infrastructure can effectively tap this market (Halal Food Council USA, 2025; Islamic Tourism Centre (ITC), n.d.-b; Pongsakornrungsilp et al., 2024). This case study emphasizes understanding Muslim traveler needs and implementing practical solutions for accessibility and appeal, contributing to economic sustainability.

7. Policy Recommendations

To promote growth, ensure sustainability, and enhance the impact of Halal Tourism, strategic policy interventions at local, national, and international levels are crucial.

- *Establish global standards and certification frameworks*: A pressing need exists for clear, internationally recognized standards and a unified certification framework for Halal tourism (Credence Research, 2025; UN Tourism, 2024). These standards, developed with international bodies and national authorities, must align with the UN Sustainable Development Goals (SDGs) for a holistic approach to environmental protection, social equity, and economic viability. A unified framework enhances trust, transparency, and market access.
- *Invest in capacity building and training programs*: Comprehensive training for all tourism stakeholders – management, staff, chefs, guides, transportation providers, and community members – is essential. Training should cover Halal compliance (e.g., food preparation, prayer facilities) and sustainable tourism best practices (e.g., environmental management, cultural sensitivity, community engagement) (Chantarungsri & Alam, 2024; Islamic Tourism Centre (ITC), n.d.-b). This equips the workforce to cater to Muslim travelers responsibly.
- *Foster robust public–private–community partnerships*: Strong collaborative partnerships between government, private sector, NGOs, and local communities are vital (Wahizan Saidin et al., 2025). Such multi-stakeholder collaboration is essential for integrated planning, resource mobilization, infrastructure development, and ensuring inclusive, equitable, and beneficial tourism initiatives (Chantarungsri & Alam, 2024). These partnerships also aid effective marketing.
- *Implement targeted marketing and awareness campaigns*: Strategic marketing is needed to promote Sustainable Halal Tourism. Campaigns should position it as an ethical, inclusive, family-friendly, and environmentally conscious option appealing to a wider audience (Wahizan Saidin et al., 2025). Awareness campaigns are also needed to educate host communities, dispelling misconceptions and fostering a welcoming environment (Rachmat et al., 2019).
- *Support research, innovation, and technology adoption*: Continued investment in research is necessary to understand evolving Muslim traveler needs and emerging trends and to explore innovative sustainable tourism approaches (Khan et al., 2024). Encouraging technology adoption – mobile apps for Halal services, online booking platforms, data analytics – enhances traveler experience, improves efficiency, and promotes sustainable practices (UnivDatos, 2024).

8. Conclusion

Sustainable Halal Tourism is a transformative force capable of steering the global tourism industry toward a more ethical, inclusive, and responsible future. By integrating Islamic principles of stewardship, balance, and mindful consumption with sustainable development objectives, stakeholders can collaboratively create tourism experiences that are spiritually enriching, environmentally friendly, culturally respectful, and equitably beneficial for host communities.

The market trajectory indicates significant and sustained growth, with values projected to exceed USD 400 billion and Muslim tourist arrivals over 200 million in coming years (Credence Research, 2025; Future Data Stats, n.d.; Ghani, 2025; Tehran Times, 2025). To capitalize on this potential sustainably, addressing challenges like standardization and infrastructure is imperative (Chantarungsri & Alam, 2024; Credence Research, 2025; Islamic Tourism Centre (ITC), n.d.-b). Embracing opportunities from technology, faith-based wellness, and cross-cultural collaboration will be key drivers (Ghani, 2025; Islamic Tourism Centre (ITC), n.d.-b; Pongsakornrungsilp et al., 2024; UnivDatos, 2024). Case studies from Malaysia, Turkey, and Japan demonstrate diverse successful approaches, offering valuable lessons on strategic planning, government support, industry engagement, and cultural sensitivity (Bozkort & Tümbek Tekeoğlu, 2024; Islamic Tourism Centre (ITC), n.d.-a; Pongsakornrungsilp et al., 2024). By focusing on environmental, socio-cultural, and economic dimensions with concrete actions and community involvement, Sustainable Halal Tourism can contribute to broader sustainability goals (Chantarungsri & Alam, 2024; Harini et al., 2025; Hidayat et al., 2024; Pongsakornrungsilp et al., 2024). With well-considered policies, increased awareness, and commitment to innovation, it can evolve into a leading model for global tourism, demonstrating that faith, culture, and sustainability can converge for ethical and inclusive travel.

References

Adinugraha, H. H., Al-Kasyaf, M. Z., & Nasaruddin, R. B. (n.d.). *Applying Muslim-friendly tourism principles in destination management: Evidence from Aceh, Indonesia*. https://journal.uii.ac.id/IJHI/article/view/39516

Ahmed, H. M. (2025, March 4). *Finding Halal Australian beef & lamb in Japan- your tourist guide*. Tazij Halal Meat. https://www.tazijhalalmeat.com/post/finding-halal-australian-beef-lamb-in-japan-your-tourist-guide

Battour, M., Mady, K., Salaheldeen, M., Elsotouhy, M. M., Elbendary, I., & Boğan, E. (2022). Ai-enabled technologies to assist Muslim tourists in halal-friendly tourism. *Journal of Islamic Marketing*, *14*(5), 1291–1309. https://doi.org/10.1108/jima-01-2022-0001

Battour, M., Salaheldeen, M., Mady, K., & Elsotouhy, M. (2021). Halal Tourism: What is next for sustainability? *Journal of Islamic Tourism*. https://jistour.org/pdf/350_6%20M.%20Battour%20et%20al.%2079-90.pdf

Bozkurt, A. D., & Tümbek Tekeoğlu, A. N. (2024). Turkey's tourism strategies: Building spiritual and cultural experiences through anchoring. *Turkish Yearbook of Tourism*, *9*(4), 693–709. https://doi.org/10.15170/TVT.2024.09.04.06

Chantarungsri, C., & Alam, A. (2024, May 12). *Sustainable strategies for halal tourism infrastructure in the digital age: Integrating architecture, urban planning, and technology*. https://proceedings.ums.ac.id/iseth/article/view/5358

Credence Research. (2025, March 22). *Halal tourism market size, growth, share and forecast 2032*. Retrieved May 12, 2025, from https://www.credenceresearch.com/report/halal-tourism-market

Future Data Stats. (n.d.). *Halal tourism market size & industry growth 2030*. Retrieved May 12, 2025, from https://www.futuredatats.com/reports/halal-tourism-market

Ghani, F. (2025). *Niche to mainstream: Evolution of halal tourism in global travel industry*. https://www.aljazeera.com/news/2025/2/1/niche-to-mainstream-evolution-of-halal-tourism-in-global-travel-industry

Halal Food Council USA. (2025, March 28). *How halal food certification supports sustainability and ethical practices?* Retrieved May 12, 2025, from https://halalfoodcouncilusa.com/how-halal-food-certification-supports-sustainability-and-ethical-practices/

Harini, S., Rahmawati, R., Silaningsih, E., Nurhayati, I., Mutmainah, I., Rainanto, B. H., & Endri, E. (2025). Development of halal tourism villages based on local culture and sustainability. *Tourism and Hospitality*, *6*(2), 55. https://doi.org/10.3390/tourhosp6020055

Hidayat, A., Astuti, B., & Supardin, L. (2024). Development of sustainable halal tourism model through halal tourism attributes. *Pakistan Journal of Life and Social Sciences*, *22*(2), 21747–21762. https://doi.org/10.57239/PJLSS-2024-22.2.001541

Islamic Tourism Centre (ITC). (n.d.-a). *Sustainability boosts the concept of muslim-friendly tourism and hospitality*. Retrieved May 12, 2025, from https://www.itc.gov.my/sustainability-boosts-the-concept-of-muslim-friendly-tourism-and-hospitality/

Islamic Tourism Centre (ITC). (n.d.-b). *Sustainability boosts the concept of muslim-friendly tourism and hospitality*. Retrieved May 12, 2025, from https://www.itc.gov.my/sustainability-boosts-the-concept-of-muslim-friendly-tourism-and-hospitality/

Khan, G., Khan, F., & Munir, S. (2024). Are halal hotels green? An exploratory study from Malaysia. In J. Fraedrich, M. Pirtskalava, T. Khoshtaria, H. Terzi, M. Bayirli, & B. Al Serhan (Eds.), *Contemporary business research in the Islamic world*. GIMAC 2023. Springer Proceedings in Business and Economics. Springer. https://doi.org/10.1007/978-981-97-5400-7_5

Marlinda, A. P., Tamara, A. P., Sambora, R., & Jatmika, S. (2024). The social impact of halal tourism policy in South Korea: Apart from the economic sector. *Asian Journal of Political Science*, 1–24. https://doi.org/10.1080/02185377.2024.2441678

Nor, N. (2023). A systematic literature review on the development of halal tourism: Review protocol guided by roses. *Russian Law Journal*, *11*. https://doi.org/10.52783/rlj.v11i3.2051

Peristiwo, H. (2021). Impact of the COVID-19 pandemic on Indonesia halal tourism transportation. *Journal of Digital Marketing and Halal Industry*, *3*(1), 19–36. https://doi.org/10.21580/jdmhi.2021.3.1.7814

Pongsakornrungsilp, S., Pongsakornrungsilp, P., Chouykaew, T., Niyomdecha, H., Chansamran, S., & He, Y. (2024). Integrating sustainability and cultural sensitivity: Clustering Muslim tourist lifestyles in the Andaman Coastal Cluster, Thailand. *Sustainability*, *16*(21), 9542. https://doi.org/10.3390/su16219542

Rachmat, R., Puspitasari, T., & Puspitasari, W. (2019). The role of halal tourism in improving economic and social welfare: A case study of Lombok Island, Indonesia. *Journal of Islamic Marketing*, *10*(2), 523–537. https://doi.org/10.1108/JIMA-03-2018-0049

Rahmawati, Y., Alhassan, U. M., A'la, A. M., & Rosyidi, L. N. (2025). Empirical study on the determinants of Muslim tourists' visit to Japan: Do Muslim-friendly facilities and culture matter?. *Journal of Islamic Marketing*, *16*(2), 353–372. https://doi.org/10.1108/jima-07-2022-0188

Raj, R. (2020). Motivation for Muslim travellers to the holy city of Jerusalem. *International Journal of Religious Tourism and Pilgrimage*, *8*(6), Article 2. https://arrow.tudublin.ie/cgi/viewcontent.cgi?article=1503&context=ijrtp

Solimar International. (n.d.). *Exploring the power of community-based tourism in the Bangladesh Sundarbans*. Retrieved May 12, 2025, from https://www.solimarinternational.com/5355-2/

Takeshita, S. (2019). Halal certification or ingredient disclosure. *Journal of Islamic Marketing*, *11*(3), 765–781. https://doi.org/10.1108/jima-07-2018-0129

Tehran Times. (2025, February 3). *Global halal tourism market projected to reach $410 billion by 2032*. https://www.tehrantimes.com/news/509378/Global-Halal-tourism-market-projected-to-reach-410-billion-by

UN Tourism. (2024). *UN Tourism outlines vision on how to develop halal tourism*. Retrieved May 12, 2025, from https://www.unwto.org/technical-cooperation/un-tourism-outlines-vision-on-how-to-develop-halal-tourism

UnivDatos. (2024). *Halal tourism market trends & growth analysis 2032*. Retrieved May 12, 2025, from https://univdatos.com/reports/halal-tourism-market

Wahizan Saidin, W. S., Irwan Ibrahim, I. I., & Azilah Anis, A. A. (2025). Halal total quality management: Enhancing standards in the Malaysian tourism industry. *International Journal of Research and Innovation in Social Science*, *IX*(I), 3141–3158. https://doi.org/10.47772/ijriss.2025.9010255

Zainol, M. A., & Mustafa, E. (2021). Accommodation needs and preferences among international Muslim student travelers. *Journal of Tourism, Hospitality and Environment Management*, *6*(24), 01–12. https://doi.org/10.35631/JTHEM.624001

Printed and bound by CPI Group (UK) Ltd, Croydon, CR0 4YY

06/04/2026

14854898-0004